Roy B.C. July 1, 1939



Rev. Kenneth V. Hanley.

# PSYCHOLOGY OF RELIGION

# PSYCHOLOGY OF RELIGION

*Revised and Enlarged*

PAUL E. JOHNSON

PSYCHOLOGY OF RELIGION



*Library of Congress Catalog Card Number: 59-8198*

PRINTED IN THE UNITED STATES OF AMERICA

# PREFACE

Everything changes but the law of change, said Heraclitus; and after thousands of years we can see that laws also change. For the "laws of nature" are actually human descriptions of orderly events as we perceive them from our limited point of view. New discoveries offer startling visions of these events from changing perspectives that open the mind to fresh revelation. We live in a mobile society on a moving planet coursing in endless space. Yet the mystery within one person is evidently as deep as the mystery beyond us. And the change within a growing person may be as decisive as in the world around him.

Nowhere among the social sciences do we find a rate of change accelerating more than in psychology. Unless perhaps it might be in the religious perspectives of contemporary man. In the years since I began writing the first edition of *Psychology of Religion,* a creative and unique period of history has been lived through. Not one of us stands where we stood then, and no one views life as he did at that time. It is a strange predicament to find that what was said then does not represent what we would say now.

To be honest with the reader, I cannot let the book stand as it was in the earlier version. If we are to have authentic dialogue, we must communicate in the present mood. If we are to meet in this living moment, we need the truest contemporary word we can offer to each other. The interpersonal psychology proposed then was a flickering candle that has grown to clearer light casting beams more steadily in widening circles. With the help of others working on this frontier, we are now able to discern more distinctly the meaning of religious encounter as the meeting of I and Thou.

The new edition is not a revision in the sense of minor corrections here and there. The rewriting is so basic in theory and application that the outcome is largely a new psychology of religion. The aim is to invite psychology to meet religion as ultimate concern, and religion to meet psychology as one person seeking response from another.

Many exciting conversations have brought us to this meeting. How can we acknowledge the priceless moments of search with fellow students and the piercing insights like sparks from the hammer and anvil of clashing debate? Special gratitude goes to James Dittes of Yale University for penetrating and critical suggestions; to William Douglas of Boston University for reading certain chapters; to James Scroggs for preparing the index; to Mildred O'Connor, Diana Good, and my wife, Evelyn, for typing the manuscript; to publishers who have granted permissions; and to all who have challenged and roused to sharper focus the religious concern.

PAUL E. JOHNSON

# CONTENTS

# 1 THE PSYCHOLOGICAL STUDY OF RELIGION

## 1. *Approaching Religion*

A certain man had two sons who were preparing to follow their father's vocation in the ministry of the church. When they came home from the theological school where they had been studying, they were warmly received in a hearty family reunion. Sometime after the evening dinner the conversation turned to theology, and it soon became apparent that the young men had departed from some of the beliefs of their father. As the differences became sharper, there were violent arguments far into the night, in which emotions became explosive. No one was willing to yield his position under pressure of attack, and finally when they had exhausted their ammunition and patience, they separated to fall wearily into bed. By morning temperatures had cooled to the point where some reconciliation was needed. Coming to the breakfast table, the father said, "I have decided to enjoy my religion and not argue about it all the time." These are two approaches to the meaning of religion.

In approaching religion one may be naïve or critical. We are naturally naïve before we are critical. The word comes from the Latin *nativus*, meaning "native"; to be naïve is our native, unaffected attitude toward life situations. Naïve experience is the fountain of all human developments, the source of arts and sciences. Seeing and hearing provide the stuff of artistic appreciation. From these sensible delights come the raw materials to construct song and symphony, rhythmic dance and graphic portrayal, sculptured form and architectural symmetry. From naïve interest in nature and curiosity about how things work come the first crude experiments and the long progress of science and invention. In each field refinements outgrow naïve beginnings, yet without the one the other could never be.

Naïve religious experience is the spontaneous interest that wakens life to awe and wonder. The vastness of the heavens or the intimate delicacy of a petal may bate the breath in wonder. Thunder and tempest may overpower human frailty in awe of mysterious powers. The steady growth and decay of life through the seasons may suggest a controlling order of cause and effect. The quiet hush of forest or sunset may impress a man with a strange sense that he is not alone. What child of nature can escape these glimpses of another world around and yet within the familiar forms? Before investigation of these naïve experiences the sense of mystery grows within us. After examination there remains a feeling of invisible backgrounds that underlie and overarch the visible life of our world.

In this state of innocence we are informed by social traditions. Words are spoken to indicate absent objects, and names refer to events beyond the range of pointing fingers. Invisible powers are designated by ideas and symbols that represent them. "Mana" among the Melanesians means a mysterious power that works good or evil. "Manito" among American Indians is a great spirit whose power is sought and feared. So everywhere people have their traditions by which the mysteries are named and clothed with character and function. Individuals growing up in such traditions accept and employ the concepts of their people to interpret the mysteries that confront them.

The naïve mind accepts traditions without question—that is, without questions implying doubt. For such a mind, to question is not to doubt but to invite the answer from a respected authority. Children ask of parents, parents of priests, priests of sacred books. The answers are not individual opinions but the voice of tradition. There is no room for debate unless authorities disagree, in which misfortune the issue is to be decided, not on the merits of the case, but on the superiority of one authority over another.

The advantages of authoritarianism are well known. Authorities offer stability and security. But the cost of authority is high. Stability may block the way of progress, and security may rest on falsehood. When authorities err, no way is provided for correcting the established errors. A critical method is needed.

There are two critical approaches to religion: the philosophical and the scientific. Philosophical inquiry interprets the reality to which religion refers. Each religious experience refers to an event of religious concern. The philosophical task is to consider the claims of religious experience and investigate the whole system of reality to which it refers. Questions about God—his existence, nature, and purpose—are philosophical problems. The truth of particular religions and their teachings, the reality of the goods of life in this world and the next (if any), are questions for philosophy.

Theology is associated with philosophy in the study of truth and reality as a whole. Both search beneath appearances for the undergirding reality; both press beyond the local view to larger perspectives. Either may be taught by authority, yet both employ critical analysis freely. There is this distinction. A theology views the whole from the standpoint of one religion and draws more deeply from that historic tradition. A philosophy of religion aims to view all religions impartially and evaluate each from a universal point of view.

In what sense is theology called the queen of the sciences? To Thomas Aquinas it was the dedication of all human knowledge to the most ultimate of all Being. The biblical and dogmatic theologian may give attention to revelation of the supernatural to the neglect of the naturalistic sciences whose knowledge is human and regarded as inferior. But when theology speaks of man and his destiny, this cannot be a one-sided conversation, for the natural sciences of man also have something to say. Psychology in particular has become a rival authority on the soul of man in relation to the biological and social meaning of this life. The dialogue between theology and psychology is, therefore, accelerating in tempo and volume until it is no longer possible for theologian or psychologist to ignore each other. At no time in history since the psalmist asked, "What is man, that thou art mindful of him?" has there been so vast and illuminating research into the nature of man. The mystery of personality is not to be captured in verbal abstractions or facile generalizations. The complexities of human nature are involved in dynamic and conflictual motivations that invite the research of psychology. Not that psychologists have the answers to the questions theologians ask, but they are aware of the profounder depths in man and join in the search for truer understanding.

The scientific approach is, first of all, description. Its task is to gather, classify, and arrange facts in systematic order. From these facts general principles are inferred. The work of science is done with ever-increasing thoroughness, and new facts are continually added. Yet the inductive leap from data to conclusion comes to probability rather than final certainty. As science depends on philosophy for its presuppositions, so philosophy depends on science for its data and many of its inferences. An adequate philosophy of religion will consider the facts available through scientific description and analysis.

Scientific studies of religion include the history of religion, the sociology of religion, and the psychology of religion. History of religion explores primitive cultures and buried antiquities to find the earliest forms, and traces the development of each religion through the centuries. Sociology of religion investigates the place of religion in group life and examines the interaction of social, economic, and political factors with religious values. The psychology of religion looks within human experience to understand what religion means to persons. It is intimately related to the other scientific studies. History and sociology both employ psychology to interpret the meaning of religious forms and activities, for they would otherwise be mere dusty records and lifeless patterns. Psychology of religion goes to primitive cults and historical faiths to secure data for its study. Social organizations, customs, and standards contribute to the psychological meaning of religion.

How is general psychology related to psychology of religion? In one sense general psychology is the root from which psychology of religion stems. There are other roots, such as psychiatry and psychoanalysis, concerned from the medical approach with mental health and therapy for the ills of the mind. There is pastoral psychology, concerned from the approach of the pastor with the needs of persons in relation to the religious community. There is religious education, concerned from the teacher's approach with the potentialities of spiritual growth and the conditions of learning. Yet these are extensions and applications of theory arising from general psychology as the taproot of all.

Psychology of religion is strictly speaking a development of general psychology reaching in the direction of religious behavior to comprehend its meaning. There are other branches which also spring from this taproot of general psychology and join together in viewing life from their specialties. Social psychology studies the meaning of persons and their roles through interpersonal relations which are basic to religious behavior. Psychology of personality studies the dynamic motivations of persons as they perceive and strive for goals important to religious development. Abnormal and clinical psychology study the devious ways in which persons seek to communicate their needs in verbal and nonverbal behavior of vital concern to the religious life. It is evident, therefore, that psychology of religion does not stand aloof in remote isolation but is deeply involved with other psychological studies in seeking the religious quality of human life.

## 2. *Early Forecasts*

Psychology is one of the youngest of modern sciences. Yet the description of human experience and behavior is probably the oldest of all studies. The earliest records of every known culture relate the doings and sayings of men and women. Exploits of heroes, often magnified to superhuman stature, make up the songs and stories told and retold before writing was invented. The odes and legends of ancient China, Japan, Israel, and Greece recount events in which the ancestors dared to suffer and achieve. As these literatures unfold, they reveal emotions and desires, ideas and ideals, that constitute the inner side of behavior. Much of this lore is permeated with religious attitudes.

The psychological data of religion are therefore as old as human history. Facts are mingled with fancies, however, and interpretations are largely naïve. Heroes change at will from human to animal forms, become invisible, fly through air, journey into the earth and undersea. The sun stands still or rides too close to the earth and burns the crops; axheads float; waves become horses; dragons ride the clouds; armed soldiers spring up from dragons' teeth. Good and ill fortune result from charms, curses, fates, or unwitting mistakes. But gradually through these bewildering irregularities there develops a sense of order and justice. Glimpses of moral law appear in the Chinese Tao, the Greek Moira, the Hindu Karma, and the Hebrew Decalogue. From these hints of law and order in man and nature come early premonitions of a scientific view.

So is the way prepared for psychology of religion. If psychology is the systematic description and critical analysis of human behavior, it appears astonishingly early on the human scene. We have found descriptions of human behavior at the dawn of recorded history. As these descriptions become more systematic and critical, the pioneer work is well begun. The naïve myths and crude legends are brought before the bar of reason and quite thoroughly overhauled. While yet in popular favor they are trimmed, refined, reinterpreted, or rejected entirely by more daring thinkers.

Ikhnaton (Egyptian Pharaoh *ca.* 1375-58 B.C.) fearlessly rejected the religious traditions of two thousand years, departing from the priests and temples of the past to found a new religion of inner appreciations. Here is thoroughgoing criticism of a powerful intrenched religion and the systematic creation of a lofty monotheism. From the hymns and records that survive, it appears that religion was understood as an emotional experience.

The ancient Hindu psychologists developed a remarkable science for analyzing religious experience. Vedanta thinkers explored the mystical rise of superconsciousness. Sankhya followers defined the powers of the individual soul as related to the organs of sense and motion. They formulated psychological problems clearly and analyzed processes with subtle understanding. They also invented yoga exercises for mental control and religious concentration.

Gautama Buddha (563-483 B.C.) was systematic in his analysis of human behavior. He conducted experiments testing the typical methods of holy men, pursuing rigorous self-discipline and fasting even to the point of unconsciousness. When six years of such experiments brought no peace, he reached a theory similar to that of Freud in its premise that the cause of suffering is desire, as it was also similar in the conclusion that enlightenment or insight is essential to its cure.

Jeremiah (650?-585? B.C.) is the psychologist of the Hebrew prophets. He identified himself with his people but was always their unyielding critic, reproving their follies (10:3) and pleading with them to return from their deceits to the true way of life (15:19). Yet he suffered the anguish of conflict and subjected his distress to tragic appraisal. The profound stirring of his emotions and convictions reveals the psychology of his doubts and faith.

Socrates (470?-399 B.C.) represents the critical spirit in Greece. His conviction that "the unexamined life is not fit for human living" propelled him on a dangerous career of upsetting the established beliefs and popular illusions of his time. In his trial and facing of the death penalty he calmly examined the resources of personality. He rejected the traditional gods of his people and found his deity revealed in conscience, a spirit that guides from within and sustains a man in life and death.

Christian thinkers have notably advanced the psychological understanding of religion. To Jesus the heart of religion is the inner spirit, and he constantly turns from the external to desires and motives, affections and thoughts, that become the decisive issues of life. Murder begins in anger, adultery stems from lust, profanity from irreverence and insincerity, enmity from selfishness and hatred. In confronting his accusers and wrestling with crucial decisions, he brings into bold belief the power of love devoted to God in eternal perspective.

Paul and Augustine expound conversion, the inner conflicts of flesh lusting against spirit, the frustrations of a divided will, the expulsive power of a new affection, the integration of a greater purpose, the peace and power of devotion to a religious cause. Each one records and acts from the dynamic of vivid religious experiences which hurls him forth into larger destiny. They define issues that have engaged theologians to modern times.

Blaise Pascal (1623-62) was a pioneer at the frontier between modern science and theology, whose experimental approach in mathematics and physics was open to religious experience. His search for truth was the passion of his life, and when he turned from external things to the inner world, he was equally precise in observation of psychological facts capable of measuring and testing. Yet he was not bound by dogmas of naturalism and rationalism to exclude the spiritual and emotional concerns of the religious life. He continued the investigation and extended it "to those mysteries which are hidden from sense and from reason."[1] Psychologists are indebted to him for inventing the calculating machine, which has become the cornerstone of statistical research. Theologians and psychologists of religion are intrigued by the dramatic religious experience which he recorded as "Fire, Certitude, Feeling, Joy, Peace," as well as by his effort to bring his science and his religion together in a personal affirmation.

The psychological approach to theology, so characteristic of many dis-

[1] *OEuvres*, II, 92. Quoted in Emilé Cailliet, *Pascal: Genius in the Light of Scripture* (Philadelphia: The Westminster Press, 1945), p. 69.

cussions, received its modern impetus from Jonathan Edwards (1703-58) and Friedrich Schleiermacher (1768-1834). Schleiermacher is generally considered the pioneer in revolting against the rationalism of philosophers and stressing religious experience as the feeling of absolute dependence. But in Boston, July 8, 1731, Edwards preached on "God Glorified in Man's Dependence," thirty-seven years before Schleiermacher was born. In *A Treatise Concerning the Religious Affections* (1746) he argues the insufficiency of reason in religious revelation. His decisive ability to communicate the urgency of authentic religious experience aroused his contemporary New England to a great revival. And yet these emotional stirrings he sought to keep within the reasonable bounds of sober responsibility through sound education.

Søren Kierkegaard (1813-55) cannot be surrounded in a paragraph, for he was a man of brilliant contrasts whose seminal contributions have waited a century to burst forth in our time. As the fountainhead of existentialism he holds a startling power over this age in his vivid portrayal of the subjective meaning of personal existence, the living pathos of despair, and the deeper sources of faith. His psychological analyses of dread, despair, and fear [2] are worked through in a religious perspective to the white-heat intensity of a crucible. From the lonely melancholy of a childhood lived in virtual isolation through devotion to a stern yet wistful father, he was suspended in foreboding until his father's death. Then he struck out recklessly in three directions: (*a*) to study theology and attack the Danish church, (*b*) to propose and renounce marriage with Regina, and (*c*) to publish a stream of epochal writings which brought upon him the anger and ridicule of his contemporaries. By the keenest of perceptions he dissects the inner life in its contrasting moods and brings to those who search with him a deepening understanding of religious potentialities. As the full thrust of his passionate search gains momentum, he gathers to his banner a growing company of those who challenge the complacent finality of abstract reason in the rigid forms of established tradition.

Kierkegaard was not the only one to revolt against the seductive abstractions of speculative philosophy. Psychologists who had dwelt in the halls of philosophy became restless and moved from contemplation to the laboratories of science. Johann Friedrich Herbart (1776-1841), who in 1809 succeeded Immanuel Kant in the chair of philosophy at Königsberg, wrote his two most important books in psychology (*Lehrbuch zur Psychologie* in 1816 and *Psychologie als Wissenschaft* in 1824-25). He became the father of educational psychology that would become empirical, mathematical, and dynamic. To him psychology was metaphysical more than experi-

[2] Kierkegaard's trilology consists of *Fear and Trembling*, *The Concept of Dread*, and *The Sickness unto Death*. All are translated by Walter Lowrie and published by Princeton University Press.

mental, yet he opposed the faculty psychology which had divided the mind into separate parts and by his insistence upon actual experience was a bridge from the speculative to the experimental approach.

Gustav Theodor Fechner (1801-87) performed the first experiments which became the foundation for the modern scientific psychology.[3] He was the son and grandson of village pastors in southeastern Germany, and when his father died, he lived from the age of five to fourteen in the parsonage of his uncle. He was graduated in medicine from the University of Leipzig. Turning immediately to physics, he published a series of brilliant researches and was appointed professor of physics at Leipzig. Five years later in 1839 he resigned the chair because of ill health and suffered acute distress for three years. This crisis from which he eventually recovered had a profound effect upon his religious life and his study of the soul. He came to believe that mind and matter are so identical that consciousness pervades all things. From that point he moved into a field of research which he called psychophysics and developed methods of measurement fundamental to psychology with his experiments on lifted weights, visual brightness, and tactual and visual distances. When in 1860 he published his *Elemente der Psychophysik,* he set experimental psychology upon a course which has resulted in a veritable avalanche of scientific investigation. It is worth noting that his work was the product of religious devotion in seeking to understand the nature of the soul in relation to the world.

### 3. *Scientific Psychology*

Wilhelm Wundt (1830-1920) is generally regarded as the first psychologist to develop psychology as an independent science. He was born in Baden, the son of a Lutheran pastor, and was educated by a vicar with whom he lived until he entered the *Gymnasium,* and the universities, first of Tübingen, then of Heidelberg and Berlin. While yet a student he was already publishing significant research, and upon receiving his degree as doctor of medicine from Heidelberg, he remained in that university to teach physiology and to introduce in 1862 a course on "psychology from the standpoint of natural science," which title was in 1867 changed to "physiological psychology." In 1875 Wundt came to the chair of philosophy at the University of Leipzig, where he opened the first psychological laboratory in 1879, known as the *Psychologische Institut.* It was here that a whole generation of experimental psychologists was trained and became the pioneers of the new science in

[3] See Edwin G. Boring, *A History of Experimental Psychology* (2nd ed., New York: Appleton-Century-Crofts, Inc., 1950).

Europe and America. The researches of Wundt and his students appeared in the journals he founded, and his own writings came to 491 items for a total of over 53,000 pages in psychology and philosophy. His *Physiologische Psychologie* (1873-1911) was thoroughly revised five times, and his *Völkerpsycholgie* (1900-1920) came to ten volumes.

To Wundt psychology was the science of experience, and its data are phenomena. He saw the work of psychology as the analysis of conscious processes into elements, and the discovery of the laws by which they are related. The element was to him not a static unit but a dynamic mental process. He emphasized the law of psychic causality that operates as one side of psychophysical parallelism. Another emphasis was his law of psychic relations, that any psychic content acquires significance from its relationships. His law of psychic contrast notes that opposites mutually reinforce each other; while his law of psychic resultants notes how association operates by fusion, assimilation, complications, and memory. Apperception is ever active as a constant stream of consciousness. While he did not bring religious experience into his laboratory, yet he did offer to his students psychological concepts and experimental contagion which led to psychological studies of religion.

On the American continent psychology was also taking pioneer strides, in which a psychology of religion was soon to be a frontier of research. The first American psychologist to study the empirical data of religion, so far as we can discover, was Granville Stanley Hall (1844-1924). He was born on a farm in Ashfield, Massachusetts, and decided to prepare for the ministry. After graduation from Williams College in 1867 with his major interest in philosophy and evolution, he attended Union Theological Seminary in New York City for one year and then on borrowed money went to Germany, where he studied philosophy (1867-71) at Bonn and Berlin. Returning to Union he received his degree in divinity, and after ten weeks as preacher in a country church he became professor of English and philosophy in Antioch College (1872-76). The publication of Wundt's *Physiologische Psychologie* captured his interest in the new psychology. He decided to go to Leipzig to study with Wundt, but on the way he was invited to Harvard as tutor, and while there he studied with William James, a young teacher only two years his senior, and completed the first American Ph.D. degree in psychology in 1878 with a laboratory dissertation on the muscular perception of space. Then going to Germany he went first to Berlin and then to Leipzig, where he lived next door to Fechner and became Wundt's first American student at the time of the founding of the laboratory.

Returning to Harvard he lectured on education, and then in 1881 he was invited to the new Johns Hopkins University to lecture and in 1883 to become professor of psychology. There in 1883 he opened a psychological laboratory and in 1887 founded the *American Journal of Psychology.* Two years later he became the first president of Clark University at Worcester, Massachusetts, and guided its development as a graduate university with emphasis upon research and instruction. He was also professor of psychology, founded a psychological laboratory, a department of pedagogy, and the American Psychological Association (1891), becoming its first president. He brought with him the *American Journal of Psychology* and launched three more journals, one of which was the *Journal of Religious Psychology* (1904-14).

It was on February 5, 1881, in the second of his series of twelve public Harvard lectures that Stanley Hall first reported his empirical studies of religious conversion.[4] He refers to data collected by correspondence, and study of the records of the Fulton Street (New York) noon prayer meeting. He contends that religious awakening is associated with adolescence as the time of sex maturing and general impressionability. This conclusion was briefly restated in an article printed a year later in the *Princeton Review* entitled "The Moral and Religious Training of Children and Adolescents," reprinted in the *Pedagogical Seminary,* I (June 1891), 196-210.

With this beginning the questionnaire method invented by Francis Galton has become one of the leading methods used in the psychological study of religion. In his fuller treatment of "adolescent psychology of conversion," [5] Hall tells how he gathered replies by inserting questions in the weekly papers of the Methodist, Baptist, Congregational, and Presbyterian denominations over a period of years, as well as inquiries made at educational institutions and religious meetings. From these replies he studied the age of conversion for 4,054 males (including data gathered by others) and concurred with Starbuck that sixteen is the age of most frequency. He was impressed by the similarities and covariants of religion and love best seen at adolescence, and took William James severely to task for denying the relationship of sex and religious awakenings. Hall was one of the first to introduce psychoanalysis to American psychologists by inviting Freud and Jung to lecture at Clark University in 1909, both of whom were to contribute to psychology of religion.

Among the students working with Hall at Clark University, Burnham, Daniels, Lancaster, Leuba, and Starbuck published research as journal articles on the psychology of religious conversion between 1891 and 1897. It was Leuba and Starbuck, however, who continued to follow a career of

[4] *Adolescence: Its Psychology and Its Relation to Physiology, Anthropology, Sociology, Sex, Crime, Religion and Education* (New York: D. Appleton & Co., 1904), II, 292.

[5] *Ibid.,* pp. 281-362.

research in psychology of religion, and to them we may well give attention.

James H. Leuba (1868-1946) was a lifelong scientist of religion whose published writings were all devoted to psychology of religion. He was born the son of a watchmaker at Neuchatel in Switzerland, instructed in the Calvinist faith and joined the church without enthusiasm due to "puzzled misery" over the irrelevancy of the creed and catechism. When the Salvation Army held meetings in his town, he was drawn to the moral ideal of no compromise with evil and had a violent conversion which he considered "perhaps the most beneficial" experience of his life.[6] Yet as a student at the University of Neuchatel he met the conflict between the "truths" of science and religion by siding with science. Upon graduation from the university he came with his family to New York City, where for two years he was secretary of the French Y.M.C.A. Then after one year of teaching French and German, he went on a scholarship to study psychology at Clark University.

For his doctoral research he chose to study religious conversion, and the dissertation was published in the *American Journal of Psychology* in 1896. To gather his data he conducted interviews with a large number of Christian converts who gave firsthand information on their experiences. He thereby introduced another method of investigation that psychologists are using with more confidence than the questionnaire, since it provides opportunity to explore questions further and secure more adequate information by sharpening issues in face-to-face conversation. This was not long after the time that Freud in Vienna published with Breuer the *Studien Über Hysterie* (1895) based upon psychoanalytic interviewing. The use of cathartic interviewing, however, antedated this publication.[7] Leuba in his study took the naturalistic point of view that has characterized his interpretations, implying that there is no difference in kind between religious and nonreligious consciousness, that religious truth is inferred like any other from experience and subject to error.

In 1897 he was appointed at Bryn Mawr College to organize a department of psychology, and from that time on, whenever he could spare time from his teaching, he returned to his "favorite subject of research" with unabated interest in psychology of religion. His first two books (*A Psychological Study of Religion*, 1912; and *The Belief in God and Immortality*, 1916) were devoted to the psychological origin, development, and function of ideas of God and immortality. He found beliefs arising from two sources:

[6] *Religion in Transition*, ed. Vergilius Ferm (New York: The Macmillan Co., 1937), contains brief autobiographies by Leuba, Starbuck, and Coe.

[7] See Josef Breuer and Sigmund Freud, *Studies on Hysteria* (Standard Ed. Vol II; London: The Hogarth Press, 1955), pp. x-xiv.

the need to explain by assigning causes and the need to seek help in the struggle for life. He concluded that science propounds better answers and methods than religion by which to meet these needs. Another study (*The Psychology of Religious Mysticism,* 1925) traced mystical claims to natural causes.

Edwin D. Starbuck (1866-1947) published the first full-length book on psychology of religion,[8] consisting of research studies which he began in 1893. He was born in a Quaker family near Indianapolis; and following his graduation from the University of Indiana and a period of teaching mathematics at Vincennes University, he came to Harvard in 1893, devoted to a scientific study of firsthand religious experience. He was soon giving out questionnaires, one on conversion, another on the breaking of habits, and a third on the lines of religious development. He was encouraged less by Münsterberg than by James and C. C. Everett, who was dean of the Divinity School. Many stormy oppositions came from those who resisted such examination of religious experience, but he persisted and found significant consistencies, such as the age of conversion near pubescence, the likeness of habit breaking to conversion, and the signs of dissociation and recentering in conversion not unlike the phenomena of split personality described by Prince and Janet.

Then taking a Harvard Master's degree and his questionnaires, he moved to Clark University to continue for the Ph.D., which he completed in 1897. His studies of conversion and religious growth were first reported in the *American Journal of Psychology* in the same year, 1897, and more fully in his book *The Psychology of Religion* (1899), giving a detailed account and interpretation of the questionnaire returns.

At Stanford University for six years (1897-1903) he conducted seminars in the psychology of religion centering upon the genetic psychology of the God-idea among high-school, college, and adult populations as secured by questionnaires. In the years 1906 to 1930 at the University of Iowa and from 1930 at the University of Southern California, he and his graduate students were engaged in extensive character research issuing in many series of publications.

One must respect the scientific work of Starbuck, which remains undiminished by the erosions of time. Taking as his premise that "there is no event in the spiritual life which does not occur in accordance with immutable laws," he met as "great orderliness and sequence among the facts of emotion" as does the physicist in his laboratory. He did not fear that science would threaten the message of religion with extinction, for it can

[8] *The Psychology of Religion: An Empirical Study of the Growth of Religious Consciousness,* with a Preface by William James (New York: Charles Scribner's Sons, 1899).

bring only a "little coherency and constancy" into the midst of that which is forever flowing, to "explore a little into the ever-enlarging region of the unknown," fully aware that most of the mystery of religion will remain beyond our grasp.[9]

In this pioneer book he undertook a "purely empirical study" into the causes and conditions of religious growth in individuals. His data consist largely of autobiographies written in response to a set of questions. Recognizing the limitations of introspection, the imperfections of memory, the meager power to describe subjective events, the variable personal equation, and the difficulties of analysis in such complexities, he yet sought common elements which might suggest the laws of growth. The questions were framed to separate facts from opinions and call forth vital and essential experiences of a general character. In the sampling his attempt was to have data as representative as possible of the American Protestant population with regard to sex, age, church connection, and vocation and taking into account the "limits within which inductions are valid." The number of cases for studying the age of conversion was 1,265, of whom 254 were females and 1,011 males. The number of 192 cases was followed by more intensive study of the motives and forces leading to conversion, the mental and bodily affections, the conscious and subconscious factors, and the character of the new life.

For studying the lines of religious growth not involving conversion, he brought together 237 cases of whom 142 were female and 95 male. In this part of the study he considered features of the religion of childhood; then coming to adolescence, he studied spontaneous religious awakenings, storm and stress, doubt, alienation, the birth of a larger self, and substitutes for religious feeling. Following adolescence he found a distinct turning into adult life which he characterized as a period of reconstruction. In this epoch the adult person was working out a standpoint of his own, interpreting life for himself. He was then more likely to have a positive faith though it need not be conventional. Starbuck studied the adult religious life in reference to external influences, beliefs, religious feelings, motives, and purposes in which growth is likely to be without definite transitions.

In treating the data extensively gathered, Starbuck made a careful analysis of the records. Where data were incomplete or obscure, he followed up with further questions. His next step was to develop categories inductively by using "enormous specially ruled charts," folded into books for convenience, which were ruled horizontally and vertically. Each case was scattered horizontally along the chart, with care to bring similar facts under one another in the vertical columns. These columns fell gradually

[9] *Ibid.*, p. 10.

into groups of columns, and eventually new groupings emerged, with vacant columns to catch new items. In this way individual cases were kept intact, yet relations among them were shown so as "to view the facts of experience more objectively, and thus to allow them to speak for themselves." [10] After analysis and classification came generalization by statistical summaries presented in charts and graphs showing percentages and comparison of all data.

Finally, the tendencies appearing in these massed results were "interpreted in their larger bearings." The correlation of the facts were first shown in their own sphere and then in larger relationships of the contextual field. For example, feelings experienced at the critical moment of conversion were cast in relation to that which preceded them to trace sequences which might be causal or genetic. Mental and bodily affections were seen together in psychophysiological relatedness. Comparisons were made of the lines of growth with and without conversion. Biological maturing was viewed in the context of conscious-unconscious processes, feelings, and rational insights, as related to social customs in religious communities. We sense the stirrings of a dynamic psychology, though pre-Freudian in viewing the unconscious mores as automatic, habitual processes rather than the interplay of surging desire and repression. Yet he does see that spontaneous awakenings are "the fructification of that which has been ripening within the subliminal consciousness." [11] There is awareness that phenomena antecedent to conversion have significance in a double sense either as causal or as "an index on the surface of what is going on beneath." [12]

George A. Coe (1862-1951) was another son of the parsonage whose interest in psychology of religion was lifelong. He was born at Mendon, New York, in 1862 and upon graduation from the University of Rochester studied theology and philosophy at Boston University for four years, then at the University of Berlin. For eighteen years he taught philosophy and psychology at Northwestern University (1891-1909) and for the next eighteen years psychology of religious education at Union Theological Seminary and Teachers College of Columbia University. In 1899 he plunged into psychology of religion with "A Study in the Dynamics of Personal Religion," in the *Psychological Review,* incorporated the following year in his first book, *The Spiritual Life* (1900). The empirical research herein reported is historically significant for the methods employed at this early date. Starbuck had noted the varieties of experience clustering about re-

[10] *Ibid.*, p. 15.

[11] *Ibid.*, p. 108.

[12] *Ibid.*, p. 109.

ligious conversion and intimated that "much depends upon the temperament." Coe undertook to investigate these temperamental factors.

He made an intensive study of seventy-seven persons, mostly college students whom he found healthy in mind and body, who had positive moral and religious training. The average age of the fifty-two males was 24.8 and of the twenty-five females was 22. He constructed a list of questions not only to record facts but also to reflect the personality of the writer in anticipation of projective and personality tests used today. After securing these written personal documents, he then had interviews to crossexamine, clear up doubtful points, and gain new important facts. A scale was constructed to guide him in "objective observation of temperamental manifestations." Interviews were had also with friends and acquaintances of the persons examined to gather impressions and observations from them. The reports of independent observers were collated and checked off against one another. Such observations were conducted in the manner of the recent "situational testing" to gain an all-around view of the person through his behavioral responses. Finally, he employed hypnotic experiments to get at the facts of suggestibility.

In reference to religious conversion he found that many expected a striking transformation, but a number of these failed to experience it. There were seventeen in Group I who expected a transformation and experienced it; there were twelve in Group II who expected transformation but did not experience it. A careful study of temperaments indicated that sensibility was predominant in Group I and intellect in Group II. Those in Group I showed slow-intense and prompt-weak temperament traditionally known as melancholic and sanguine; while those in Group II exceeded them in both promptness and intensity (choleric temperament). Mental and motor mechanisms were also studied, as dreams, hallucinations, and motor automatisms. Of Group I there were eight persons who had either hallucinations or motor automatisms. But of those in Group II who sought transformation in vain, only one had either hallucination or automatism.

Suggestibility was studied by hypnotic experiments. Behavior under suggestion was of two types: passive to accept suggestions without resistance and spontaneous to resist and act contrary to suggestion. Of the fourteen persons given hypnosis in Group I (those expecting and receiving a striking transformation) thirteen were of the passive type. Of the twelve persons in Group II (expecting but not receiving a striking transformation) nine clearly belonged to the spontaneous type, one was entirely passive, and two open to some doubt. From all data compiled in these studies he inferred that trances, visions, and automatic behavior were essentially hypnotic and that suggestion has played an important part in both individual experiences and epidemic manifestations associated with religious conversion. He did not, however, slip into the error of assuming, as Leuba seemed to do, that to find psychological mechanisms related to religious experiences explained them or proved they were nothing but mechanical events.

> The ultimate test of religious values, however, is nothing psychological, nothing definable in terms of *how it happens,* but something ethical, definable in terms of the *what is attained* of loving trust toward God and brotherly kindness toward men. . . .
>
> The worth of the experience depends, not upon the presence or absence of suggestion, but upon whether it includes a decision and a renewal that reach deep into the springs of conduct.[13]

During these years in the closing decade of the nineteenth century, William James (1842-1910) was preparing the classic study which was to be the most influential of all, first given as the Gifford Lectures in Edinburgh (1901 and 1902) and published as *The Varieties of Religious Experience.*[14] To comprehend the genius of this work, we must view it in the context of his whole life and times, which come to vivid focus here. He was born in New York City, the first of four sons and a daughter in a family of rollicking good humor and exciting conversations in which each was encouraged to assert his opinions on equal footing against the others. The father, Henry James, was an ardent seeker who turned from law to theology, revolted against the Princeton Calvinism with the founders of Union Theological Seminary, believed mightily in the resources of religion with no hope in the church as an institution, traveled incessantly to cultural centers of Europe, parlored with the great liberals of his day, and met the public as author and lecturer. Yet he never arrived at a satisfactory resting place and held his freedom above the confining restraints of a vocation.

William was educated on a wide circuit around the Western hemisphere, at home everywhere and nowhere, impelled restlessly from art to science, from medicine to laboratory science, from physiology to psychology and philosophy. He became the senior American psychologist while assistant professor of physiology at Harvard University by first offering in 1875 a course in "Relations Between Physiology and Psychology." He was contemporary with Wundt of Leipzig in opening a laboratory in 1876 in which instruments were used for psychological experiments. But he soon ranged beyond the laboratory, taking psychology into the department of philosophy in 1877, and the following year contracted to write *The Principles of Psy-*

[13] *The Spiritual Life: Studies in the Science of Religion* (New York: The Abingdon Press, 1900), pp. 144, 146. Questionnaire studies and content analysis of 1,117 hymns shed further light on temperamental factors in religious experience.

[14] *The Varieties of Religious Experience: A Study in Human Nature* (New York: Longmans, Green & Co., 1902).

*chology,* published twelve years later. The experimental approach was carried out from the functional stream of consciousness moving goalward into the roomy vistas of his philosophy as radical empiricism and pragmatism.

Within William James was a perpetual conflict of scientific naturalism with religious supernaturalism. As a student at twenty-five in Germany he wrote his father that he was a thoroughgoing naturalist against the claims of supernatural religion. Yet after his father's death in 1882 he wrote to his wife that he must understand "the value and meaning of religion in Father's sense, in the mental life and destiny of man." [15] It was not until the publication of his *Principles of Psychology* that he was able to do this, but then he turned to an intense study of religious and moral experiences. When in 1896 he was invited to prepare the Gifford Lectures he began at once a psychological study of religion.

While he was closely associated with Starbuck and the other psychological pioneers in this historic decade, and though he drew upon biographical documents which Starbuck shared with him, yet his psychological approach was significantly different. For they came to the task as experimental psychologists seeking the quantitative evidence of numbers by statistical methods. Truly they had their reward as have the many psychologists who followed them to the present time. But James did not arrange quantitative data in statistical patterns; no charts or graphs appear in his book.[16] Instead, personal documents are profusely used as case studies to present the primary data of firsthand experience, described by the persons who experienced them. Other psychologists sought to ascertain by statistical averages what is normal for large populations. James was seeking to discover what is unique in the religious experience of individual persons, however varied and abnormal they might be. For in this way he hoped to find what is most personal and authentic in religious experience no matter how extreme it appears by conventional standards. He distrusted bigness and sensed that popular averages, like crowds, conceal the unique meaning and flavor of personal life.[17]

From his passionate interest in the nature of persons as they are, wrestling with their destiny through conflict and stress to become what they desire to be, he welcomed the evidence of abnormal psychology. He knew from his

[15] R. B. Perry, *The Thought and Character of William James,* II. (Boston: Little, Brown & Co., 1935), 322.

[16] In his Preface to Starbuck's book he says: "Such statistical arguments are not mathematical proofs, but they support presumptions and establish probabilities, and in spite of the lack of precision in many of their data, they yield results not to be got at in any less clumsy way." (*Op. cit.,* p. ix.)

[17] He defines religion as "the feelings, acts, and experiences of individual men in their solitude, so far as they apprehend themselves to stand in relation to whatever they may consider the divine" (*op. cit.,* p. 31). This individualism is reaffirmed by Allport.

own distress and nervous disorders the depth and poignancy of the human spirit longing for health and religious wholeness. He could identify with the sick soul who through the anguish of acute suffering is better able to sound the profounder meaning of human existence and sense more urgently the need for religious salvation. His own health was often precarious. In the summer of 1899 his heart was damaged by overexertion when he became lost on a mountain-climbing expedition and struggled all night and into the next day to find his way home. It was at this time he was writing *The Varieties of Religious Experience,* and much of it was written from bed when he was able to work only two or three hours a day.

From his medical training he brought a strong interest in the pathological and a recognition of its significance for understanding the nature of man, not as repulsive or deforming but as human in a larger sense through suffering and struggling for wholeness. He was able to perceive the diverse and conflictual strivings of the emotional life as functional to growth and fulfillment. He described the *Varieties* as a study of morbid psychology mediating and interpreting the value of "exceptional mental states," gaining a dignity for the religious life otherwise frequently lost or rejected. This position has been reaffirmed by the work of Boisen, who also sees the religious potentialities of psychosis and crisis. In this James is emphatic.

> It would profit us little to study this second-hand religious life [determined by imitation and retained by habit]. We must make search rather for the original experiences which were the patternsetters to all this mass of suggested feeling and imitated conduct. These experiences we can only find in individuals for whom religion exists not as a dull habit, but as an acute fever rather. But such individuals are "geniuses" in the religious line; and like many other geniuses who have brought forth fruits effective enough for commemoration in the pages of biography, such religious geniuses have often shown symptoms of nervous instability. Even more perhaps than other kinds of genius, religious leaders have been subject to abnormal psychical visitations. Invariably they have been creatures of exalted emotional sensibility. Often they have led a discordant inner life, and had melancholy during a part of their career. They have known no measure, been liable to obsessions and fixed ideas; and frequently they have fallen into trances, heard voices, seen visions, and presented all sorts of peculiarities which are ordinarily classed as pathological. Often, moreover, these pathological features in their career have helped to give them their religious authority and influence.[18]

Here the wisdom and pragmatism of James come into play. His wisdom saved him from the reductionism that plagued Leuba and Freud, enabling him to perceive that origin does not determine value. He notes the fallacy of discrediting states of mind by calling them nothing but expressions of

[18] *Ibid.*, pp. 6-7.

organic disposition or pathology. Medical materialism is a "too simple-minded system of thought" when it finishes up the apostle Paul by assigning his vision on the Damascus Road to a lesion of the occipital cortex or to epilepsy. His pragmatic test directs attention to the "consequential fruits for life" as more significant than the roots. His empirical criterion for appraising religious experience was not origin but "the way in which it works on the whole."

By radical empiricism James meant to say that nothing is so important as concrete experience. In the religious enterprise the most vital concerns are ultrarational and to be settled not by the abstract reasoning of the philosophies and creeds but by moments of living experience. The thesis of the *Varieties* is that though some manifestations of religion may be absurd as creeds and theories, yet the life of religion as a whole is man's most important function. The facts of religious experience are not secondary but primary evidence in their own right, and these he will respect for their testimony of invisible realities which they reveal. This he called "piecemeal supernaturalism" to indicate how the Beyond is revealed in "what goes on in the single private man."

> The struggle seems to be that of a less articulate and more profound part of human nature to hold out, and keep itself standing, against the attempts of a more superficial and explicit or loquacious part, to suppress it. The profounder part believes, but it can say so little. . . .Just see, they will say, *how* absurd. Yet I must shape things and argue to the conclusion that a man's religion is the deepest and wisest thing in his life.[19]

What we have in the work of James is a clinical approach to religion in contrast to the experimental. He finds the person most alive at times of crisis and enters with him into the turbulent emotional conflicts to comprehend the meaning and direction of his life thrust. He is a dynamic and therapeutic psychologist of religion who sees the drama of human life in the struggle through conflictual stress to goals of growing fulfillment. For him the religious concern is as deep as life itself, for it moves in the life and death struggle for the saving wholeness that will unify the self-defeating divisions of life. With Freud and Jung he affirmed the epochal importance of the unconscious forces and resources of personality. He did not, like Freud, hold the psychosexual libido at the center of the struggle. But he did, like Jung, hold psychic energy boundless as a mother sea, whose tides flow in and out of the personal subliminal life and through whose larger relationships saving experiences may come.

[19] From notes made by William James in preparation of the *Varieties*, quoted in Perry, *op. cit.*, II, 327.

We have noted different approaches which may be taken into the meaning of religion. Most often the human person is naïve in his natural approach to any situation until he is taught and conditioned to be otherwise. Then he may put his spontaneous interests under the leash and guide his attention to critical analysis and appraisal. Critical studies of religion may be philosophical and theological to view the whole creation on a grand scale from large perspective. Or the critical approach may be scientific and bring religion under exact and meticulous scrutiny by the working tools of history, sociology, or psychology.

In this chapter we have briefly traced the relations of these approaches to one another. Having glanced around at this context to get our bearings, we now set our course in a psychological direction. We acknowledge the importance of the long past in which beginnings have been made. And we mark the rise of scientific psychology with its new approach to religion in all the vigor of a youthful enterprise. In the next chapter we will examine contemporary psychologists of religion.

# 2 CONTEMPORARY PSYCHOLOGIES OF RELIGION

We have traced the history of psychological interest in religion through William James into the twentieth century. To this point psychology was an infant science, or as Coe would say a quasi science, taking its first experimental baby steps. The results were meager and the field of operation narrow, but the young psychology would one day be a science like its older brothers, the physical, biological, and mathematical sciences and its peers the social sciences. In the twenty-three years from 1879 when Wundt and James turned to psychological laboratories to 1902 when James published *The Varieties of Religious Experience,* the progress is notable and pathways have been opened that will become a network of highways by our mid-century.

How shall we map the highways of contemporary psychology? Whatever design we use to classify psychologies is projective from our own perceptions as we look forth upon the maze of roads crisscrossing one another to place upon them the imprint of our organizing attention. In the first edition of this book psychologies were classified into three groups reminiscent of the Hegelian dialectic. I suggested three ways of looking at mind: the subjective, objective, and synoptic points of view. The subjective view studies mind from within by introspection, as the structural psychology of Hume, Titchener, and Locke; the dynamic psychology of James, Thorndike, and Woodworth; and the depth psychology of Freud, Jung, Adler, and Rank. The objective view studies mind from without by external observation, as the behaviorism of Pavlov and Watson; the functional psychology of Dewey, Angell, and Mead; and much of experimental psychology. The synoptic view studies mind in perspective, as the Gestalt psychology of Wertheimer, Koehler, and Koffka; the personalistic psychology of Allport; the interpersonal psychology of Sullivan; and the field psychology of Lewin.

Having sorted these psychologies into such groupings, I then asked by what methods they gathered scientific data on religion. We noted that subjective studies of religion employed biographical, questionnaire, and psychometric methods. Objective studies of religion employed archaeological, anthropological, and experimental research. Synoptic studies of religion followed historical investigation, social and religious surveys, and systematic analysis and interpretation. It may be convenient to perceive psychologies in such a design, but not altogether satisfactory. Actually there is a good deal of overlap, and one comes to feel constrained by rigid categories into which a vast amount of subtle and complex discrimination is pressed to fit the scheme. Psychologies by this time have broken over boundaries, acknowledged the merit of other positions, and moved toward integration, leaving shells of the past as outworn fossils.

And yet groupings are significant not only for the convenience of the observer but to hold in view useful distinctions and relationships. It is more efficient to travel by a map which gives an overview of the terrain than to follow one's course without reference to directions or destinations. Too, it is well to recognize that no single road is the only way of proceeding to a destination, but that alternative routes are available. Designs are projections of what we see and intend to do according to interest and purpose; which means we are free to drop one and pick up another. This we are going to do in laying aside the earlier classification for a new one useful to our present study. Viewpoints were then classified according to methods of investigation; now we will classify psychologies according to theories of religion.

In the fourfold design to be submitted here, many psychologists may be associated in each grouping. But as this is an overview rather than an exhaustive account of details, it will be convenient to select one or two leading exponents of each viewpoint. The conflictual theory will be represented by Freud and Boisen. The collective theory will be represented by Jung. The personalistic theory will be represented by Allport. The interpersonal theory will be viewed with Moreno and Buber.

## *1. The Conflictual Theory*

The conflictual theory of Sigmund Freud (1856-1939) is important because of the ascending influence of psychoanalysis upon the culture of our century. Freud was born in Freiberg, Moravia, the first-born of a young and loving mother (age 21), who nourished in him faith and a sense of destiny; and a patriarchal father (age 41), who punished him as dispenser of righteous judgment like Yahweh, who thundered the moral code. His next brother, Julius, displaced him and died when Sigmund was eighteen months old. His playmate John was his nephew yet one year older, a dear rival of whom he said: "We loved and fought each other."

The culture of Judaism was his religious homeland. In his *Autobiography* he says, "My parents were Jews, and I have remained a Jew myself." He was enriched by this heritage of literature and proverbs; he was devoted to its great ethical principles and imbued with heroic willingness to suffer for a cause. Yet he was skeptical with alert and canny realism and viewed rituals as a nuisance unrelated to the ethical imperatives. Actually this religion was for him a cause of sorrow and deprivation; he saw his father insulted and unable to claim justice. Sigmund himself was denied professional advancement in Vienna because he was a Jew and eventually had to face the anti-Semitic persecution of the Nazis and flee to London.

The culture of science was his vocation and measure of truth. His devotion to truth was his greatest passion, and he did not hope to gain by other means what science does not give. For he worked in the nineteenth century, when science was engaged in constant warfare with the claims of religious dogma. His scientific culture was an unbroken naturalism in which natural law was all-embracing and ultimate. From these naturalistic presuppositions supernatural religion was to him an illusion, and religious concepts were but images of the mind or psychological projections of inner needs.

Psychoanalysis was to Freud a theory of human conflict and a therapy to heal the conflict. Within every personality he found an endless struggle of conflicting energies to express and repress primitive impulses emerging from the unconscious. The libidinal impulses which he called the id would drive recklessly to destruction unless repressed by the moral censorship of the superego, acting for the parents and other authorities in the life of the growing child. These conflictual strivings arise inevitably in the family as the young child enjoys the nourishing affection of the mother and becomes a rival of the father for the mother's love. This was named the Oedipus conflict for the son in Greek mythology who unknowingly killed his father and married his mother, and who was struck with such remorse on learning his true identity, that he destroyed himself. This dramatizes the conscious or unconscious conflicts of the child needing love and security amid the rivalries of desire and denial in learning to live as a member of society.

Whether in the distant beginnings of prehistory or in the beginning of life in the present family, Freud saw the origin of religion in such conflicts. When the child is disobedient and asserts himself against the father, he will feel guilt and need reconciliation. When he is helpless and unable to control the world, he will feel weak and in need of the father's strength. He learns both to fear and to admire the father as the one to deliver him in time of need. When he is older and goes forth as an adult, he may again be unable to control the world or his own aggressive impulses. Then he may regress to childish dependence and long for the father to bring him deliverance from guilt by reconciliation and from weakness by faith in one who is more powerful than himself.

Religion to Freud was a consoling fiction, unsupported by external events but well supported by inner wishes. As early as 1904 he spoke of the mythological and religious view as "nothing other than psychological process projected into the outer world." [1] In 1907 he noted the compulsive character of ritual acts and concluded that religion might be called a "universal obsessional neurosis." [2] In 1910 he further described religion as rooted in the parental complex:

> "Psycho-analysis has made us aware of the intimate connection between the father-complex and the belief in God, and has taught us that the personal God is psychologically nothing other than a magnified father." [3]

From his studies of totemism and monotheism [4] he inferred that religious history arises from the murder of the father or leader, and the need to restore and honor him by deification. It is easy to personify the forces of nature as a father to whom the sons may appeal for protection against danger and anxiety.

In *The Future of an Illusion* (1927) he granted that "religion has performed great services for human culture" [5] by restraining asocial instinct and that it may protect the true believer against certain neurotic afflictions. Yet he would avoid such "symbolic disguisings of the truth" by a rational effort to replace neurotic survivals with intelligent control of the instincts. He would aim to overcome childishness by education to reality, to rely upon one's own resources and learn to endure with resignation.

These quotations will have further consideration in Chapter Ten. For the present we must recognize how the psychoanalytic work of Freud has provided the impetus for a continuing stream of psychological studies of religion, provoking lively controversy and inviting fruitful research. Jung, Adler, Rank, Reik, Flügel, Bergler, Fromm, Jones, Money-Kyrle, Sanders, Lee, Cole,[6] and others have explored the meaning of religion in psychoanalytic terms. Anthropological and case methods have been employed to study

[1] *Psychopathology of Everyday Life.*

[2] "Obsessive Acts and Religious Practices," in the *Collected Papers,* II (London: Hogarth Press, 1924), 25-35.

[3] Quoted by Ernest Jones, *The Life and Work of Sigmund Freud,* III (New York: Basic Books, Inc., 1957), 354.

[4] *Totem and Taboo* (New York: W. W. Norton & Co. [1913], 1952); and *Moses and Monotheism* (New York: Alfred A. Knopf, Inc. [1937], 1955).

[5] (London: Hogarth Press, 1928), p. 65.

[6] See Bibliography for titles.

cultural and personality patterns, tracing parallels and reaching conclusions by analogy (which is more suggestive than conclusive). The concepts of these conflictual thinkers are usually governed by naturalistic assumptions, and the outcome is frequently reductive, disposing of religious claims by reducing them from conflictual to regressive psychic mechanisms.

The conflictual theory of Anton Boisen (1876- ), however, offers a counterthrust to the reductive procedure of Freud. Boisen was born in Bloomington, Indiana, and upon graduation from Indiana University in 1897, was a teacher of Romance languages at his alma mater until 1903. Then he studied forestry at Yale University and worked for three years in the United States Forestry Service before turning to theology. At Union Theological Seminary he specialized in psychology of religion with George A. Coe with special reference to mysticism. For five years he was a rural pastor and then a Y.M.C.A. worker overseas in the First World War. On his return he was engaged in a state survey for the Interchurch World Movement until 1920, when he decided to re-enter the pastoral ministry. While waiting for the call to a church, he was absorbed in writing out the meaning of his religious experience. At that time there came upon him an overpowering idea of a coming world catastrophe, in which he was involved. He was so disturbed that his family committed him to a mental hospital, where for three weeks he was in a violent delirium which he says was indelibly burned into his memory. The diagnosis was "catatonic dementia praecox," and his family was told not to expect his recovery. After a temporary recovery of four and a half months, he entered another severe disturbance of ten-weeks duration.

From this mental illness he did recover, however, and out of that experience came his vocation to be the pioneer full-time chaplain of a mental hospital and to bring religious resources to the mentally ill. He was intensely interested in the meaning of psychoses and dedicated himself to research into the religious implications of such experiences as reported in his books and the journals of religion and psychiatry. From the inner awareness of what psychosis meant to him as well as from his study of other persons in mental illness, he formulated the hypothesis of a significant relationship between acute mental illness of the functional type and religious conversion, as of the apostle Paul, George Fox, and many others well known in the history of the Christian Church. What he finds in common between psychosis and conversion is this, that both arise out of "inner conflict and disharmony, accompanied by a keen awareness of ultimate loyalties and unattained possibilities."

Religious experience as well as mental disorder may involve severe emotional upheaval, and mental disorder as well as religious experience may represent the operation of the healing forces of nature. The conclusion follows that certain types of mental disorder and certain types of religious experience are alike attempts at reorganization. The difference lies in the outcome. Where the attempt is successful and some degree of victory is won, it is commonly recognized as religious experience. Where it is unsuccessful or indeterminate, it is commonly spoken of as 'insanity." In those constructive transformations of the personality which we recognize as religious experience, the individual is relieved of his sense of isolation and is brought into harmony with that which is supreme in his hierachy of loyalties. He succeeds in effecting a synthesis between the crisis experience and his subsequent life which enables him to grow in the direction of inner unification and social adaptation on a basis conceived as universal.[7]

In his intensive study of 173 schizophrenics, Boisen found one characteristic common to all: they are isolated from their fellows through social failure and loss of self-respect. In their psychosis they experience a sense of the mysterious, a sense of peril, and a sense of personal responsibility. They have ideas of death, of cosmic catastrophe, conflict, rebirth, of a mission to be fulfilled. Among three typical reactions of panic, self-deception, and drifting he found the panic most conducive to recovery as breaking up rigid defenses and erupting into a new life. Mental illness is a problem-solving approach to life, an effort to resolve intolerable conflict and find unification in a new perspective. The religious concern of guilt and personal responsibility is working through to ethical reorganization by identification with ultimate loyalties. In this way the suffering may be remedial and the illness not necessarily evil but a purposive effort to come through crisis to higher unification.

While Freud and Boisen agree that religious experience arises in conflict, they differ sharply in viewing the outcome of such experience. To Freud religion is a neurotic solution that appears to him regressive and reductive. But to Boisen religion offers sound and mature healing of conflict by working through crisis to ethical responsibility productive of larger loyalties. Not every such attempt is successful, and when the goal is not achieved, the person or group may revert to deception or drifting. Religious groups as well as individuals are aroused by crisis to creative growth. Yet before or after crisis they may settle down into uncreative patterns of careless or conservative custom. This seems to indicate to Boisen, on a broad base of evidence he has gathered from religious groups, that crisis serves a creative purpose in society even as the heightening of conflict may in mental healing and religious conversion.[8] At this point there is a meeting of conflictual

[7] *The Exploration of the Inner World: A Study of Mental Disorder and Religious Experience* (New York: Harper & Bros., 1936), p. ix. Used by permission of the publisher.

[8] *Religion in Crisis and Custom: A Sociological and Psychological Study* (New York: Harper & Bros., 1955).

psychology and crisis theology. Religion here is not escape from reality but confrontation of reality.

Anton Boisen, who has survived many of his contemporaries, continues at Elgin State Hospital (Illinois) as Chaplain Emeritus, active as ever in research and writing, attending professional meetings and giving valued counsel to his younger colleagues. His conclusions are well supported with empirical evidence which he gathers by methods of social survey, clinical records, case studies, statistical and graphic analysis, as well as historical and theological correlations.

## 2. *The Collective Theory*

The collective theory of religion, here represented by Carl Gustav Jung (1875- ), emerges out of conflict to overcome conflict. It has been the work of conscious intelligence to analyze and separate into conflicting parts, but deeper than such divisions is the encompassing unity of the unconscious, which Jung undertakes to explore. As the son of a Swiss Reformed pastor his interest in religion has been continuing and profound. He studied medicine at the University of Basel, practiced psychiatry at Zurich, and became one of Freud's early supporters. By 1913, however, they came to basic theoretical differences that caused a gulf between them. These differences will be examined further in Chapter Ten, yet they need to be outlined here in noting contemporary psychologies of religion. Freud was an individualist who emphasized the separateness of each person, and he was an analyst who saw the conflictual forces of personality as essentially irreparable. By psychoanalysis he sought to enable his patient to release defenses and recognize the nature of the conflicts and thus to tolerate them by making the unconscious conscious. Jung acknowledges the polarities and oppositions in man, but to him they are as complementary as the colors of a spectrum, capable of blending and unification. And as a collectivist he finds the whole more basic than the differing parts, the source of all healing and wisdom. To him the personality has no boundaries, for the personal unconscious moves out continuously into the racial unconscious. From this oceanic psychic energy of universal dimensions he draws the ultimate answer to every question and particularly religious questions.

Religious experience, as he sees it, is an uprushing from the collective unconscious of dynamic energies and symbols of timeless and universal meaning. Psychology is purely empirical and does not raise metaphysical questions, nor does it explain away the mystery but seeks to describe religious phenomena. Contrary to Freud, who internalizes religion as the product of subjective wish-motives, Jung externalizes religion as arising from sources of unconscious energy beyond the individual consciousness. This is no fantasy but a revelation of a numinous power from beyond, which is experienced as mysterious otherness. This otherness is evidently indefinable except by symbols or archetypes which recur in many cultures as indicative of the racial unconscious of mankind. To deny the meaning of this vast unconscious is to impoverish life by separation from the ultimate sources of vital energy. To repress conflicting energies is to defeat the wholeness of life which can be achieved only in their integration.

To find these common symbols or recurring archetypes, Jung turns from one religion to another for evidence that underlying our differences the universal will appear. This need not be one culture borrowing from another, for such ideas spontaneously emerge from a common substratum more basic than the differences. A central dogma of Christian theology is the Trinity, which meets the triad archetype in the ancient religions of Babylonia, Egypt, and Greece, signifying the dynamic progression of father-son duality through a unifying third. The cross is a focal symbol of Christianity elaborated in many designs and meanings of quaternity. The mandala circle of four parts recurs in the religious symbolism of the Orient, as an archetype signifying the meeting of opposites in unifying wholeness. The Mass is a living mystery dramatizing the sacrifice and sacred meal found in totemism, and the act of God present to the worshiper in transforming the creatures of bread and wine into the spiritual symbols of incarnation.

> The archetype is "that which is believed always, everywhere, and by everybody," and if it is not recognized consciously, then it appears from behind in its "wrathful" form, as the dark "son of chaos," the evil doer, as Anti-Christ instead of Saviour—a fact which is all too clearly demonstrated by contemporary history.[9]

Religious symbols are not invented but have grown out of the basic conditions of human nature which Jung believes are everywhere the same. The conflicts are to be resolved by these reconciling symbols appearing in dreams and myths, or historic culture and religion. For the archetype is not merely a symbol as a sign but a very complex and dynamic meaning that is able to unite the individual at deeply unconscious levels with his race. The goal of religion is to be one with the universal psyche, not to submerge consciousness in a sea of unconscious oblivion, but to enrich and integrate personal consciousness by ultimate resources. The ultimate dimension to which Jung seeks to be related is impersonal psychic energy or spirit, as in the absolute idealism of Hegel and the pantheism of Hindu

[9] *Psychology and Religion: West and East,* tr. R. F. C. Hull (New York: Pantheon Books, Inc., 1958), p. 117. Used by permission of the publisher.

monists. It is characteristic of collectivism to subordinate the individual person to the impersonal whole. This tendency appears in theories of religion offered by Durkheim, Ames, King, Dewey, and Wieman.[10]

Now in his ninth decade Jung continues to practice psychiatry in Zurich, surrounded by his family and associates in the institute named for him. His researches in religion and mythology, symbols and rituals, customs and beliefs, extend into most of the cultures of the world; as well as dreams and visions from many sources, and the symptoms and hallucinations of psychiatric patients. An authorized English translation of his *Collected Works* is being published by Pantheon Books of New York and will exceed eighteen volumes. His research methods include experimental studies of complexes by the word-association test; case studies based upon dreams and free associations, using the methods of internal consistency and active imagination; and comparative studies of religion, mythology, and occult sciences such as alchemy and astrology. It may be too early to predict the outcome of Jung's fertile ideas, but to date, his influence is apparently greater in religious than psychological channels.

### 3. *The Personalistic Theory*

The personalistic theory represented by Gordon W. Allport (1897-     ) is a counterthrust against both the conflictual theory of Freud and the collective theory of Jung. Allport was born in Indiana, one of four sons of a physician and younger brother of psychologist Floyd Allport. He was educated at Harvard University, receiving in 1922 the Ph.D. degree in psychology, with additional study in Berlin, Hamburg, and Cambridge universities. He has taught at Robert College, Istanbul; Dartmouth College; and since 1930 at Harvard University, where his theories and writings have come to a significant place in contemporary psychology.

His personalistic psychology, which he expounds persuasively, is set in opposition to every collectivism that would subordinate the individual person to a common denominator whether statistical averages, populations, types or archetypes. He is the protagonist for the uniqueness of individual personality, which may be lost in the mass of numbers and scientific generalization. He invites fellow psychologists to invent scientific methods to study the individual in his unique self-consistency, congruent with his own style of life, rather than to reduce him by quantitative measurements to common traits and general abstractions.

He is also set in opposition to every reductionism that would reduce the

[10] See Bibliography for titles.

whole to parts or the living behavior to segmental instincts and mechanisms. The present is not to be explained altogether by the causal determinism of the past, for present motives may function autonomously; and the meaning of behavior cannot be grasped apart from the future goal and the intention to reach it. Facile reductions of conscious intention to unconscious motivation are self-deceptive and misleading, like the work of a detective who overlooks the obvious clue to explore the hidden sutleties of his theory. Why overlook conscious determinants? Has the person no right to be believed in what he thinks he is trying to do? "What drives behavior, drives now"; and we do not understand personality by overlooking contemporary motivation, the goals and aspirations of conscious, rational foresight.

"A narrowly conceived science," he observes, "can never do business with a narrowly conceived religion." Yet it would be absurd to suppose that psychology and religion cannot meet or work together harmoniously for human welfare. Allport as a psychologist brings his science into conversation with mature expressions of religion, that larger understanding may result from the encounter. It is consonant with his future-oriented psychology that he recognize man's religious quest for the meaning and destination of his life. Also that each individual person will pursue and discover this meaning as his own in a unique sense.

The unique character of a mature religion is integral with the central intention of the individual person. To act mentally is to intend a goal. Intention may be defined as the conscious striving of an individual for a goal which he undertakes to reach. Its direction is toward a future destination, and his future is what concerns a person most of all. For the growing business of every person is in becoming more than he has been. Faith is a personal affair, which no one else can provide or prescribe for the individual. Faith is a motivating belief in the validity and attainability of some goal set by desires yet appraised as a true value. The forward thrust of these future-oriented desires involves such aspirations as longing for a better world and for the fulfillment of one's own potentialities in the ultimate context of life.

The mature religious sentiment does arise through social interdependence, even though each individual will discover it for himself. It is possible, therefore, to identify and delineate characteristics which are representative, even among individual variations, of the nature of what it means to be religious in a mature sense. In his book *The Individual and His Religion*, Allport gives a psychological description of the religious sentiment:

The maturely productive religious sentiment, I have argued throughout these pages, is an interest-system within the structure of an individual's personality basically like any other well-developed interest-system. Like other mature sentiments it is *well differentiated,* which means that the individual at various times can view its sub-parts and their relation to one another; it is *dynamic* in its own right, that is, it plays an important autonomous part in the motivational life of the individual regardless of its own origins; it is *productive of conduct consistent with the nature of the sentiment,* and engenders a conscience appropriate to the values involved. Because of its special nature, however, the religious sentiment in some respects does differ in degree if not in kind from other mature sentiments. It is certainly more *comprehensive,* since it aims to join all experience into a single meaningful system. It is likewise a *uniquely integral system* in that it aims to give one leading directive to the life as a whole. Finally, because of the limited certainties that plague any religious belief, there is an *heuristic* quality to this sentiment: it is held with loyalty for the very purpose of discovering all the good and all the truth that may issue from it.[11]

Allport has worked to broaden scientific method in psychology. He notes that either the investigator may choose to study behavior in terms of universal variables (nomothetic) or he may focus upon the individual case (idiographic). There is need for both, and in his research he complements one with the other. Expressive behavior is studied by psychological tests and repeated observation of gesture, voice, handwriting, and muscles used in tasks to discover stable characteristics of a consistent style of life. Matching techniques and cluster analysis are employed to correlate data. Personal documents, questionnaires, and case studies are used to integrate information on the complexity of individual personality. Direct methods of conscious appraisal are considered essential in spite of the current preoccupation with indirect methods.[12]

Other personalistic psychologists of religion are Coe, Pratt, Knudson, Strickland, Brightman, Bertocci, and Walter Clark.[13] Allport has associated with William Stern in Germany and social psychologists in America, though his psychology is unique as his own individual personality.

## 4. *The Interpersonal Theory*

The interpersonal theory is a vigorous counterthrust to each of the three theories, redirecting and extending dynamic principles inherent in them. A frontiersman who contributed to the development of interpersonal psychology is Jacob Levy

[11] *The Individual and His Religion: A Psychological Interpretation* (New York: The Macmillan Co., 1950), p. 124. Used by permission of the publisher.

[12] See the chapter on "Allport's Psychology of the Individual" in Calvin S. Hall and Gardner Lindzey, *Theories of Personality* (New York: John Wiley & Sons, 1957).

[13] See Bibliography for titles.

Moreno (1892- ). He was born in Bucharest, Rumania, the first of six children, three boys and three girls. His father, a merchant, and his mother, a housewife, were Sephardi, or Spanish Jews, and his mother tongues were Spanish and Rumanian. At the age of four he went to Bible school and began to read the Bible in Hebrew. When he was six, his family moved to Vienna, and there he learned German and attended public school and the university, where he pursued studies in philosophy, theology, and mathematics before turning to medicine and completing the doctor's degree in 1917. While a medical student he was a research assistant of the Psychiatric Clinic at the University of Vienna, and in the year 1911 he met Freud and attended one of his lectures. But the analytic reductionism of Freud left him cold, for he was already moving in another direction.

Moreno recognized the deep conflicts of life, but to him they demand a creative solution in religious dimensions. He was not satisfied with the religious institutions which were preoccupied in conserving the traditions of the past but was more impressed by the dramatic dialogue of Jesus and Socrates. His idea of God was of the Creator on the first day of creation, acting spontaneously to bring into being a new world. And spontaneity became to him the basic principle motivating behavior in creative action. With this as the revolutionary principle to change life from confining rigidity to creativity, he saw the need of a new religious movement employing the new discoveries of science.

In the spring of 1914 Moreno published in Vienna the first of a series of poetic writings entitled *Einladung zu einer Begegnung* (*Invitation to an Encounter*), which is evidently the first literary definition of encounter, the concept which has become central in the existentialist movement. To describe the encounter, he portrays two persons exchanging eyes to comprehend and know each other:

> A meeting of two: eye to eye, face to face.
> And when you are near I will tear your eyes out and place
> them instead of mine, and you will tear my eyes out and
> will place them instead of yours, then I will look at
> you with your eyes and you will look at me with mine.[14]

The literary magazine *Daimon*,[15] of which he was the editor, carried in the February issue, 1918, a dramatic dialogue by Moreno entitled

[14] (R. Thimms Erbe, Wien II, Darwingasse 4, 1914), p. 5. At that time he used as his pen name Jacob Levy. There were six annual publications until 1920 entitled *Invitation to Encounter*, followed by six others published at that time anonymously.

[15] Published by Bruder Suschitzky in Vienna.

"Einladung zu einer Begegnung: Die Gottheit als Autor" ("Invitation to an Encounter: The Godhead as Author"). In this article (page 6) appears the term "interpersonal communication" ("zwischenmenschlichen Verkehr"). The term "interpersonal relations," which Robert MacDougall used in 1912, came to prominence in his book *Who Shall Survive* (1934) and in the journal he founded in 1937, *Sociometry: A Journal of Interpersonal Relations*. During the years 1918-20 Martin Buber was a contributing editor of *Daimon*, and his articles appeared side by side with Moreno's, prophetic of the role each would have in the history of interpersonal theory. The I-Thou concept of God was the keystone of the interpersonal arch as documented in their publications of 1920-23. *Das Testaments des Vaters*, 1920 (*The Words of the Father*), contains dialogues of direct address in the form of *Ich und Du*.[16] Buber's *Ich und Du* (1923) is the definitive statement of the I-Thou relationship.

Moreno is best known for his pioneer work in sociometry, psychodrama, and group therapy. What is not so well known and yet is clearly stated in his writings is that the basic motivation for all of his work is religious. "The theory of interpersonal relations is born of religion." [17] Sociometry (the psychological and experimental measurement of interpersonal relations) he began first with a community of displaced persons at Mittendorf near Vienna, 1915-17. The classic study he conducted at the Hudson (New York) Training School for Girls, 1932-36, during which the essential concepts and procedures of this science were developed. Here the sociometric test invited the girls to decide with whom they would and would not like to live, and the psychological currents were shown in sociograms. In this way the emotional dynamics of group life were revealed and therapy for personal needs was provided.

Psychodrama had its beginning in Vienna with the Theater of Spontaneity, which Moreno first conducted in 1921. He found the legitimate theater stifled by the practice of giving the actor lines to memorize written by another, to portray a character which he was not, on a shrouded stage with the audience in darkness. He invented the open stage in the center of the room with access from the audience all around. His theater invited actors and audience to portray their own dramatic situations from the here and now, and to speak impromptu, without written lines, in response to one another. He perceived this as a kind of dramatic religion, a theater to call forth the spontaneously creative self and learn with God what it means

[16] Published at first by Moreno anonymously, now as *The Psychodrama of God*, by J. L. Moreno (New York: Beacon House, 1947). Note pp. 110-11.

[17] See especially the "Preludes" in *Who Shall Survive?* by J. L. Moreno (rev. ed.; New York: Beacon House, Inc., 1953). The quotation is from p. xxxi. Used by permission of the publisher.

to be a creator.[18] This became the therapeutic theater to heal the distresses and conflicts of the inner life by allowing the patient to act them out in the face-to-face encounter of psychodrama. This method has been widely used in schools, churches, and hospitals to provide catharsis, role learning, and the working through of individual and social dilemmas.

Group therapy is another development in which the theory and practice of Moreno have played a significant role. Group treatment was given by Joseph H. Pratt, M.D., at the Boston Dispensary as early as 1905 for tuberculosis and by 1930 for psychosomatic disorders. But it was Moreno who diagnosed the structure of interpersonal relations in small groups, and from this he went on to employ interaction within the group as psychotherapy. In 1931 his monograph on *Application of the Group Method to Classification* was published by the National Committee on Prisons and Prison Labor. The following year he opened his address to the American Psychiatric Association in Philadelphia with this definition: "Group psychotherapy is a method which protects and stimulates the self-regulating mechanisms of natural groups—through the use of one man as a therapeutic agent of the other, of one group as a therapeutic agent of the other." [19]

The study and use of the small group has become a notable achievement of the behavioral sciences since 1930. Group therapy has proved effective with delinquent youth, alcoholics, patients, students, and parents. Experiments in group dynamics have resolved social conflicts and improved human relations in the community, the school, industry, and religious groups. Role perception, group discussion, and democratic decision have been facilitated through these experiments significant to psychology of religion.

With undiminished spontaneity Moreno carries on these many lines of activity from Beacon, New York, where he conducts institutes, directs psychodrama, supervises students, edits publications, and participates extensively in professional societies. The concepts and experimental methods which he has fostered are so widely used that his part in them will probably be forgotten long before the fruits of his labors have fully appeared.

The interpersonal theory of man has come to further development in the work of Martin Buber (1878-     ). While Moreno has been at work with interpersonal relations in psychiatry and the social sciences, Buber has been pioneering a philosophical anthropology of I and Thou. He was born in Vienna, fourteen years before Moreno, in the year 1878, of a famous Galician rabbinical family. His early youth was spent in Lemberg, steeped

[18] *Das Stegreiftheater* was published in Vienna in 1923, translated as *The Theatre of Spontaneity* by J. L. Moreno (New York: Beacon House, 1947). See pages 4, 12, 13, 95, 96, for references to the religious dimension.

[19] *Who Shall Survive?* p. lv.

in great Hebrew traditions in which piety and culture flowered in the spirit of the Enlightenment. During his student years at the universities of Vienna, Berlin, Leipzig, and Zurich he devoted himself to philosophy, literature, and art among the great thinkers of that day. His early scholarship illuminated the Chassidic movement of ethical mysticism within the human community, and his dialogic view of man makes him, now at Hebrew University in Israel, one of the prophetic voices of our time.

His most influential book is a slender volume of poetic beauty published as *Ich und Du* in 1923 and translated as *I and Thou* in 1937.[20] Later writings on this theme were published as *Between Man and Man.*[21] We have noted that Moreno and Buber were associated in the literary journal *Daimon* and that both were concerned with the encounter of person with person. How much they may have influenced each other is not altogether clear, but they moved in a common stream of fertile significance, the interpersonal theory of man and God. Buber does acknowledge a germinal idea which Feuerbach gave in his *Principles of the Philosophy of the Future* in 1843:

> The individual man for himself does not have man's being in himself, either as a moral being or as thinking being. Man's being is contained only in community, in the unity of man with man—a unity which rests, however, only on the reality of the difference between I and Thou.[22]

Buber sees that man is incomplete as the single one; he is not himself in isolation. Neither does he find his fulfillment in the crowd by submerging himself in the collective mass. Real life is in meeting, lived in the relation between man and man. This meeting is the life of dialogue in which one person addresses another, turns to him to make him present and perceive what life means to him. As we communicate person with person, my whole being says something to you, and your whole being speaks something that enters my life.

In this dialogic relation the person whom I encounter is not the object of my experience; he is the subject who addresses me as subject. There are two primary words, each indicating a relation. If I say the primary word I-It, I am defining a relation to a thing, and my attitude is that of separation from an object. The I of such a connection has no present, only the past in which things are classified. The living experience of the present arises when I confront Thou in this moment. The real, filled present occurs in meeting in which there is living and mutual relationship. The primary

[20] R. G. Smith, tr. (Edinburgh: T. & T. Clark, 1937; reprinted in New York by Charles Scribner's Sons).

[21] R. G. Smith, tr. (New York: The Macmillan Co., 1947).

[22] *Grundsätze der Philosophie der Zukunft,* quoted by Buber in *ibid.*, pp. 147-48.

word I-It can never be spoken with my whole being. But when Thou is spoken, the speaker takes his stand in relation. I become a person through my relation to Thou.

Man does not become a whole self alone or in reference to objects, but only in relation to another self. The whole self is a unity of opposition, in which tension and conflict arise from the essential duality of personal existence. This Buber calls the inborn Thou, which from birth will always be over against my singleness. To enter into a relation is to accept this tension of duality as essential to my being and to live the life of confrontation. So ultimate is the meaning of relationship that Buber finds in every relation the eternal Thou revealed. Not by turning away from human persons do we meet God, but God meets us in all of our interpersonal relationships. "In each Thou we address the eternal Thou." [23]

God is not one object to be inferred from another as philosophers do by abstract reasoning, for this reduces Thou to It like any other thing. "God is the being that is directly, most nearly, and lastingly over against us, that may properly be only addressed not expressed." [24] God in the direct relation of encounter is not an idea in the abstract sense of logical argument, induced or deduced from some other givens. Rather he meets us as Thou in the present moment of living relationship. He is not to be proved or disproved but known in the dialogue of personal relationship. Religious experience for Buber is at once psychological in the intimate sense of meeting and theological in the affirmation of ultimate Being so revealed.

Though not himself a psychologist, Buber contributes significantly to the psychology of religion in submitting data and description of the religious life which psychologists will seek to understand. He further sharpens our focus upon the nature of man and offers a frame of reference for contemporary study that gives meaning and dignity to the human encounter.

We have surveyed four contemporary theories of man in psychoreligious context. There is much to learn and much to question in each of them. The conflictual theory sees man as a profoundly complex personality, who is caught in the distress of internal contradictions and struggling desperately to grow into productive maturity. His religion according to Freud operates like an obsessional neurosis seeking protective security through reconciliation with a father symbol. The depth of the conflict is affirmed by Boisen, and the cure he finds to be a religious conversion whereby a person becomes responsibly related to larger loyalties.

The collective theory also rises from inner conflicts yet sees them as complemental tendencies capable of mutual support when integrated into larger wholeness. The religious thrust is an overpowering invasion of psychic

[23] *I and Thou*, pp. 6, 79.
[24] *Ibid.*, pp. 80-81.

energy from the collective unconscious, whose mysterious meaning is to be discovered in archetypes or universal symbols, appearing in many cultures as racial memories to inform and guide the individual as he wrestles with his destiny to fulfill the hidden potentialities of his being.

The personalistic theory is dubious of all collectivisms which submerge the uniqueness of the individual and of all instinctual or segmental views that would reduce him by causal determinism to a lesser creature of the past. The direction of the growing person is forward, and his business, according to Allport, is to overcome the blocks which arrest his becoming and move into effective maturity by new motives to replace former ones. The religious sentiment may well be instrumental to effective maturing by outreaching neurotic regressions in response to an all-embracing system of values. Mature religious behavior follows conscious intention to worthy goals by orientation to the future.

Interpersonal theory finds the essential nature of man in his encounter with another person, without which he can know neither himself nor the fullness of the living present. This is what personalistic psychology overlooks in its effort to explicate the uniqueness of the individual. It is what collectivism loses in the mass which submerges the individuality recaptured and enriched by the relation of person with person. It is what conflictual psychoanalysis misses in viewing man "from the bottom up" as a product of infantile and primitive wants, and what interpersonal dialogue addresses as I confronting Thou in the relation of whole and present being.

It is evident that every theory of man emerges from a philosophy whether latent or manifest. For theory is constructed of principles which assume universality in one way or another. Psychological research will continue to gather significant data by ingenious methods to fill in needed details and at times to upset established theories. But data are only a collection of meaningless items in a heap of confusion until viewed in the clarifying and integrating perspective of a theory. Facts and theories are not interchangeable parts from mechanical assembly lines. They are the tools fashioned by a purposive intention to wrestle with elusive unknowns and hold a steady course to a goal we may decide to seek.

## 5. *Religion and Personality*

Defining religion is a difficult task because religion is so complex. It is one of the broadest terms that language provides, for religion works with the largest ideas man has conceived. As a collective noun it covers a vast array of human interests and activities. In the name of religion what deed has not been done? For the sake of religion men have earnestly affirmed and contradicted almost every idea and form of conduct. In the long history of religion appear chastity and sacred prostitution, feasting and fasting, intoxication and prohibition, dancing and sobriety, human sacrifice and the saving of life in orphanages and hospitals, superstition and education, poverty and wealthy endowments, prayer wheels and silent worship, gods and demons, one God and many gods, attempts to escape and to reform the world. How can such diametrical oppositions all be religious? Yet which of them can be excluded without an arbitrary denial of historical facts?

An adequate definition of religion must be general enough to include all types. Many definitions are constructed by the doubtful device of mistaking some part for the whole. It is possible to classify definitions of religion by the chief aspect indicated. Leuba classified them in three groups as emphasizing the intellectual, emotional, or volitional aspect.[25] To these may be added others such as social and institutional definitions, theological definitions, and synthetic definitions that seek to unite these aspects in a larger view. We may well begin with a general definition.

*Religion is response to a Sustainer of values.* This statement aims to include as many aspects and varieties of religion as possible. Any response, whether fear or trust, any action or attitude that recognizes a power able to control values, is religion in the broad sense. Any Sustainer—or many—who can save or destroy, give or withhold what one may need or desire, is indicated. A Sustainer may be personal (as a Father) or impersonal (as a process), human (as a parent) or divine (as a Wholly Other), natural (as scientific forces) or supernatural (as magical powers), individual (as in monotheism) or societal (as in humanism) and institutional (as in patriotic devotion to the nation). This definition excludes neither magic nor demons, neither codes of laws nor ethics; it includes devotion ofanimals to masters, children to parents, lovers to beloveds, and patriots dying for a fatherland. The essentials of religion are (*a*) desire for values, (*b*) conscious dependence upon a power who is able to sustain such values, and (*c*) responses considered appropriate to realize the values by reference to such a power.

With this inclusive view as a background, a more distinctive definition is needed to differentiate religion. It must distinguish what is meant from what is not meant, drawing clearly the line between the designated and the undesignated. For a term that connotes everything denotes nothing. Religion will need to be distinguished from magic and myth, social custom and organization, science and philosophy, ethics and aesthetics, though it may have points in common with them. A differential definition will point to what is essentially unique.

*Religion is personal devotion to ultimate Being, who is believed to offer*

[25] See his *A Psychological Study of Religion* (New York: The Macmillan Co., 1912), pp. 339-60.

*creative potentialities for human life through enlarging relationships.* The most unique trait, the distinguishing mood of religious experience, is ultimate concern.[26] Psychology cannot prove or disprove the existence of ultimate Being. But neither can psychology ignore human belief in such a Being. Careful observation will reveal that religious devotion is not content for long with the local and proximate but insistently seeks the eternal and ultimate. It is natural to respond to a local Sustainer of value, who may satisfy a desire or give security for the moment. Yet every moment points beyond itself since its fulfillment cannot satisfy for long. The finite person is ever fragmentary and incomplete. But in knowing this he transcends the fleeting moment, looks before and after, and longs for Someone greater and more complete to answer his loneliness. He may try one remedy after another to ease his restless search, but nothing transient will hold him, and soon again he takes up the endless search for that which will give ultimate and faithful response to his deepest need.

Other hungers may be satisfied with food at hand, and if the supply is constant, a person may grow fat and lazy in this security. But a religious longing of ultimate concern is not so. For this is a hunger that no thing will satisfy, and no material supply will give the answer sought. The ultimate quest is for a Being who confronts me in living relationship as I search for him. I am determined to meet Thou, for nothing less will give my life ultimate significance. The creative potentialities are not the I-It relation to a thing or any number of things. Rather as Buber shows in his account of the religious encounter, the ultimate meaning of I is to be discovered only in meeting Thou. Who is Thou? This is the ultimate mystery and fascination of man's persisting quest. The full-rounded answer is beyond finite vision, yet the experience of meeting Thou is the essence of religion and the testimony of those who do not give up the ultimate concern.

These are the religious seekers who believe that the creative potentialities of our life are to found in the meeting of I and Thou. Every meeting of person with person is an adventure pregnant with unknown potentialities. And every meeting is an interpersonal relationship that may increase or decline in value. To exploit another person is to meet him as It, and treating him as a thing to serve as means to my ends, such a relationship declines in value. To reverence another person is to meet him as Thou with honest appreciation of his worth and dignity as a creative center of valuing experience. Such a relationship has creative potentialities for mutual growth and discovery of what it means to be a person in a giving and receiving of value. To meet a finite person in this way is not to make him the ultimate

[26] Thomas Mann wrote, "Religion is man's ultimate concern." See the Preface to *Order of the Day* (1930). See also Paul Tillich, *The Dynamics of Faith* (New York: Harper & Bros., 1957).

Thou, for he is local and transient in relation to me. Yet to meet a person in full respect and appreciation is a step toward ultimate confrontation. Every true meaning is, therefore, at once a revelation and a participation in widening relations. For it is through such enlarging relationships that religious seekers come to ultimate concern and by personal devotion sense the creative potentialities of human life.

Religious meeting is interpersonal. It belongs in every case to persons for whom the meeting has meaning and worth. A religious value may refer to an other, but it also refers to a subject who cherishes it. Religion therefore moves and has its being in the realm of personality. The experience of religion is a personal experience; its value is intelligible only to persons. Psychology of religion seeks to explore the meaning of religion in the relationships of human personality.

There are two ways in which religious studies may evade personality. One may take a microscopic view of religion by studying the minutiae of its minor details, the jots and tittles (dots of *i*'s, crossing of *t*'s) in literal devotion to words, or the postures and genuflections of formal ceremonies, thus missing the vital meaning of religious experience for personality as a whole. Another may take a telescopic view of religion as a cosmic process in a comprehensive unity of impersonal pantheism, submerging personality in the larger whole as a wave subsiding into an ocean of engulfing Being. Either view, whether microscopic or telescopic, lacks the perspective of personality and distorts the understanding of religion. These distortions psychology of religion seeks to correct by focusing upon religion as personal experience.

Personality is a unique center of individual life striving for goals through dynamic relationships. Not all of these goals have ultimate meaning; many of them are sought for immediate satisfaction. But as each goal is reached, it becomes a starting point for other goals. In the ongoing search for a goal beyond goals and a relationship beyond local relations, a person may develop the ultimate concern of religion.

Scientific psychologies have sometimes been microscopic, explaining behavior in atomistic terms without recognizing the perceptive work of personality as a whole. The reflex arc, stimulus-response, association of ideas, instinctive urges, unconscious mechanisms, may be useful concepts but are fractional segments of the whole personality in action. While the specializing tendency of a science may come to know more and more about less and less, the generalizing tendency of a philosophy may come to know less and less about more and more. Some psychologies of religion are overphilosophical, taking a telescopic view of distant processes beyond the legitimate range of psychology. Psychology will recognize the objective reference of all experience to enlarging relationships, but it does not aim to investigate the nature of God or the transempirical reality of a cosmic continuum.

The psychology of religion here set forth aims to follow a moderate course between the rocks and shoals of the microscopic and telescopic fallacies. In so doing we must consider personality-in-relations the unit of our investigation. Responses are to be seen as intra-activities of personality, yet they respond to other persons in outgoing relationships. This may be called interpersonal psychology, for a person is one who meets other persons in relationships that mutually determine and are determined by the dynamic complexity of his growing life.

# 3 RELIGIOUS EXPERIENCE

## 1. *Thresholds of Religious Awareness*

To be conscious is to have experience. The limits of conscious experience are called "thresholds" or "limens." Experimental work has been conducted to discover the points at which persons become aware of auditory, visual, and gustatory stimuli. But these sensations, once thought to be the final elements of psychological analysis, are neither specific nor reliable data but abstractions from larger empirical unities. Gestalt psychology has demonstrated that perceptions are total patterns of meaning, not summations of atomistic sensations. Perceptions are organized by persons into meaningful wholes. "No Gestalt without a Gestalter." [1] Thresholds are, therefore, boundaries of personal significance that are raised or lowered by the person's selective responsiveness.

What does it mean to be conscious and have experiences? In waking from deep slumber you have a typical experience to analyze. One may be roused by some disturbing stimuli such as light or sound waves. The effort to wake up meets resistance and perhaps resentment at being disturbed from drowsy comfort, but one responds by groping for a meaning. "What's that?" The light may then be recognized as coming from a window—which means morning. The noise may be identified as the ringing of an alarm clock meaning, "Time to get up." With that recognition a dilemma arises, "Do I have to get up, or can I stay in bed a while longer?" Then one gropes for perspective by recalling yesterday with its unfinished business and forecasting today with its plans and responsibilities until a decision is made and action taken or action deferred.

There are evidently four steps in this procedure of becoming conscious: (*a*) There is *awareness*, or selective attention. From waves of stimuli beating upon his receptors, a person selects relevant ones by attending responses. Intensity, suddenness, or repetition of light or sound stimuli have arousing effect. Yet the motor set, interest, or response of the person also directs at-

[1] William Stern, *General Psychology*, tr. H. D. Spoerl (New York: The Macmillan Co., 1938), pp. 114, 179.

tention (literally, "a-tension" toward something). (*b*) With this comes a process of *search*. What is going on? One is alert enough to be aware of a disturbance without yet fully knowing what it means. Awaking is an exploratory process, focusing perception upon the total situation, seeking more information about it. (*c*) The next step is a *judgment* of recognition. This is the daylight that means morning, the sound of an alarm clock meaning "Wake up!" Perception grows clearer as the mind gropes for understanding. Every judgment is a relating act, bringing this event into relation with others and seeing them together. The range of interpretation is enlarged by other items from the memory of the past and the prospect of the future. (*d*) From these insights conscious experience now integrates into *purpose*. There have been purposive, or goal-seeking, tendencies throughout in selectivity, search, and judgment. But the purpose now becomes the problem, or focal issue, in a conscious effort to make a decision. Something needs to be done, in this case the getting up and on to the tasks of the day. As one recognizes the morning time that means another day, he foresees goals and engages in the consideration of means to serve the ends in view.

Religious experience is not so simple as this, yet the religious consciousness upon analysis yields the four operations noted above. There is *awareness* of religious stimuli [2] and *search* for religious meanings. There is interpretation issuing in *judgments* of recognition and value. There will be *purposes* to do something to attain religious goals. Religious consciousness is not a world separate from the secular consciousness. The structure of all experience appears to have these four characteristics though the content may vary. The nature of religious experience does not contradict or escape the natural order of consciousness.

Such intricate behavior as perception is far removed from the naïve view of a raw mind stamped with the exact image of a raw object. Each individual perceives a given reality in his own characteristic way shaped by his expectations, the sum of his previous experiences, and the goal-direction of his personal intentions. The spread and flow of events will be cut up and organized by his language and culture. What he perceives will be the meaning the person gives to a situation in his transaction with it. J. S. Bruner reports an experiment of showing to different observers the picture of a man with head bowed. Persons with a religious orientation perceive the man as praying. Other persons with economic orientation perceive the man stooped as at work. Each one perceives what he is set or prepared to to see and to which he brings a personalized meaning as his interpretation. Perceiving according to Bruner is a three-step cycle of (*a*) expectancy

[2] A religious stimulus may be defined as any event which initiates a religious response, as toward a Sustainer of values.

with the "tuned organization," (*b*) input of information from the environment, and (*c*) confirming the expectancy hypothesis.[3]

Does the person in religious awareness use the natural perceptions, or does he have a special sense beyond them? To begin with, we should admit the place of sensory perceptions in much of our religious experience. To perceive the beauty of a sunset or the splendor of a starlight night may call forth joyous reverence. To sense the boisterous terror of a storm at sea may impel men to call upon their God for mercy and help. To hear persuasive preaching, scripture reading, and singing of hymns may lead to a religious conversion. To see the holy symbols of a High Mass may hold one in rapt attention upon the divine meanings. Religious awareness stoops to use the lowliest of perceptions and elevates them to sublime heights of admiration and devotion.

The language of religion is rich in sensory imagery:

> O taste and see that the Lord is good. . . .
> I will lift up mine eyes unto the hills, from whence cometh my help. . . .
> I saw . . . the Lord . . . high and lifted up, and his train filled the temple. . . .
> Speak, Lord; for thy servant heareth. . . .
> When I consider thy heavens, the work of thy fingers, the moon and the stars, which thou hast ordained; what is man, that thou art mindful of him?
> (Pss. 34:8; 121:1; Isa. 6:1; I Sam. 3:9; Ps. 8:34.)

By enlarging interpretation, perceptions are woven into the meaning of an eternal Presence.

This brings us to the other part of the question: Does religious awareness employ a special spiritual sense? William James finds evidence for an affirmative answer. In his chapter on "The Reality of the Unseen" he cites numerous illustrations of supersensible recognitions, leading him to conclude:

> It is as if there were in the human consciousness a *sense of reality, a feeling of objective presence, a perception* of what we may call "something there," more deep and more general than any of the special and particular "senses" by which the current psychology supposes existent realities be originally revealed.[4]

Though he does compare this type of experience with hallucinations, yet he considers vivid experiences of divine presence convincing to the one

[3] "Personality Dynamics and the Process of Perceiving," Robert R. Blake and Glenn V. Ramsey, eds., *Perception: An Approach to Personality* (New York: The Ronald Press, 1951), pp. 121-47.

[4] *Op. cit.*, p. 58. Italics are in the original.

who has them and decisive in the permanent fruits of character. The outcome of his investigation seems to be that intuitions may be either illusory or real but are more apt to bring certainty than shallow rationalism.[5]

What the psychologist now perceives is that all recognitions are supersensible. Every perception of what we may call "something there" is deeper and more general than any of the particular senses. This is quite as clear to the physicist after Einstein as it is to the psychologist. L. K. Barnett says: "In accepting a mathematical description of nature, physicists have been forced to abandon . . . the world of sense perceptions." [6]

In this going beyond the senses science joins with religion. The ultimates of physics are invisible, supersonic energies, and relations by which the events of the physical order are perceived. It is no more possible for the scientist than for the religious seeker to limit his perceptions to the obvious surface data of the five senses. Psychology has buried the controversy of rationalism versus empiricism by showing that reason is the integration of experience, while experience is charged with dynamic meanings that exceed and enrich the data of the senses. To perceive is always more than passive reception of sense impressions; it is active insight relating them into the meaning of a whole situation.

Rudolf Otto criticizes the above passage from William James as naïve, contending that James resorts to mysterious hypotheses to explain religious perception.[7] To Otto this feeling of reality is objectively given as "a primary, immediate datum of consciousness" not deducible from other data. This unique datum of a "Wholly Other" he calls the "numinous," from the Latin word *numen,* meaning the divine force or potency ascribed to objects or beings regarded with awe. "This mental state is perfectly *sui generis* and irreducible to any other." [8] It is a direct perception of reality independent of other forms of knowledge.

Albert C. Knudson joins with Otto in finding the source of religious experience in a unique religious a priori. He distinguishes four different kinds of experience: sense experience, aesthetic experience, moral experience, and religious experience. "Man has a native capacity for each of them." They are "structural in human nature, . . . unique and underived." No one of them can be deduced from, or reduced to, another. The religious a priori is a

[5] "If you have intuitions at all, they come from a deeper level of your nature than the loquacious level which rationalism inhabits. . . . The unreasoned and immediate assurance is the deep thing in us, the reasoned argument is but a surface exhibition." *Ibid.,* pp. 73-74.

[6] *The Universe and Dr. Einstein* (rev. ed.; New York: William Sloane Associates, Inc., 1957).

[7] *The Idea of the Holy,* tr. J. W. Harvey (London: Oxford University Press, 1923), p. 10 n.

[8] *Ibid.,* p. 7.

unique endowment, or potentiality, consisting not in specific content but in the capacity to have religious experiences.[9]

The thrust of this argument is that religious experience is an authentic perception of a unique relationship. It is a living encounter of a person who is I confronted by the Other who is perceived as Thou. It is contended that every person has such a religious capacity as deeply rooted and essential to his human nature as sense, aesthetic, or moral experience. Consequently, religious experience is unique and of its own kind, not to be reduced to another kind of experience. Against this view Freud[10] would say that religious experience is an illusion, a disguise to cover the infantile longing for dependence which a child may have on a human father. In his struggle for independence the growing child revolts against his father to displace him and claim for himself the throne of ascendance over rivals. Then he suffers guilt and disillusionment in meeting the demands of real situations. He learns that he is not sufficient unto himself; he repents of his aggressive pride and seeks to restore the relationships he has injured.

What then is the illusion? Is it the perception of the other person or of oneself? It may be either or both, for we are subject to error in all perceptions. What Freud offers here is an analogy between the family relations of the growing child and the expanding relations of the mature adult to his universe. If it is possible to distort one's perceptions in the family, it is no less possible in relation to our universe. Scientific perceptions may be as illusory as religious ones, which Freud demonstrates by his notable work in exposing the errors of his fellow scientists. His own perception of religion may be an illusion, and he would be the last one to deny that any human knowledge is beyond the danger of error. What emerges now from his study of religion is that our religious perceptions need to be examined again and again to free them from error, for nothing less than the truth can make us free.

The question with Freud as with James and Otto is whether there is actually an objective event or real Presence to answer our religious perceptions. Three positions are taken in wrestling with this question. Freud decides there is no ultimate Being, and consequently religious perceptions must be illusory. Otto decides there is in reality the Wholly Other, and consequently he finds religious perceptions to be authentic. James is unable to decide, and consequently he takes a pragmatic view that we have a right to believe so long as contrary evidence is not conclusive. What they demonstrate to the alert observer is this: Religious perceptions are personal decisions. But are not all perceptions, whether of sense or aesthetic or moral

[9] *The Validity of Religious Experience* (Nashville: Abingdon-Cokesbury Press, 1937), p. 146.
[10] *The Future of an Illusion.*

values, personal decisions? In our haste we make dogmatic assertions, but what we mean to say is: "This is how it looks to me."

In every perception we seek for objective evidence by relating appearances and impressions into whole meanings. But when you integrate the data of your experiences into a judgment, you are making a personal decision. "This I decide it to be." "This, all things considered, I must do." Passing recognition of a cloud screening the sun may lead to an instant decision, "It is cloudy," followed by another decision to put on a coat to keep warm. Religious perceptions call for personal decisions of even greater moment, for they involve the destiny of life as a whole. Religious decisions are essentially cumulative, each one leading to the next situation of choice until the whole of life is brought into response to the ultimate Being. To commit my life to a religious cause is not the end but the beginning of ongoing and integral actions by which life gains a decisive direction. In lesser responses to local needs almost any Sustainer of value may suffice. But in the course of ultimate concern a religious decision is irrevocably committed to faithful and eternal Being.

Such Being we neither prove nor disprove. That is beyond the limits of scientific psychology, to be referred to philosophy and theology. Yet they who once offered proofs for God are now in deeper humility saying that proof is not ours. It is only the little proposition that can be surrounded by proof near at hand. The ultimates in every discipline of knowledge are incapable of proof. They are axioms and postulates to acknowledge as necessary to give order to confusion and meaningful relatedness to the fragments of our perceptions. In psychology of religion we are to observe the behavior of persons who respond to the perplexities and goals of human life with ultimate concern. For this is what it means psychologically to be religious.

What empirical tendencies may be taken as clues to distinguish religious from nonreligious experiences? Religious awareness will be seen to arise in devotion to values. Briefly we may note three characteristics of religious experience: (*a*) Religious experience is a value experience: a preference for interests and needs worth realizing. (*b*) Religious experience has a divine reference: an objective outreach to a supreme value and source of ultimate values. (*c*) Religious experience is a social response: to confront Thou in a potentially creative relationship. These movements in religious experience will be explored as we proceed.

## 2. *Interest, Need, and Value*

At the thresholds of religious awareness we have discovered psychological tendencies that are present in all experience. This raises the question of the uniqueness of religious experience. What makes some experiences religious and others nonreligious? The previous section reached the conclusion that religious traits arise in concern for ultimate value. The next step will therefore be to analyze the psychological development of values, particularly religious values.

Value stems from interest and need. Whatever satisfies interest or need has value. R. B. Perry defines a value as "any object of any interest." [11] Interest is a personal response of attention. It literally means tension between events. From our viewpoint interest may be defined as an attentive attitude toward situations that seem to affect one's values. Perry describes interest as a motor-affective act, attitude, or disposition of favor or disfavor. It is characteristic of human attitudes to be for or against. This spontaneous response of preference is what recognizes objects of interest as values. Yet Perry enshrouds his concept with a cloak of mystery: "An act is interested in so far as its occurrence is due to the agreement between its accompanying expectation and the unfulfilled phases of a governing propensity." [12]

Expectation is clearly an aspect of interest, but his reference to a "governing propensity" is a more difficult puzzle. By this term he makes reference to a general determining tendency in control of the organism. The implication is that interests are controlled by instincts or mechanisms that push them into action. In relating these determining tendencies to instincts he does not mean hereditary reflexes. Behavior is too variable and modifiable for that. To him instinct is an inherited propensity, a specific disposition to learn. This is called a "driving adjustment" that responds to external and internal stimulating conditions by tending to release particular sets of random acts to particular goals. The propensity is thus merely a tendency to respond to stimuli by repeated efforts until "success" is attained. If instinct is reduced to nothing more than a persistent tendency to react to stimuli, we may wonder what after all is left of the instinct.

William McDougall [13] contends that the inherited and relatively unchanging tendencies of human character are of two main classes: general and specific. In addition to the general tendencies arising from the constitution of mind, he describes a number of specific instincts of flight, curiosity, self-abasement, self-assertion, and so on.

To multiply instincts in this way raises the dilemma of where to stop. In later writings[14] McDougall adds food-seeking, gregariousness, mating, acquisitiveness, laughter, the migratory instinct, and other propensities. E. L.

[11] *A General Theory of Value* (New York: Longmans, Green & Co., 1926), p. 115.

[12] *Ibid.*, p. 183.

[13] *An Introduction to Social Psychology* (Boston: J. W. Luce & Co., 1908), pp. 47-84.

[14] *Outline of Psychology* (New York: Charles Scribner's Sons, 1923), pp. 130-76; *The Energies of Men* (New York: Charles Scribner's Sons, 1933), pp. 97-98.

Thorndike finds almost as many instincts as situations to which organisms respond. His catalog of unlearned tendencies or "gene-caused propensities" seems to approach infinity. In defense of their large number he argues that the genes provide tens of thousands of specific details in making the sizes and shapes and colors of the parts of man's body—Why then should instinctive tendencies be less elaborate? [15] He does omit the religious instinct as well as McDougall's instincts of self-abasement and self-assertion, Freud's death instinct, and many others, such as the herd instinct, the maternal instinct, rivalry, acquisitiveness, pugnacity, and self-preservation. Why omit some of these and not others? His reply is that genes are not deities and do not deal in magical powers. But why is one instinct less magical than another?

McDougall agrees in rejecting the religious instinct, for religious emotion is no single and specific expression of one instinct. It is too complex and diversified to be the product of a single motive but develops in various ways from multiple causes.[16] Formerly, religious instinct was generally accepted, but today one can scarcely find a psychologist to defend it. Religious experience grows out of many needs and interests basic in human nature, but to single out one of these is oversimplification, and to reduce empirical facts to instinct is unempirical.

The difficulty in every instinct theory is a fallacy of abstraction. Instincts are not facts, as popular thinking may assume, but theoretical inferences from facts. The inability to agree upon the nature and number of instincts is a typical difficulty in dealing with concepts that reside not in concrete facts but in the mind of the theorizer. Instincts are defined as unlearned tendencies "prior to experience and independent of training." But who can know what is prior to experience and independent of modifying conditions? It is maintained that sucking is an instinct because it appears so early in life. And yet the baby makes random motions, exploratory and experimental, in the first feeding that indicate learning is taking place. There is further possibility of prenatal practice in thumb-sucking and experimenting to learn. Other so-called instincts are delayed and defended on the principle of maturation. Yet who can deny that learning is possible during the maturation period? If there is any situation in which every possibility of learning is excluded, a test case might be made. The best experiments appear in animal behavior, but it would be careless analogy to infer that human learning is identical with animal behavior.

Gordon Allport and Peter Bertocci have conducted a stimulating debate on these theories of motivation. Allport views the purposes of different peo-

[15] *Human Nature and the Social Order* (New York: The Macmillan Co., 1940), pp. 300-301.
[16] *Introduction to Social Psychology*, pp. 91-92.

ple as too diverse to be traced to a few primal motives shared by all. When they seek the same goals, it is obvious that they are influenced by a similar environment and culture; they learn from one another the methods of attaining them. Interests and traits develop in response to situations that invite them.[17] Bertocci replies that one cannot explain the similarity of goals by appealing to similarity in culture, for the culture itself needs to be explained by reference to the cause of cultural similarity.[18] If individuals did not have common motives to begin with, would they ever create a common culture? Is not human life equipped with common goal-seeking propensities or purposes? Allport also recognizes purposive motivations, but arising from contemporary goal seeking (functional autonomy), modified by learning, and individualized by divergent temperaments and abilities.[19] Bertocci proposes a synthesis of propensities, sentiments, and traits. He suggests that traits can be one of the levels at which vital energy organizes itself into the life of an individual. Sentiments to him are "not adequate to explain the persistent and continuously functioning characteristics of given individuals which are uniquely expressive of their form of adjustment rather than their environment." [20] Allport cannot accept the proposal to regard attitudes, sentiments, and traits as merely proximate factors in motivation. "To my way of thinking they offer so ultimate a representation of human motivation as psychological knowledge today warrants." [21]

The debate over instincts has followed the course of psychoanalytic theory to the present time. Freud [22] perceived the whole economy of personality as a struggle of instinctual urges for pleasure in opposition to the restraints of civilized society which he called the reality principle. Libido was his term for the psychosexual instinct emerging from primitive biological needs, which might be repressed in the hidden dynamics of the unconscious but never eradicated. In later writings he saw these erotic urges as life instincts struggling against the aggressive death instincts. By instinctual he meant innate and primal sources of dynamic energy driving blindly yet insatiably goalward for reduction of restless tensions. What these sources of energy are, he did not presume to know. He recognized that such concepts are un-

[17] *Personality: A Psychological Interpretation* (New York: Henry Holt & Co., 1937), p. 112.

[18] "A Critique of G. W. Allport's Theory of Motivation," *Psychological Review*, XLVII (1940), 509.

[19] "Motivation in Personality: Reply to Mr. Bertocci," *Psychological Review*, XLII (1940), 535-45.

[20] *Op. cit.*, p. 531.

[21] "Motivation in Personality," p. 553.

[22] *New Introductory Lectures on Psychoanalysis*, tr. W. J. H. Sprott (London: Hogarth Press, 1933, p. 124.

known constructs "superb in their indefiniteness" and referred to the instincts as "our mythology." None of his theories has been more controversial than this, and most of the revisionists and neo-Freudians who differed with him have departed in one way or another from his instinct theory.

In view of the abstract and dubious implication of "instinct," it might be wise to give up the term for a better one. The better concept from our point of view is "need." Needs may be organic (as hunger is), arising from lacks in the vital processes. They may be psychological and sociological in the growing range of interests and activities. This avoids the ambiguity of unlearned inheritance by recognizing that needs are constantly changing through learning and modifying conditions. Needs are "dynamic, unique, personal, and ultimate." They meet the purposive goal seeking of Bertocci and the demand of Allport that "what matters most to me is that all of these units of motivational structure be regarded as dynamic, unique, personal, and ulimate." [23]

The dynamic psychology of Henry Murray arises from the theory of specific needs that motivate personality.[24] He classifies needs as viscerogenic and psychogenic. The organic needs which he calls viscerogenic include air, water, food, sex, lactation, urination, defecation, harm avoidance, and sentience. The psychogenic list of twenty-nine items includes such needs as acquisition, conservance, order, recognition, defendance, dominance, deference, blame avoidance, affiliation, succorance, and exposition. The effort to specify concrete needs is useful, but his recourse to universalized needs common to all falls again into the abstraction of instincts. In fact, the resemblance of his list of needs to familiar instincts is striking, as is also his concept of a hidden force which drives the organism.

> A need is a contruct (a convenient fiction or hypothetical concept) which stands for a force (the physico-chemical nature of which is unknown) in the brain region, a force which organizes perception, apperception, intellection, conation, and action in such a way as to transform in a certain direction an existing, unsatisfying situation.[25]

An abstraction is "a convenient fiction or hypothetical concept," and if there is any single organic force that does all that the above statement claims, it is as mysterious as the magical genes of Thorndike. We can agree with Murray (*a*) that need is the immediate outcome of certain internal and external occurrences, (*b*) that it is not a static entity but comes and goes and changes, (*c*) that each need is unique, and (*d*) that there are similarities

[23] "Motivation in Personality," p. 553.

[24] *Explorations in Personality* (New York: Oxford University Press, 1938), pp. 52-96.

[25] *Ibid.*, p. 123.

among human needs. A need arises from an inner feeling of tension that seems to impel striving toward a specific goal. Yet needs tend to attach themselves to objects by a cathexis of desire or purpose. The focusing of needs upon specific objects and the images, interests, and emotions thereby excited become a need-integrate or complex.

A larger integration of need theory is presented by A. H. Maslow [26] in a progressive movement to higher goals. He would give up all attempts to make atomistic lists of drives or needs as theoretically unsound. For this implies that they are equal, isolated, and mutually exclusive; while in fact a particular desire may be a channel through which several other desires are expressed. What he finds is a hierarchy of fundamental goals or needs as motives that pull from before rather than push from behind. The physiological needs such as hunger are prepotent if the organism is starving, but when hunger is satisfied, it is no longer a determining want. Safety needs may become dominant until they are gratified. Then belongingness and love needs emerge as dominant, and with them esteem needs come into focal attention. Even if these basic needs are all satisfied, there will be discontent unless one is doing what he is fitted for to realize his potentialities in self-actualization. The desire to know, the aesthetic, moral, and religious values, are higher needs which ascend as basic needs are met. For human life is endlessly dynamic and holistic in seeking values through enlarging relationships.

Such needs are modifiable and adaptable to the complex situations in which a person lives. And yet the person is more than a product of his environment. He becomes what he is potentially designed to be. There are self-determinants within the organism that impel his strivings and set the goals he will seek. They can and will be modified by learning, and yet they offer continuing motivation as they develop in response to environmental situations. Needing never ceases, but no one need is independent or insatiable. Human needs can disappear as animal instincts do not. The gratification of one need creates another. For man never gives up his quest for values nor is long content with the already attained. He seeks ever more ultimate value goals.

From interests and needs values develop. To be aware of a need is to value the event which will fulfill it. To be interested in a value is to desire it enough to give attention and goal-seeking effort in that direction. A value becomes a goal of appreciation and preference, which one strives to realize. In seeking such a valued goal, the means that promise to serve that end are also valued. Instrumental values are means that serve intrinsic values as ends.

[26] *Motivation and Personality* (New York: Harper & Bros., 1954).

This will help us to understand the nature of religious values. From the needs of personality there arise goal tensions in dynamic relations of interest. In seeking goals of value, attitudes of preference and desire become potent, overlaid with other attitudes of fear of thwarting and failure. In this mingling of desire and fear the person suffers anxiety and knows the distress of finite insufficiency. If in humility he now confesses his need and seeks the larger resources of supernatural power, he becomes religious.

Wherever a need becomes crucial to the whole meaning of life, the search for value takes on the serious intent of a religious quest. Not all values are religious, yet when essential needs are urgent enough and human abilities insufficient, a religious search for fulfillment may become the ultimate concern. The seriousness of this concern is shown by Kierkegaard in his analysis of dread,[27] which he describes as a sympathetic antipathy of fascinating distress. This dread is a dizziness of freedom which seizes the human spirit gazing down into its own possibility and grasping at finiteness to sustain itself. Yet because the person is finite, he will be disappointed in his efforts to realize his possibilities. He will fall into internal and external conflict, which will force him to exercise choice between contradictory values. Whatever he may choose will leave other needs unmet, for he is that conflictual creature who has infinite possibilities to desire but only finite capacity for their realization. His very possibilities thus become his dread and his despair; his very finitude impels him to need the ultimate Thou.

The long debate among psychologists over instincts and needs is very important to our understanding of religious aspiration. It is also basic to our understanding of man caught in the toils of this tragic human conflict, forever wanting more than he can reach.

Why does man want what he wants and strive always for that which is beyond his grasp? Is some demonic force driving him furiously from behind, some irrepressible instinct of causal determinism that dances him like a puppet? If so, man is a victim of mechanical forces over which he has little if any control and to which he will submit, however much he agonizes to do otherwise. If man is the puppet of impersonal forces, he can talk of religion piously, and even go through ritualistic motions compulsively, to no avail; for he is a lost soul beaten down inexorably by a fatalism of heedless necessity. If this is the instinct theory of Freud, is it not inevitable that he will see religious aspiration as an illusion?

Yet as the evidence accumulates, we are impressed by the amazing capacity of the human organism to learn from experience in ever-new and surprising ways. So decisive in fact are the changes which persons achieve through learning that even the necessities which were considered inexorable

[27] *The Concept of Dread*, tr. Walter Lowrie (Princeton, N. J.: Princeton University Press, 1944).

yield to the flexible and spontaneous alternatives of human choice. This decisive power of learning Freud could not long deny, and as an honest scientist he gave equal place in his later theory to learning as a counterforce to instinct. What the person learns from his relations to parents and others whom he fears and admires will be introjected or taken into himself to oppose and modify the primitive instincts. The stage is set for interminable conflict, yet out of these decisive conflicts will emerge the creative character who in the travail of his suffering brings forth the arts and values of civilization. In spite of his discontents, and even because of them, man is able to grow through conflictual learning into productive maturity. It is in wrestling with conflicts of his own nature and turning outward to reconcile his conflicts with the Other that a person becomes religious. Freud may return to the childhood conflict with the father as the primal religious motive, yet Buber finds the religious experience fulfilled in the present moment of living encounter with Thou.

Through this debate we come to a question of basic import to any psychology of religion. Is religion natural to man, or is it learned? The weight of the dilemma will be seen in its consequences. If religion is native, then you may argue that it is essential to the fulfillment of human life, and apart from religion man is lost without the central meaning of his search. To view man as naturally religious is to sense how urgent it is to provide for this crucial need. But another might take the contrary view and hold that if religion is native, it is determined by compulsive instincts to serve unconscious needs other than the conscious meanings of religion. To this view the religious behavior would then be a deceptive mask to disguise a selfish gratification with respectability. Nativity can thus be used, as it often is, to argue religion either up or down.

On the other hand, if religion is learned, then you may infer it is not reducible to a segmental drive like fear or to compulsive neurotic obsessions, for it is rather the conscious intention arising out of reasonable learning to respond to the One who is ultimate in value. To view religion as an outcome of learning is to act religiously from a present motive to confront Thou and so to fulfill the highest meaning of life. But another might take the contrary view that if religion is learned, it is a superficial form of behavior that imitates what others do to conform or to have prestige and win approval. This would be to view religion as optional and unessential to basic human needs. So learning may also be used to argue religion pro or con.

To cut through the double knot of this dilemma, it is well to acknowledge that we are confronting here the basic paradox of man, to be resolved only by searching more deeply into his existential nature. The contradiction is deeply rooted in the nature of man as a person in conflictual relationships. It is because man is a finite person with infinite possibilities that he ventures upon the religious quest. He is naturally finite, yet he learns of infinite possibilities which he cannot reach alone. Thus he will never be content to endure the finite loneliness of self-sufficient isolation. His inborn need (which has been called instinctual) may drive but cannot guide him to the ultimate fulfillment he seeks. Religious learning is the discovery of ultimate resources to meet infinite longings of the finite spirit. Such learning is a confrontation in the present moment to know that I am finite before that which I perceive as the infinite Thou.

# 4 RELIGIOUS EXPERIENCE (*Cont'd*)

## *3. I and Thou*

Psychology is one of the most useful of the modern sciences for the understanding of man and the guiding of growth to fulfill his amazing potentialities. We may not hope to comprehend the intricate meaning of religious experience without psychological analysis. And yet we cannot overlook the subtle and misleading fallacy of psychologizing true values by reducing them to fictions. Animal psychologists may reduce human motives to the model of the rat in a maze; pathologists may see all persons as falling into the syndromes of neurotics and psychotics. Though disciplined scientists may be cautious in claiming to explain all by a simple formula, others are likely to move to hasty conclusions that religion has been explained away as a "projection" or an "obsessional neurosis."

Against this deceptive reductionism of human complexities to the simplicities of scientific parsimony, Gordon Allport has made effective protest. He shows the poverty of reducing the unique individuality of personality to abstractions and common elements of mind-in-general. He notes that the elements employed in such analyses are not true parts of the living whole. He warns against the trivial view that adult religion is merely a repetition of the experiences of childish immaturity. It is not surprising to find religious concerns entangled in the desires of infantile and neurotic personalities, for their religious needs may be genuine indeed. But the religious integration of a mature person attains larger perspective.

> The healthy person in possession of normal intelligence, insight and emotional maturity knows that he cannot solve life's problems by wishful thinking or cure his partialness by fictionizing. To cure his partialness he must find something more convincing than partialness itself. Hence the developed personality will not fabricate his religion out of some emotional fragment but will seek a theory of Being in which all fragments are meaningfully ordered.[1]

[1] *Becoming: Basic Considerations for a Psychology of Personality* (New Haven, Conn.: Yale University Press, 1955), p. 94.

To engage in an enterprise of such dimensions as religious living will involve the whole personality. Unconscious dynamics will have their part, yet the larger meaning of it is not reducible to unconscious mechanisms. For religious perspectives are integrating to bring together conflicting impulses into intentional living in view of the whole meaning of life. The conscious ego, the person at the center of these experiences, is the integrating agent who asks searching questions and makes religious decisions. "Who am I and what is my destiny?" "What am I to do in the face of these religious meanings?" "How can I devote myself to the religious way of life?"

A man is different from animals in that he is able to transcend the impulsive desires of the moment and wonder about his destiny in binding together past and future. He is able to perceive himself as a person in relation to his world. Without this transcendent awareness religion would be impossible. For a man's religion, as Allport says, is "his ultimate attempt to enlarge and complete his own personality by finding the supreme context in which he rightly belongs." [2] This perspective outreaches the local scene to an objective world extending beyond what his senses behold. His effort is to find his place and purpose in relation to the whole of this otherness.

No religious experience is merely subjective without objective reference. An argument for solipsism, contending that mind has knowledge of nothing beyond itself, is a *reductio ad absurdum.*

Like the dunce cap, solipsism is a device to put on others and is not intended for one's own head. Those who wield solipsistic threats intimidate by waving absurdities over the heads of opponents in argument. If one actually believed that doctrine and wanted to be consistent, he would not attempt to convince others, who are as nonexistent as empty space and as unapproachable as the other side of the sun. Psychologists and philosophers with rare exceptions are all engaged in studying mind in relation to the objective world.

When J. H. Leuba suggests that the religious person invents his own god,[3] he surely does not mean to say such a person is entirely cut off from reality. For he recognizes the co-operation of men not only with other men but with "hyperhuman" forces of the real world. What he seems to mean is that the gods of religion are inductions from experience and that human experience manifests "a Force tending to the creation of an ideal society." The reality is actually there; the invention is man's interpretation of it.

What we insist is that religious experience is response to objective reality. The presence of objective reality seems undeniable; at least it is assumed by everyone in practical activity and scientific labors. What reality is like is a

[2] *Individual and His Religion,* p. 142. Used by permission of The Macmillan Co.

[3] *Psychological Study of Religion,* p. 10.

question of interpretation. To physics it is a system of electronic forces, largely invisible yet moving at high speed and power in orderly ways. To religion reality is also powerful and largely invisible, but vastly different from physical nature in value and responsiveness.

With divine powers we seek to co-operate in a way different from that employed with physical powers. Physical powers are treated mechanically by push and pull, prediction and control. Divine powers can be neither pushed nor pulled, predicted nor controlled arbitrarily. The divine Being is treated as an Ultra-Person to be respected and invited. He responds not to command or coercion but to petition and persuasion. Even though the divine Being may not be recognized clearly as personal, yet he is treated as a person in every religious attitude.

The distinction between physical and spiritual is not one of amount of power. It is one of quality and kind of power. Things may be as powerful as high explosives, but they are not talked to as capable of understanding ideas. Spirits may be vaguely and weakly conceived, but they are viewed as responsive in personal ways to offering and invitation. Man responds socially to spirits because he expects spirits to respond in kind to him. There is a kinship of interest and comprehension, of asking and answering, that makes interpersonal relations widely different from impersonal relations.

The interpersonal relation of religious experience is perceived as I and Thou. As the religious person looks forth upon his world and searches for the meaning of it all, he meets the Other who is seeking him. This was the experience of Moses as he came to the burning bush on Mount Horeb and marveled that in the remote wilderness he was not alone. He was addressed by a Being who entered into conversation with him, and though mysterious the communication was intelligible and personal so as to change the whole course of his life (Exod. 3-4). He protested against the insistence of this Other and tried to talk his way out of the demands, but there was no escape from the conviction of reality brought upon him in this meeting. He continued through the portentous years that followed to work out his religious vocation in the context of that relationship.

It is in such meetings of I and Thou that man attains his most distinctively human characteristics. There is a double principle here at work which Martin Buber[4] calls distance and relation. The first movement is the "primal setting at a distance" as a man recognizes existence independent of himself which he perceives standing over against him as wholly other. Wherever you meet man, he finds himself in contradiction toward that known and unknown world which is beyond and in opposition to him.

The second movement which man undertakes is to enter into relation with

[4] "The William Alanson White Memorial Lectures," *Psychiatry*, XX (May, 1957), 97-129.

the otherness that confronts him. No one is content to recognize the contradiction of self and other without doing something to enter into relation with that which confronts him. To do this the man must exercise a synthesizing apperception of "making present," or bringing the distant into personal experience and holding the relationship in vivid awareness. To recognize what another man is at this moment wishing, feeling, and thinking is to grasp him as more than a component but a self-being in existence as I am. So a person confirms what he is and may become in relation to another person who is affirmed as independent yet related to him.

The essence of religious experience is interpersonal meeting. Such experience arises in the reverence of profound appreciation for the Other, the Thou to whom I devote my concern. I am not the object of the religious quest, but the seeker for that which is greater than I. Meeting the Other is to discover not a religious object but a subject who responds like a person. There is mystery here beyond the limits of knowledge, yet recognition to know and be known. A voice speaks from the mystery beyond and enters into conversation which reveals significant meaning. At least this is the claim of those who report what revelation and prayer mean to them in religious meeting. From the animism of primitive religion to the monotheism of a world religion the nature of religious meeting is experienced as person to person.

Local religions are egocentric in asking a Sustainer for what I desire as my value. Great religion is theocentric in seeking values other than mine and offering myself to a larger purpose. When religion is ultimate concern, the question is not merely what do I desire but what is required of me in the service of the highest purpose. This imperative note of obligation is heard in the greatest and most moving religious experience, well documented in the scriptures of the ethical religions. When the response of I and Thou is mutual, it becomes responsibility to fulfill, as in the Hebrew covenant, the faithful requirements of the relationship.

Interpersonal conversation means acceptance of both otherness and togetherness. This is true of every real meeting of man with man. For mutuality is interpersonal, not collective. Each person participates in a partnership with each person who confronts him in active relationship. Psychological and religious fulfillment is not in one or the other alone, nor in both of them crowded into one collective mass submerging personal identities, but rather in the dialogue between them where they live on speaking terms together. Truth means that men communicate themselves to one another as what they are. Genuine dialogue turns to the partner in open and honest communication. Each speaker means the partner as the unique person he is, not merely to perceive him but to receive him, confirming and accepting his personal being. As each one brings himself fully into the dialogue to say what is actually in his mind, he makes the contribution of his spirit without reduction or shifting ground. For every person stands in objective relations to other persons, and these relationships are essential to his religious life.

It is the ultimate Thou whom the religious person seeks most of all. For the finite is incomplete and needs the Infinite; the creature is not self-sufficient and needs the Creator. Does this reduce the value of the finite persons who meet us in a religious quest? Is the ultimate concern to forsake all lesser concerns? This problem has led some religious seekers to the monastery and the hermitage. Kierkegaard meets this dilemma heroically and decides to sever his engagement with Regina that he may give undivided attention to God. He wrestles with the question in his writings and resolves that he must devote his singleness to God as the Single One. "He who communicates it [the truth] is only a Single One. And then its communication is only for the Single One; for this view of life, 'the Single One,' is the very truth." [5] He flees the crowd as distracting and corrupting that he may be single in his devotion to the ultimate One.

With this view Buber is in sharp disagreement, and to explore the question enters into debate with him across the century that stretches between. The I-Thou relationship is not exclusive but inclusive of other relations. It is the ultimate Thou who reveals himself in every interpersonal meeting as a lesson in the meaning of dialogue and a representative of the nature of Being. Does the Creator deny himself in his creation or affirm his actuality in these relationships?

> Creation is not a hurdle on the road to God, it is the road itself. We are created along with one another and directed to a life with one another. Creatures are placed in my way so that I, their fellow-creature, by means of them and with them find the way to God. A God reached by their exclusion would not be the God of all lives in whom all life is fulfilled. . . .
>
> Religion as specification misses its mark. God is not an object beside objects and hence cannot be reached by renunciation of objects. . . . He is not to be found by subtraction and not to be loved by reduction. . . . I cannot answer the lifelong address of God to me without answering at the same time for the other . . . for our human way to the infinite leads only through fulfilled finitude.[6]

It is possible to deny such ultimates by devoting one's energies to the pursuit of proximate goals and instrumental values. The psychologist as scientist may draw the boundary of investigation around his laboratory and

[5] *The Point of View of My Works as an Author* (London: Oxford University Press, 1944).

[6] *Between Man and Man,* pp. 52, 58, 61. Used by permission of The Macmillan Co. and Routledge & Kegan Paul, Ltd.

statistical coefficients. Yet as a person his life goes beyond these boundaries to more ultimate concerns. He is aware of distances beyond the co-ordinates of his science and postulates a universe of intricate yet orderly and intelligible relations. He enters into relationship with other persons in mutual appreciation and responsibility. Whatever the language may be, he participates in dialogue of person with person and may consequently know the flavor of I and Thou.

## *4. Religious Emotion*

Motions and emotions go together. They are related in language and life. In language both come from the same root, "to move." In life they represent dynamic or motivating tendencies. Psychologists and psychiatrists give enlarging place to emotional factors controlling behavior. Devious experiments have been conducted to discover and measure emotions. But emotional life is not well understood and remains one of the baffling obscurities of present-day psychology.

This difficulty results from the prevailing style of conceiving emotions impersonally. The usual approach has been to analyze them into elements and to classify them by abstract and atomistic schemes. They have been reduced to sensations of pleasantness and unpleasantness. The somatic basis of feeling has been studied, and graphs have been made of pulse rate, breathing rate, and electrical changes of the body under emotional excitement. Emotional effects of glandular secretions and biological needs and strivings have been noted. But the outcome has been contradictory and inconclusive.

William Stern believes that feeling will be properly understood only as this atomism yields to a view of personality as a whole.[7] Emotions encompass all experience and subordinate all other mental activity to them. Feelings and moods are nuances, casts, and tones that pervade and suffuse the entire consciousness. He calls feeling embedded experience characterized by subjective nearness to the person. It has a formlessness that is difficult to describe directly without crystallizing it into ideational patterns. Cognition and acts of will are *Gestalten* and tend to form salient patterns; feeling is *Ungestalt,* fluid and diffuse, yet very influential in both ideas and action.

Emotions are dynamic and telic tensions of personal experience. They are usually aroused by interacting external and internal conditions of personality. Stimuli from the external world and stimuli from within organic processes and consciousness mingle with attention, perception, memory, anticipation, purpose and judgment to produce emotional tensions. Needs, interests, and values arise in these emotional processes and play the role of both cause and effect. They are goal strivings which are

[7] *Op. cit.,* pp. 513-74.

never experienced without emotional qualities. Organic and psychic needs awaken interest in values that will satisfy them. To need something is to endure the risk of gaining or losing it. To value something is to have satisfaction in its realization and dissatisfaction in its loss. Emotion is thus the qualitative experience of tension toward goals.

Emotions have polarity because "the activity of the person maintains multiple polarized tensions" [8] that are reflected in consciousness. The polarity consists of the fluctuating success and failure which every person experiences in reaching his goals. The dynamic resurgence appears in the expending and accumulating of energy, as felt in experiences of excitement and tranquillity. Transitive feelings are exciting when striving toward goals, pleasant while approaching goals, and unpleasant when receding from them. Resultant feelings are tranquil when telic activity is concluded, pleasant when fulfilled, and unpleasant when not fulfilled. These unstable fluctuations of mood result in an inner strain known as ambivalence. One may have ambivalent religious feelings in the alternating love and fear of God. Gradations of feeling occur, with variations in intensity, breadth, duration, depth, and genuineness of personal experience.

What stimulates emotion? In animals whose brains have been removed, scratching the back or pinching the tail may produce snarls from a dog or hissing and clawing from a cat; but these are evidently reflex actions. Conscious beings respond emotionally to situations that mean danger, success, or frustration. The same object or event, such as lightning, frightens one and not another according to its meaning for him. A child knows not whether to laugh or cry at a parental slap until it is clear whether it is a "spank" or a "love pat." The James-Lange theory that emotions result from bodily actions rather than causing them is a partial view of the total situation. Bodily action may accentuate emotion (as in the famous case of fear caused by running from a bear), but running away from a rabbit does not cause fear. Is it not the recognition of danger from the bear and no danger from the rabbit that makes the essential difference? And the recognition of this meaning is the idea that stimulates the emotion.[9]

We may talk of a pure emotion, but who has ever met one? If we should have a pure emotion, we could not recognize it, for recognition adds an idea to the emotion. Emotions are not things to be separated or divided, but activities of persons responding. A dynamic and integral view sees the various aspects of life united in total responses of the personality as a whole.

[8] *Ibid.*, p. 533.

[9] "The intensity of the anxiety is proportionate to the meaning the situation has for the person concerned. . . . The therapeutic task, therefore, can only be that of finding out the meaning certain situations have for him."—Karen Horney, *The Neurotic Personality of Our Time* (New York: W. W. Norton & Co., 1937), p. 44.

The half truth in the James-Lange theory is the fact that body and mind interact. Bodily activity accentuates fear, even as fear whips up the circulation and neural tonicity for vigorous activity. Yet both the emotional and bodily activity are responses to occasions that mean danger by persons who recognize the need for flight or resistance. The whole truth points to emotions as interrelated with every interest and activity of the psychophysical life. To be emotionally aroused is to feel with the whole body from the tip of the toes to the roots of the hair impulses that interact with conscious ideas and judgments of need and value. If in any situation one decides it does not matter, the emotion subsides. If he sees purposes threatened and thwarted, he is stirred up to excited responses of the total personality to defend his values.

Religion is deeply rooted in human emotions. There are those who find the origin and development of religion specifically in the emotional life. In my view religious interests permeate every aspect of experience. No experience is vital or dynamic without emotional support, and since religion is concerned with the deepest needs and highest worths of life, it will naturally be charged with emotional urgency. The most intense feelings appear in the most vital experiences. Indifference results from lack of interest; and when religious interest fades, emotional content drains off and religion dries up in formalism or neglect. Liberal religious sects that neglect emotion for rationalism fade and decline. Without emotional motivation religion is of doubtful value except as a relic in a museum. Even museum relics have value only as they awaken interest and stir responses. Yet what a far cry from the warmly intense emotion of personal religious experience to the detached curiosity touching museum interests!

What stimulates religious emotion? Religion is affected by any and all interests vital enough to satisfy needs and increase values. Persons need to survive and grow in constant development of values; they need to communicate values in interpersonal relations; they need to create and construct new values for the enrichment of all; they need to mingle admiration and humility in reverence of ultimate value. Religion is deeply involved in efforts to meet all these needs and to sustain all these values. And the more clearly their worth is recognized, the more emotional we become about them. We have so much at stake in the risks of life and society, in creating and appreciating these values, that we are rightly aroused emotionally to protect them from loss and enjoy them more abundantly. The complex organization of interests and emotions around a value object is known as a sentiment. The organization of sentiments around permanent goals is known as a disposition.

It is in the reverent sentiments and dispositions that we become most directly and vividly aware of religious values. When man confronts Thou, he may well be stirred to the depths of his being by the supreme significance of that event. A thorough analysis of such emotions is made by Rudolf Otto in *The Idea of the Holy*. He finds the essence of religious experience in a constellation of emotions of creature-feeling. The fundamental element in strong and sincere religious emotion is the *mysterium tremendum*, which combines (*a*) a sense of awe more solemn than fear, a dread of the divine wrath; (*b*) a realization of the unapproachableness and power of the divine majesty; (*c*) energy and excitement in the urgency of the living God; (*d*) a stupor of wonder and astonishment before the "Wholly Other"; and (*e*) fascination, alluring rapture, and complete surrender to the supernatural object of devotion.

How are religious emotions different from other emotions? The distinctive feature is the ultimate concern of the I-Thou relationship. Otto considers awe, wonder, and fascination nonrational, but these emotions are aroused by cognitive reference to Thou. The more tremendous Thou is judged to be, the more emotion rises to significant intensity. Fear of a bear is as different from "fear of the Lord" as one perceives them to be different. One may fear a God of wrath; but if God is interpreted as a Father who pities his children, fear gives place to trust and love. "Fear of the Lord" is a complex of emotions of profound awe and reverence. Otto vividly describes emotions arising from recognizing a God of power, wrath, and unapproachable mystery. But to those who perceive God to be forgiving, redeeming love, the religious emotions will be somewhat different. They experience the gentler feelings of gratitude, trust, peace, and devotion in loyal service.

J. H. Leuba ably disposes of the theory that fear is the primary emotion in religion. If fear is conspicuous in primitive religion, it is not because of the intrinsic qualities of primitive religion but rather because of the insecurity and danger that dominate primitive life. Even there fear is mingled with other emotions and steadily yields to modification. In the emotional progression of religion fear changes to awe, reverence, admiration, gratitude, and a sense of the sublime. And in the higher civilizations today fear and awe have been largely displaced by other religious emotions. In contrast to the wave of fear that provoked religious revivals in the time of Jonathan Edwards, quite different emotions prevail in our generation. The theology that stressed God's wrath, the wretchedness of this life, and the torments hereafter aroused fear. Changing ideas of God, man, and eternity may change these emotions. Leuba finds three causes for the decline of fear: (*a*) in civilized society occasions for fear have become fewer (except in war and calamity); (*b*) modern education make us more reflective and less emotional, thereby converting emotions into controlled reactions; and (*c*) recognition of the inadequacy of fear as a method of meeting danger turns us to more intelligent responses. The characteristic religious sentiments of our time are sympathy, love, trust, hope, courage, fortitude, and forgiveness; these prove more effective for the needs of modern living.[10]

Religious emotions, sentiments, and dispositions are complex. No single feeling or meaning characterizes all varieties of religious experience. Objective situations condition emotional responses. Whatever God means to you will define your religious emotions. Your ideas of the divine purpose and the goal of human destiny will be significant. And subjectively how you feel about religious values will decide what you do about them. Religion may be as flat as your indifference or as vital and urgent as your sense of great issues at stake. If you believe in an ultimate Being and feel deeply your need of divine assistance, you will be serious about religion. Emotions arising from such beliefs reverberate through all of life and affect every deed and decision.

Emotions may be constructive or destructive. Fear spreads panic, and anxieties result in hesitation and inefficiency. Anger and despair, likewise, produce inaccurate fumbling and random responses. These distressing emotions are destructive of poise, stability, and efficiency. They defeat the values sought by disorganizing the personality. And their effects are undesirable—indigestion, circulatory and nervous disorders, illness, weakness, and unhappiness. Other emotions are constructive in creating stability, joy, and success. Faith, hope, and love are the justly famous trilogy that serve as constructive forces in personality and society.

How does religion influence the emotions? Can we expect religion to control the emotional life so that the destructive tendencies will be curbed and the constructive tendencies strengthened? There is convincing evidence to this effect. Faith, hope, and love are more characteristic of the great religions than fear, despair, and rage. The typical religious concern is to wrest the largest meaning from every circumstance of life. This essential hope that characterizes religious experience is a constructive emotional force, giving the worshiper stability and integration for effective living. Trust and love cast out fear and despair, transforming destructive emotions into constructive energies of harmony, confidence, and peace.

William James distinguishes the constructive and destructive impulses as healthy-mindedness and morbid-mindedness. His lecture on "The Religion of Healthy-Mindedness" gives numerous case studies to demonstrate how religious concern helps one to live serenely and well. By positive suggestions of personal faith, enthusiasm, recollection, and the eloquent example of others, many are cured of diseases and kept from evil and despair. This is achieved not by the moral methods of effort and strain but by religious methods of surrender and trust in a supernatural power. His lecture

[10] *Op. cit.*, pp. 126-50.

on "The Sick Soul" explores the destructive tendencies of morbid fear, pain, despair, and their urgent need of a redemptive religion of deliverance. No refined optimisms or moral consolations can meet these deeper needs, but only a religion that is complete enough to offer a way of salvation. The divided self has to be united, and the natural man born again to a spiritually adequate personality.

What brings about such changes, says James, is "the way in which emotional excitement alters." [11] New interests become "hot parts" of the field of consciousness; former interests become cold. From these centers of dynamic energy come the constructive emotional forces for the remaking of personality. How this happens we do not know. He uses mechanical figures of speech, points to the unconscious, and suggests a wider self through which saving influences come. Psychology will trace results more clearly than causes, and beyond the immediate environment does not presume to explain the ultimate causation of these religious changes.

This we know: Religious motivation rouses life from indifference to interest, from inhibiting to facilitating energies. For life is inevitably a venture into vast unknowns with the limited resources of finite existence. The finite predicament is one of boundless possibilities and endless insecurities. The historic thrust of religion is not to deny the danger of human living with opiate or fiction, however one may be tempted to do so. A mature religious person is willing to live dangerously and accept insecurity to meet Thou and wrestle with the mystery of human destiny. The contribution of this ultimate concern is to put the trivial in its place for the sake of a larger meaning, and the fear in its place in courageous devotion to a greater purpose than being safe. The effectiveness of such religion is to enhance the meaning and value of life through dynamic relationships.

## 5. *Types of Religious Experience*

The varieties of religious experience are many and profuse. To classify them accurately is next to impossible, and yet they cluster and come together in polarities of similarity and contrast. The resemblances that draw religious persons together are most clearly seen in contrast to the differences that set them off from one another. Those whose religious experiences are alike tend to affiliate sympathetically into sects aware of their mutual interest. At the same time they are often joined by opposition to another point of view against which they unite. In tracing types of religious experience, I shall present them in pairs of contrast.

*a*) The *individual* versus the *social*. One type of religion emphasizes in-

[11] *Op. cit.*, p. 195.

dividual experience. Ezekiel was an individualist who declared, "The soul that sinneth, it shall die" (18:4). Each person is individually responsible to his Creator. Hermits have forsaken society for the privileges of solitude. Others find religion a social experience and do not understand why people ever want to be alone. To them religion has a social origin and a social purpose in the development of interpersonal relations. Religious life is a fellowship, and salvation is through brotherhood in a beloved community. Introvert and extrovert tendencies have been noted to affect all experiences of life; these basic individual differences turn religious interests inward or outward. If the religious encounter is a meeting of I and Thou even in solitude, then the lonely individual is not alone but face to face in every moment of worship. Yet Kierkegaard, the individualist, decides he must renounce Regina for the Single One; while Buber the interpersonalist decides to meet Thou in every relationship.

*b*) The *active* versus the *passive*. The active type of religion is well known. The first religious facts are religious acts. Primitive religion is active in ceremonies, dances, sacrifices, and ritual. Religious leaders demand action. "This do, and thou shalt live." (Luke 10:28.) Good deeds are required of the Buddhist; deeds of penance are expected of the Roman Catholic; deeds of service are stressed among Protestants. Moral achievement and reforming zeal appeal to many. The passive type finds meaning in silence and quietism. Hours spent in meditation and prayer seem more important than busy rounds of frantic activity. Salvation is not by deeds of merit but by faith and divine grace. Self-surrender is a way to let go of the world and make room for spiritual power. A Buddhist controversy over this point was represented by the "monkey-hold" sect teaching that man must exert himself to be saved, reaching up and holding on as the baby monkey to its mother; and the "cat-hold" sect teaching man not to struggle but to relax in faith and be saved by the upholding divine power, as the kitten is held by its mother.

*c*) The *formal* versus the *informal*. These contrasting types are evident in services of public worship. Formal services are rich in symbolism, ritual, and ceremonies. Art and images, incense and rhythmic beats, impressive architecture and elaborate decoration, processions and recessions in dramatic pageantry, traditional prayers, genuflections, and intonations make up the content of formal worship. It has dignity, antiquity, and a funded meaning to excite emotions and aspirations. But others may react against this weight of formality and seek religion in simplicity. A Friends' meeting, with its bare walls and silence, is an austere protest against formality, offering instead the spontaneous utterance of prayer and testimony as the spirit moves. Aesthetic symbols give way to free and democratic comradeship in which God dwells in the heart as an inspiring, guiding inner light.

*d*) The *conservative* versus the *progressive*. Religion may be perceived as an effort to conserve values. The conserving tendency to save what is worthy is evident in every religion. To this extent everyone is conservative who cares for any value enough to maintain it. But when effort to preserve outreaches the effort to grow, we have the conservative type. The traditional ways of the past are then considered unquestionably superior to the new ideas of the present. The new departures are resisted as betrayals of the glorious treasure of the past. In opposition to the conservative is the progressive, who is more eager to grow than to preserve the past. He welcomes change confidently, believing that progress is possible, ready to forego the security of the attained for the adventure of the not yet attained. The progressive is liberal in his generous welcome to the "wave of the future," and he may be radical in uprooting the past to reform the present.

*e*) The *tolerant* versus the *intolerant*. The tolerant person seeks to be open-minded and broad-minded. He delights in differences, seeing in diversities the enlargement of the interests and values of life. He expects to find good in all religions; he may consider one religion as good as another. To the intolerant this is "fatal apostasy" from the only true revelation. Tolerance is feared as a betrayal of unique and unapproachable superiorities, and despised as a weak and foolish compromise that degrades the best to the level of the worst. To one of strong and dogmatic convictions there is only one true religion or right way of life. Other creeds are false, other gods are no gods, other churches a scandal of false pretension. It may be observed that formal and conservative types tend to be intolerant. But this is not the whole story, for informal and progressive types may be just as dogmatic and scornful of any who disagree with their enlightenment.

*f*) The *affirmative* versus the *negative*. Affirmative religion is optimistic and healthy-minded. It stresses the abundant life and seeks to enlarge all values. It looks up, not down, forward, not backward; facing the sun, the shadows fall behind. Evil is forgotten or excluded as unreal and unhealthy; sin and error are to be avoided by filling the mind with truth and goodness. Trust, rather than fear, is the dominant emotion. It emphasizes the desirable by positive suggestion and constructive development. Negative religion is pessimistic and suspicious of human nature. It sees every desire as a temptation luring life to destruction, and it hopes to save life from evil by cutting off desire. It prohibits with "thou shalt nots" and hedges the good with stern commands to keep it pure from corruption. It glories in sacrifice, denial, and a martyr's crown. The ascetic discipline strengthens character by the enduring of hardship and by training for great labors.

Here are twelve types of religious experience set in six pairs of contrast. They are not exhaustive, but they are typical of prevalent tendencies in religion. Any type pushed to its ultimate extreme means distortion. Each needs the corrective of its opposite to save the religious life from partiality and imbalance. The dialectic of Hegel advances by uniting antitheses in a higher synthesis, moving on to other oppositions and yet higher unities, canceling out of the unworthy and reclaiming the worthy. The religious life is a symphony of many moods and melodies in contrast and harmony to endow the finite with infinite possibilities and to fulfill the rhythm of growing relationships.

Having noted these contrasting types of religious behavior, it is even more pressing to inquire why religious persons are what they are. What is each person trying to do in his characteristic style of religious expression? It is evident that religious experience does not have exactly the same meaning to all. And it appears that each one is quite congruent with himself and likely to persist in his own religious pattern. Is he inner-directed from the particular need of his own unique individuality, or is he other-directed from the expectations of his religious group? Again we are impaled on the dilemma of whether religious motivation arises from native need of the individual or is acquired by learning through interpersonal relations. And we are not able to deny either set of motivations, for they interplay in the religious search.

We must continue to explore in the following chapters the why of religious behavior. At this point in our inquiry let us remind ourselves that the religious life is a venture of faith impelled by the urgent need of a finite person to reach out for answers to the infinite potentialities of his conflictual nature. In his outreach he may follow any of the contrasting modes of behavior noted above as types of religious experience. Through this outreaching he is likely to persist in what becomes his characteristic style of behavior.

Does the religious person persist by virtue of reinforcing habit or fresh discovery? It appears that many and perhaps the majority of those who persist in religious behavior are moved by reinforcing habit. They are the legalists and ritualists who occupy themselves with the externals of religion. They may be regular in church attendance and always in their place to carry on the routine observances with invariable repetition, but who miss somehow the profounder stirrings of the spirit. They are willing to do their duty, but the horizons are limited and the duties are usually routine.

In sharp contrast to such routine is the vivid experience of those who are vitally aware of fresh religious discovery. To them the religious moment is an encounter with Thou in the awe and wonder of tremendous mystery. Prayer is an authentic inner experience of communion with the divine, and worship is an elevation of the spirit in repentance and renewal, aspiration and dedication. Such a person will return often to take his bearings and refocus the direction of his desires in harmony with the larger purpose to which he devotes himself. To him the religious quest is the motivating center of all he does. He lives and moves and has his being in a relationship of ultimate concern.

Such devotion is defined by Walter H. Clark [12] as *primary religious behavior*. He distinguishes this authentic sense of religious discovery from the *secondary* religious behavior of those who have translated a once vital experience into punctilious observance of a formal duty. Still further removed is the *tertiary* religious behavior of those who have never known a firsthand religious experience but merely follow a routine in unfeeling repetition. He insists that the meaning of the primary is so different from the secondary religious behavior that conclusions drawn from one cannot be applied to the other. Yet psychologists more often present data from the secondary behavior than the far more significant primary behavior. And it is customary for many investigators to conclude that religion is reducible to its least meaningful forms. William James gave his attention in the *Varieties* to those "for whom religion exists not as a dull habit but as an acute fever" (p. 8), believing the findings would prove more significant than to study secondhand religion which is only a dim copy of original experience.

In this chapter we conclude that the most authentic religious behavior will be primary first-person experience. This is not to discount secondary religious behavior which in its way may be a sincere devotion to duty. Yet experimental psychology finds a law of effect, that learning is extinguished where the effect is lacking in value. In so far as tertiary religious behavior approaches a minimum of value, it is probably on the way to extinction. If this religious behavior continues, there must be some reward in meaning and value, though not to be confused with the primary experience of confrontation.

[12] *The Psychology of Religion* (New York: The Macmillan Company, 1958), p. 23. Note also the attack of Jonathan Edwards upon the Half-Way Covenant in New England churches, in which reputable persons were permitted to enjoy the privileges of the church without making full profession of religious faith.

# 5 RELIGIOUS GROWTH

## 1. *Developing Religion*

The best place to begin is at the beginning. But like the end of the rainbow, beginnings are difficult to find. Artificial events can be staged and scheduled so that the public may be seated in neat rows to see the curtain rise or hear the whistle blow. Natural events are different. They come silently and unexpectedly, without publicity or fanfare. And before we arrive on the scene, the beginning is lost in later developments. Historical beginnings are notably obscure. Something is beginning every minute, but those present lack the perspective to know what is going to be significant enough to preserve for posterity. When posterity gathers sufficient perspective on a development to ask how it began, the origin is erased by the passage of the time that made the history.

The origins of religion are hidden. Somewhere in the prehistoric ages men somehow developed religious traditions that were well established when the first written records were made. The discoveries of archaeolgy and anthropology have pushed history back thousands of years into the formerly unknown past and have added priceless records to the early chapters of man, but religious beginnings are still beyond view. More light will yet be shed on these distant antiquities as the results of further research accumulate. What do we know about the early development of religion?

*a*) The beginning of religion was *humble*. As Jesus was born in a stable, so religion first appeared in lowly surroundings—unworthy, one may think, of its later glory. Primitive superstitious beliefs and rites may seem repulsive to refined tastes, but origin does not determine value.

*b*) Religion from the first was *complex*. Most explanations oversimplify the origin of religion. It has been suggested that religion begins in fear or wonder, totem or magic, instincts or spirits. But these are partial explanations, half-truths or less, for the whole truth is far more complex. Whatever concerns life in the complexity of its interests and values concerns religion.

*c*) Religion aims at *social values*. As far back as we can see, religion is devoted to human welfare. It performs strange and sometimes destructive acts, but always for what is thought to be a larger good. Its basic motive is to create, conserve, and increase values. The highest values and purposes are the concern of religion.

*d*) Religion is therefore *urgent*. To the primitive mind the mysterious powers are not to be taken lightly. They control destiny and must be approached cautiously and reverently. Religion was serious business then, perhaps more so than today, if needs were greater and resources fewer. When the values of life are at stake, there is reason to be earnest. In times of crisis religion usually comes into the foreground. The more urgent the need, the more men seek for a response.

*e*) Religion develops in *persons*. This includes the intrapersonal adjustive activities of the individual as well as the interpersonal activities of individuals in social relations. Persons are creators and sustainers of societies. Primitive tribes may appear to submerge persons, but the person is the subject of every religious experience, the one who serves and is served by religious values.

Growth is the basic need of life. Every living thing seeks to complete itself. "Fullness of life is the goal of life, the urge to completeness is the most compelling motive in life." [1] Hadfield shows how this law of completeness works physiologically toward health by restoring wounds and deficiencies to wholeness, and psychologically toward self-realization by seeking to harmonize all complexes and sentiments into unified expression. Morally we strive toward perfection and religiously toward holiness or spiritual wholeness. Other needs may be tangential, but the urge to grow is the never-ending demand for completion. We are born to grow, and our natures are eager to be moving along lines of fulfillment. Without growth life slips instantly into decay and decline. There is no standing still. We must either grow or die.

Religion is life seeking completion. Without growth religion declines. To grow is, therefore, a religious imperative. Otherwise religious experience is but a memory and religious activity an empty shell of hollow formality. Religion is a resource for human growth, serving the growing needs of persons and societies. To serve life well, religion must keep apace with human growth at every stage of development.

What produces religious growth?

*a*) Situations of *need* are conducive to religious growth. Crises often turn men to religion because they are dramatic exposures of urgent need. But for those who have eyes to see, life is constantly in need. Only the blindness of conceit misleads us to suppose we are self-sufficient. To realize that we are

[1] J. A. Hadfield, *Psychology and Morals* (New York: Robert M. McBride & Co., 1925), p. 61.

forever incomplete is to sense our deep need of Thou to answer the need. To know insecurity from hour to hour, to meet disappointment and loss, is to feel the need of more ultimate resources.

*b*) Experiences of *fulfillment* encourage religious development. If there were no answers to prayer, who would continue to pray? Unless something is found, would it not be futile to search? No illusion can long survive its exposure. Religion does not live except where something happens. Those who earnestly and intelligently seek religious values find their needs satisfied, and trust because they trust not in vain. Magical superstitions pass away as cumulative experience shows them to be unfounded and useless. False religious ideas and foolish petitions also fall before the tests of experience. But true religion survives and grows through its convincing results. Fulfillment is essential to religious growth, to encourage and nourish its developing life.

*c*) Between every vital need and its true fulfillment stands a *personal venture*. Religious faith is a courageous adventure, quite different from a tentative opinion. It is a personal decision to undergo risk, to suffer the consequences, and to carry on a faithful life. More people lose their religion through neglect than from any other cause. Mere activity is not enough, for that may be nothing more than random motions and meaningless repetitions. Saying prayers is a meaningless exercise if the mind wanders while the tongue mumbles careless syllables. Religious living is a rigorous discipline that touches all of life; it is a vocation in which every action and attitude is to be aligned with the overarching purpose. Religious growth is more than cognitive belief or a stir of emotion; it is a fine art to perfect by faithful practice. To live with God and fellow men in harmony and service for the sake of meaningful values is the artistry of religion.

## 2. *Religion of Childhood*

If the origin of religion is mysterious in the distant past, what shall we say of the individual child who is born this morning? He comes before our eyes and acts out his growing life where we can know him by firsthand observation. Yet the causes of his growth are also a mystery. What does he seek as his ultimate concern? How is he to become a religious person? The inner meaning of his religious behavior is hidden in the complexities of his nature. He may not be able to communicate the full range of his religious meanings to us. And he may not fully understand them himself. The best we can do is to observe what he does and listen to what he says as a growing person. There will be many gaps, but from the evidence obtainable the psychologist with sensitive empathy will infer some glimpses of what he is seeking to do and what religion is meaning to him.

We have found the sense of need to be the primal motivator of human life and specifically at the root of religious concern. The newborn infant does not have to wait long for his needs to arise. In the first moments of birth the need for oxygen is a crisis so urgent that his fragile life depends upon it to survive. Hunger for nourishment is another need that does not long delay. It is from the pain of these needs that the baby comes to sharp conscious awareness. And out of this anguish he struggles and reaches out to be fulfilled. Yet he cannot thrive on chemicals alone; he needs security and love. When he is comforted by the mother's tenderness and not until then does he begin to know the spiritual fulfillment of his native desires. He now takes up the lifelong search beyond the physical satisfiers for interpersonal relations in which he is valued, respected, and loved.

Without such insistent needs he would not become a religious person. Even in its minimum form religious behavior is a seeking out of vital needs to invite some response from a Sustainer of values. From his first pangs of need and his outreach to fulfill them the infant begins to search for interpersonal relations. If then he does not cry in vain and his need calls forth an answering response, he discovers that he is not alone in this strange world. He learns that someone knows him and responds to his need in faithful love that justifies his growing expectations. His vital concerns are now projected toward someone who is concerned with him to fulfill his needs. For he learns that he is not sufficient in himself to attain fulfillment, that he must find the completion so urgently required in the one who responds from beyond.

Such a wordless dialogue every infant enters into when his only language is a cry. He is evidently too limited in his experience to know the full meaning of religion. But he is not too young to know ultimate concern, for his very life depends upon the answer to his cry. You may remind us that he is not fully aware that his life depends upon the answering person. But with all his being he cries in a desperate sense of urgency that speaks of ultimate concern. His need is the ultimate so far as he knows it, and he struggles with his whole being to win the response from beyond himself.

In this way, it seems to me, he is making a personal venture. He is throwing himself without reservation into the violent crying forth of his need. And he will not give up until he is heard or exhausts himself and loses consciousness in fitful sleep. There cannot be much faith at first, and his cry sounds the note more of despair than hope. But if he is heard and wins the response to his cry, there is the first ground of his faith. Day by day he will make the effort to see if his grain of hope will grow into faith. The faithful person who is always ready to respond is the essential answer to his cry for faith. And by learning that he will be heard in the regular response of the faithful person, he is gaining the embryo resource of a religious faith.

It is the nature of growing life to be constantly interdependent. The newborn infant is a whole organism of functioning cells and processes which are interdependent upon one another. And yet he is unable to survive in isolation. He is interdependent with his environment in a field of co-acting responses by which the resources of his growing life are sustained. He must interact with human persons if he is to become a person himself. This has been shown in that a feral child who is adopted by animals will develop animal behavior lacking the distinctive traits of human behavior. The growing person is not bound to arrive, nor can he ride on the back of animal instincts to become a person. He will become a person with religious concern only by learning through interacting with a faithful person the meaning of his finite search for response from beyond.

Learning is motivated by stimuli from the dynamic environment, especially by interpersonal relations. It begins at birth and continues to death. Learning is of the utmost importance for growth and contributes to the majority of human developments. Learning conditions all forms of behavior and experience: motor skills, language, personality traits, social adjustments. Religious development results from learning with a faithful person to seek the answering One. The rate of learning is probably highest in early childhood. It has been contended that persons learn more in the first year than in any other. Aptitudes for learning are present from birth, and the list of first-year achievements is very notable.

When is the best time to begin religious training? The earlier the better. Before birth is not too soon, or even before the birth of the parents. For the family is the first school for childhood learning. If the parents are sincerely faithful to respond, there is the first requirement for the religious development of children. Long before formal instruction is set up, the child is learning by suggestion, imitation, and adjustment to the attitudes of others. The religious opportunities of infancy are greater than we realize. First impressions are indelibly lasting. To neglect the first years and begin later is to omit the foundations without which the whole structure is insecure.

What are the religious needs of childhood? It will be well to consider three periods: infancy, ages 1-2; early childhood, ages 3-6; and later childhood, ages 7-12.

*a*) *Regularity* is the first need of infancy (ages 1-2). This is physiological, as somatic rhythms call for regular supply of nourishment, sleep, and exercise. But it is even more a psychological need. Infants learn only by repetition. Their pattern of life must have stability and order to establish associations and meanings. No single item has meaning until it is associated with another item in a series of relationships. Chickens learn to associate the appearance of the farmer with food and flock eagerly around him because he regularly supplies the food. The rapidity of learning is shown by an experiment with newborn infants who where given the bottle just after a buzzer had been sounded for five seconds. By the time they were four or five days old, they had established the association, so that when the buzzer sounded, they opened their mouths, performed sucking motions, and decreased other activities.[2] Desirable habits and trustworthy character require regular associations in which causes and effects of conduct are consistent enough to teach lessons of good and bad. A secure basis for religious experience is a dependable, trustworthy environment to answer the outreach of need. The infant's first revelation of God may come through this experience of regular and responsive interpersonal relations.

*b*) *Affection* is another religious need of infancy. Infants who are not shown affection develop withdrawing attitudes that lead to antisocial traits and unhealthy emotions of fear and antagonism. Lack of affection is a major cause of neurotic and delinquent tendencies.

> In examining the childhood histories of a great number of neurotic persons I have found . . . the basic evil is invariably a lack of genuine warmth and affection. A child can stand a great deal of what is often regarded as traumatic—such as sudden weaning, occasional beating, sex experiences—as long as inwardly he feels wanted and loved.[3]

Gentleness, kindness, and tender care develop social responses and healthy emotions. Yet child care may be overprotective. Too constant solicitude encourages a helpless dependency that retards growth. Infants need to be left alone enough to develop their own resources and grow self-reliant, yet to learn that someone will answer when they call. God may be known to children in the love of parents and friends. If our love were wiser, it would be more divine.

*c*) *Religious example* is also needed in infancy. Relationship to a living model is one of the first and best ways of learning. Long before a vocabulary is acquired for verbal instruction, children learn by observation. How is a child to develop a sense of values? By sensing what parents hold worthy. To the infant, parents stand for God. They perform the functions of God, creating and sustaining the living values of their children. They provide whatever is needed and receive from the infant responses of dependency, trust, petition, and gratitude that are nearest to the religious emotions. Now

[2] D. P. Marquis, "Can Conditioned Responses Be Established in the New-born Infant?" *Journal of Genetic Psychology,* XXXIX (1931), 472-92.

[3] Horney, *op. cit.,* pp. 79-80.

when these godlike parents show attitudes of reverence and devotion to a yet higher source of values, the child is deeply impressed. Whatever moral and religious traits parents desire children to have may best be shown in themselves.[4] Emotions are very contagious. Parents who maintain harmony instead of conflict, faith not fear, hope not despair, will inevitably communicate these emotions to children. Trust in God and fellow men need not be argued for. If trust is practiced, it will be eloquent.

*d*) In early childhood (ages 3-6) the *discovery of persons* is a constant adventure which begins in the first months of life. The infant at first may only dimly distinguish between persons and things. Pets and parents are pushed and patted around as mechanically as inanimate objects. Then comes a dawning recognition that persons respond in ways that things do not and do things that squeaking, rolling toys cannot do. Crying brings attention and cooing invites affection from parents. Persons are thus appealed to as understanding and as responsive to persuasion. In the discovery of other persons the infant comes to know himself as a person. Social consciousness is prerequisite to self-consciousness and religious awareness. With the mastery of language by the age of three, he is able to conceptualize himself as a person, like yet different from other persons. When God is accepted by parents as present in the home, he seems to the child like a member of the family. Prayer is as natural as family conversation. The invisibility of God may be a problem, and yet parents are also invisible when they leave the room. Pictures and stories of God that portray him in crude anthropomorphic terms are to be avoided, yet the fatherhood of God is meaningful to any age. Ideas of God need to grow steadily with enlarging understanding, until his traits are viewed in a cosmic sense.

*e*) *Co-operation* is another outreach of early childhood. As soon as persons are discovered, they are sought to play the game of co-operation. Nothing interests children more than the give and take of responsive interaction. Games as simple as tossing a ball back and forth or picking up and throwing down seem never to become stale. Participation is a social adventure, and those who take time to play with children win their loyal devotion. If parents are too busy to respond to these invitations, they miss the finest opportunities to demonstrate participation. Seeing the aloof individualism of adults, children also take on that stubborn social resistance that blocks effective communication. Religion is I seeking to co-operate with Thou through all of the relationships of life. Lessons in co-operation are therefore basic to religious growth. Every co-operative root does not bear religious fruit, but without the roots no fruit may be expected. In early

[4] R. V. McCann, *Delinquency: Sickness or Sin* (New York: Harper & Bros., 1957), asserts that lack of "adequate models" is a cause of delinquency. A weak, absentee, or criminal father is correlated with delinquent behavior in the son.

childhood participation is so eager and spontaneous that its cultivation is a natural development. For the happiness of the child and the welfare of his future society, co-operation belongs in the first lessons of life. In this way families will learn the meaning and value of religious response.

*f*) *Sharing* is a needed social art to learn in early childhood. It is a mutual response of giving and receiving values. Children usually receive more than they give, with consequent danger of selfishness. By and large, selfishness does more damage and breeds more misery than any other practice. And selfish habits are firmly rooted in childhood from infancy. Personality disorders and social failures of later life have their beginnings in selfish attitudes of childhood. Learning to give up desires and possessions to others, learning the joy and justice of exchanging gifts and services, are lessons essential to religious as well as social living. For religion is an interpersonal experience of sharing the best values of life, with outgoing interest through enlarging relationships. When prayer is selfish petition for private advantage, it dips beneath the religious level to unsocial magic. Prayer becomes religious in asking good for others and seeking mutual welfare. As soon as children begin to pray, they may learn to pray unselfishly and find religion a way of wider participation with others.

*g*) In later childhood (ages 7-12) *curiosity and exploration* are leading interests. Having acquired a vocabulary, the child uses it violently to ask questions. His stay-at-home days are over. At school and roaming about the neighborhood he is eager to find out everything there is to know about his world. These jumping, shouting question marks often drive adults frantic with their insatiable curiosity. Busy and impatient parents may resist the noise and resent the questions as a nuisance to be outlawed for disturbing the peace. But a question is the best tool of understanding. Every question should be respected, for it is a sign of readiness to learn. Questions about sex and the story of life are not to be evaded but calmly and openly considered, for no other time will be so appropriate to understand these vital mysteries. Questions about God and religion are not easy to answer well: first, because they are difficult to explain; and second, because, like sex, they have emotional halos. Wise parents will think ahead and clarify their own religious concepts against that day when they must justify the faith that is in them. No one knows the hour when a leading question will open the mind of childhood, but blessed is he who is prepared to answer well. Even better is the mutual search with the child that shares with him the exploring adventure.

*h*) *Integration and self-control* are important agenda of later childhood. In these years physical growth is slower but firmer, knitting bones, muscles, and nerves together in closer co-ordination. Explorations collect oddly assorted curiosities, as incoherent as the contents of a boy's pocket or a girl's dresser. These fragments, dumped into a heap, need to be organized into an orderly system. And the older child cannot be organized permanently by anyone but himself. The mother may clean his room periodically and put things in order, but they do not stay that way. The important thing is to learn for one's self the satisfaction of being neat. Fortunately, the child has at this age strong tendencies toward independence, toward making his own decisions and thinking for himself. Coercion is resented by children, who respond better to invitations that captivate interest than to orders that forbid. Tempers and moods need to be controlled from within by the development of the poise and dignity of self-respect and social responsibility.

Life should grow increasingly purposive and responsible. A religious purpose can give meaning and unity to life. Children at this age may become earnest, loyal followers of a religious purpose. Or they may rebel against the ideals and expectations of their elders to follow primitive impulses recklessly in angry defiance or covertly in sullen resistance. The forces of conflict are deep and incessant in every personality. To understand this basic struggle in each person will enable us to be more tolerant and helpful to the growing child. Integration and control may be stimulated from without but actually develop from within.

### 3. *Religion and Adolescence*

Youth is what everyone wants except those who have it. Why does everyone want youth? First, because it seems so gay and bright with promise. Second, because we miss it later on and find no way to return to it. Why is it not desired by all who have it? First, because it is not so easy as it looks; no age has more perplexing problems and inner tensions to work out. Second, because youth is impatient for the not yet attained—impatient to explore the future, cross frontiers, and win a responsible place in the world.

Adolescence means "growing up to," or growing toward, maturity not yet attained. Youth has the advantages and disadvantages of a halfway house; it is on the way yet not at the goal. It is somewhere between childhood (vehemently disowned as helplessly innocent) and adulthood (often resented as somber and subdued by the cares of the world). A young person is very sure that he has outgrown and rejected his childish past, while at the same time he secretly suspects that he has not come into his future estate of manhood or womanhood. Reluctant as he may be to admit it, he is not yet all here, and he knows it to his sorrow.

There is no more decisive time in life than adolescence (ages 12-24). For the young life is then at the threshold of many opportunities. Children are so busy growing they have little time for anything else. The developments of childhood should build sturdy foundations of health, neuromuscular skills, social adjustments, mental abilities, moral and religious ideals. Taking a step at a time as they do, children are not in a position to gain perspective and understand themselves. Physical growth is very rapid in the early months of adolescence. And then youth has time to pause long enough to size up his situation, take his bearings, and gather resources to go ahead.

Physiological changes of puberty are significant in growing up. Maturation of organs, glands, hair, voice, and figure indicates a new cycle of life. A person is the same yet not the same. Certain habits, attitudes, and characteristic features maintain identity. The continuity of growth preserves the developments of the past, and nothing ever learned is entirely lost. But the changes of adolescence gradually renew almost every aspect of personality. Psychologically, adolescent personality expands in many directions. Four dimensions at least may be noted.

*a*) *Personal experiences deepen.* Emotions have a depth heretofore unknown to the adolescent personality. Periods of storm and stress, well known at this age, are in part reverberations from glandular developments violently stimulating the emotions. Mood swings from elation to depression; outbursts of temper and variations of temperament are unpredictable and often unmanageable while the adolescent is trying to learn how to live with his new feelings. To ask him why he feels as he does is futile, for he probably does not understand his own unexpected emotions. These upsurgings of vitality are indications of larger capacities for sensing the values of life. Appreciations are awakened and refined. There is keener sensitivity to ranges of values undiscovered before.

Religious experience is enriched by deeper reverence and satisfaction in communion with God. Church symbols, traditions, and fellowship become meaningful and mysteriously inviting. Worship, once mere formal repetition, glows with vivid awe and mystery. Prayer may inspire ecstasy and meditation aspire toward heroic sacrifices and achievements. Life changes to a technicolor of rainbow brightness. It is not surprising that religious awakenings come so naturally in adolescence, for new capacities and sensitivities make possible richer experiences and deeper appreciations of all values.

Under favorable conditions, religion occupies a very important place in the life of the maturing boy or girl. It satisfies his groping for a fundamental, synthesized understanding of the whole realm of experience. It gives him a sense of values, a sense of personal relationships and obligations. It facilitates the formation of high ideals of unselfish service. It gives him help in attaining that self-control and self-discipline which characterizes strong personality. It reinforces his moral character. It aids him in resolving many conflicts of impulses and desires, and thus assists him in attaining sound mental health. Praise, prayer, and other elements of worship may enrich and deepen his life, and add much to its wholesomeness and happiness. Religion in reality involves personal devotion to a Supreme Being, and can provide a unifying force for all that is highest and best in the youth's nature.[5]

*b*) *Social interests broaden.* The discovery of persons has been noted as one of the great events of early childhood. Now the adolescent discovers persons in a new sense. Persons were then convenient or inconvenient objects to do things for you and with you. Now they become creatures to admire, to exclaim and wonder about. When boy meets girl, the heart beats faster, and though they may have been in the same neighborhood for years, they now see each other as for the first time. Interpersonal encounters are more intensive in emotional response and eager desire to be together. Social interests are more extensive as one friend after another comes into favorite focus and circles of friends grow larger. Children often prefer older friends, but adolescents are devoted to associates of their own age and count every minute lost that is not spent in the company of one or more of them. To be with the crowd is the life, until couples begin to pair off and the later adolescent comes to prefer the only one. In either case social consciousness is keen and social approval means everything.

A boy of seventeen writes: "And in the last year I made a wonderful discovery. That is that the people one sees all about and who seem a formless mass with no individuality at all are composed of vitally different personalities all of whom are more or less disposed to talk about themselves. Experience is practically tapping on your back if you will only turn around. There was the taxi driver whose father had been a blacksmith in Haiti and who after having married a Negro woman refused to send his half-breed children to a Negro school. Incidentally, this fellow had about the most sensible political views I have ever heard. All this I gathered in while riding a few miles."

Another boy the same age writes: "I now also realized that it was not enough to classify a teacher as nice or not nice (a nice teacher could have bad qualities and vice versa), in fact it grew on me that a teacher had to be classified in two separate ways: as a teacher, and again as a person. With the ability to see a teacher in more than one light came a real interest in the characters of the people round me; each of my friends took on a new color."[6]

Religion at this time expands socially. The conscience becomes sensitive to new social values and responsibilities. The anguish of guilt and remorse broods over social blunders and personal inadequacies. Ideals of perfection

[5] Fowler D. Brooks, *The Psychology of Adolescence* (Boston: Houghton Mifflin Co., 1929), pp. 341-42. Used by permission of the publisher.

[6] From *The Adolescent Personality,* by Peter Blos. Copyright, 1941, D. Appleton-Century Co., Inc. Reprinted by permission of Appleton-Century-Crofts, Inc.

and hero worship tantalize the ineptitudes of adolescence. The pain of self-consciousness causes one to pass through awkward stages to increasing grace and skill, learning thereby to aspire and work for desired progress. In this time of high idealism youth dreams of turning the world upside down and building a better world. Such dreams are not to be discouraged; they are the best hope of human progress and deserve a larger place in the councils of adult leadership. The religion of youth develops social enthusiasms that are worthy of being encouraged. The sharp sense of social need, the courageous challenge of old and intrenched wrongs, the eager desire to serve, and the readiness to make sacrifices for a cause are characteristic of youth. They are likewise essential to religious and social progress. Unless we keep our religion young in this sense and our social order flexible to constant change in every generation, the civilization we cherish will fall into decay.

*c*) *Intellectual powers heighten.* This social sensitivity does not, however, mean slavish servility. The normal adolescent has a mind of his own and intends to use it. The center of authority moves inward from external commands to self-demands. It is not unusual for young people to flaunt their independence. In struggling for a sense of worth and a place of respect in society, they insist, rightly or wrongly, upon making their own decisions. Freedom to think and decide is their right and should be exercised throughout childhood. College freshmen show wide contrasts at this point. Those who have had practice in deciding for themselves at home sail out into the larger freedoms of college on a steady keel, but those who have had everything decided for them are helplessly at sea. They either flounder in depths of dependent homesickness or careen wildly about tossed by every wind of opinion and wave of impulse. Parents who tire of sharp criticisms and long arguments should recognize that adolescents need to try their logical wings and heighten intellectual powers if they are to grow in wisdom.

Religious experience needs to grow intellectually. Childish concepts of God and miracles, heaven and hell, biblical inspiration and revelation, religious duties and devotion, need to grow up. Doubts are not to be feared, but welcomed, as symptoms of independent judgment. Adolescent doubt may be exaggerated by some writers, and doubts are often induced by social expectation and imitation. But the basic cause of doubting is the emerging reason, seeking to understand and to find coherent meanings for the contradictions of experience. Children may be taught narrow, inflexible religion incapable of expansion or of harmony with mature experience. To teach this kind of religion is to court needless conflicts that finally turn many away from religion, which they come to identify with superstition. Foolish teaching of religion, like the popular stories of Santa Claus, makes bitter skeptics who distrust the whole business and resent those who have deceived them. Everyone needs a sound philosophy that will meet the tests and stand the shocks of modern life. As intellect develops in childhood and adolescence, continuous growth should enlarge religious concepts. Young people need freedom to think, stimulating problems to solve, and democratic guidance through comradeship with mature minds who are honestly facing and creatively thinking through their own problems.

*d*) *Life purposes lengthen.* The aims of childhood are transient and temporary. A baby cries for the next meal and reaches for what dangles before his eyes. Children live from day to day, an hour at a time, a hand-to-mouth and step-by-step existence. Young people begin to sum up days into weeks, months, and years. They save pennies and dimes until they have enough to purchase some long-desired treasure. Through a round of social dates, whirling off with one friend after another for the thrill of the moment, they come to think of going steady and planning for marriage and a home. After many years of doing one task at a time and hoping the next one will not turn up too soon, they come eventually to think about a vocation to follow through life. As purposes lengthen into destinies, the most important decisions of life are made. We may ponder why these far-reaching decisions are made before young people have the wisdom of age. Older and less democratic societies have permitted the elders to decide these questions for youth. But our observation is that youth do about as well and that with added responsibility judgment matures to reach sounder conclusions.

The long purposes and destinies of life involve religion. "Why live?" and "What shall I do with my life?" are essentially religious questions. They raise perspectives of the total meaning of life that draw together beginnings and ends. If we are here for a purpose, we ought to discover what that purpose is. If there is a purpose, it concerns not only us but the world at large. A vocation is more than a job to finish or an occupation to consume time and space. A vocation is essentially a purpose as long as life. Literally it means "a calling," of God to do his will. It is a commission, or sending forth, under divine orders. "Who will go?" "Here am I; send me." No religious experience is adequate without this sense of divine vocation to give direction and continuity to living. To find such a life purpose is to settle the deepest issue of life, not once for all, but every day. For purposes may fail unless they are reaffirmed and renewed from day to day. Living on purpose means enacting that intention into every thought and mood, every deed and development.

### *4. Religious Maturity*

Every age is a crisis, the crisis of how to grow. For life is a constant battle with decay. Health is a winning battle of victorious living; disease, senility, and death are losing battles. In biological terms this is known as metabolism, the ratio of building up (anabolism) to the destruction (katabolism) of living cells by which energy is provided for vital processes and activities. Retarded growth is one of the most pitiful tragedies of life. Nature sometimes falters and leaves human wrecks—in stunted forms, withered limbs, or defective organs. Mental retardation is even more serious, as seen in those whose clouded intelligence is unable to rise above the mental ages of infancy or early childhood. Social retardation is evident in the maladjustment of those whose immaturities appear in timid withdrawing or aggressive delinquency.

Religious immaturity is not so startling, yet it is quite as tragic as other retardations. When religion fails to grow, the results are religious cripples who are stunted, deformed, blind, or deaf in spiritual life. Jesus evidently considered this more serious than bodily injury. (See Matt. 5:29-30.) But not many take the spiritual life as seriously as that. Religious cripples and morons are so common that we scarcely notice them. Many adults cherish a retarded religious experience that misfits present needs and disqualifies them for larger adventures.

To arrive at maturity is something, but not enough. To continue growing through the long years of adulthood is the problem. For maturity is one of the most dangerous threats to growth. It is the age of settling down into hardening forms that resist change. The average man develops very little after the age of twenty-five. Whether a college graduate or an unskilled laborer, he is not likely to change radically the established pattern of his life. He learns no more than is necessary, develops almost no new interests, makes no major reforms, and acquires surprisingly few ideas beyond those needed in the daily routine of his business. This stagnation does not mean that he is incapable of further growth, for educational experiments have shown as great, or greater, capacities for learning in the later years. We stop growing psychologically, not because we must, but because it is easier to keep familiar habits and follow the settled ways of the good old days.

Childhood delights to grow; adolescence demands it. We expect children to grow, sending them to school and to play that they may have every growing advantage. We are sure that adolescents have much to learn, and we urge them to cast aside childish pranks and take on the full stature of manhood and womanhood. But when young people get their growth, as we say, when they have a steady job and a home of their own, they are to settle down and tread the old beaten paths of those who have gone before. Having taken their last fling and bidden farewell to youth, these young adults are put in lock step with their grandparents and expected to keep in line. Why should there be no more adventures after the age of twenty-five? Why complete one's education so prematurely when learning ought to be as long as life? Our society is sadly at fault to establish these humdrum customs of treadmill routine as the style for maturity. Is it the machine-age civilization or short-sighted, dumb assent that truncates growth so sharply at the threshold of maturity, making drones and robots of adults?

There are at least five major tasks for maturity to accomplish. They involve the whole personality and yet are distinctly religious problems for mature religious growth.

*a*) *Self-knowledge.* It takes years of living to know oneself. To understand one's abilities is the product of many experiments to see what one can do best. A child is ready and eager to try anything, not knowing where his aptitudes lie. By maturity one should have a fairly clear idea where he can best succeed. Quite as important is it to know his limitations and realize what he cannot do. Knowing his limitations, the next problem is to accept them and live cheerfully within his own range of growth. Religious aspiration seeks perspective in humility before the Creator, yet hoping that many limitations are relative and trusting in the power of continued growth. Religious self-knowledge corrects both conceit and inferiority in the devotion to a larger destiny motivated by ultimate concern. It seeks the optimal pattern of life—to learn what is best and then proceed without hesitation to do it.

*b*) *Controlling desire.* Children are attracted like flitting butterflies to every bright spot of interest. They want what they want when they want it, but not for long. Youth is overpowered with desires. New powers and waking capacities supercharge them to excesses. Like inexperienced drivers, excited to have so much power, they open the throttle recklessly, forgetting the need of control. A mature person, like an experienced driver, knows the dangers that go with power and is more alert to the value of control. Control of lower desires for the sake of higher ones is a religious art. If one is sincerely religious, he lives for a purpose, and by that ongoing intention he controls his unruly impulses. To accept a divine calling is to have a larger responsibility, to trust a higher guidance, and to find the peace of resignation to a higher wisdom.

*c*) *Larger resources.* Motor skills are learned in early childhood. Social skills are won at the expense of awkward attempts and constant adjustment. By later adolescence a fairly complete set of habits has been acquired for the ordinary routine of later years. It is the misfortune of most adults to be content with habits already acquired and to coast along on past achievements. It is estimated that human beings are 20 per cent efficient most of the time. In a crisis we may rise to the occasion and make some heroic rescue by a superhuman feat of strength and endurance. Then, without further incentive we drop back into the familiar mediocrity. More constant stimuli are needed to rouse us to the higher ranges of possible achievement. Religious motivation is a constant source of greater achievement. Dedication to a divine purpose is a tremendous incentive to heroic living, and those who are committed to the ultimate are more apt to rise to their best efforts. By aspiration and inspiration, by faithful practice and progress, maturity may develop larger resources to meet the demands and expectations of the religious life.

*d*) *Wisdom of experience*. Intelligence has been defined as ability to learn by experience. Experience increases self-knowledge, control of desire, and efficient skills—that is, if one is able to learn from his experiences. Otherwise he makes the same mistakes over and over again. But if one can learn, every experience becomes his teacher. Wisdom is more than facts or skills; it is a true sense of values. Wisdom is a sound judgment—not a hasty opinion but a sense of the whole meaning of life. Religious maturity has this wisdom of experience. A religious person is intent upon the business of living. He cultivates the inner life, welcomes every interpersonal relationship, and evaluates every experience as a possible divine revelation. He refers his perplexities to larger perspectives and seeks to view the situation as a whole. It is therefore in religious maturity that ever-growing experiences may ripen into the fruit of wisdom.

*e*) *Growing faith*. The faith of childhood is a flower of innocence. The faith of adolescence drops childish petals to put forth intelligent fruit. But the faith of maturity is like a tree whose roots are deep in the stream of experience, whose trunk is sturdy enough to bear the brunt of the elements, that brings forth fruit in season. Having weathered many storms, such faith is proved worthy and able to stand. Faith so tested is more than dumb assent; it grows into faithfulness. Belief grows into trust; it rises above the merely intellectual and becomes a venture of one's whole existential being. "Though he slay me, yet will I trust in him." (Job 13:15.) The faithful are full of faith. They are also filled with courage, patience, and unshakable determination to march in the line of duty. Seasoned faith is the salt that loses not its savor but flavors, purifies, and preserves.

It is true, as Allport notes,[7] that most criticism of religion is directed to the immature forms. There is no denying that immature persons may be religious, and if so they will exploit religion for self-gratification. Rigid and compulsive dogmatism, holier-than-thou intolerance, insatiable need for reassurance, obsessive ritualism, fear of unpardonable sin, and regressive dependence are immature religious attitudes. But it is fallacious to generalize, as Freud has, that all religious behavior is consequently neurotic or immature. The error here is in confining religious behavior to the "defensive

[7] *Individual and His Religion*, p. 54.

functions of the ego" rather than in the forward intention of the reality principle.

If psychology is to illuminate the meaning of religion, there is need to follow "the course of becoming to its ultimate frontiers of growth." [8] No shred of evidence is to be left out in any stages or varieties of growing personality. Mature religious sentiments are described by Allport as differentiated in richness and complexity, with many interests and successive discriminations woven into continuous reorganization. They become master motives which supply their own driving power. They consistently orient and direct behavior to comprehensive and integral goals. The mature religious person is willing to take risks in advance of certainties; he is tolerant of doubt and frustration yet willing to devote himself to the ultimate meaning of life so far as he is able to discern it.

## 5. *Experiment and Integration*

Growth is an interacting process of experiment and integration. To grow, we must try the untried. The infant begins his experiments in random motions to explore and develop potentialities. Walking and talking are difficult skills to be learned by renewed efforts. Social adjustments to enlarging circles of persons are exciting experiments in the fine art of living with others. Mental growth is measured by the mastery of problems of increasing difficulty.

But experiments alone never produce growth. Whatever is gained by experiment needs to be appropriated by integration; otherwise experiments would remain forever in the futile disorder of random activity. A chicken runs frantically about a coop, dashing against one side and then another in foolish experiments. A child of two years will look around, take in the situation as an integrated whole, and walk straight to the door. Many people saw lamps swinging, apples falling, and teakettles steaming before Galileo, Newton, and Watt drew their conclusions therefrom. Learning by experience is bringing the lessons of experimentation to a synthesis of understanding.

Experiments without integration are centrifugal. They strike out and fly off in various tangents like the knight of Stephen Leacock who mounted his steed and rode furiously in all directions. They decenter life in distraction and confusion. The multiple appeals and distracting stimuli of the contemporary scene tend to shred interests and scatter purposes. The speed at which we dash along is not conducive to poise or concentration. There is no lack of exciting adventures, but how to unify the many fragments of living into a whole life is the unsolved problem.

[8] Allport, *Becoming*, p. 98.

Integration of personality means the effective co-ordination of interests, emotions, and intentions. This unified, harmonious functioning of all one's powers brings a sense of well-being. The balanced wholeness of a character formed by good habits is referred to as integrity. The unintegrated person is disorganized, loose, contradictory, and unpredictable. Careful studies show that the average child in grades 5 to 8 is ethically unorganized. Integration of character traits is a specific achievement, not well provided for in current education.[9]

Dissociation is a disintegrative tendency. Many problems are so perplexing and distressing that, instead of making a direct attack upon them, one may dispose of them by ignoring or evading them. Running away from, postponing, or repressing unwelcome issues are well-known devices of escape. Ernest M. Ligon defines lust as an "intense emotional attachment of any sort which is not integrated with the total personality." [10] A lustful eye roves and a lustful heart is never satisfied but is always craving new excitements and experiments. Pure desires are integrated to a faithful purpose, but lusts refuse to remain true or constant. These evasive tendencies lead to serious nervous disorders.

Integrations are often incomplete and immature. A childish devotion to a father or mother may become a fixation that prevents mating and marriage. Childish impressions of God as a kind of Santa Claus may preclude larger theistic perspectives. Dogmatic devotion to the old-time religion may block normal growth to religious maturity. Integrations are needed at every stage of growth to consolidate gains and prepare for continued advance. But no integration is to be final. Finality paralyzes growth.

What prevents the integration of personality? We have noted that contradictions are inherent in the nature of man. Every person desires many more values than are possible—first because of his finite limitations and furthermore because they are contradictory alternatives in opposition to one another. These dynamic conflicts are so deep and relentless in every person that he is bound to suffer the anguish of frustration. If he follows his impulses, he will be divided and torn apart by their distracting demands. If he seeks to control the impulses for the sake of a unifying religious purpose, he is in for a long struggle. The dynamic counter-forces are so powerful and insistent that we may not expect an easy solution. Psychologists are likely to consider the conflicting desires necessary to the formation of character and welcome the struggle to shape or sublimate the impulsive nature into a more creative life.

A realistic view of man cannot overlook the disruptive forces entangled

[9] See Hugh Hartshorne and F. K. Shuttleworth, *Studies in the Organization of Character* (New York: The Macmillan Co., 1930).

[10] *The Psychology of Christian Personality,* pp. 142-43.

in these frustrating conflicts. The predicament of human life is serious and critically dangerous both for the individual person and society at large. We can destroy ourselves; this much freedom we have. Yet as we stand on the brink of destruction, we also stand on the edge of creative achievements by exercising what freedom we have to discipline our desires and move forward to enlarging responsibilities. If these recalcitrant desires and angers foster in us the pride and deceit of self-sufficiency, the dangers are accentuated. The need for integration may centralize upon an inferior motive, and whatever unity so attained may drive on to destructive effects.

The more deeply we understand man, the more urgently do we come to his need of religion. It is evident that no easy solution or superficial remedy can avail. From the depth of this new humility we realize that no person is sufficient unto himself or able by his own resources to attain his potentialities. The finite creature with infinite possibilities will hate and destroy himself unless he seeks beyond himself the answering response. Not every religious venture reaches the goal, but the ultimate concern that declines to settle for the trivial is moving in the direction of larger fulfillment.

In the early stages of religious growth experiment outruns integration. Curiosity invites the child to search for the new and unknown. Questions fly off alert minds at amazing speed. Answers and traditions that satisfy the elders only stir up the younger generation to more questions. Every suggestion is worth trying; every idea might be a revelation. The not discovered is more challenging than the already found, for it offers new adventures. This is one reason for the bewildering variety of religious beliefs and activities. In the history of religion every possible interpretation and experiment seems to have been tried (as also in science, morals, and politics). Whatever experiments have not been tried will no doubt have their turn. The experimental times are the progressive stages in growth.

Then come the conservative tendencies of maturity. As experiments are sifted out, men tend to agree more upon common conclusions. The random adventures of immaturity become the positive directions of maturity. A new science (like psychology) is still in a state of volatile disagreement, but an old science (like physics or chemistry) has a larger body of integrated and accepted knowledge. Experiments continue, but they tend to fill in the gaps of theory rather than overthrow the established order. When a revolutionary hypothesis, like relativity, comes along, it offers a new integration and experiments are devised to verify it. Religious progress has the advantage of a long history, and there are now signs of converging among creeds and practices. Maturity settles many of the conflicts and distractions of youth, but its danger is in surrendering experiment for the comforts of integration. In order to keep growing, religion needs to be equally vigorous in experiment and integration.

Out of the despair and hope of this struggle, there may come a religious conversion. To venture forth into a religious decision is in one sense a crucial experiment. It has been called by Pascal the great wager, betting one's life on God. If the venture succeeds, the divisions of life may find unity in a greater integration. These possibilities we are to consider in the following chapter.

# 6 CONVERSION

## *1. Dynamic Relations*

Herbert Spencer, in his search for a formula that would be inclusive of life in its biological, psychological and sociological aspects, defined life as "the continuous adjustment of internal relations to external relations." [1] In this brief sentence is contained a useful generalization, not unlike Einstein's theory of relativity in scope and intent. Each theory succeeds in bringing a vast array of complex data into meaningful order by a principle of dynamic relatedness. Life is continuous adjustment. This is the basic assumption underlying all of the biological and behavioral sciences, that life is never inert but always mobile, intent upon a goal in dynamic striving to go and do something. To live is to adjust to the complex and delicate demands of a precarious existence.

A living organism may be described as irritable protoplasm. Yet every organism is more than a mass of cells; it is an organizing unit of structures and functions whose internal relations are constantly changing through mutual interdependence. And these complex internal relations are continually adjusting to the external relations of the environment with which the organism is interdependent. To adjust is to be flexible and adaptive enough to meet changing conditions by appropriate responses. This is necessary for survival. To live is to respond appropriately to the multiple and often confusing demands of internal and external relations.

Because no organism is self-sufficient, this life depends upon outreach to resources beyond itself. This outreach is *selective* not to environment in general, but to that particular resource which will satisfy a specific need. And the outreach is *responsive* in a two-way mutual interaction. When a baby robin is hungry, you can see him open his mouth and reach out imploring food. But he will starve to death unless there is an answering response from the parent, who captures a worm and gives it into the open

[1] *Principles of Biology* (New York: D. Appleton-Century Co., 1897), I, 80.

mouth. When the baby robin grows and learns to dig for himself, he must select and respond to the behavior of the worm or the insect he would capture. In every such relationship there is an interaction of giving and taking whereby one organism adjusts to the response of another. The baby robin was giving forth a cry or postural response of the outstretched mouth to the parent, who in turn responded by giving food, which was then taken into the baby to meet the need and nourish growth. The parent was giving her energy and skill to take the worm, who was giving himself, though reluctantly, to feed the need of the baby robin. So internal relations are adjusted to external relations and reaching forth seeks the answering response from beyond.

In the previous chapter we have considered the behavior of the human infant in reaching out for food by insistent crying until someone comes to answer his need. But he is not satisfied entirely by a chemical formula from a bottle, important as this may be to his survival. He also cries for tender loving care and will not be satisfied without it. His affiliative need is more insatiable than hunger, for it continues when food hunger is periodically extinguished. This means that persons are more important to him than any thing, and his behavior will be continually motivated in one way or another by his concern for interpersonal relations. He may be so disappointed in these relationships that he will turn against the persons who are most significant to him. Or he may be partially satisfied in ways that induce him to persist in the search for ever more satisfying interpersonal relations.

Life grows toward whatever it reaches for. Yet the human being is often diverted by his conflicts from the outgoing and open relationship with other persons, to become defensive, anxious, or hostile. In this he may distort his perceptions of others and see them as threatening enemies rather than co-operating allies in the venture of his goal striving. He is then likely to fear the open encounter with other persons and eventually to shrink the area and freedom of his interpersonal relations. This retreat and distortion is self-defeating by reducing the larger meaning and outreach of life. It is counter-religious behavior.

Religious behavior seeks the largest possible adjustment of life, for it is concerned about the ultimate relationships. Not content with partial adaptations to local conditions of the moment, religion seeks adjustment to the whole meaning of all relations in the total perspective of eternal destinies. To follow the outreach of religious response is to see man seeking the largest values in their utmost completion. The range of adjustment measures the life, yet not in a merely quantitative sense, for religious concern is seeking a quality of life that has meaning in the giving and receiving of outflowing affection, known in the New Testament as agape or unselfish love. The religious quest as we have discovered before is a meeting of I and Thou in profound reverence and devotion.

But no one is wholly religious or irreligious, even as no person is entirely outgoing or retreating in relation to other persons. For conscious desires are tangled at their roots with unconscious and primitive impulses that are contradictory. Man is a creature of conflicts so deeply involved that they are inherent in his nature, and try as he will, he cannot escape them by his own efforts alone. Consequently, the inner life of man is embroiled in rebellions and divisions that undermine his stability and keep him forever on the verge of dismay. His religious quest though insistent is inconsistent and fluctuating even in the most faithful seekers between elation and despair. Like every other aspiration the ultimate concern is fraught with the discontent of one who is determined not to delude himself. If he foresees infinite possibilities, he will also know his finite limitations. And the more ultimate his devotion, the deeper is his humility in the awareness of his own fickle and unsteady nature.

These internal and external relations are dynamic in a dual sense. They have the power to disrupt and to fulfill. They are never static but ever seeking and striving to attain the unattained. In this sense they are unstable and ready at any time to disrupt closures which have been made. The integration at any point is subject to upsetting by new experiments. Nothing attained is final either to satisfy the present or hold against the future as secure beyond question.

In the other sense these relationships have the power to fulfill what cannot otherwise be whole. For the isolated individual is fragmentary and lonely. His nature demands affiliation with other persons in larger relationships. The religious quest is motivated constantly by the disruptive need of the unfulfilled person and the fulfilling power of ultimate relationship.

## 2. *Conflict and Crisis*

Human personality is at once the best known and the least understood of all forms of existence. Each person knows himself best from inside information of his own experience and what it means to him to live through it. He can feel his own shadings of mood from moment to moment, the ebb and flow of his emotions, and the crosscurrents which are almost but not quite ready to do or decide. Yet there are shadowy unknowns in the unconscious depths of his nature that impel or restrain him in a baffling interplay of conflicting tendencies. From his dream and fantasy life come intimations of surprising wishes and fears that imply the ongoing of secret plots and counterplots in his life drama.

As he wrestles with this mystery, every person becomes a problem to himself. "Man has always been his most vexing problem," as Reinhold Niebuhr says.[2] He is the only animal who is able to perceive himself as an object and by so doing to transcend the life of momentary experience to judge his own behavior in larger perspective. This self-consciousness which sets him apart so complicates his behavior that he is divided against himself and unable to act on pure impulse. He looks at himself and questions his own impulses, whether to follow or resist them. He may start to act, then hesitate and come to a standstill while he ponders the situation and asks himself if it is better to do this or that. So he checks and contradicts himself by the inner separation of self-consciousness.

Out of these contradictions come the possibility of freedom and the necessity of making choices. Human life is a series of forked-road situations, in which choices are inescapable. If a person is stubborn and refuses to go either way, that too is a choice. The more conscious he is, the more alternatives he confronts and the more decisions he has to make. "The more consciousness, the more self," as Kierkegaard says.[3] And the more self-awareness, the more alive a person is. Becoming a person means this heightened awareness of "I-ness," in the experience that I am acting in response to the events of my world.

Yet for this new dimension of self-awareness man must pay a considerable price. Out of the very contradictions that provide his freedom come the distresses of conflict. Life can never be simple or easy for a conscious person. He must forever contend with the competing demands of a complicated world and the clashing desires of a complex inner life that give him no rest. Like Adam, the prototype of every man, he is lured by the unknown, tempted by untasted possibilities, seduced by the one he loves, forbidden by highest authority, caught in conflicts of desire, overcome with guilty remorse, and driven forth to wrestle and sweat in a world of contradiction and uncertainty.

In these struggles who will not suffer anxiety and dread? Through such experiences every person must pass in the process of his self-realization. Anxiety is the psychological climate of conflict and uncertainty, in which alternative possibilities clamor for attention and choice in either-or situations. "Dread is the first reflex of possibility," says Kierkegaard,[4] "a glimmer and yet a terrible spell." It is the "dizziness of freedom" [5] in the tempting-

[2] *The Nature and Destiny of Man* (New York: Charles Scribner's Sons, 1941; 1949), p. 1.

[3] *The Sickness unto Death,* tr. W. Lowrie (Princeton, N. J.: Princeton University Press, 1941), p. 43.

[4] *The Journals,* ed. and tr. Alexander Dru (London: Oxford University Press, 1938), p. 967.

[5] Kierkegaard, *Concept of Dread,* p. 55,

forbidding stress of diversified options and alluring contradictions. Out of such anxiety a person comes to heightened awareness and passionate intensity of unique individuality. In this way he discovers his finitude and sin; he knows that he is incomplete, and yet he knows that he is not alone. He confronts Thou in the depth of his anguish and the height of his aspiration.

Freud also finds basic conflicts in every personality. From a "seething cauldron" of excitement known as the id, primitive desires press impulsively and persistently for gratification. So irrational are they that if they have their way unrestrained, they will come to reckless destruction. In so far as these primitive impulses conflict with the standards of conduct established by society, they are met by a restraining No from persons in authority, such as parents who speak from the urgency of their own conflictual struggles.

As the growing child admires and fears his parents, he will identify with them and model his behavior after theirs. To the young child his parents seem omnipotent in the ability to gratify their desires, and he seeks to be like them in such traits as will gain him his desires. Also he needs their approval, for they are so close to him from day to day that he cannot tolerate the anxiety of their disapproval. A two-way relationship develops in which the child reaches out to identify with the parent and then to introject or take into himself their most insistent demands. So he will internalize their moralistic demands and regulate his conduct by the introjected authority they represent.

This internal authority, which Freud named the superego, is set against the impulsive id from which it derives its energy. There are two ways in which the superego operates. The conscience incorporates the punishments from the parents and continues to bring the punitive force against the impulsive life. In this eternal warfare the person suffers incessant guilt and moral anxiety which intensifies the distress, and punishes himself for trivial and unrealistic guilt feelings.

Another response of the growing person is to incorporate the approvals of the parents as the ego-ideal. This is the positive and rewarding effect of identification that motivates the person to strive for perfection at any cost to his contrary impulses. In his drama of urging and checking forces the drive for perfection collides with the drive for id pleasure, and the outcome is a civil war of interminable psychic struggle and intolerable feelings of guilt. In the lure of pleasure he is forever guilty, and in the light of the ideal he is forever condemned. He becomes his own accuser, and as the conflict is internal and largely unconscious, it is inescapable.

At the center of the conflict is the ego, aware of the demands of society and serving as the executive function that seeks to adjust to this reality principle. But its energy is derived from the impulsive life of the id, and the demands of the pleasure-seeking id are constantly upon the ego. The person is again in conflict which is inescapable, and he requires the utmost ingenuity to work out compromises between the conflicting demands. In this three-way conflict the moralistic demands of the superego operate against the reality seeking of the ego as much as against the pleasure seeking of the id. And the insistent demands of the id are striving against the restraints of the ego as well as the superego. To manage these recalcitrant forces the ego activates a series of defenses to repress the painful conflicts. But these defenses only drive the conflicts into the unconscious, where they continue their underground warfare in explosive dynamics that disturb the whole personality.

Neo-Freudians like Horney and Sullivan give priority to interpersonal relations over instinctual drives. Impulses of love, anger, and fear are responses to other persons who are perceived as approving or disapproving. These relations to other persons, which Freud also emphasized in his later years, are introjected to constitute the dynamic character of personality. Disturbing relations set up anxieties and neurotic defenses that react in perpetual conflicts. The neurotic person is not free to make realistic choices, for he is locked in conflicts of equally compelling forces driving in opposite directions, neither of which he wants. A person so blocked is stranded with no way out unless a radical change in him is accomplished affecting his relations with other persons.

Likewise William James[6] recognized the sick soul as a divided self caught in basic conflict. Even when he may prosper and appear happy, he is haunted by a feeling coming from a deeper region of the precarious uncertainty of every good. A vigorous mind like Goethe can look back on his life from seventy-five years and say, "It has been nothing but pain and burden." Luther, when he had grown old, confessed, "I am utterly weary of life." This sense of failure and futility may vitiate all gains and infect any happiness with contradiction. Confronted with evil and loss as a finite person whose days are numbered, it is easy to fall prey to despair and melancholy. "I must first pass a sentence of death," said Bunyan, "upon everything of this life." The vitality of feeling that was once heightened to the anguish of acute distress may then turn to numbness and apathy. Again the cloud of anxiety may come to a storm of panic fear or settle down into obsessive compulsions to perform strange rituals in vain efforts to cope with fear.

Boisen[7] from his own experience and research is able to give an inside view of mental illness. He finds the focus to be an intolerable sense of personal failure and guilt. Three different reactions have been noted: (1) drift-

[6] *Op. cit.*

[7] *Exploration of Inner World.*

ing, withdrawing, and giving up the struggle; (2) delusion, self-deception, and projecting blame elsewhere; (3) a desperate attempt at reorganization. The first two are not conducive to recovery. They result in social isolation and progressive distintegration of personality with no fighting spirit or will to get well. But in the third reaction a person is willing to acknowledge the seriousness of illness and take radical steps to reconstruct his whole life. The more acute the crisis, the better is the prognosis, as there is less opportunity for drifting or deception when the distress is all-engrossing.

In this acute crisis he discovers healing power at work in psychotic illness, when it is a desperate attempt at reorganization of a way of life that had become intolerable. It may issue in a dramatic religious experience akin to conversion. In profound distress there is ultimate concern for the whole destiny of life. There may be honest confession of failure and guilt with earnest desire to enter upon a new life. In the study of historical religious leaders like Jeremiah, Ezekiel, Paul, Luther, George Fox, John Wesley, Bunyan, and Swedenborg he traces conflicts similar to mental illness but emerging into religious conversion. In a religious crisis a person feels that he is confronting Thou, while his fate hangs in the balance. In these periods of ultimate concern creative forces are exceptionally active, as are forces of destruction also in the heat of seething emotions that intensify the struggle. In such eruptive and decisive experiences the person may have a religious conversion to change the whole course of his life.

Crisis is inevitable for man. Conflicts are inherent in the dynamic structure of his personality and emerge to acute distress in his self-conscious awareness. Human growth undergoes critical periods in birth, puberty, marriage, parenthood, climacteric, aging, grief, and dying. There will be frustrating situations to confront and intrapsychic conflicts to suffer. Minor hurts and problems may be healed and adjusted, but underlying them is the deeper wound of perpetual conflict at the center of his being. It would be superficial to deny this basic disturbance and gloss it over with optimistic rationalizations. There is nothing to be gained in hiding or belittling the seriousness of man's predicament.

Is there no way out of this unyielding conflict in which every person wars against himself as his own worst enemy? Freud saw the psychic conflict as interminable, and while he did much to understand and heal the sufferings of his patients, he remained pessimistic about ultimate solutions. Kierkegaard, who took an equally serious view of man's predicament, believed there was a way of salvation open to man by renunciation and singleness of devotion to God in faith that only God can give. James and Boisen agree that the crisis of conflict and despair is of fatal proportions and that there will be no easy way out. The solution is to be found in religious conversion, which is a revolution decisive enough to transform the whole personality.

If such a conversion is possible, the crisis may not be altogether evil. It may be an unusual opportunity to deal with life in a new and creative way. Until problems confront us, we do little serious thinking at all, and only then do we engage in active search for solutions. A crisis arouses heightened awareness and acute perceptions to sense danger and cope with the situation. It causes a desperate search for resources by which to meet the need so vividly experienced. It brings into sharp focus a person's role in the situation, his relationships and his responsibility to do what is best at such a time. Actions are to be weighed more seriously, and questions are asked as to why this is so, what it means, and what is required.

Not only does a crisis serve to awaken and mobilize resources for the individual; it has the same effect upon a social group. Boisen[8] has shown by extensive research that times of crisis are the most creative periods in the history of religious movements. What the crisis of mental illness may do for an individual personality as a religious conversion, so the acute distress of economic depression may do in launching and augmenting a religious revival as in the Pentacostal movements around 1930.

Where there is little awareness of need, there is little concern for anything. But where the need is great, human concern rises with the sense of urgency to ultimate pitch. Religion as ultimate concern is a quest for the greatest value and destiny of life. When local values are lost and the familiar props of complacency fall, then our little securities are broken and we know they are helpless to save us. Desperate need calls for greater resources than our customary defenses and feeble futilities. When the half-gods go, we turn to the ultimate Thou, realizing as never before that no other will be relevant to our ultimate concern.

Every person is insufficient in his own isolation. This we learned at an early age and found answers, if we were so fortunate, in the sustaining love of our family relationships. But then we clamored for independence and gained a certain pose of self-sufficiency by relying just enough on faithful relations to keep our balance in an unsteady existence. We might do so well for a while as to forget that we are finite and gain a deceptive illusion that we are sufficient and secure.

But when the crisis strikes, we learn again what had been so easily forgotten. Now we know our need, and after vain efforts to regain the self-sufficient pose, we must turn one way or the other. Either we hide behind defenses that cannot save but only foil us, or else we must honestly confess our folly and seek with ultimate concern for Thou. If we turn in that direction, the outcome may be a religious conversion.

[8] *Religion in Crisis and Custom.*

## 3. *Toyohiko Kagawa*

To understand religious conversion, we must have intimate knowledge of individual persons. Similarities do appear among the many who have known conversion and from whom significant tendencies may be seen as general principles. Such tendencies are not to be overlooked, but let us first come face to face with a religious person whose conversion is the decisive event of his life. In the vivid experiences of this devoted Christian of Japan, we may follow the dynamic effects and radical changes which flow through a religious conversion.

Toyohiko Kagawa was born in Kobe, July 10, 1888. His father was the headman of nineteen villages in his native province of Awa and later became a cabinet minister as secretary of the Privy Council of the emperor in the Meiji era of enlightened reign. Then in the port city of Kobe he pioneered in transportation and met financial failure in this venture. It was here that Toyohiko was born, one of four children of the geisha dancer who became his father's favorite concubine. As a child he knew the warm affection of the loving mother and admiring father who took legal steps to adopt him as a legitimate son. But in his fourth year both of the parents died, and he was deprived of the love he had known. He was sent with an older sister to live with the stepmother and paternal grandmother in the ancestral village of Awa. There was no welcome for him here where the two elderly women lived a solitary life amid the ruins of a grander past. To them he was an unwanted interloper left in their reluctant care. The stepmother rarely spoke to him, and the grandmother discharged her anger upon both children in beatings that caused hatred to burn within him. The sister never played with him, as she was eccentric and hysterical, eventually becoming an invalid.

When he entered primary school, he was so insecure that he felt like an intruder there and had no courage to seek the friendship of other children in the neighborhood, except for one companion who was the son of a tenant farmer on the estate. In his loneliness his chief solace was to commune with nature in the bamboo grove or the sand dunes along the river. As he learned to read, he entered a fascinating world peopled with history and legends, ideas and adventures, that occupied many waking hours.

He was regularly sent to the Buddhist temple to learn from the Confucian classics of filial piety and loyalty in all the relationships of life. From the Buddhist teachings and ritual he sensed a mystic awe and quiet reverence that nourished the religious mood in him. When he came to the age of ten, he was recognized as the master of the house and sent to represent the family at the New Year's ceremonies of the village, and to receive and record the rent from the tenants. He also assisted in tilling the soil, setting out rice plants in the spring mud and harvesting the rice in the fall, cutting grass for the horse, fishing in the river, or nursing baby birds and animals as his playmates.

Then as a neighbor child was dying, he was accused of injuring her, and though the rumor was unfounded, it swept around the village until he felt that everyone must blame and scorn him. He went to see the sick girl, to offer her the little fund of savings from eggs he had sold, and though innocent to ask forgiveness of her parents. He was so moved to weeping and sorrow that he could not touch food. Life seemed intolerable to him.

At this time the eldest son of the family returned for a visit, and Toyohiko asked permission to leave the village and go to school elsewhere. He was sent to live with a wealthy uncle at Tokushima, and in this city he entered the Boys' Middle School. He was an eager student, but he was repelled by the low moral tone of the other boys, and as he declined to join them in riotous conduct, he became the target for their banter and was lonelier than ever. In melancholy anguish he was lashed by storms of hopeless despair.

> I have shouldered the cross of lofty principles and shining ideals, but when the dream of life ends will there be anything left but a cold corpse? I am denied even the hope of existence as a corpse. I will be reduced to ashes. Ashes the goal toward which I move! The thought of it drives me mad. When I think that those ashes will be beaten, driven by the rain and washed away into the gutter, a violent choking sensation sweeps over me.
>
> There is nothing to do but to drift with the clouds and be driven by the rain. Oh, that the thunders would roll and the rain descend in torrents! Or that the ship of life would suddenly sink and I could go down with it in peace.[9]

In this school one of his teachers was a Christian. And he found a welcome in the homes of two missionaries, where tea was served in a spirit of hospitality and where with other students there were exciting conversations, laughter, and singing. As he began to read the Bible, he was deeply moved by the life and teachings of Jesus. The missionary spoke of a God who loves and forgives. As Kagawa read and reread the Gospels, he saw the possibility of new life. He knelt and prayed, "O God, make me like Christ!" This prayer became the dedication to a new life purpose. His clouds of melancholy yielded to the rising sun flooding him with light.

When he announced his conversion to Christianity, he met bitter opposition from the uncle in whose home he was staying. Yet he continued in prayer to commune with God and witness to his new faith. When he declined to renounce this faith, he was disowned by his uncle and disin-

[9] William Axling, *Kagawa* (New York: Harper & Bros., 1932), p. 18. Used by permission of the publisher.

herited by his family, going forth from the sheltering roof with only the clothes he was wearing at the time. Taking the life of poverty, he devoted himself to serve the poor in Christlike love, a mission from which he has never turned aside.

At the age of seventeen in 1905 he entered the Presbyterian College in Tokyo, where he read passionately and ranged widely in the fields of philosophy and the social sciences. Finding a beggar in the street, he brought him to his dormitory room and shared his food and bed with him. His generosity to those in need was unbounded. He gave not only his meager funds but his shoes and clothing to those in distress. Convinced by Tolstoy that violence is futile, he publicly espoused the cause of pacifism during the Russo-Japanese war and thereby suffered the blows and epithets of his fellow students, yet he forgave them and prayed for them.

In the second year of college he came to advanced stages of tuberculosis and after many hemorrhages went to a seashore village in search of healing. For a year of nearly fatal illness he wrestled with the ravages of disease and doubt. Yet he continued his reading and on the pages of old magazines wrote his first novel, later published as *Across the Death Line,* which circulated 250,000 copies and put him among the foremost writers of Japan. He took an interest in the fishing folk of the village and brought them a Christian message of hope and faith.

The following year, though not healed, he had come to terms with death, which had no more terrors for him. He entered the Kobe Theological Seminary to prepare for the vocation of a Christian minister. While a student there he devoted his evenings to preaching on the streets of the Shinkawa slums. As he saw the poverty and disease that held these people, ten thousand of them crowded together in filth and vermin, living in houses six feet square with little hope of a better life, his heart went out to them until he decided to cast his lot with them.

At the age of twenty-one he moved into one of the windowless huts in the Shinkawa slums, where for over fourteen years he ministered to the needs of those around him. Whoever asked for food or lodging was welcome to share his small hut until often every inch of floor space was used at night, and his rice gruel was thinned out to serve all those who came. To supplement his monthly scholarship from the theological seminary, he swept chimneys to earn money so that he could feed his guests. Preaching on the streets and teaching the children who came to his Sunday school, he was sought by families in illness, crisis, and death. He was robbed but he always gave willingly what was asked until he scarcely had a garment to clothe himself. He was beaten and severely wounded, but he would not strike back or defend himself. If it was necessary to flee, he would return at once and carry on his work regardless of threats and dangers. And never did he ask for police protection.

As he visited the sick, comforted the sorrowing, and fed the hungry, he was constantly bringing his witness that God is love. At six o'clock in the morning he would be at the street corner preaching in the rain to those who were going to work, and at the end of the day he would be speaking of God's love for them. One time he adopted a starving infant and nursed him through illness to health. Preaching in one of the factories, he met a young woman named Spring, who encouraged other workers to attend his meetings and who eventually married him, willing to live in the little hut and share it with the many homeless who came for shelter. In time they added a room for a dispensary and another for a hostel to accommodate their needy guests. Rather than turning from men to God, he met God in the slums. Said he in his *Meditations:*

> God dwells among the lowliest of men. He sits on the dust-heap among the prison convicts. With the juvenile delinquents He stands at the door, begging bread. He throngs with the beggars at the place of alms. He is among the sick. He stands in line with the unemployed in front of the free employment bureaus.
>
> Therefore, let him who would meet God visit the prison cell before going to the temple. Before he goes to church let him visit the hospital. Before he reads his Bible let him help the beggar standing at his door.[10]

In this close contact with the diseases of the slums, he took them upon himself also. When his eyes were affected with glaucoma, he nearly lost his sight and had to live in darkness for many months to regain a partial vision. His wife suffered a similar affliction, and both of them were handicapped by limited vision. Yet they bore the burdens of the poor gladly and rejoiced that they were counted worthy to suffer for them.

Books were his constant companions, and he pursued knowledge with unflagging zeal, ever alert to understand the meaning and problems of life. He studied the life around him with eager and thoughtful interest. "The slums are a laboratory of life and of human society," he declared. "Some people think of me as administering palliative remedies, but I am an industrious scientist. I am researching life at one of its outbreakings in the social order." [11] His second book was *The Psychology of Poverty,* a study of its causes and cure. When in 1914 he came for two-years study at Princeton University, he also investigated social services and labor movements.

The effect of industrialism in Japan was to draw populations into congested slums where factory conditions were unregulated at that time by

[10] *Ibid.*, p. 28.

[11] *Ibid.*, p. 45.

labor legislation. Kagawa found that low income was correlated with high infant mortality, tuberculosis, alcoholism, crime, and prostitution. "Humanity by rights should not denegerate to such a state. If it comes to this it would be far better for them to be dancing, crying monkeys among the island forests in the South Seas." [12] So he became the cofounder of the Japan Federation of Labor.

In 1921 the Kobe dock workers went on strike with the slogan "Follow Kagawa!" The police had decreed regulations making it unlawful for laborers to form associations. Kagawa disregarded the decree and organized the strikers into the first striking labor union in Japan, issuing a manifesto to the nation, in which he stated:

> Laborers are personalities. They are not commodities to be bought and sold according to a scale of wages based on the market price. Furthermore, they must be given the right to organize. For this reason we who belong to the army of producers make the following proclamation:
>
> "We are not machines. In order to develop our own individualities, to personalize society, and to secure a social order which will provide the producers a real culture and give them security as to their livelihood, we demand the right to regulate our own circumstances." [13]

At this historic moment Kagawa opposed the use of violence, even though the soldiers were called out and the police sought to prevent their meetings. Every day Kagawa addressed them to guide and uphold their morale. He went personally to the employers and public authorities with their demands. He was black-listed as an agitator, arrested and thrown into prison. While he was in prison, his book *The Shooter at the Sun* was launched into wide circulation, and he was formulating in his mind, though denied paper and ink, another popular novel, *Listening to the Voice in the Wall.*

When he was released from prison, he was welcomed by a thousand laborers at night, carrying lighted paper lanterns and banners with shouts and songs, escorting him to his home in the slums. As he labored to improve their working and living conditions, he also pleaded for their rights to education and recreation, freedom of marriage and migration, freedom of speech, association, organization, and religious worship.

> The laborer must have no mean opinion of himself. Away with self-depreciation! Be conscious of your worth as a laborer and glory in your role.
>
> The producer's course is in creation. . . . Be calm! Be steady! Let the imperialists and the capitalists do their worst. It matters not what the radicals and extremists say.

[12] *Ibid.*, p. 47.

[13] *Ibid.*, p. 50.

There is but one course for the laborers. That is production motivated by love. . . . Intelligently, accurately swing your hammer and watch the results. Unions are necessary, but labor problems can only be solved by the inner awakening of the laborer.[14]

The plight of the farmer was also serious in overpopulated Japan, where 85 per cent of the area is mountainous and landholdings small, where interest rates where high and debts interminable in the prevailing tenant system. Kagawa saw the defeated farmers drifting into city slums in a vain attempt to improve their sordid lot. So in this same year 1921 a group of peasants met in Kagawa's hut and organized the first independent peasants' union. Later in the year an All Japan Peasants' Conference was held, and the Japan Peasants' Union was publicly launched with its magazine, *The Soil and Freedom*. The union took the part of small landowners and tenants against the landlords, arousing a storm of controversy and opposition. It promoted legislation to protect the rights of the tenants and settle their disputes with owners. It proposed to take an active part in elections and stood for national ownership of the land. Its program included education for rural people, rural co-operatives, credit unions, better housing and sanitary conditions, scientific agriculture and crop insurance.

Kagawa guided this agrarian movement into farseeing constructive channels away from violence and selfish interest to the improvement of rural life for all. He toured the country speaking to the peasants, crusading for the new freedom of scientific farming, new crops, co-operative enterprise, education, and love. Though acclaimed everywhere, he was bitterly opposed by intrenched authorities and the police, who obstructed his work and denied the right of assembly.

Not only was he opposed from the conservative right when he attacked predatory capitalism, advocated the socializing of community wealth, and offered a social order in which love and co-operation would replace the profit motive and competition. He was quite as viciously attacked from the left by the advocates of class strife, materialism, and antireligious Communism. Left-wing labor leaders issued a manifesto: "Bury Kagawa, the hypocrite, who is unceasingly striving to make dupes of us, of the propertyless class. This false humanitarian taking advantage of us, hides behind the beautiful name of religion and scatters a deadening anaesthetic among us." [15]

In the face of these attacks Kagawa held aloft the Christian way of life as the hope of the world. If social reconstruction is to realize the goal, he insisted, it will have to be motivated by the spirit of Christ willing to suffer

[14] *Ibid.*, p. 55.

[15] *Ibid.*, p. 78.

and die for the saving of all. Man-made morality has brought evil upon evil and strife against strife. Laborers and peasants need a movement toward brotherhood in the spirit of the carpenter Jesus. Likewise, there is hope for the capitalist who will voluntarily reduce his own profits and standard of living to lift the whole level of society, to socialize capital and turn from acquisitive to co-operative ways. In all walks of life we need the Christlike spirit to purify motives and desires, to cease discrimination between rich and poor, to love all men and women and children as belonging to one family.

Then came the earthquake of 1923 which killed 100,000 people and left two thirds of Tokyo in ruins. Transportation and communications were shattered, and fires swept far beyond control. The time had come for reconstruction, and Kagawa was invited to serve on the Imperial Economic Commission. From this strategic post he was able to help the nation rebuild its economic life and at the same time introduce some radical social reforms. One of these was the Anti-Exploitation Land Act, providing that land held for speculation might be confiscated and turned to productive use. In 1925 the law against trade unions was repealed giving labor the legal right to organize.

Kagawa was drafted to serve on the government's commissions on unemployment, on labor exchanges, and on emigration. He was frequently urged to run for Parliament for the Labor Party, but he declined to do so, though he worked and contributed to the campaigns of other proletarians. He did not want to hold any position that would separate him from the poor or be a barrier to his work with them. At the crisis of the economic depression in 1930, he was called by the mayor of Tokyo to become chief of the Social Welfare Bureau at a nine-thousand-dollar salary per year. This he declined but did serve as chief advisor without salary to reorganize and extend the program of social welfare. He started eleven new social settlements, secured shelter for the homeless, fed the hungry, provided medical service and visiting nurses, initiated unemployment insurance and employment agencies.

In 1926 Kagawa was called by the Imperial government to rebuild the slums of the six largest cities of Tokyo, Osaka, Yokohama, Kobe, Kyoto and Nagoya. During this period $10,000,000 was appropriated for the purpose. Narrow alleys gave place to well-paved and sewered streets; the huts reeking with disease and filth were replaced with modern municipal apartments with room for sunshine and fresh air. But this was not enough as Kagawa viewed the situation. He said:

> Better housing conditions alone are not enough. This must be followed by other social legislation. There must be a minimum wage, sick aid, unemployment in-

surance, old-age pensions, and mothers' pensions before poverty can be wiped out.[16]

Then foreseeing the drift toward war in the rising tide of militarism, Kagawa in 1928 organized the National Anti-War League of Japan. The international situation was worsening, and the hopes of the millions around the world were drowned in the flood that rushed into the Second World War. But Kagawa was not one to give up in the face of opposition and he drew into his movement against war laborers, peasants, progressive political thinkers, scholars, literary and religious leaders. A platform was adopted with three planks:

1. We are opposed to war and all preparations for war.
2. We are opposed to all aggressive imperialistic political, economic, and uplift movements.
3. We are opposed to the advocacy of aggression, to imperialistic utterances, and to the oppression of weaker groups and peoples.[17]

It may appear that on this battle line Kagawa met his greatest defeat. For in Japan as in many other nations the history of our century has been bathed in blood and the whole of human society subjected to military ends of destruction under the deceptive guise of "winning the peace." Probably no other principle of his Christian devotion has cost him more than his unyielding stand upon nonviolence. It was his nonviolence that discredited him to many in the ranks of labor and the peasants who listened to the violent doctrine of class strife. This stand lost to him the political following he once had, the influence with the government, the press, and the nationalistic "patriots." He was denounced as a traitor to his own people, a tool of American or Russian interests. During the war he was virtually a man without a country. But he would not waiver or sidestep his convictions. Instead he gave his full energy to what he considered the central issue of all, the work of an evangelist who so long as he has breath will not cease to preach the gospel of Jesus Christ and salvation through love.

Knowing well that this cannot be the work of one man alone, he sought to draw together the Christian forces of Japan in a united, nation-wide, and continuous extension of this gospel of forgiving love. In 1929 this was named the Kingdom of God movement, with a central committee to coordinate the work of many participants and a weekly magazine to help keep the lines of communication open. When a national conference was held of representatives of the three religions of Japan—Shinto, Buddhism, and Christianity—to emphasize common ground, he appealed to them all to

[16] *Ibid.*, p. 87.
[17] *Ibid.*, p. 103.

cast off the shackles of the past and pioneer in the work of love. "God desires mercy, not ritual."

It is beyond human calculation to measure the lines of influence streaming forth from one person who gives his life wholly for others in religious devotion. Whatever we see is the obvious. But there are consequences far beyond the manifest which flow from decisions enacted into life purposes. Not every religious conversion is permanent or fruitful in the ongoing course of human life. What are the marks of a genuine conversion?

## *4. Conversion and New Life*

A genuine religious conversion is the outcome of a crisis. Though it may occur to persons in a variety of circumstances and forms, and though we may find many preparatory steps and long-range consequences, the event of conversion comes to focus in a crisis of ultimate concern. There is in such conversion a sense of desperate conflict in which one is so involved that his whole meaning and destiny are at stake in a life-or-death, all-or-none significance. Unless a person is aware of conflict serious enough to defeat him, and unless he is concerned ultimately enough to put his life in the balance, he is not ready for conversion. If in such a crisis a person reaches out to Thou, willing to give all of himself to this relationship, and out of mingling despair and hope decides to enter a new way of life, he may be radically changed in a religious conversion.

William James put it this way:

> To be converted [is] the process, gradual or sudden, by which a self hitherto divided, and consciously wrong, inferior and unhappy, becomes unified and consciously right, superior and happy, in consequence of its firmer hold upon religious realities.[18]

Let us note some of the preparatory steps leading to the religious conversion of Toyohiko Kagawa. In the first four years of his life he knew how to cry out of his need and receive the answering response of a loving mother. He learned to recognize and reach out to persons in sustaining and stimulating relationships of approval and affection. Then at the death of his parents he suffered the shock of grief and separation, as the persons upon whom he most depended for the meaning of life were taken from him. This loss was not readily healed, for they were irreplaceable and the foster parents to whom he was sent did not welcome him.

Their stern demands and punishments through his growing boyhood would inevitably form in him a punitive superego. His daily life at home

[18] *Op. cit.*, p. 189.

and at school was governed by the watchful eyes and commands of his task makers, and if he rebelled, he was bound to suffer the more. There were moments of freedom when he would go into the bamboo grove or along the river to enjoy the leisure and fantasy of a boy at play. But even then he was not entirely free from discipline, for he knew when he must return to his tasks and that he would suffer unless he obeyed. The punitive superego introjected the taskmaster into himself, and there could be no escape from the inner monitor.

In these years he was not alone. Though he was a lonely boy in feeling himself a stranger at home and at school, he learned to find companions in trees and plants, in the flowing stream, the sky, the clouds, and the rain. The fish, the birds, and the baby animals were companions to him, as well as the people he met in books and the heroes of the Confucian classics. Already the ego was busy reaching out to the real world around him to seek relationships to fill the emptiness within and help to reconcile the conflicting demands of the pleasure-seeking id and the stern superego. He was living in the presence of Thou when he painfully came to terms with the stern requirements of his home and when he was joyously meeting the mystery of nature in the larger forces of the world beyond.

Then came another crisis which shattered the world of his boyhood as death had closed the world of his childhood. He was accused of wounding and causing the death of a neighbor girl. This was the more devastating because he lacked the sustaining love and approval of those upon whom he was dependent at home. If he felt that his schoolmates and their families in the village were also blaming him, where could he turn for moral support? His conscience was also punitive and well conditioned to accuse him even though he knew that he was innocent. Surrounded by accusers and without support from his own conscience, he could well find his predicament unbearable.

Out of this acute distress he turned for help to his eldest brother, asking for a way of deliverance by going to school in another city where he might begin again a new life. When this request was granted, he entered the Middle School, hoping to find companions with whom he could feel at home. But even there he was pursued by the punitive superego, giving him no rest from conflict. He could not permit himself to enjoy the moral laxity of his schoolmates, for he felt guilty beyond endurance already and held to high ideals as the hope and guiding star of one lost at sea. But this separated him from his fellows who became his accusers for wanting to be different from them. He seemed to be cut off from life by his conflicts, and with no hope in sight he tottered on the brink of despair and suicide.

At this point his concern was ultimate, and the conflict was so intense he must make a decision of some kind. Three alternatives were before him.

First, he might throw off moral restraints and let the primitive impulses have full sway. This would evidently unite him with his fellow students and settle the conflict in favor of the pleasure-seeking id. To do this would have taken him recklessly along the exciting road of lust and aggression until he would deteriorate to the point of destroying himself and his usefulness to humanity. If he had followed this course to the end, he would be lost in oblivion having wasted his potentialities and returning eventually to the bottomless misery of self-accusing guilt. But this he could not do because his superego was too strong to yield and his capacity for guilt too foreboding.

A second alternative might be to invest his utmost energy in the superego, to uphold his moralistic defenses and repress the lusty impulses. This would not put the conflict to rest but would drive it underground, where the warfare would continue in the unconscious. He would then become a defensive personality, whose unrelieved tensions would drive him compulsively toward unattainable perfectionism, manifest in hard self-righteousness and scorn for any who yielded to temptation or gave vent to their impulses. In following this course to the end, he would become an unloving legalist without sympathy for his fellow men but compelled to punish them as he did himself for the sin of being human. He would make no real friends in his extreme aloofness but re-enact the relentless anger against life of his punitive grandmother. Along this road whatever he did would have the flavor of bitterness in the mood of stern rejection of life that becomes a living death.

A third alternative, and the one most often followed, would be to seek a compromise between these conflicting drives without renouncing either one. To put the ego at the disposal of both contradictory forces would engage the whole energy of life in a cloak and dagger game of deception and attack. Outwardly the mask of the persona would show a pious front of conventional righteousness. On every occasion the person would seek to gain the favor and approval of others by appearing respectable. He would not dare openly to show his true feelings or expose himself to the danger of detection. He could not afford to stand out with a minority where he would be unprotected by the mass who seek cover. Yet all the while behind the mask of conventional propriety he would be plotting to gratify a selfish lust or vengeful spite in secret ways to destroy others without hurting himself.

If this seems overdrawn like a murder mystery, then we may tone it down to the mildest conniving to have my way in any little advantage and gratify my secret vanity in the most trivial folly or harmless conceit. And yet even in the "harmless" play of fantasy and the tiniest trick of self-indulgence, there is division within the personality of the one who so indulges himself.

The unity of purpose and integrity of character is by so much undermined, and even where no major offenses occur, the valor of heroic living is lost in the trickle of endless compromise. If this is our course, we are caught in the net of our own cunning.

The young Kagawa wanted none of these alternatives. In the anguish of such conflicts he had come to the point of profound despair. The intensity of his search had led him to question the meaning of life and wonder if his own life was worth continuing. There had been anguish before, but in the moment of this crisis he fully engaged in the struggle of life and death. In this ultimate concern he was searching desperately for an answer to the predicament of the finite person whose infinite possibilities beckon insistently just beyond his reach.

Then a Christian teacher introduced him to the Bible and missionaries whose faith in the gospel of Jesus was contagious. He began to see possibilities of a new life leading out of conflict into love. He stood before Thou as the central reality of life, the answer to his desperate search. Whether his conversion was to come in public or private is beside the point. It was public in the sense of meeting other persons who responded to his search with answering love. It was private in the sense of personal encounter with Thou and the decision that no other could make for him to give his life into this ultimate way of religious devotion.

Actually, Kagawa moved beyond the three alternatives to find the answer in a fourth, which became for him the course of a new life. How shall we describe the fourth alternative? In Freudian terms we may say that he invested his full energy in the ego ideal. This was a radical change from the punitive superego, in which heretofore he was bound in the defenses of the moralistic conscience. After the death of his loving parents he had to identify with the unloving and punishing authority figures in the ancestral home. The negative character of this identification had made him over into their image, and as much as he hated them, he was bound to live by their demands. He was a victim of the guilt and resentment that molded him into a defensive alien person even in the midst of his fellows.

But the event of conversion was to change the dynamic motivating center of his life from the restraining conscience to the creative ego ideal. In Christ he found the heroic model he sought to become and so identified with him that the Christ ideal was introjected to become the motivator of a new life. As Paul would say: "Not I, but Christ liveth in me." With all the pent-up and repressed passion of his intense emotional longing he wanted to be like the man who was homeless, despised, and acquainted with grief; yet in the midst of his fellow men was everywhere at home, always loving and joyously alive. His life was vital and abundant because each moment he confronted his heavenly Father and from him received overflowing love to minister to the needs of those around him. "O God," he prayed, "make me like Christ!"

To Freud it might seem childish to seek the answering response of a heavenly Father. But to Kagawa it was the threshold of a new maturity. Rather than regressing to fantasy and helpless dependence, he met the realities of human conflict with courage and firm decision. When opposed by his uncle, he stood his ground as man to man and held to his decision bravely though it cost him the loss of family and inheritance. In the new security of his relationship to Thou he was willing to take the risk of poverty and even to give away the shoes from his feet and the clothing from his back. Before his conversion he was aloof from his fellows, but in this new life he is so openly related to them that he shares his bed with the beggar. Before his conversion he was a defensive person desperately seeking to save himself, but now he accepts without defense the filth and the vermin, the blows and diseases of his fellows. From the privileges of aristocracy he responds to the needs of the poorest in the dregs of society's slums.

What becomes of the crippling conflicts he was trying so desperately to repress? He no longer hides them in unconscious repression but calls them forth into the open arena of public life. He welcomes the lusty primitive impulses to conscious enjoyment of passionate expression. But not by self-indulgence; rather he pours out his passion like Jesus to save others at any cost in face of every opposition. He unleashes the restraining conscience to positive and irrepressible action in generous self-giving to right the wrongs and heal the sorrows that others suffer. He ceases to blame or condemn anyone, even the ruffians who knock out his front teeth or the police who cast him into prison. The punitive drive is transformed into supportive therapy to care and to cure the ills of life around him. Paul was converted from punitive legalism of "thou shalt not" to generous outgoing "thou shalt love thy neighbor as thyself." In this wise Kagawa was also converted from his stand-off moral defenses to overflowing agape love for the outcast and the enemy.

It is significant to note that such conversion does not bury conflicts but instead accepts and fulfills them. Though Kagawa stood with Jesus upon the principle of nonviolence, he nonetheless entered passionately into conflicts with full energy and devotion. The intense struggle with tuberculosis upon which he was soon to enter gives indication that his inner conflicts were not evacuated. Out of his desperate struggle of life and death forces within him comes the novel which sounds the note of a battle cry, *Across the Death Line*. Referring to himself as a fighting pacifist, he does not at all mean that he has given up the struggles of conflict, but that he chooses to fight with spiritual and constructive weapons rather than lethal and destructive ones.

One reason I entered the slum is my fondness for fights. Not because they often end in murder, but because of the whole-souledness which characterizes the contestants. Not because of the foul words which fly and the abuse which is exchanged, but because justice is struggling for victory. Not because the swords flash, but because blood is being freely offered up. When the red blood flows, man recovers Adam's original undisguised soul. I wanted to see that naked soul.

When the swords flash through the air and the red-hot charcoal braziers fly through space, when the red blood flows and the corpse lies prone in the narrow alley, I give myself to quiet thought and prayer. Man's soberest and sincerest moment is when he sees life freely given.[19]

In the conversion of Kagawa the four contemporary psychologies of religion which we considered in Chapter Two may all find illustration. The conflictual theory of Freud and Boisen is well documented in the central place that conflict holds in the life of Kagawa leading up to and following his conversion. The analysis of his conflictual struggle is clarified by the theory of Freud, while the outcome of his conversion is better understood in the view of Boisen that new life comes in wrestling with the existential crisis and giving oneself into a creative relationship with the Other.

The collective theory of Jung may find in Kagawa the invasion of psychic energy from the archetypes of Son and Father, and of conflict reconciled in the mandala form of the cross. Integration of conflictual forces is not by repression but in the return of the repressed and the bringing into fulfillment of basic oppositions into complementing harmony of expression. From introversion of self-concern he goes to extroversion of concern for others, yet without denying the one for the other but fulfiling the potentiality of both in the outgoing devotion of his individuation.

The personalistic theory of Allport may find in Kagawa the creative power of futuristic motivation, as he steps from the restraints of the past into the fulfillment of intentional devotion to future goals. The principle of functional autonomy is demonstrated in his conversion, which achieves a new system of motivation by which to follow a new and unswerving course of mature productivity. The peripheral and segmental distractions are brought under the discipline of his propriate striving. There is no regression or arrest of growth but a steady, consistent, and expanding becoming through an all-embracing religious theory of life.

The interpersonal theory of Moreno and Buber will find in Kagawa the vast effects of the encounter of I and Thou. So long as he kept behind his defenses, he was a lonely and defeated person, unable to resolve his conflicts or save himself by his desperate striving. The formation of his boyhood character was the resultant of his interpersonal relations and their

[19] Axling, *op. cit.*, pp. 104-5. Used by permission of Harper & Bros.

conflictual structure which he introjected into himself. The crisis which led to conversion was intensified by the breakdown of the interpersonal relations from which he felt excluded and through which he brought self-accusation upon himself. The turning point came as he was made welcome to feel at home in other relationships with Christians and their God as revealed in the passionate drama of Christ.

It was this encounter which changed Kagawa from a fearful creature of restraints to a fearless man of action. The therapy which wrought this radical change was action therapy. From the hopeless brooding of despair he turned to the outgoing dramatic action of face-to-face encounter with friends and enemies. Instead of restraining his impulses, he gave them forth in spontaneous love to those he met in each present moment of living. He gave freedom to his emotions openly and generously yet always channeled by one purpose to fulfill the mission of Christ. His joyous spontaneity burst forth in prayer and praise of God, in poetry and novel, in art and scientific research, in his outreach to beggars and his willingness to take them into his own hut. His spontaneous impulses were disciplined always by dedication each day to the larger perspective of his love, and they bore fruit in new energy, new ideas, and new programs to better the life of laborer, peasant, prostitute, and of every person worthy to grow from childhood to stronger maturity and enjoy the best of life God with man can achieve.

If religious conversion can do this, it is not to be shrugged off as wishful thinking or mere illusion. Where the results are inconsequential, there is reason to infer that the conversion was not genuine. But, you may be asking, is conversion necessary for everyone? Why trouble the contented persons who face no crisis or see no need for a new life? We may hear various replies to this question, and they are entitled to honest consideration. When we put this question, however, in the ultimate sense of the nature of man, we perceive that life for every finite person is a crisis. For no person is self-sufficient or able to fulfill his needs from within himself alone. He is incomplete, and to live at all he must depend upon resources beyond his own. Consequently, the very existence of man from moment to moment is a crisis. He may evade or deny the issue of his finitude. He may even claim that he is content to be what he is for the limits of time he can stand his ground, and then let him die without regrets and no questions asked. But in this defiant pose he deceives no one more than himself, who is too stubborn to acknowledge the infinite possibilities that might enlarge and enrich the meaning of his life. There is no crisis more serious than the pride that refuses to face the crisis. There are none so blind or so much in danger of defeat as those who will not see. The crisis is here whether we assent or not, as deep as our finite need and as great as our unformed potentialities by which to realize the meaning and integrating purpose of life.

## 5. *Revival and Survival*

There are those who scoff at religious revivals or quarrel with the methods by which religious groups may conduct evangelistic meetings. This is to be expected in a culture of such diversity as ours, in which there is freedom to differ in religious beliefs and practices. Some prefer the gigantic mass meeting, others the individual work of personal evangelism, and others the face-to-face interaction of the small group. Others will prefer none of these and ask only to be let alone. But when it becomes clear that the crisis confronting us will not pass, that it is inherent in our finite tendency to court defeat by cutting ourselves off from larger potentialities, then our concern may be ultimate. Then we may see that life is forever a crisis by the very terms of our finite existence, that our human aspirations will defeat us until we reach out for a response from beyond ourselves. Revival is ncessary for the survival of all that we hold most ultimate in this restless search of human life.

To no one in our time has this crisis become more decisive than to those who call themselves Alcoholics Anonymous. They number well over 100,000 persons who have come to admit defeat in their effort to control the excessive use and devastating effects of alcohol. They are those who admitting this have found in religious conversion a way of changing life for themselves and others whom they seek to help. The approach of one alcoholic to another is not to condemn him or exert holier-than-thou pressure on him to reform. It is rather to accept him as an alcoholic who is sick and so allergic to alcohol that he will not be able to indulge without disaster. The approach of one alcoholic to another is to understand him with all the distresses, frustrations, and evasions that make up his way of life, in his futile compromises between the moralistic superego of punitive restraint and the pleasure-seeking id of reckless indulgence. The one who sponsors another alcoholic on the road to recovery will come to him anywhere at any time, respond to every request for assistance, and introduce him to a group in which each will share his problem with others and all will sustain one another in the group dynamics of faithful interpersonal relations. There are now some 4,500 groups in this and forty-one other countries.

Out of the crises of repeated defeat and despair these alcoholics have sought and found a way through religious conversion to new and victorious life. The principles which have emerged in their struggles have been formulated as the Twelve Steps of their journey to a better life. They have emerged inductively from trial and error until they have been validated as true in the experiences shared and the lessons learned. The problem of alcohol is but a symptom they find of deeper causes in personality which they seek to change. The steps are not easy to take; they are often deferred and evaded until the repetition of failures convinces them to distrust the easier way and decide to go the whole way of complete humility and teachableness.

## THE TWELVE STEPS

1. We admitted we were powerless over alcohol—that our lives had become unmanageable.
2. Came to believe that a Power greater than ourselves could restore us to sanity.
3. Made a decision to turn our will and our lives over to the care of God as we understood Him.
4. Made a searching and fearless moral inventory of ourselves.
5. Admitted to God, to ourselves, and to another human being, the exact nature of our wrongs.
6. Were entirely ready to have God remove all these defects of character.
7. Humbly asked Him to remove our shortcomings.
8. Made a list of all persons we had harmed, and became willing to make amends to them all.
9. Made direct amends to such people wherever possible, except when to do so would injure them or others.
10. Continued to take personal inventory and when we were wrong promptly admitted it.
11. Sought through prayer and meditation to improve our conscious contact with God as we understood Him, praying only for knowledge of His will for us and the power to carry that out.
12. Having had a spiritual awakening as the result of these steps, we tried to carry this message to alcoholics, and to practice these principles in all our affairs.[20]

These steps are characteristic of conversion as viewed in this chapter. The conflicts of these persons have intensified to a desperate struggle which comes to a crisis in which they are unable to deny that they are destroying themselves and their relationships with those they love and care for most. Until they set aside deceptive pride and honestly admit their inability to manage the conflicts alone, they go on repeating failure after failure. When these struggles bring them to see the depth of their finite need, they begin to reach out for a Power greater than themselves as their only hope. They may not clearly comprehend this mysterious Power, but the turning point comes in a decision to turn over their lives to the care of God as they understand him. If they cannot yet believe in God, they may begin by trusting their lives to the care of the group that sponsors them. From this reaching out in ultimate concern comes an answering response demonstrated in the concern shown them by the sponsoring alcoholics. Then as new life and power comes to them through such relationships, they can see how growth is possible through interpersonal devotion. I will require Thou to grow into the larger fulfillment of maturing potentialities.

[20] *Twelve Steps and Twelve Traditions* (New York: Harper & Bros., 1953). Used by permission of William G. Wilson, cofounder, Alcoholics Anonymous.

It is evident in the sequence of these steps that no conversion will instantly change everything forever. The seeker must take one step after another no matter how painful or difficult it may be. He will have to become a pilgrim dedicated to distant goals that call for ongoing experiments in faithful devotion to the main purpose to which he gives himself. He will fail and slip back into the old and familiar descending steps that have led before to his defeat. Then he must make a searching and fearless inventory of himself, confessing to God and another human being the exact nature of his wrongdoing. After such faltering he must come to the point at which he is willing to have God remove these defects and to ask God to do so. He must systematically right so far as possible the wrongs he has committed to others that his human relations may be sound and constructive. He will need to practice meditation and prayer daily to face Thou and gather strength and guidance to proceed on the next stage of the journey. He must reach out constantly to others in need and devote his energies generously to helping them on their journey to the better life.

The experience of every persisting seeker will vindicate the need for renewal of the I-Thou relationship if one is to follow the road of faithful becoming. Revival again and again is necessary to survival of the religious life. This is as necessary spiritually as the physical health and growth which require food and exercise. Mere survival is not the chief end of man but the fulfillment of his highest potentialities, and this ongoing development is to be attained only in faithful relationship.

There are resistances and counterforces that will oppose these ardent devotions, clamoring for rest, ease, and the reduction of tension by lessening the goal. No one is finally secure beyond temptation or the imminent danger of defeat. To mistake religious conversion as a once-for-all-nothing-more-to-do finality will surely be to go down to defeat and bring discredit upon the genuine validity of that conversion. The enemy of growth is arrest, as Allport says; and whatever the diversion may be that slackens the intention, it is not to be taken lightly for it may bring the downfall of all we have attained. Eternal vigilance to renew and revive the fullest devotion is the price required of religious growth.

Conversion experiences may be as varied as life itself in the multiple ways that life finds to reorient and regenerate its flagging energies. A new birth is a major change in life whether sudden and dramatic or quiet and inconspicuous. The essential mark of authentic conversion is the completeness of the devotion and transformation. The age of conversion as well as the style of conversion may respond to expectations of the religious group. Studies of conversion have been made by psychologists, as we have noted in Chapter One, since 1881. The average age of conversion has been occurring earlier, as shown in the following table.

AGE OF CONVERSION[21]

| *Studies* | *Date* | *No. of Cases* | *Average Age* |
|---|---|---|---|
| Starbuck | 1899 | 1,265 | 16.4 |
| Coe | 1900 | 1,784 | 16.4 |
| Hall | 1904 | 4,054 | 16.6 |
| Athearn | 1922 | 6,194 | 14.6 |
| Clark | 1929 | 2,174 | 12.7 |

Starbuck in 1899 found the most prominent preconversion experiences in descending order to be depression and pensive sadness, calling on God, restless anxiety and uncertainty, sense of sin, loss of sleep or appetite, feeling of estrangement from God, desire for a better life, doubt and questing, earnest seriousness, weeping, and nervousness.[22] He found the following motives leading to conversion: social pressure and urging, the following out of a moral idea, remorse for sin, fear of death or hell, example or imitation, response to teaching, self-regarding motives, and altruistic motives. Central factors in conversion experiences he noted as spontaneous awakening, forgiveness, public confession, sense of oneness, self-surrender, determination, and divine aid. Emotions following conversion, as listed by Starbuck, are joy, peace, acceptance and oneness with God or Christ, happiness, bodily lightness, weeping or shouting, partial disappointment, relief, struggle and sense of responsibility, load lifted from body or heart, and subdued calmness. Conversion was seen to be a crucial and necessary experience to resolve conflict and attain larger life.

E. T. Clark, in his questionnaire study thirty years later, classified three types of religious awakening: (*a*) definite crisis (in emotions and attitudes), (*b*) emotional stimulus (less intense, no special change, but some event recalled as stimulus to awaken religious consciousness), and (*c*) gradual awakening (religious life flows on like a stream, enlarging and growing, striking no obstructions and forming no cataracts). In contrast to

[21] Starbuck, *op. cit.;* G. A. Coe, *The Psychology of Religion* (University of Chicago Press, 1916); G. Stanley Hall, *op. cit.;* W. S. Athearn, *et al., Indiana Survey of Religious Education* (New York: George H. Doran Co., 1924); E. T. Clark, *The Psychology of Religious Awakening* (New York: The Macmillan Co., 1929).

[22] *Ibid.*, p. 63.

the emotional crises prevalent in Starbuck's study, he finds the crisis type far outweighed by the tendency of gradual growth.

The more radical awakenings of crisis tend to occur about the age of seventeen—which coincides with earlier reports of Starbuck and Hall. But when religion develops as a gradual process, the awakening comes as early as twelve years. If the process is interrupted or resisted at this age, it is then deferred about five years and requires an emotional crisis to overcome obstructions. The later the conversion comes, the more intense and revolutionary it is, for the changes are more drastic and difficult. The sterner theology of the past discouraged gradual growth by the theory of original sin. But E. T. Clark finds that only 10 per cent of his group seem to have heard of the stern theology, while the majority think of a God of love and forgiveness. The theology of the next generation, another thirty years after Clark's study, accents both the judgment and forgiveness of God. The relation of theology to type conversion is indicated in the following table:

THEOLOGY RELATED TO TYPE OF RELIGIOUS AWAKENING[23]

| *Group* | *No. of Cases* | *Definite Crisis* | *Emotional Stimulus* | *Gradual Growth* |
|---|---|---|---|---|
| Total | 2,174 | 6.7% | 34.7% | 66.1% |
| Stern Theology | 176 | 34.6 | 34.7 | 30.7 |
| Confirmation | 133 | 2.2 | 5.5 | 92.3 |
| Above 40 Years | 81 | 35.8 | 30.9 | 33.3 |

Viewed in perspective, conversion is an incident in the process of religious growth. Without continuous growth before and after the climax, conversion is unreal and futile. With the preparation of previous development and the continuation of later progress, it may be decisive for the whole life. The timing of a crisis may be incidental, but the growing through time is essential. A sudden conversion may speed up the developing process and yet contain the same steps of advance. These steps move in a sequence of three periods: preparation, climax, and continuation. The climax may rise to a sharp peak of contrast standing like a Great Divide between two epochs of life. It may be marked by a quiet moment of decision on a fairly even pathway of advance. Or religious growth may con-

[23] *Op. cit.*, p. 87.

sist in a series of decisions and rededications that carries forward a lifelong purpose to a worthy goal. Decisive as one hour of dedication may be, it is the constant renewal of personal devotion that holds continuing significance.

No single method of revival is enough; for each in itself is partial, and religion seeks the complete life by complete devotion. A true conversion takes all of a person and redirects the total life upon a new course. It holds the dramatic appeal of eternal destinies and divine imperatives. It offers a great adventure to lose all or win all, a decisive choice between good and evil. Religious education may seem trivial if it misses this dramatic appeal of great issues at stake. Gradual growth may seem futile unless one has a vision of the ultimate goal and is able to move decisively in that direction. The revival meeting puts the crisis now, in this very hour, with eloquent contrast between the way of life and the way of death.

This sense of urgency religion can ill afford to forget. To achieve a new religious life, therefore, requires new birth. The regenerative powers of religion are deeper than conscious knowledge; they rise from dynamic, extraconscious resources of personality. They are larger than the individual and come through the interpersonal relations of a social and creative universe. The mysteries of life and death, birth and rebirth, will not be plumbed by superficial answers. They are greater than our knowledge by as much as cosmic energies are greater than a cup in the hand of a child. To experiment with mysterious powers is the work of science and the devotion of religion. Each in its way will explore the possibilities open for larger life.

# 7 PRAYER AND DEVOTION

## 1. *Spontaneous Prayer*

Prayer is the natural language of religious experience. The native language of all life is a cry. As birds and animals cry out to express emotions and to signal to others, so the first language of every human being is a cry. We understand the cries of infants to mean hunger, loneliness, pain, or joy. For the same motives prayer is offered, as situations of need call forth these responses. Even as a sharp pain may come to vocal expression in a groan, or a startling surprise produce a cry of fear, so prayer is the inevitable outburst of emotional distress. Primitive men preface prayers with rudimentary sounds, as whistling, clicking, or wailing, which reveal prelinguistic backgrounds. People of our day are likely in moments of stress to ejaculate, "O God! Help me!" as a spontaneous expression.

Friedrich Heiler is undoubtedly correct in taking this cry for help as the original form of prayer.[1] From the wordless cry wrenched from one in danger or distress, prayer expands to elaborate forms, phrases, and conventions. Whatever the form and however elaborate the foliation, the taproot of prayer is the elemental sense of need. In years of comfortable living some forget to pray; but if danger or anguish becomes urgent enough, most men pray irresistibly.

Prayer is as natural as conversation. One turns to speak to a friend to communicate ideas and share experiences. And if no one is listening we talk to ourselves subvocally. But prayer is not meant to be talking to oneself. Those who pray believe that they are addressing an Other, invisible but none the less real. The sense of a real Presence is the condition of prayer, in which the first person *I* speaks to the second person *Thou*. The exact nature of the Other may be unknown, but he is sought as a Person who can hear and help. Magic and science are mechanical operations with impersonal powers. Prayer is interperonal, a person-to-person call asking for an answer. Dynamic ten-

[1] *Prayer*, tr. S. McComb and J. E. Park (London: Oxford University Press, 1932), p. 11.

dencies to interact with other persons come naturally to expression in language and prayer.

If prayer is natural for some, is it for all? It seems to be the universal language of religion everywhere. From age to age and land to land, whether among primitive tribes or sophisticated church members, religious aspirations rise in prayer. If

> Prayer is the soul's sincere desire,
> Uttered or unexpressed,[2]

then we may agree that everyone has sincere desires. Yet many sincere desires are not offered to a Thou who is trusted to create and sustain values. If we take prayer as conversation with God, this excludes (*a*) those who do not believe in a God, (*b*) those who seek to evade God because of fear or guilt, and (*c*) those who feel no unmet needs or think prayer of no avail. There are many who do not often pray, yet there are few who never pray.

When do people pray? A group of Minnesota young people of college age in 1933 reported praying in situations of wonder and admiration, fear, great responsibility, joy and contentment, need, temptation, and love. When asked what they prayed for, they suggested the following subjects: physical needs (including food, health, and weather), protection, forgiveness of sin, guidance to know the way, strength to carry on, humility, security in God's presence, vision to see ahead, intercession for family and friends, gratitude for God's help, petition for God's compassion, power to endure hardships, to be used for God's will on earth, help to live better and avoid former mistakes, the purifying of heart and mind, peace of soul, courage to dare, greater faith that God is ever with us, greater confidence in mankind, ability to discern the value of life, ability to serve fellow men more effectively, the church and its leaders and members, the tempted, God's kingdom, and better world conditions.[3]

No psychology of prayer can overlook needs, for every prayer comes to focus upon a need. The range of human needs varies with the specific situations in which people find themselves, from the elemental physical needs for maintaining life to the more sophisticated needs listed by these young people. We may define a need as a force organizing personal action to improve a situation. Whenever the tension of need is urgent enough, a person does something about it. He may think, fret, worry, weep, or curse; or he may act overtly by going somewhere, exploring, experimenting, inventing, working, or striving to control. He may appeal, persuade, argue, plead, bargain, or promise to co-operate with a person who seems able to help.

[2] James Montgomery (1771-1854), "What Is Prayer?"

[3] P. E. Johnson, "When College Students Pray," *Christian Advocate,* CIX (1934), 179.

The social appeal of interpersonal outreach to Thou for an answering response is in the direction of prayer.

There are many needs of which we are not conscious. One is not conscious of the need for air until deprived of it. Of most needs we are conscious only intermittently. Our need for food and water is recurrent with the rhythm of organic requirements; the need for security varies with the awareness of risk and danger. We become conscious of needs as we come to the margin of loss and gain in values. New needs may be created by education, or advertising, or observation of what others enjoy. The needs of our civilization have multiplied beyond all expectation with progress in science, technology, and economies of abundance.

Human prayers follow human needs. The more urgent the need and the less adequate we feel, the surer we are to pray. If a need is trivial, it may not matter enough to pray; if one can meet the need independently, he may see little reason to call for help. So prayers rise and fall with the ebb and flow of need. Does this mean that prayer is a confession of weakness? Relatively, yes—though it would be truer to say that it is a confession of inadequacy. Self-sufficiency is self-deception. No one is omnipotent; everyone has situations of need when he is inadequate.

It may be objected that this view turns one to prayer only as a last resort, when every other means has failed. The objection is accepted and sustained by the facts of human behavior. Most people pray intermittently, when special needs arise. Theirs is a faith that God helps those who help themselves. Why ask for help as long as one can help himself? Should not each person do his best to solve his own problem? The sturdy virtue of self-reliance seeks to go as far as possible without prayer. The time will come when needs overbalance adequacy; then, but not till then, do many resort to prayer.

This observation gains support from a questionnaire study conducted by Murray G. Ross [4] of 1,720 youth who replied to the question "Why do we pray?" Their replies are summarized in the following table:

PERCENTAGE OF 1,720 YOUTH WHO REPLY TO THE QUESTION "WHY DO YOU PRAY?"

| | Per Cent |
|---|---|
| God listens to and answers your prayers | 32.8 |
| It helps you in time of stress and crisis | 27.2 |
| You feel relieved and better after prayer | 18.1 |
| Prayer reminds you of your obligations to man and society | 10.7 |
| It's a habit you have | 4.0 |

[4] Murray G. Ross, *Religious Beliefs of Youth* (New York: Association Press, 1950), p. 63.

| | |
|---|---|
| All good people pray | 0.9 |
| One takes a chance if one doesn't pray | 0.5 |
| Other replies | 5.8 |

Less than 15 per cent of these young people replied that they never prayed at all. Only 4 per cent prayed merely from habit, and less than 1 per cent were willing to admit that they prayed because all good people pray or because one takes a chance if one does not pray. More of them saw prayer as a social responsibility to be aware of obligations to other persons. More than 18 per cent prayed because they felt better after prayer. The two strongest motives for praying were for help in time of stress or crisis, and the belief that God would listen and answer.

Is there one need more basic than others that will move a person to pray? To our interpersonal view the most imperative human need is for a responsive relationship. The demand for relationship is the meaning of the infant's cry saying that he will not be comforted until the answering person responds to him. From this cry for response we trace the unfolding verbal systems of language and prayer reaching out to address and be addressed. The outreach is seeking to encounter the answering person, for as Buber shows, real life is meeting. This dialogic relation begins in making the distant Other present and orienting one's behavior to the goal of this living relationship.

Prayer as we understand it is first addressed to a human Thou. It would be instructive if we could remember accurately the first feelings of infancy. What we have to do is to infer from observed behavior and empathy to sense what we would feel in the infant's predicament. His cry carries a note of urgency as if he suffered acute psychosomatic distress of body and mind together. We infer that he may be cold, wet, hungry, and bombarded by unaccustomed stimuli disturbing the unconscious bliss of sleep. More than this we infer that he feels lonely, separated, estranged, and incomplete in his isolation. His first cry is no doubt a protest as well as a plaintive plea for help. If someone comes to answer his cry for help, he learns that he is not altogether alone. He knows he does not cry in vain, and he will cry again to address a Thou and call for the answering response.

This we have noted before, and we return to the crying infant to find a clue to the psychology of prayer. Here is portrayed the finite predicament of the lonely person who is incomplete in himself, addressing his plea to a Thou who will respond with the relationship he desperately needs. No other need is so persistent as the need to relate, and no other activity is so important to him as the dialogue with a responsive person. If no one answers his call, his grief is unconsolable. He becomes emotionally ill and does not want to live, for nothing else will satisfy his regnant need or justify the intolerable emptiness of his existence. If the answering response comes only now and then with no way of predicting the response, he suffers insecurity and emotional instability. If he is rejected repeatedly by his most significant other person, he will become antisocial or criminal, either withdrawing to avoid the hurt of rejection or striking back in angry bitterness to retaliate and punish those who deeply hurt him at the center of his utmost need. Attitudes toward God may also follow these alternatives in praying.

If then prayer arises out of this basic need and is as natural as a conversation, we are not surprised to find that most people are inclined to pray. The need to relate is insatiable, not to be extinguished but reinforced by every fulfillment. And one relationship prepares for the next, not to close the circuit in finality but to open the circuit to new relationships in the outreaching and endless search to complete the fragmentary existence of the finite person. This finite quest is not readily fulfilled because the need is ultimate. Consequently, the growing life is always reaching out for a more ultimate relationship. In his eagerness to possess a needed relationship, an anxious person may often hold another to himself to gratify his egocentric need. The other person may be exploited for my advantage and used as a means to the selfish end of my gratification. But this reduces the Thou to the level of a thing, and no one can satisfy his basic need by such an I-It relationship. Even the haughty slaveowner who reduces other persons to chattels and drives them to do his bidding is not content but hungers the more for someone to love, someone to whom he may give ultimate devotion.

It is not uncommon to find prayer that seeks to exploit Thou and use God to gratify selfish demands. James B. Pratt [5] calls such prayer subjective and proceeds to show that it is self-defeating. For when prayer or worship is an exercise conducted to gratify my own needs, it is only my effort to do something for myself, in which the Other is so insignificant as to be merely instrumental. In that form of egocentricity I will eventually find other means to serve myself and discredit the broken circuit of prayer as an outworn formality. Which indeed it is, when I have already broken the praying circuit by reducing Thou to It and resorting to magic to get my desires by mechanical manipulation.

In contrast to this, true prayer is objective worship addressing Thou as ultimate Being who is worthy of reverence in his own right. He is not sought to gratify my need or do for me what I ask. Such prayer seeks God more than his gifts, for he is the intrinsic and ultimate goal of the finite quest. If the basic human need is relationship, then to come before him in

[5] *The Religious Consciousness* (New York: The Macmillan Co., 1920).

humility and address him in gratitude for his presence is to enter into the ultimate relation. To pray is to offer myself to Thou in a living encounter which intensifies and enhances the whole meaning of life. I am fulfilled not by self-seeking but by other-seeking, not by grasping from the Other but in self-giving to the Other. For self-seeking breaks the circuit and leaves my ego at the center, while other-seeking completes a dynamic circuit to fulfill my fractional existence in larger wholeness.

This is demonstrated on the human level in the interpersonal relationship of address and response, in which each person accepts and cherishes the other for his own intrinsic worth. And where each person gives to the other his utmost devotion, we find a communion that fulfills within these limits the meaning of the I-Thou relationship. Such communion the mature religious person seeks in prayer, and there are many who believe they have the answering response from God. The nature and activity of God are beyond the scope of psychology to verify or deny. Though stopping short of the ultimate at the boundaries of natural science, yet psychologists will listen respectfully to the reports of those who claim to have responses from God. They will examine such evidence as comes to them and submit it to the categories and procedures of empirical psychological analysis.

Broadly speaking we may consider two alternatives in assessing the experiences of prayer. If prayer is autosuggestion, it may be classified as meditation, and as such it will count as a practice worth cultivating to attain perspective on the conflictual strivings of daily life, to choose goals wisely, to set the course by which to move toward them most effectively, to compose or harmonize jangling emotions, and to bring so far as possible the contradictory forces of personality into unified integrity. In meditation one may learn from the written or spoken words of others and even address fictitious or absent companions. But the person is solitary in meditation, and while he may think about other persons, he is yet isolated with his own thoughts. He is not whole but incomplete until he enters into dialogue with another person. For this reason solitary confinement in a prison cell is so great a deprivation that men call it a living death.

If, on the other hand, prayer is a living encounter in the present moment, the entire meaning of life is transformed in such a relationship. The broken circuit is completed in the meeting of I and Thou, and what was feeble or futile before becomes dynamic with new motivating energy. Those who report the answering response from Thou are transformed like Kagawa, who found a new dimension of life. By regular practice of prayer they are refreshed when weary and renewed when discouraged and defeated. Fragments of meaning come to wholeness in the experience of meeting Thou. Confused and contradictory impulses are integrated around a central purpose to give more than to receive, to minister rather than to be ministered to. Opposition and conflict do not weaken religious purpose but actually call forth more passionate self-giving devotion. They are not like those who call in vain, for they seem to have a response.

Yet there are others who do not give so convincing a report. Remembering Clark's distinction between primary, secondary, and tertiary religious experience, we may conclude that the majority are not so blessed in prayer. There are the heroes of the faith who like Jacob wrestle mightily with the mysterious Thou until they receive the blessing. And there are many who misunderstand the potentiality of prayer or give up too early at the first disappointment and look for an easier shortcut, who care more for the next meal than the ultimate and turn more readily to material gain or pleasant comforts. Each one follows his own perceptions, and praying has different meanings to different people. Granting that it is natural to pray and that most people pray now and then on occasions that to them may seem appropriate, we may also agree that prayer for many who call themselves religious is a rather dim view of secondary value.

We have noted the practice of spontaneous prayer. It is impromptu, intermittent, and reserved for times of stress. This is the primitive and childlike use of prayer. But as men and women mature in the wisdom of experience, they see that spontaneous prayer is not enough. For the needs of life are persistent. One may live a hand-to-mouth existence without a thought beyond the next meal, but the risks and deprivations of life are too hazardous for a provident man. One may take no thought of his health until illness lays him low, but preventive medicine prepares to maintain health reserves before it is too late. To see and anticipate these needs is the most successful way of meeting them. Instead of waiting for emergencies to strike, the well-organized person plans and provides in advance to meet them more efficiently. Mature prayer is a preventive and sustaining procedure by which life may be held at higher levels of constant resourcefulness.

To understand this principle of larger spiritual preparedness is to move from spontaneous prayer to disciplined prayer. Instead of praying on the impulse of a mood, one may employ prayer to prevent distraction and come to difficult situations resourcefully. By frequent practice in the spiritual exercises of prayer, it may be possible to develop powers and controls, attitudes and habits, that will prove more adequate to every situation. Those who desire these results enough will order and discipline the hours of every day to cultivate the inner resources of faithful devotion. Prayer in this way comes to be more than a "desire uttered or unexpressed," more than a cry or conversation. Prayer is then the conscious experience of genuine concern and faithful communion with Thou.

## 2. *Ways of Discipline*

Those who are most devoted to prayer cultivate the inner life systematically. Like workmen who keep faithfully at a chosen task, or artists who know that excellence demands long hours of regular practice, or athletes who submit to rigorous training to be strong, they follow a schedule of daily spiritual exercise. Among those who make a business of prayer three religious vocations arise: the mystic, the prophet, and the priest. We may well study their methods.

The mystics are specialists in prayer. They have a passion for the ultimate Thou, in the light of which physical things are dark and unreal. Believing in the infinite value of spiritual reality, the mystics are ready to sacrifice material goods as worthless and the appeals of the senses as deceptive illusion. To them prayer is the highest privilege and the deepest responsibility of life. In prayer they invest the working day, coming to prayer as a scientist to his laboratory, eager to discover reality, faithful to labor unsparingly, alert to improve methods of experiment and research.

The mystics of various religions—Hindu, Buddhist, Hebrew, Christian, and Moslem—have developed methods accepted as standard. From similar devotional experiences have come devotional exercises common to mystics everywhere. These are often referred to as the "ladder of prayer" or the mystical ascent to God. Four steps are noted, which may be described as awakening, purgation, meditation, and union.

*a*) *Awakening* is the first step in religious encounter. Experiences urging toward mysticism may be dissatisfactory human conditions, inner restlessness and conflict, hunger for a better state, vision of the splendor of a larger life, or a foretaste of ecstatic joy. It may be a conversion or a vivid and compelling reawakening. Augustine decided, "I know nothing other than that the fleeting and falling should be spurned, the fixed and eternal sought after." [6] Pascal wrote, "From half-past ten to half-past twelve fire, joy, certainty." [7] Suso declared, "O my heart's joy, never shall my soul forget this hour." [8] A vivid, firsthand experience of spiritual value is essential.

*b*) *Purgation* is the negative path of renunciation. The logic of renunciation is that devotion to the mystical purpose requires purification. The natural life is distorted by carnal desires and material values, a false universe of egocentricity. The earnest devotee seeks to correct his perspective by clearing away whatever is not in harmony with true reality. This stripping away is represented by the threefold monastic vow of poverty, chastity,

[6] *The Soliloquies of St. Augustine,* tr. R. E. Cleveland (Boston: Little, Brown & Co., 1910), p. 8.

[7] From the *Memorial,* quoted in Evelyn Underhill, *Mysticism* (New York: E. P. Dutton & Co., 1911), p. 228.

[8] *Leben und Schriften,* quoted in *ibid.*, p. 225.

and obedience. Mortification is a self-discipline to break up the old selfish habits, abandon the comforts of least resistance, and take on new spiritual daring. The aim is to produce a definite vitality and efficiency as athletes do in the physical exercises of the gymnasium and the field.

c) *Meditation* is voluntary concentration upon the object of devotion. Recollection is used in the sense not of remembering but of collecting the self together, narrowing attention to focus on one aspect of reality—a word, name, or attribute of God, a verse of scripture, or an incident in the life of Jesus. This leads to another stage known as "orison," or quiet relaxation. The struggle for concentration yields to surrender of the will to God, a turning from doing to being. Orison is not the prayer of petition, but a trustful waiting, a wordless communion, a silent yearning of the soul, an opening of the spiritual eye to gaze upon the glory of God. Contemplation is often named as another step beyond meditation. It means self-forgetting attentiveness, an illuminating act of the whole personality in devotion to God.

d) *Union* is the goal of mystical discipline. A merging or absorption of self with the all Being is sought by pantheists. An intimate sense of personal fellowship with God is the aim of theists. Hypnotic states of ecstasy, rapture, and trance are welcomed by some; depressive states of darkness and separation are endured at times as emotional reactions of fatigue and relapse. Beyond these emotional extremes true mystics seek a transforming of character that will become a permanent incarnation of the divine in the human. "Not I, but Christ liveth in me," said Paul (Gal. 2:20). "My life shall be real, because it is full of Thee," declared Augustine.[9] In such complete devotion to Thou may come a new sense of divine strength, freedom, and serenity. A person so dedicated and inspired becomes a radiating center of spiritual vitality and love overflowing to others.

Prophets are also men of prayer. They are fully as devoted to the religious cause as the mystics, but they follow another discipline. The mystic is regulated by the aim of self-control, while the prophet is directed by the aim of social action. The mystic is an individual who turns to God in private devotions; "so must the single soul be allowed its own single love." [10] The prophet is devoted to social welfare and identifies himself with the common life of his people.[11] He broods with God over the evils of his time and cries out the divine message of repentance and reform. The urgency of social

[9] *Confessions* X. xxviii.

[10] *The Essence of Plotinus*, ed. G. H. Turnbull (New York: Oxford University Press, 1934), p. 96. The social implications of this are also stated by Plotinus: "This does not make the man unfriendly or harsh; giving freely to his intimates of all he has to give, he will be the best of friends by his very union with Divine Mind."—*ibid.*, p. 37.

[11] Note Moses, praying God to forgive his people, ". . . and if not, blot me, I pray thee, out of thy book which thou hast written."—*Exod.* 32:32.

needs possesses the prophet until he can bear it no longer, and he is compelled to throw his life recklessly into courageous action with God so serve others.

Although mystics may also be prophets and vice versa, greater clarity is gained by noting the emphasis of each. Prophetic prayer arises in concrete need and comes to a vigorous emotional expression. Mysticism is calm, aesthetic contemplation, but prophecy is stormy in emotion and urgent in ethical demands. It takes the form of ardent petition and intercession for others by eloquent persuasion. Abraham pleading with God to save Sodom argues persuasively, "Wilt thou also destroy the righteous with the wicked?" and, "Shall not the Judge of all the earth do right?" (Gen. 18:23, 25). Prophetic prayer freely confesses sin and unworthiness.

The yearning for vision of God is not an experience for the prophet alone but one to share with his people. "The Lord God hath spoken, who can but prophesy?" (Amos 3:8.) The practical social emphasis is evident in the prayer of Jesus for his disciplines, "For their sakes I sanctify myself, that they also might be sanctified through the truth, . . . that the love wherewith thou hast loved me may be in them" (John 17:19, 26). Francis of Assisi felt it was a great shame when he found anyone poorer than he, and prayed for grace to love more truly. The prophet therefore is disciplined by his keen sense of need, his responsiveness to God's relevation, and his devotion to the bringing of men to God in ethical and religious reform.

The priests are also men of prayer. They take up prayer as a religious vocation and work faithfully at the task of praying. But their discipline is not the self-control of the mystic or the social action of the prophet. Priestly discipline is ritual. The life of prayer is regulated in the temple by tradition and authority. Spontaneous prayer is too chaotic and inexact for institutional use. Extempore prayer consequently yields to literary editing. Fluid expressions set into forms that become norms. The present experience is subject to the authority of the past with its cumulative traditions and meanings. In this discipline priests feel obliged to be correct, to utter their prayers in good style, according to the established proprieties. So develops a priestly liturgy for public prayer and a breviary for daily offices.

Each of these disciplines has its psychological value. Priestly prayer is rich in traditional symbols, aware of historical continuities, precise in well-ordered expression, effective in literary and dramatic power, solemn in dignity, and impressive in social resonance. Priestly prayer gathers up the experience of the group and distills its essence into a fragrant expression. But repetition may result in sterile, hollow formality. Then prophetic revolt breaks forth as a cleansing moral imperative.

> I hate, I despise your feast days, and I will not smell in your solemn assemblies. . . . Take thou away from me the noise of thy songs; for I will not hear the melody

of thy viols. But let judgment run down as waters, and righteousness as a mighty stream. (Amos 5:21-24.)

And when social service grows weary or reforms are lost in failure and despair, the sources of spiritual vitality may be renewed in the transforming mystical experience of communion with God. Each discipline supplements the others in kindling anew the flame of devotion.

It may well be noted, as Walter Clark [12] does, that these disciplines become ways of life going beyond prayer to represent different approaches to religion. He describes the prophet as one who has immediate experience of God in common with the mystic, but the prophet departs from the mystic in carrying out his religious vocation. The prophet has a sense of mission as the mouthpiece of God, a concern for rightness of living, a reliance on intuition, and a highly individualized interpretation of religious truth. The prophet is of this world, and he lives in history. He enters the arena of social and political conflict to speak for God and righteousness. He is more apt to be found preaching than praying or meditating. He is less introvert and more extrovert than the mystic, more masculine than feminine in temperament, going forth to aggressive social action and reform.

The priest is the religious conservative in contrast to the prophet as the religious liberal. To the priest God is known through tradition and the institution in which he is revealed. His first loyalty is not to himself and his personal experience, nor to the people who fall short of righteousness, but to the institution whose servant he is. In worship he prefers ritual and liturgy, and distrusts the enthusiasm and freer innovations of the prophet as dangerous experiments. Both of these have their part to play in the religious drama, and both have their characteristic dangers.

> The prophet may become extremely egotistic, while the priest may become simply fussy and dull. The prophet may advocate change simply for change's sake, while the priest may resist all change. The prophet may stimulate disorder, while the priest fosters rigidity. The prophet may fragment the religious institution, while under the priest it may die of dry rot. The prophet may conceive a vested interest in stirring up the people, while the vested interest of the priest may be to keep the people contented. If religion is in any sense the "opium of the people," it is the priest who stands guilty of having prepared the prescription.[13]

A fourth type of religious leader considered by Clark is the religious intellectual. He is the man of thought, most often known as the theologian, and he also has an important function to perform. He has his own way of becoming aware of spiritual reality through logic and reason. Yet his concern

[12] *Op. cit.*, pp. 291-306.

[13] *Ibid.*, p. 302. Used by permission of The Macmillan Co.

for religious experience is apt to diminish as his passion for abstract truth rises to ascendancy. Unlike the mystic and the prophet his belief is secondhand. Unlike the prophet his interest may be to appraise righteousness rather than to practice it, to study history rather than to change it. He recognizes the complexity of situations and is inclined to suspend judgment until all the evidence is in. He is an explorer in the field of ideas, and religion needs the calm and penetrating perspective of the thinker who faithfully and fearlessly sifts out the truth from error, who punctures illusions, articulates his searching doubts, and reconstructs religious intuitions into theological systems.

Conflicts among these four types of religious discipline occur whithin the individual person as well as social movements in the history of religion. A theological student with whom I explored the religious search was struggling with these conflicts within himself. He yearned to be an intellectual, and yet he had chosen the priestly role of the churchman. He experimented with and found effective results in the mystical practices of prayer and meditation, yet sought to speak for God in his Sunday pulpit and take the role of the prophet in promoting social justice and guiding the scourge of war into the paths of peace. His dilemma was intensified by the complexity of the roles of a Christian minister, who may choose to follow one or another of these disciplines.

This may warn us from the error of setting these disciplines in final and irreconcilable opposition to one another. For they do overlap, and it is well to recognize that while they seem often to contradict, they are actually capable of supporting one another. This we find to be the case with Kagawa, who was able to integrate the conflicts and enrich the meaning of life by employing them to serve one great purpose of religious devotion. He might be classified as a flaming prophet who has a message of righteousness and a dynamic energy of social reform. Yet he is equally the mystic who is revived and counseled daily through meditation and prayer. He is the intellectual who carries his research to the slums to find the causes of poverty and writes books that stir the minds of multitudes. Yet through all his activities he is a churchman who has the priestly function of reconciling men to God. In his religious devotion all of the disciplines join. In suffering he is able to rejoice and in darkness to know the inward light even if the outer world fails him. He says:

At the center of things there is a heart. On the yonder side of darkness there is light. Deprived of sight, I discern that light flooding in through the darkness.

To me all things are vocal. Oh, wonder words of love! The bedding, the tears, the spittle, the perspiration, the vapor of the compress on my eyes, the ceiling, the matted floor, the voice of the chirping sparrow without, all are vocal. God and every inanimate thing speak to me. Thus even in the dark I feel no sense of loneliness. . . .

Prayer continues! Prayer continues! Daily my prayer continues! . . . Be the sky clouded or clear, my prayer continues.

Given the gift of life, I must pray—pray for God's Kingdom, pray for the world. Simply because I am doomed to dwell in the dark is no excuse for allowing my soul to devote itself to self-centered musings.

In the darkness I meet God face to face. In the darkness my soul is clothed in white raiment and, purified, ascends to the holy of holies, into the very presence of God. The darkness itself is a holy of holies of which no one can rob me.

That's it! That's it! It is not I that believe in God. It is God who is bringing me to the birth. Here lies the reason for this long blindness. This is the purpose back of this wearisome confinement. I am being born, born of God. God has some great expectation regarding me. I must not give way to despair because of pain or sorrow. God is bearing me in his womb. . . .

I realize that a lot of work is waiting. But work is not the purpose of my life. I am given life that I may live.

It is impossible for me to stupidly moon away this present precious moment in boredom by idly thinking of tomorrow. My life is focused in this one moment. My present task is here and now to fellowship with God on this bed of pain.

I am not thinking of tomorrow or the next day, nor even of this day's sunset hour. I am concerned only with being, this present moment, without any sense of tedium, with God. And for me constantly praising God for the joy of the moments lived with Him there is no such thing as tediousness.[14]

## 3. *Psychological Effects*

Spontaneous prayer arises from urgent need. Disciplined prayer acknowledges the needs of finite life and seeks dynamic resources to fulfill them. What needs can prayer meet? How effective is prayer for any purpose? Work achieves visible results. By appropriate action one can walk a mile, build a house, or bake a loaf of bread. What does prayer accomplish? Can prayer transport, build, or bake? Prayer is no substitute for action; neither is intelligence, trust, or kindness. But action may fail for lack of intelligence, persons are ill for lack of trust, and poverty is unrelieved without kindness. Not all action is constructive; not all work is successful. Mere busyness is futile if one does the wrong thing. What can work accomplish without foresight, skill, and co-operation?

Religion is a delicate balance of many factors. Every value achieved is a product of insight and action, appreciation and constructive labor, desire and effort toward fulfillment, organization and social co-operation. The

[14] Axling, *op. cit.*, pp. 153-54. Used by permission of Harper & Bros.

achievements of prayer result from its proper use. Prayer does not work as a substitute for a steel chisel or the wing of an airplane. It does not replace muscular action in walking or faithful study in meeting an examination. These are not the proper uses of prayer. But prayer may help to calm the nerves when one is using a chisel in bone surgery or bringing an airplane to a landing. Prayer may guide one in choosing a destination to walk toward, and strengthen one's purpose to prepare thoroughly for an examination.

In the psychological realm of motivation the effects of prayer can be observed. This is the field in which the operation of prayer may appear to be most appropriate. The inner life of tensions and desires, stresses and problems, is the dynamic area of spiritual energies. What are the psychological effects of prayer? Those who pray report the following experiences:

*a*) *Awareness of needs and realities.* As prayer arises from needs, so needs become clearer in praying. The realities of life are faced with One who knows all; self-deception is laid aside, and deeper honesty opens truer understanding.

*b*) *Confession and sense of forgiveness.* To confess needs, failures, and anxieties is a purging emotional catharsis. In the prayer of confession one may find assurance of forgiveness and harmonious adjustment to a larger, interpersonal destiny.

*c*) *Trust and relaxation.* Prayer in faith and hope releases tensions, brings peace of mind, disposes of worry and fear, and undergirds insecurity with basic confidence.

*d*) *Perspective and clarification.* Prayer aims to see life steadily and whole in the perspective of God. As a cluttered desk is put in order, so in prayer confused experiences are sorted out and brought to clearer order. Prayerful meditation solves problems and works out practical plans of action.

*e*) *Decision and dedication.* In this clarifying perspective goals come into view and purposes move toward them. Dedication of self to a cause relieves indecision and becomes a dynamic motor set to effective action. Such a decision is a first step in unleashing latent powers to achieve.

*f*) *Renewal of emotional energy.* In the sense of meeting Thou one may have creative experiences of elation, inspiration, and expansion of emotional resources. Such experiences are euphoric and energizing.

*g*) *Social responsiveness.* The prayer experience of meeting Thou overcomes isolation and loneliness in feeling that we are not alone. There are moral support, courage, and virility in this feeling of social response. In praying for and with others, one becomes socially sensitive to their needs and more ready to co-operate for the good of all.

*h*) *Joy, gratitude, and reconciliation.* Prayer affirms values, enlarges appreciation, and recognizes present good. These affirmations give a joyous undertone, awakening gratitude and reconciling one to sorrow and loss. Whatever comes, one is better prepared to meet it in this spirit.

*i) Loyalty and perseverance.* Prayer is an act of devotion and renewal. Loyalties are fostered by affirming ultimate goals and giving one's self in faithful devotion. Rededication in prayer develops persistence to carry on in the face of obstacles and fatigue.

*j) Integration of personality.* Amid the distraction and contradiction of many appeals prayer focuses attention upon a supreme loyalty. In the conflicts of unruly desires prayer recollects the major purpose and unifies the energies along the channel of this dedication. Those who pray faithfully manifest a basic integrity that gives life poise and inner peace.

This account of psychological effects may appear to some as an overstatement, but to those who have explored the resources of prayer it will seem an understatement. Not all praying is so effective, for prayer is often misused and misunderstood. Prayer is bound to fail, as is any other instrument taken out of its proper field and put to magical rather than experimental use. The prevalent neglect of prayer indicates the misunderstanding and misuse of it. The total value and influence of prayer are beyond calculation because the consequences affect the hidden recesses of personality and permeate in subtle yet pervasive ways the intricate relationships of life. But in the psychological functions listed above, prayer is well employed. Prayer with none of these results is futile. If prayer has even one of these effects, it is well worth while. Rightly used, prayer may have enlarging effectiveness in the psychological needs of personality and the outgoing dynamics of interpersonal relations.

Experimental psychologists speak of the law of effect to indicate that behavior is regulated by the effect of previous efforts. In experiments with learning, the animal in a maze may step on a grid which gives him a painful electric shock. When this event is repeated time and again, the animal will learn to avoid the grid, and his behavior is regulated by that punishing effect. In another experiment the animal who presses a lever is rewarded by pellets of food. When this event is repeated, he will learn to press the lever when he is hungry, and his behavior is regulated by the rewarding effect. Experiments with human subjects give further supporting evidence to the law of effect. Behavior that has no effect in meeting a need will be extinguished because it is inconsequential. On the other hand, behavior that has desirable consequences will be continued and its motivation reinforced. Likewise, the behavior that is consistently punished by its consequences will be discontinued. And the learning, whether positive or negative, is guided by the effect of the behavior.

This may provide us with a psychological principle by which to deal with the question why some religious persons pray more than others. The effects of praying will no doubt guide the practice of prayer. The child who prays that his dead mother return to life and care for him as before may decide that prayer does not work. The mother who prays for a sick child who gets well may be reinforced in her desire to continue praying. Those who pray for rain and receive a downpour may be rewarded and believe it is good to pray for rain. But on other occasions if such prayer does not bring rain, those who once prayed may consider prayer to be useless as it seems to have no effect upon the weather.

Whatever the experiment we undertake, it is to be evaluated in terms of discoverable effects. "By their fruits ye shall know them." In practice we are all likely to employ the pragmatic test of considering the consequences. So in praying we are not unmindful to whatever effects may be known, and by the accumulating empirical results we gather evidence to guide the course of future behavior. One student found silent communion to have a notable effect in refreshing his spirit, renewing his purpose, and helping him to concentrate on the main business at hand. By these effects he was reinforced in the motive to continue his prayer and meditation. Likewise in his sessions with a counselor he came to a new understanding of himself and by this effect saw the value of more open communication with his wife and more searching examination of his own conflicts. In both counseling and prayer he was awakened by confrontation to seek the enlarging dimension of relationship.

In the maturing of a religious person there are steps to take along a journey toward ever more ultimate goals. To the child the parents may appear to be ultimate, and in his dependent need he reaches out prayerfully to them as the ones to give him a responsive relationship. But he will eventually discover other companions who may come to focal significance in his expanding frontiers of exploration. The mystics follow a ladder of ascent to guide the onward journey of their prayer discipline, until they come to the eventual sense of union with Thou as the ultimate goal of their quest. To the maturing religious seeker every step of the ascending way of prayer is pressing on to a more ultimate relation. The self-centered desires by which we begin the experiment of prayer eventually are recognized as foolish and vain petitions. The gifts once sought are seen in truer perspective to be paltry baubles, vanishing into insignificance before the one great need of ultimate concern which is the encounter of I and Thou.

Looking again at the list of ten psychological effects we have discovered as fruits of prayer, they now flow together in a surprising unity. Each of these effects emerges from a relationship more ultimate than the specific result. All together they may appear to meet a succession of various needs which at first glance might seem unrelated. But actually they are by-products of a deeper fulfillment of which they are the characteristic resultants. There is one need so basic that it is prepotent over all others, the need for relationship. And there is one resource for religious growth so deep that all others are derivative therefrom, the meeting of I with Thou. It is the sense of living encounter in the present moment that spontaneously creates new life and opens the way to follow onward a path without end.

### *4. Religious Devotion*

When prayer follows this endless path to the ultimate Thou, it is more than the experience of the moment or a fleeting vision that comes to return no more. The ladder of ascent is a journey that moves on from stage to stage, to a goal that may be reached but never overpassed. There will be ups and downs and plateaus when the struggle may seem futile and the rewards invisible. But the faithful religious seeker will continue to press on when others turn back and to weather the storms of doubt and despair that would beat down the more vacillating fair-weather friends. For the life of prayer becomes the dedicated faithfulness of religious devotion.

To the Hebrews their relation to Thou was wrought into a covenant whereby each party was bound to uphold a mutual pledge. The fathers from Abraham on had met Thou and entered into a compact that obligated each one to fulfill. God had said, "If you will be faithful and not rebel or go after other gods, I will be your God and you shall be my people." The entire religious history of Israel as portrayed in the Old Testament pivoted around this covenant. Every prayer to Thou was based upon this basic agreement, every sin was measured in terms of it, and every victory was a new evidence that it is being fulfilled. When afflictions and disasters fell upon the people, there was no doubt that someone had sinned and the penalty fell to show that the covenant offers the only true way of salvation. To ensure faithful devotion, religious laws were formulated covering the entire range of human behavior seen in relation to the righteousness of God and the obligation of man to live in concord with the covenant.

In some such way the ethical religions of the world perceive their responsibility to Thou as requiring faithfulness at all times and in all circumstances. In this perspective of constant responsibility the act of prayer is like a jewel sparkling in its setting. It may be otherwise to those whose prayer is a spasmodic outcry from a belated moment of direst need. But for the person who follows a discipline of consecutive praying, each prayer is another step along the way of his endless devotion. He prays to meet Thou, to collect his wandering mind, to reaffirm his basic purpose, to acknowledge his dependence as a finite person upon more ultimate resources, to confess his sins and follies and seek the answering forgiveness, to take his bearings and seek further guidance to pursue his course faithfully. He reaches out to Thou in communion of love and gratitude, in need of waking and refreshing energies, to renew his ebbing life and dedicate himself to ultimate devotion.

Yet the psychology of religious devotion is very perplexing. Why does a sincere person who wants to be religious find it so difficult? Man may be incurably religious, but he is just as persistently irreligious. The confessions of saints as well as the more conspicuous faults of sinners bring a convincing weight of testimony. The earnest religious life never ceases to be a struggle against temptation and resistance. Whoever takes religion as an easy way of life has less than a complete devotion.

Psychological analysis may help to disclose some causes of difficulty in religious devotion. How is such devotion possible? What are the inner resistances that distract and defeat singleness of purpose? Religious devotion includes the following psychological processes: (*a*) interest in and attention to spiritual values; (*b*) conscious decision, choosing the way of life that offers these values; (*c*) identification of self with the religious purpose of loving service; (*d*) renunciation of other interests that conflict and lead away from this devotion; (*e*) progressive integration of personality around God and his will for life.

If these five psychological factors are essential to religious devotion, what is it that so often prevents fulfillment of them? Personality is not one stream of energy flowing in one direction. Rather do we find many streams of energy playing upon each other in crosscurrents and counterforces that swirl around in all directions. Whatever unity we have is won against heavy odds. For personality is a dynamic unity of multiple and contradictory tendencies.

Each step in the progress of religious devotion is met with its own particular resistances. (*a*) Religious interest is rivaled by other interests, whose secular attractions appeal seductively to the senses. To concentrate upon any object, especially the invisible, intangible objects of religion, is to wage a battle against diversity. (*b*) Deciding for a religious goal means deciding against other goals that may seem even more delightful. To make any decision is to reject other possible goods and overrule other alternatives. (*c*) Identification with a religious cause will require holding this first among competing interests and diversions of life. Selective attention and loyalty to a religious purpose require a high degree of control. (*d*) Renunciation may not be so difficult in the first enthusiasm of a great decision. How to endure and re-enact that renunciation hour after hour is the lifelong test. (*e*) Progressive integration is easier said than done, for it involves the difficult art of taking each developing interest and obligation as it comes and reorganizing the shifting kaleidoscope of life into new unities of consecutive purpose. To follow any course consistently is a running combat with fading spans of attention, contrary desires, comfortable inertias, frequent doubts, and the surprising perplexities of constant readjustment.

To observe this in life, let us study the concrete situation of a woman who had found success in England as a college teacher and the author of two novels and a play. She describes herself [15] as an agnostic humanist dwelling among good pagans who lived in charity with their neighbors but scornful of religion as superstition. She had great plans for her literary future. "I was, it seemed, completely self-pivoted and from a settled centre thought myself prepared to help and comfort my neighbor—within reason, of course." [16]

Then in her forty-third year something happened that she could not well explain. The first impression was of meeting head on a full charge of some strange Power. It was in the year 1934 after conducting a party of past students and staff from the college to the Passion Play at Oberammergau that she came sight-seeing to a medieval church in Nuremberg to observe the carvings by friends of Dürer. As she was tired, she sat down in a chair alone in the church except for a verger at the far end. She was gazing at the tomb about twelve feet away, quite relaxed and thinking idly with her eyes open. What happened she calls Encounter, and she can best give in her own words the meaning of the experience.

It was as if I had moved, in my mind, away from the central place, as if I had always sat on a throne in mid-consciousness, administering my affairs, and *had stepped down.* It was positive, and I cannot, by taking thought repeat it. It had the stillness of humility shining with surprised joy, the quality of joy seen sometimes on the face of a very young child when he recognizes unexpectedly, someone he loves. I had the impression it was momentary, the time taken to switch on a light, or to press a button.

Then, precisely, as if that moving off the centre of my own consciousness had set some machinery going, it happened. How can I explain! I can only use negatives.

I saw nothing, not even a light.

I heard nothing, no voice, no music, no nothing.

Nothing touched me. Nor was I conscious of any Being, visible or invisible.

But suddenly, simply, silently, I was not there. And I was there. It lasted for a moment, yet it was eternal, since there was no time.

And I knew as certainly as I know I am trying to write it down, as certainly as I know that I live and eat and walk and sleep, that this world, this universe is precisely as we see it, hear it, know it, and is at the same time completely

[15] In *The Following Feet* by Ancilla (Greenwich, Conn.: The Seabury Press, 1957), which is a confessional study of her spiritual pilgrimage.

[16] *Ibid.*, p. viii. Used by permission of The Seabury Press.

different. It is as we see it because we are of it; it is also and at the same time wholly *other*.

A completely colour-blind person suddenly aware of colour? More fundamental than this.

A dog in a library sniffing his master's familiar book suddenly enabled to read it?

Robert Bridges's wolf and the first inklings of thought? (*The Testament of Beauty*, line 319.) But it was not an inkling, it was complete. Yet I do not know in what ways the earth appeared different. It was not different materially. It still had form, and colour, even good and evil, and animals and people, but it was conceived differently, as a whole, perhaps, as a spiritual entity. And it filled me with awe and grave joy and certainty, since I knew for always that so it was and no other, and that all was well; that it was the answer to all questions. I had no vision of God or any person, no vision of Christ, or of any spiritual being. Yet it was all that is, and there was no God, and equally no Not-God. It was whole and of the spirit. No words can make it clear. All I can say is that the wholeness seemed akin to that part of me that I should call spirit, as if my spirit were part of it and could not be separated from it.[17]

She had no idea how long the experience lasted, believing that it was momentary yet with a clear impression of timelessness. It was whole and complete, not to be analyzed, fussed over, or frittered away. It was a secret inner discovery, a kind of knowing yet not by the customary methods of knowing, too sacred to tell to anyone else or to classify with any other experience she had before. She did not pray, she did not speak, but left the church alone, rather stunned and not quite sure of herself. She felt strange and unprotected, yet she was fully aware she had come to a moment that would change everything as the turning point of her life. What she had long denied, since giving up the religious moods of childhood had come to her so surely that she could never doubt it. Having thus known, she could feel that she would always know and that for her the world was all new.

This moment of encounter became the focal center of her life from that time on. Friends and associates noted a difference in her, as if she did the same things but in a different context. Though changes in the pattern of her life came slowly through the following years, yet she felt that the change was completed in an instant and that what followed was an unfolding of it. At first she feared a recurrence of the experience, feeling she could not endure it. Then as fear subsided, there was a great longing to "see" again. But neither prayer, nor discipline, nor passivity, nor deliberate relaxation would do it. Other experiences occurred but this was like the dividing line of history from B.C. to A.D. She could not return to life before that event but must go forward always from that as the beginning of a new life.

From her childhood she did recall the stories in her home of missionaries

[17] *Ibid*, pp. 20-21.

who went forth to the New Hebrides and the Congo to die in a short time, and what a strange sense of awe she felt. Also, as a lonely child she had a secret companion, a "God" of her own who would never stop loving and approving her whatever she did. This was her refuge as a sensitive child wounded by the least suggestion of criticism or disapproval. In panic she would feel lost, that they would not love her any more, that no one would ever love her. From this terror of the castaway her God would save her. He was always there and would always want her.

Later she rejected marriage because she felt that no one could love her and that her marriage would fail because she was unlovable. In her early twenties, desperately longing for some certainty of belief, she suddenly laughed and said to God, "I don't believe in You any more, but isn't it odd as we both know You are there all the time!" Later even that vestige of belief had disappeared for at least ten years before the Nuremberg event, and she was complacently proud to have that superior attitude of the agnostic humanist who had decided that religious belief is childish and scientific skepticism the reasonable view of the enlightened mind.

She wondered why in that 1934 encounter she was not aware of love or anything that could be interpreted as contact with a personal God. One reason she thought was her limited conception of love. Her conclusion is that she was shown love in that encounter but did not recognize it. How could the lamb lost on the mountainside know that the shepherd came in love, not to interfere with his freedom but to rescue him from a tragedy of which he was innocent? As a result of adolescent misapprehensions linked with the castaway fears of childhood she had a deep distrust of love as not for her.

> In my heart I cherished in place of love a sullen hatred of myself and human beings because I felt rejected, a hatred that in its arrogance cut me off from any real human fellowship. Passion I had known, and possessive frenzy. If this was love it seemed the enemy of all freedom, and I felt like a wild bird in a cage when I met it. To have been confronted, then, at this time by a personal Savior demanding a response to love unknown could only have made me desperate. The necessity, indeed the inevitableness, of *unhurrying chase* described in the remaining sections of this book is thence obvious.[18]

She also recognizes that in her mind there may be insufficient distinction between what actually happened and her interpretation of it. The former in spite of all attempts to describe it cannot be told, while the latter is the sum of all the historical and cultural influences to which her society was subjected. In the ancient myth of the encounter in the Garden in the cool of the day, God met Adam where he was. So her encounter could happen

[18] *Ibid.*, p. 37.

only where she was, since even if she had desired, she could not have approached him. From this point she unravels the thread in the following direction.

> Where then was I that I had to come by this path? I was lost and I did not know it. I had chosen to give the apple to Athena, that is I had chosen for myself the way of the intellect. I kept adding to myself smatterings of one language after another, reading widely and indulging in day-dreams of authorship. Church and chapel I despised as outmoded. Everyone whose thought I respected on art, on criticism, on the humanities, viewed religion as escapism, as a fairy-tale for children, above all as an offense against intellectual integrity. Yet because we were Greeks, or Humanists, we were agnostic rather than atheistic keeping in the deepest recesses an altar to the Unknown God, though not in the least desirous of knowing more of Him. It was upon that altar that the fire fell, as if One said, "You want to know? Here then is knowledge!" And I *knew* for always, though precisely what it was I knew my feeble intellect, overthrown and for once admitting the fact, could not tell. All I could stammer was that our view of the universe was about as accurate as that of a mayfly on a summer's day, and that there existed another way of knowing that made our vaunted wisdom look like a child's sand-castles when the tide comes in.[19]

Knowing this much, she was convinced now that she was not alone in the wastes of an empty universe. The encounter had opened a new dimension to her, and all life took on new meaning. She found a new joy in the beauty of nature and a new sense of relatedness to other forms of life. Strangers looking at her smiled and said, "You are happy." And she was enchanted with the joy and wonder of life throbbing in her body and tingling in her finger tips. There was a new exuberance in her teaching as she entered fully into her work with the college students. She felt creative rather than frustrated, and a phrase, "the wells are filling," sang in her mind. Ideas were bubbling for her novel, and she gave the week ends and long holidays to writing.

But then came the first stripping, and the overflowing joy was stopped. A colleague, who interpreted this exuberant joy as gloating over secret success in writing, accused her to the college authorities of neglecting the work she was paid to do in college. Though Ancilla could not see that she was guilty of neglect, she did not defend herself and, when the trouble was over, found it easy to indulge in self-pity. Her exuberance was deflated, and what had been a light touch before became the heavy tread of weariness. Her efforts to write were leaden, and when the novel was finished, no publisher would consider it. Eventually she came to see what she had not guessed before, that her writing was "sheer self-dramatization" and her dreams of

[19] *Ibid.*, p. 36.

authorship the defiant "Now I will show you what I can do" of a child who feels rejected. Otherwise they would not have yielded to the first criticism.

In the months that followed she discovered *The Imitation of Christ,* and the book came alive for her. "Why art thou so grieved for every little matter spoken against thee," she read. "Be more patient of soul, and gird thyself to greater endurance." Behind the austerities of this manual was someone who knew something related to the encounter of Nuremberg. It was like finding the footprints of some earlier traveler along a desolate road. She resolved to set some time aside every day for meditation, to seek other writers who might know what was the intention of the encounter.

It did not occur to her then to seek help from a living person. But a retired teacher returned for one year to active lecturing. Something came in associating with her to know her complete intellectual integrity and her complete humility shown in compassionate love for the most stupid of her students. Without yielding her firm integrity, she knew that the answer was to be found in a spiritual world and that materialistic humanism was not enough. Her knowledge was evidently firsthand from some personal encounter. She knew, and that knowing made her what she was. She was openly religious and participated in a sacramental worship which seemed alien to the scientific mood. Yet without discussing her faith, one could not deny that she was wrapped in a humble love that was rooted in her religion.

The second stripping came one Christmas season when, for reasons she does not explain, Ancilla was compelled to leave her beloved home in the north country and to admit that the only help she could offer the people dearest to her was to leave them, since that was their desire. By that time England had entered World War II, and with her fear of being a castaway, alienated and a stranger to reality, she turned to the darkness of London in the time of the blackout. Though rejected and refused a place in the family festivities, she had yielded and given the Other a place to speak in her. Instead of the anger and self-assertion to be expected, she had felt gentleness and pity for the suffering that must ensue.

Torn from the roots she had called home, she was at first in anguish and then going to a church for the Christmastide service, the terror passed and she felt whole. She was able to see "my mother and my brethren" in every living soul, to find her home in earth itself, with the sky for her roof. As at Nuremberg, she ceased in that moment to be the center of her own life but stepped down denying herself with consent to have it so. She accepted wartime responsibilities gladly to care for children, to show kindness to strangers whether soldiers or refugees, and to shelter her students through long successive nights of bombings. In all this she saw people differently, related to them as one who cares in moments of love and pity for them. A new relationship developed with the students she taught, in which she was more intimate and more deeply charged with mutual respect. "For the first time I went amongst them, as it were, unarmed."

In place of the writing she had thrust upon her an overbalance of lecturing, as she accepted the classes of another teacher in addition to her own, seeking in the college a substitute for all she had lost in the second stripping. She exulted in the new work but had warning from her doctor and to her surprise, when she asked for leave to recuperate, was denied with an icy retort, "You are merely putting yourself before your students." What hurt most was the dawning realization that this was so. She longed for some assurance of love to comfort her but was appalled when love was offered to her by an older student whose need of affection was great. She was unable to cease from rejecting others because she rejected herself. Her dream of heaven was a vast empty room, and she could not accept the doctrine of the incarnation because to her the Father and the Son were too personal. Needing love she could not find or give the love she sought. In her diary she wrote these lines:

> It seems that I am frustrated in my relations with people by a hatred of part of myself. In my gross imaginings my "shadow," in Jung's term normally female and of Prussian characteristics, persecutes a child, always feminine. I am both the persecutor and persecuted in the act, therefore in loving myself I hate myself. I hate the gentle child-like me. I believe that until I come to love, not to hate, the feminine me (whom I killed in my first novel), who is soft, unfretted, without tension, I shall be liable to torment people, be unable to love people and be unable to seek further, since my hatred is blocking the way. But I do not think I can break the "hate" by myself. . . . I think that I must try to see it all afresh as a child does, that I may learn to love instead of to hate. But how? I've over-intellectualized my relations with God and with people.[20]

The third stripping came when, because of limited funds at the college, she was dismissed from her teaching position. After the many years of faithful service, beginning the day at 7:55 A.M. and closing the day at 10:30 P.M. after the last student was locked in, she felt that to be dismissed this side of a pension and without warning seemed unjust. She had thought of herself as part of the college as if it were another body. The students were her children, and to serve them was her life. She loved the building and the silent chapel at night when the students slept. She could not conceive of herself apart from the college or of the college as apart from her. And yet she was a paid hand on three months contract, and now the contract had expired.

From a human point of view it was far worse than the other strippings, but though it was a shock, she knew by this time how to relinquish her

[20] *Ibid.*, pp. 106-7. Used by permission of The Seabury Press.

grasp. Thomas à Kempis had taught her how to be humbled without being humiliated. Again and again she had read his words:

> I am in thy hand; turn me round and turn me back again as thou shalt please. Behold, I am thy servant, prepared for all things; for I desire not to live unto myself, but unto thee; and oh, that I could do it worthily and perfectly!

Perhaps she had come to shelter behind the college. She awoke after deep sleep with a sense of release and freedom, as if something constricting had slipped away.

On the last Wednesday of the term the staff gave a farewell party to those who were departing. This she dreaded at first, but there was a happy, relaxed mood in the group, and a deep feeling of compassion and love flowed out to the ones who had worked and played together for so many years. While the music teacher played Chopin, while thunder rolled over the plain in the darkening light, they gathered in a compact circle around the piano. Held together by the moment of rapturous listening, the sharp edges of individuality blurred, and spirits met and fused. Here, thirteen years after Nuremberg, what had been sought was found, and as she says, the Trinity was complete in the realization of love incarnate in the relationship of person with person.

> In this year, 1947, I knew the glory in the crucified Christ, not alone in the beauty of the earth, not alone in the ineffable otherness of transfiguration, but immanent in the hearts and minds of ordinary men and women. It was the lowest rung of a new ladder, the first step of the next part of the way wherein I was to find a fuller and more permanent fellowship of which it is written that "death itself shall not unbind their happy brotherhood." [21]

This may help us to understand the ongoing forward thrust of religious devotion. Spontaneous prayer may be a momentary cry of distress for help. Disciplined prayer, along whatever route, may be followed in faithful religious practice, in a continuing search for Thou, as steady and persistent as human nature, fickle yet committed, can make of it. Such prayerful seeking and dedicated living becomes a way of devotion.

Having once known the encounter, Ancilla would not give up or turn back in her quest for the ultimate relationship. Her life of religious devotion was not the instantaneous change of a sudden conversion. The encounter was pivotal as a conversion to become the central reality by which every step from then on was guided and evaluated. And yet it was the beginning of a long journey of partial finding and relentless searching for the fuller realization yet to be attained. Her devotion was to keep on following in the face of every loss or setback, learning something crucial in each disappointment

[21] *Ibid.*, p. 124.

and pressing on through every uncertainty as one faithful to the very end.

Her journey was like an extended course of psychotherapy. Though she was unable at that time to confess the inner struggles to a priest or pastor or any human counselor, yet she was awakened and called forth by the invisible encounter. In the light of this relationship she was able to find a new perspective by which to examine the inner recesses of her own life, not once but regularly as one returns to bare his soul before the counselor. As in all counseling or psychotherapy the outward events of the day become the foil and counterthrust by which to react and interact with one another. Every disturbing incident or significant relationship brings to focus the deeper struggle and the hidden motives of one's predicament.

In the long course of her therapy she gives crucial significance to the stripping away of her defenses as outer layers to be peeled off if she was to come to the central core of her own existence and the deepest hunger of her unsatisfied life. Not one of these strippings was she ready or able to peel off by her own volition. In each case the blow came from another person in what at first seemed to be an unkind and unjust act of cruelty. Behind her defenses she could project the blame upon others and feel persecuted, rejected, and undone. But when the defense was peeled away, she could then see herself more clearly and perceive what she had been doing to protect herself from the growth she needed most.

Ultimately, she recognized the work of a loving providence in each of these blows which left her so defenseless. Though she would not have chosen to give up what was most dear to her, and though stripped of one defense she clutched more tightly to the next one, yet she came to see that each loss was opening the way for a more ultimate fulfillment. Though she was reluctant to admit it or accept it, her suffering like the cross she so resisted was to be the cost of her salvation. The pride of intellect, which was her most unyielding defense, was closing other doors and stifling her emotional life, until she was a captive of the prison she made for herself with crossbars of fear and hatred.

She had always known since childhood that love was what she wanted and needed most. But so deep was her distrust of love that she exiled it from her life by hating the self she thought unworthy and incapable of love. To cover the emptiness of that loss, she followed intellectual ambitions ardently and won success enough to hold these trophies above all else as reminders to prove that she was worthy of respect after all.

Is it not amazing that these trophies and defenses were stripped from her without defeating her deeper quest? She might easily have been so embittered by her losses that she would fall into hopeless or angry depression unwilling and unable to continue the struggle. This could have been the outcome except that she was in therapy at the time. She had the encounter to sustain and orient her through these losses toward more ultimate goals. Without the resources of this more ultimate relationship she would have been bereft indeed and might actually have gone down to defeat.

What other than the life of devotion to the ultimate goal could have turned each defeat into a spiritual victory? She might have written another novel, had another home by accepting marriage, or secured another teaching position. But in themselves these alternatives though attractive in the external rewards of prestige, might not have won the victory or brought her to the ultimate goal she sought. To give and receive genuine unselfish love was not to be achieved by any turn of the wheel of external fortune but only by a deep and transforming change within herself.

This is why the encounter was the central event in her life with power ultimately to change all other events: first because the encounter was profoundly inward where the change was needed, and second because it was dynamically related to that Other who was beyond yet evidently concerned for her loveless self. She could not at first recognize that the Other could be Thou, for she had fled from the personal relation to the impersonal security of intellectual abstractions. Only as one by one her defenses fell was she able to tolerate love and be open to the fulfillment of a loving relationship. Perhaps because the Other was so invisible and elusive, she was first able to respond to the Presence with knowledge, before she was able to give love to or receive love from a person.

When finally she was able to experience love in the human relations with her fellow teachers, she had already been standing at the threshold of loving God. Her devotion through the years of searching since the encounter at Nuremberg was not in vain, for she had given up one defense after another and gradually was coming to respond to the other as a Person. Recently she had been reading Martin Buber and learning at last that "Thou" was a possible greeting by which to address the Other. Her study of the devotional classics and her knowledge of other persons who were fulfilled in love through religious encounter prepared the way for her own discovery.

In the culminating steps of her devotional therapy she was to give and receive love in the religious dimension of I and Thou. This she found at last to heal the irreconcilable conflicts of the years and bring her into a dynamic wholeness unknown before. The resistance against the church, the incarnation of Father and Son, and the sacramental symbolism dissolved, as she was drawn into the fellowship of a welcoming congregation. No longer a castaway she had the firm sense of belonging to a beloved community and open to participate more freely in the mutual giving of love. But it was, as she says, only a beginning, "a turning of the page of my lesson book revealing how much more there was to learn." [22]

[22] *Ibid.*, p. 32.

# 8 WORSHIP

## 1. *The Search for God*

*Hindu Worship.* At the Ramakrishna Chapel of the Hindu Vedanta Society a service of worship was conducted by the swami. The altar of carved mahogany is dedicated to God, identified by the Sanskrit character *Om,* and bears the motto: "Truth is One, men call it by various names." Candles were burning, and the altar was surrounded by a profuse array of flowers, fruits, and emblems for use in ceremonies.

The swami entered, removed his shoes, and seated himself beside the altar, legs crossed, hands folded, eyes closed in silent prayer. Then, following the prescribed ritual and employing the appropriate Hindu words, chants, gestures, and implements, he enacted the earnest drama of the human spirit in search of God. The service proceeded for two hours in the following order:

1. Consecration of the room.
2. Invocation, asking the blessings of the different aspects of God, fingering the beads of a rosary, and bowing with folded hands.
3. Prayer:
   "May Thou be installed in the hearts of all devotees.
   May Thou be the Source of their knowledge.
   May Thy Divine Love be with them.
   We are worshiping Thee that thy eternal glory may be with all, that all beings may be illumined and led to Thy realization."
4. Removal of evil influences from the room with flowers, rice, and mustard seed; drawing a line of light around the worshiper as well as the devotees; clapping and snapping fingers around his head.
5. Consecration of water for worship, with gestures, prayers, and blessings.
6. Purification of the prayer rug, with prayers and a flower.
7. Purification of flowers and other emblems of worship, including eight large silver trays of various fruits, milk, honey, and holy water from the Ganges River.
8. Transformation of the constituent parts of the body. Then transformation

of the whole body, by awakening latent Divine power, through gestures and prayers.

9. *Pranayama,* or rhythmic breathing through alternate nostrils.
10. Awakening all the mystic centers of the body by praying, chanting, and touching these parts of the body.
11. Installation of the Deity within the worshiper, bowing to the floor, praying aloud, and placing a flower in the hair at the center of the head.
12. *Pranayama* (rhythmic breathing).
13. Worship of the different aspects of God: Creative, Preservative, Destructive, Masculine, and Feminine; different powers and incarnations including Christ, Buddha, Krishna, and others with five offerings: perfume, flowers, incense, light, and food.
14. *Dhyana,* or meditation in silence—body poised, eyes closed, mind focused in concentration.
15. Mental worship with the particles and chemicals of the body, mind, and emotions of love, patience, devotion, and so on.
16. Purification of another receptacle of water.
17. *Dhyana* (meditation).
18. Worship of the particular Aspect of God for the day—the Divine Mother, with offerings of flowers, milk, honey, water, use of bell, relics, mystic, circles with incense, kneeling, and chanting.
19. Special worship of other Holy Personalities, incarnations as above. Members of congregation offering flowers to Christ, Ramakrishna, and the Holy Mother. Reading from the Gospel of John, chapter 1.
20. Surrender of the fruit of worship to God.
21. Benediction: a prayer for peace, harmony, joy, and bliss in the world.

*Hebrew Worship.* The congregation gathered together for the Sabbath service at Temple Israel. In contrast to the elaborate symbolism of the Hindu worship this service was simplified to accent the naturalness of communion with God. The marble pulpit was decorated with only two stars of David and two palm branches. Large seven-branch candlesticks at either side upheld electric candles. The ark directly behind the pulpit was concealed by sliding doors bearing the star of David. Marble pillars stood at either side, and the eternal flame was burning above. The choir loft with organ and musicians was concealed by a plush curtain. Members of the congregation were provided with prayer books and hymnals, to participate at the direction of the rabbi in the following order of worship:

1. Invocation.
2. Hymn.
3. Prayers in Hebrew and English by the rabbi and congregation.
4. Chants by the cantor.
5. Responsive readings from the Psalter.
6. Hymn.

7. Prayers in Hebrew and English by the rabbi and congregation.
8. Prayers before the ark.
9. Presentation of the scroll (Torah) from the ark with blessings.
10. Reading from the Torah, or sacred law, by a thirteen-year-old boy (the confirmand) and his teacher in the religious school.
11. Prophetic reading and interpretation of a chapter in Jeremiah by the boy to be confirmed, followed by his pledge to uphold the faith.
12. Prayer on replacing the Torah in the ark.
13. Confirmation of the boy by the rabbi, welcoming him into the membership of the temple and eloquently charging him to be loyal to God.
14. Sermon by the rabbi on "Life."
15. Prayer for the sick, the refugees, and the suffering, for the nation and the victory of democracy, for all peoples and the brotherhood of man.
16. Prayer for the eternal welfare of the dead and the comfort of the mourners.
17. Benediction in Hebrew.
18. Organ postlude.

*Roman Catholic Worship.* It was Sunday morning and four masses were celebrated in the Corpus Christi Church. The people assembled in reverent spirit, genuflecting toward the altar before entering the pew and then kneeling to pray silently, guided by the rosary or the missal. The Mass was conducted in Latin, to be followed by the congregation either in Latin or in English with appropriate responses. The theme of the ninth Sunday after Pentecost, "Thou hast not known the time of thy visitation," was the need to profit by the lessons of history. The priest was attired in green vestments, the seasonal symbol of hope, carried a veiled chalice, and was accompanied by two altar boys.

1. Mass began at the foot of the altar (pure white, holding the crucifix with kneeling angelic figures, white candles, the tabernacle, and altar cards), as the priest made the sign of the cross, saying "In the name of the Father and of the Son and of the Holy Ghost. Amen. I will go into the altar of God. To God who giveth joy to my youth." Confessing and asking forgiveness, the priest ascended to the altar.
2. Introit (to enter), a psalm signifying entrance to the presence of God, read by the celebrant from the Epistle (right) side of the altar.
3. The Kyrie, "Lord, have mercy upon us," followed by the Gloria.
4. Prayer of invocation and thanksgiving.
5. Epistle, I Cor. 10.
6. Gradual (*gradus* step from where it was formerly sung), Ps. 8.
7. Preparation for Gospel (at middle of altar): "The Lord be in my heart and on my lips, that I may worthily and becomingly announce his Gospel. Amen." (Signing forehead to understand it, lips to declare it, and heart to love it.)

8. Gospel Luke 19. (People standing.) Priest read from the Gospel side of the altar, then kissed the sacred page and prayed: "May our sins be blotted out by the words of the Gospel."
9. Creed (Nicene, composed A.D. 325). Priest then faced the people. "The Lord be with you." The people respond, "And with thy spirit."
10. Sermon and announcements from the pulpit.
11. Offertory, Ps. 17. Collection received by ushers from the people. Priest uncovered the chalice.
12. Offerings of Bread and Wine. Priest lifted the bread on the paten with prayers, adding water to wine, bowing before altar. Then he blessed the bread and wine, washed his fingers, kissed the altar, and turned to the people, who responded, "May the Lord receive this sacrifice at thy hands, to the praise and glory of His Name, to our own benefit, and to that of all His Holy Church. Amen."
13. Secret (from Latin for "separated"), a petition for acceptance of gifts now separated from secular use.
14. The Preface, a hymn of praise and thanksgiving to exalt the mind for sacred actions.
15. The Canon (Greek word for rule or standard), six prayers of remembrance and four prayers of offering, half before and half after the Consecration.
16. Consecration of Bread and Wine. Priest genuflecting elevated the Host, then the Chalice, Bell rang thrice for each event. Prayers.
17. Communion. Priest received Sacred Host and Precious Blood, and distributed wafer to each of the faithful who knelt at the altar rail. Prayers and responses. Priest closed tabernacle and rinsed Chalice with wine for purification.
18. Communion Verse and Response.
19. Postcommunion Prayer: "May this heavenly Sacrament be to us, O Lord, a renewal of both mind and body, so that as we perform this act of worship we may also feel its effect."
20. Final Blessing: "May Almighty God bless you, Father, Son, and Holy Ghost. Amen."
21. The Last Gospel. (People standing.) John 1.
22. Prayers after Mass. Addressed to Mary, God, St. Michael, and concluding responsively:

"Most sacred Heart of Jesus,
Have mercy on us."

*Protestant Worship.* Sunday morning worship in the Copley Methodist Church represents another design in the human search for God. The movement of worship is clearly marked in four stages of advance, as definite as altar stairs ascending to the living Presence. Not content to remain in the sanctuary as a sheltered place, the worship culminates in a dedication of life to go forth in service to the world. The order of service is a unity of contrast and response in a rhythm of alternation, yet moving together as a united congregation to the encounter. In Protestant tradition worship has been known as a "meeting" in which persons meet together to meet God.

*I. Adoration of God*

1. Quiet. (Let the people be in devout meditation.)
2. Organ Prelude, "Prayer."
3. Processional Hymn, "Ancient of Days."
4. Call to Worship (by the minister).
5. Invocation (by the minister).
6. Sanctus (the people uniting): "Therefore with angels and arch-angels, and with all the company of heaven, we laud and magnify thy glorious name, evermore praising thee, and saying": Choir: "Holy, holy, holy, Lord God of hosts, heaven and earth are full of thy glory: Glory be to thee, O Lord, most high!"

*II. Confession of Sin*

7. Prayer of Confession (the people uniting): "Almighty and most merciful Father, we have erred and strayed from thy ways like lost sheep. We have followed too much the devices and desires of our own hearts. We have offended against thy holy laws. We have left undone those things which we ought to have done, and we have done those things which we ought not to have done. But thou, O Lord, have mercy upon us. Spare thou those, O God, who confess their faults. Restore thou those who are penitent; according to thy promises declared unto mankind in Christ Jesus our Lord. And grant, O most merciful Father, for his sake, that we may hereafter live a godly, righteous, and sober life; to the glory of thy holy name. Amen."
8. Choral Response, "The Lord is in his holy temple."
9. The Sacrament of Silence. Relaxation of body, mind, and spirit. Listen for the Voice of God.
10. Angelus Bells.
11. Words of Assurance (by the minister).
12. Word of Forgiveness (by the minister).
13. The Lord's Prayer.

*III. Affirmation of Faith*

14. Message in Song, "O rest in the Lord."
15. Psalter, "An Unfaltering Trust," responsive reading.
16. Gloria Patri.
17. First Lesson, "The Lord's Promise," Jer. 29:12-13.
18. Second Lesson, "The Comforting Spirit," John 14:15-25.
19. Call to Prayer:
    *Minister:* The Lord be with you.
    *Choir:* And with thy spirit.
    *Minister:* Let us pray. O Lord, show thy mercy upon us.
    *Choir:* And grant us thy salvation.
    *Minister:* O God, make clean our hearts within us.

*Choir:* And take not thy Holy Spirit from us.

20. Collect for Peace (all uniting): "Our God and Father, whose rule is over men and nation; bless the President of the United States and all those associated with him in authority, and grant that our country may take her rightful place in the council of nations, in securing righteousness and freedom for mankind, and in forging and maintaining a peace that shall be just, merciful, and enduring for the welfare of the whole world; through Jesus Christ our Lord. Amen."
21. Silent Intercession.
22. Prayer of Communion. Choral Response.

*IV. Dedication of Life*

23. The Offertory, Presentation, and Doxology.
24. Hymn, "There's a Wideness in God's Mercy."
25. Sermon, "With You Always."
26. Recessional Hymn, "Are Ye Able?"
27. Silence (the people bowed in prayerful dedication).
28. Benediction. Choral Response.
29. Organ Postlude, "Grand Choeur."

These orders of worship come from three religions, rich in centuries of experience and tradition. Each one is unique in the features, symbols, and beliefs that constitute its distinctive life. Yet all manifest significant traits in common. The dominant motif in every religion is the search for God with ultimate concern for the meaning and purpose of life. A sense of supreme values pervades the entire process, and with this an earnest determination to lay aside the unreal for the real, the transient for the eternal good. Physical objects are not despised; they are consecrated as a bridge to the spiritual. Natural values are not denied but blessed as means to intrinsic divine value. Human efforts are not neglected but are dedicated to the service of God and man.

These four contemporary journeys Godward may serve to introduce us to the ways of worship. We may be mystified by the forms and symbols of worship until we discover the purpose that underlies and runs through them. To discover this direction is to understand the heart of worship and see the devotion that overflows in the artistry of many radiant expressions. To explore the motives and methods of worship is to enter more deeply into the psychology of religious experience.

## 2. *Forms and Symbols*

Worship has an eventful history. The word is Anglo-Saxon in origin, but the experience belongs to every people. A contraction of "worth-ship," it refers to value. Worship is reverence for the Author of life and true values. In practice worship consists of acts designed to establish a better relationship with this ultimate Being. Men may not agree in their conceptions of who and what this Being is, nor in the methods and devices by which a better relationship is to be established; but most of them do unite in concern for the meaning and value of life. Magic and science attempt to secure values by mechanical means, understanding natural laws, and controlling impersonal forces. In contrast to these mechanical methods, religion seeks values by personal devotion and reverent appreciation.

Forms of worship present a variety of mysterious activities. The mystery is essential to the adventure, for worship seeks to cope with the deepest mysteries of life and death. The ultimate fate of values is ever shrouded in mystery, and worshipers stand in awe of the controlling Power that dispenses life and death, good and evil. Yet every act of worship has a meaning, if one is initiated to its secret. The outsider is often baffled because he does not understand what the action means to the actors. To understand worship one must be a worshiper. Appreciation is the essence of understanding, for only as we sense the symbolic value can we comprehend the meaning.

To observe every worshiping group from primitive tribe to city cathedral is not possible for any one student. If we are to view these many forms in perspective, we must rely upon the reports of others who describe what they have seen. A survey of worship in action will show the following typical forms in general use.

*a*) *The dance and procession* may be solemn in magnificent pageantry or exciting in ecstatic frenzy. Dances are employed religiously by American Indians, the Negroid peoples, whirling dervishes of Semitic tradition, and Hindu worshipers of Siva and Kali. They dramatize tradition, prepare for expeditions, or induce excitement felt as divine possession. Processions are more evident in religious ceremonies. A gold effigy of Osiris was daily presented to the setting sun, taken for a ceremonial voyage, or carried around the walls of Memphis. In the New Year festival of Babylon images of gods arrived from other temples, as Anu from Erech and Enlil from Nippur, "to take the hands of the great Lord, Marduk." [1] Processions appear in the festivities of Greek mystery cults, Jewish pilgrimages to the temple, and Moslem pilgrimages to Mecca. In these, and in Christian church worship, the procession signifies approaching the divine Presence, progressing toward the religious goal.

*b*) *Invocation* is the calling of a superior being to be present. It may be a vocal salutation, as an opening request in a worship ceremony; or

[1] S. H. Hooke, ed., *Myth and Ritual* (London: Oxford University Press, 1933), pp. 19-24.

the invitation may be extended in artistic representation of the deity and in religious symbols. Sketches and paintings of religious objects have been discovered in paleolithic caves of France, Spain, and Algeria. Sand painting and totem portrayal survive among American Indians; the modeling and carving of images has wide religious use. Judaic, Moslem, and some Christian bodies have prohibited images and turned to architecture rich in symbols and eloquent in religious meaning. Altars, pyramids and obelisks, minarets and mosques, Gothic arches and lofty spires, are invitations to meet God.

*c*) *Dramatic ritual* seeks to enact the enterprises that provide values for the group. In hunting or combat the desired results are dramatized to prepare for the event. Agricultural ceremonies enact planting and fertility, rain making, harvesting, and threshing. Myths and legends are dramatized to revive heroic exploits and honor the ancestral spirits. A ritual pattern in Egypt and Asia dramatized the death, resurrection, combat with enemies, sacred marriage, and triumph of the god. Candle burning to signify the divine presence, incense to indicate the rising spirit of prayer, sacrifice, and dedication, are dramatic elements prevalent in many religions. The Roman Catholic Mass is a dramatic portrayal of the sacrificial work of Christ.

*d*) *Sacred music,* vocal and instrumental, is widely used in worship. Rhythmic beating of tom-toms and vocal chants are used by Africans and Amerindians. Wooden drums are used in the intonation of Buddhist scriptures. Temple bells are as common in China, India, and Japan as church bells in Europe and America, calling the faithful to worship and the Deity to listen. The Hopi Indians conduct a flute ceremony with prayers and offerings for nine days. Psalms and laments have been sung in Hebrew worship from the time of the Exodus. The chorus had a prominent part in the Greek tragedies, celebrating religious mythology. Christian choral music has developed stirring harmonies that with congregational singing express the emotions of profound worship.

*e*) *Prayer* is an act of worship that takes many forms. Mechanical devices, such as prayer wheels, placing prayers in wells, waves, fires, and so forth, are little more than incantations. Repetition of sacred names, ejaculations, and ecstatic cries may have earnest appeal of urgent need and sincere devotion. Fixation of attention by posture, closed eyes, controlled gaze, or rosary seeks to avoid distraction and concentrate wholly upon the divine Being. Prayers may be called out in a loud voice to attract the deity or brought to a vigil of silence to create intimate communion. Prayer is the heart of worship. Without divine visitation and communion worship is not complete.

*f*) *Sacrifice* has been practiced in the worship of most religions. The Hebrews offered the first fruits of the harvest and flock in gratitude for divine blessings. The Vedic Aryans poured melted butter on the fire; Romans made a libation of wine; Brahmins offered horse sacrifices; followers of Mithra sacrificed a bull. Human sacrifices were offered by the Aztecs and Maoris. Offerings express gratitude or petition, expiate sin, dedicate for sacramental use, seal vows and covenants. To Christians the crucifixion of Jesus is a vicarious sacrifice for the sins of the world, reconciling God and man. Feasts are historically associated with sacrifices and renewal of devotion. The Jewish Passover and the Christian sacrament of Holy Communion (Eucharist) are feasts to re-create spiritual life.

g) *Confession and purification* recognize the evils of life and seek to dispose of them. Primitive evils may be contagious powers to quarantine by taboo or magic. With the rise of conscience evils become sins to be expiated. Lustrations are widely used by Japanese, Egyptians, Greeks, Hindus, and others for purification. The Christian rite of baptism is in the purifying tradition. Fire is a purifying energy among Celts, Romans, and Persians. Heaping sins of the people upon a scapegoat driven into the wilderness (Hebrews) or upon boats sent out to sea (Japanese) is another purifying ceremony. Navajo chant practices for the removing of evil and illness require an elaborate use of prayer sticks, plumed wands, paddles, snake sticks, ashes, powder, feathers, jewels, reeds, mush offerings, arrows, whistles, bull-roarers, flints, clubs, chant tokens, rattles, and medicines. Confession of sin brings the purification to a higher level of repentance, forgiveness, and renewal.

h) *Recitation* forms a natural part of worship. No people is without traditions cherished as a unique heritage. The reciting of these traditions is significant for the instruction of the young and for the interpretation of customs and events. Mythology is the philosophy of primitive man, attempting to answer the mysterious questions of creation, nature, life, and destiny. Every mature religion has its bible to preserve the words of life, the true teachings and history of the faith. Sacred scriptures are accepted as divine revelation, to be heeded and followed by all who profess the faith. Professing the faith brings the creed to a lofty place in worship as the affirmation and avowal of the faithful. The synagogue service of the Jews opens with the Shema and calls upon laymen to come forward and read from the Torah. Moslems listen with rapt attention to the reciting of the Koran. Christian worship gives a large place to reading and preaching from the Bible. By meditating upon the inspired word, sacred traditions are enshrined in living personalities and come to new birth through the labors of many minds.

Divergent as these forms of worship appear, they converge into a clear pattern of unity. Coming from every time and place of human habitation, these varieties of aspiration have a common center. If the symbolic meaning of each form is followed, they will all point to God, who cares and responds to the needs of persons. It is evident from a study of religious experience that worship is a reverent outreach of the human spirit toward Thou with ultimate concern.

## 3. *Why Worship?*

To understand an act of worship, one must explore what it means to the worshiper. Why does he worship? What does he seek? How does he feel about it? Each form and symbol has a history in the tradition of the group. Every worshiping attitude and aspiration has a purpose reaching out to some desired goal. Special acts carry specific meanings, to be understood by participation and interpretation. From these cultic events, general trends broaden out into universal principles of worship which we find to be procession, invocation, dramatization, music, prayer, sacrifice, purification, and recitation.

To ask why men worship in these ways is to open the question of motivation. What moves such different people to do such similar things? Evidently there are universal needs that urge their claim to be satisfied in typical ways. Human needs we have seen to be dynamic tensions arising from organic and psychic urges tending goalward. Many needs are unconscious, yet on the way to conscious awareness pain from within and stimulation from without bring them to attention. Persons who are seeking goals come to sharpen the focus of these needs and develop methods for meeting them. Acts of worship are methods of expressing and seeking fulfillment of vital needs. A psychological analysis of worship activities may clarify these motives.

There are many specific needs which human beings seek to fulfill in one way or another. Any need which is urgently desired may be sought by religious means in prayer and worship. By assiduous observation of audible and written petitions one might collect an extensive list of what is prayed for, covering a wide range of diversified needs. But such lists would be mere collections, falling short of a theory by which to comprehend the deeper meaning of such behavior.

In Chapter Two we considered four psychological theories of religion: conflictual, collective, personalist, and interpersonal. Each of these theories throws some light upon religious behavior, but in seeking to understand the meaning of worship we find the interpersonal theory most illuminating. According to this theory there is one need more basic than all others, the need for responsive relationship. Things may react, as when a rubber ball is thrown against a wall and bounces back into your hands or when light is reflected in a mirror to portray your image. We may work or play with the mechanical reactions of physical and chemical energies. But what a person needs most of all is a relationship of mutual response, which is very different from the reaction of a thing. Nothing less than a person will respond to me as a person.

I have offered the hypothesis that spontaneous prayer is a cry for an answering response, and traced this behavior from the imploring cry of the infant to the predicament of the finite person, whatever his age or condition, reaching out for some more ultimate answer to his insufficiency. We have seen how the persistent search of I for Thou to complete this crucial incompleteness has followed the disciplines of the mystic, the prophet, the priest, and the intellectual as religious ways of life. Now as we consider the meaning of worship, we find no better place on which to stand than the hypothesis of the cry of finite persons who seek an answering response. For worship may be viewed as socialized prayer, the cries of individuals joined together in search of Thou.

Whenever individual persons co-ordinate their behavior in unison, some discipline is required to synchronize what would otherwise be chaotic expression. Consequently, we are not surprised to find that worship follows a discipline to guide the participants. A religious community worshiping together will follow an order of worship, as we have noted in the first section of this chapter, established by a tradition and guided by a leader in the role of priest, though he may be designated by some other title. Congregational worship may vary from low to high degrees of formality but is everywhere subject to a traditional discipline and usually guided by a priestly leader who co-ordinates the praying of individuals according to a standard procedure. One may think of the Religious Society of Friends as an exception, as they wait in silence for the spirit to move anyone to speak, yet their behavior is regulated by a governing tradition, and elders are recognized as leaders whose words have authority in the democratic context and who close the meeting by shaking hands with the neighbor to symbolize the continuing unity of fellowship.

The theory of worship here proposed is based upon the first principle of interpersonalism that no finite person is complete in himself, but that every person most persistently seeks a responsive relationship with another person. From this basic need persons call for answering response in prayer and worship. In worship the religious community joins together to reinforce the outreach for completion in two dimensions: the vertical outreach to Thou in the ultimate sense and the horizontal outreach to other persons who unite in the fellowship of worship. In this way worship becomes the united cry of a congregation seeking the answering response with ultimate concern.

In worship we therefore find a clear demonstration of the dialogic relation, no less than in the meeting of the individual person with person. The language of worship is the language of address, and the expectation is always to invite a response. The mood of worship is the hushed excitement of the encounter, by which the worshiper comes before Thou to be humbled and elevated in overpowering mystery of the Presence. The symbols of worship carry emotional value of profound and hidden meanings, which signify to those who comprehend them the response from beyond to the human cry.

To trace the intricate design of worship in these symbols of response will clarify the basic outreach of man for relationship. Returning to the forms of worship noted in the section above as most universal among the religions of the world, let us consider what they indicate of the I-Thou relationship. We shall find that each one elaborates by symbolic expression the religious quest for the answering response. The procession will signify approaching Thou. The invocation will recognize and address Thou. The dramatization will anticipate the response of Thou. The music will offer an outburst of joy in the presence of Thou. Prayer will ask Thou to see the need of the finite creature and enter into relation with him. Sacrifice will offer to Thou some token of self-giving in this relationship. Purification will acknowledge human unworthiness and seek to be cleansed and renewed by Thou. Recitation will affirm the wonder of this encounter with Thou and the truth so revealed to guide the finite person in his journey.

*a*) *Approaching* is the intention evident in religious processions. Why do religious persons want to approach objects of worship? Curiosity, wonder, fascination, are interests that motivate approach. Insects and animals are lured by bright colors, moving objects, attractive odors, and the like. Symbols used in worship may also attract by sensual appeal, yet there are deeper motives that draw men to an invisible presence. Otto[2] describes this as the appeal of a tremendous mystery arousing awe before the overpowering majesty, fascination in the solemn beauty, and rapture in the vital urgency of divine energy. These exciting emotional responses are directed to a Wholly Other not easy to approach yet earnestly desired, unapproachable yet inescapable. Fear and hope mingle in approaching ultimate Mystery with awe-filled yet faithful concern. Trust and affection are stronger motives of approach and draw creatures to Creator, as children to parents, in love and confidence.

*b*) *Recognizing* is the intention of invocation. Approaching leads to recognition, as when two men study each other first as strangers, then, seeing the identity of a friend, smile, nod, and speak. So the worshiper in approaching a divine Person gives salutation as a sign of recognition. Invo-

[2] *Op. cit.*, pp. 12-41.

cations are offered in terms of address, to announce arrival and open communication. There is no worship without recognition of One who is worthy of worship, near enough to exchange greetings. Whatever the sign of this presence, the meaning is clearly to recognize Thou and seek a mutual response.

*c*) *Anticipating* is a mood of expectation native to worship. "Religion is anticipated attainment." [3] Not content with life as it is, worshipers hope to find a larger fulfillment. To realize this, religious ceremonies dramatize attainments, as planting and harvesting festivals or rising from the dead. Worship focuses attention upon the goal sought so dramatically that it becomes a powerful incentive to attainment. The function of ritual is to anticipate goals, to arouse zealous purposes, and to enact the efforts needed to achieve them. Such religious action is neither isolated nor mechanical, but continual and interpersonal. Worship approaches Thou reverently to address and enter into his presence with joy and gratitude or confession of need and concern. Anticipation is essential to realization.

*d*) *Praising* is a rapturous expression of gratitude that follows recognition and anticipation. To recognize divine beauty, truth, and goodness is to admire a glorious splendor. Adoration is the outreach of admiration toward the perfection one desires yet falls short of. Holding joyous attention upon God as the ideal to emulate is an elevating experience that sublimates the petty impulses of life to nobler harmonies. To anticipate these gains is to believe them genuine, already in the process of attainment. For such progress one feels gratitude and turns to thanksgiving. Praise may thus move from the Giver to the gifts received in gratitude, returning again to express appreciation to the Giver in a constant round of rejoicing. These notes of praise and rejoicing find wings in hymn and poetry. Sacred music rises to melody and harmony in expressing this delight, as a fountain overflows irrepressibly.

*e*) *Asking* is what prayer means to the average person. Worship is more than asking, but it cannot be less. Asking may seem natural to children, but it has important prerequisites. No one asks until he wants and knows what he wants. Again, no one asks except where interpersonal relationships invite the expectation of a kindly response. Knowing how, when, and whom to ask is a basic question for everyone. Not to ask indicates false pride and mock independence. Worship is an attitude of humility in which one acknowledges dependence upon greater powers and faith in their kindness and mercy. In this attitude it is as appropriate to ask for future goods as to give thanks for past ones. Asking is an expression of courtesy, not to command or demand, not to receive dumbly, but to offer petitions in deference and trust.

[3] Hocking, *The Meaning of God in Human Experience*, p. 31.

*f*) *Offering* is the act of giving some valued thing to another. This is the intention of the sacrifices which have taken so many forms in the history of religion. But why do people give to One who seems to have everything without lack? Evidently because giving is itself a value. There may be uses for gifts in a religious cause, as giving for missions or to feed the starving. But greater than any gift is the act of giving itself. The religious meaning of giving is dedication of life to God. When it is voluntary, as the free offering of life for others, it becomes a holy deed of complete devotion. "Greater love hath no man than this, that a man lay down his life for his friends." (John 15:13.) No worship is complete without a genuine offering in this sense, to carry the devotion from emotion to consecrated action. Such offering has objective value and influence beyond the individual as a means of outgoing affectionate energy.

*g*) *Renewing* is one of the elemental needs of life, because of fatigue, error, guilt, and conflict. Distressed by depletions, mistakes, quarrels, sins, and frustrations, the finite person will ever need to be renewed. Worship is a means of grace by which to restore broken spirits. Rites of purification give symbolic cleansing to cancel evils and heal diseases. In the temple vision of Isaiah the holiness of God made his own guilt unbearable until his lips were cleansed with a live coal from the altar. (6:1-9.) Standing in the divine presence makes this need acute and demands purgation to renew life to wholesome purity and effective power. Until one is cleansed and energized, he is not fit for the religious life and mission. He will need to return again and again to worship, to renew the vows and resources of heroic living. For renewal is a constant need and worship a constant opportunity.

*h*) *Affirming* is a constructive act of rejoicing in the truth. No mere dumb assent is worship, but a creative assertion of what makes life most worth living. To recite a creed is to declare a faith with conviction, as a code to live by and die for. To read scripture is to discover new insights and recover lost treasure. It is easy to forget, and even the greatest experiences fade in time. Only renewed insights survive. To Wordsworth poetry arises from "emotion recollected in tranquillity." Sperry points out that remembered emotion may be more significant than emotion first felt. He finds worship an "occasion for that recollection in tranquillity by which we possess ourselves permanently of the certitudes which have been ours." [4] The great affirmations bear reaffirming, for instead of wearing out, they gain in meaning as we grow in understanding.

We have noted that all forms and intentions in worship point to a central focus of devotion known as God. The verbs expressing these intentions are active, transitive verbs. Worship is an act moving out to a Goal. A wor-

[4] *Reality in Worship* (New York: The Macmillan Co., 1925), pp. 194-96.

shiper is not passive; neither is he content to talk to himself in autosuggestion. He is reaching out to Thou, who has what he lacks and who may fulfill what he needs. Worship is approaching, recognizing, anticipating, and praising God; asking, offering, renewing, and affirming God. God is the goal of every act of worship. Men may not agree as to what God is, nor be able to prove that he is; but in worship they believe they are addressing Thou, who is good enough and great enough to respond.

True worship, therefore, has objective reference. Pratt [5] has distinguished between subjective and objective worship. Objective worship aims to affect or communicate with God; subjective worship seeks to influence the worshiper. From historical and contemporary practices he shows how the objective worship, as in the Catholic Mass, turns from man to God. Cathedrals are constructed and ceremonies conducted for God, not for the congregation, who may be unable to see, hear, or understand the words intoned in a foreign language as the priest faces the altar and addresses God, who is the Host. Subjective worship in ancient Buddhism or modern humanism ignores God as too unreal or impersonal to hear prayer, and performs rituals for the human effect. Much of Protestant worship is subjective in aim, placing a pulpit at the center, reading and preaching, singing and enjoying harmonies, to create a mood and instruct the congregation.

In conclusion Pratt shows that subjective worship follows the law of diminishing returns. If the churchgoer understands that public ceremonies are put on as a show to make a psychological impression on him, he will not be deeply impressed. He may be entertained and edified, but more as a passive spectator than as an earnest participant. Eventually he will come to distrust the sincerity of the performance staged for his benefit. For if nothing objectively real happens at church, his attendance will become a matter of convenience, mood, and impulse, subject to the relative interest of competing attractions. Lack of reality is a cause of indifference toward worship.

We may go a step further, to ask whether the subjective aim without objective reference is worship at all. If worship is reverence for Thou, then activities which ignore God fall short of the essence of worship. A visit to a prominent humanist society will be instructive. The "Sunday Morning Meeting"—not designated divine worship—was held in a theater. The service opened with organ preludes and continued with a hymn by Rudyard Kipling addressed to the "Spirit of Truth." Instead of Scripture the leader read a passage from the dean of an Eastern university. In place of prayer he gave an "Aspiration on the Rising Generation," followed by organ re-

[5] *Op. cit.*, pp. 290-309.

sponse and instrumentation by a string trio: The second hymn was addressed to the congregation:

Who will say the world is dying?
  Who will say our prime is past?
Sparks of good, within us, lying,
  Flash, and will flash to the last.
Still the race of hero spirits
  Pass the lamp from hand to hand,
And the growing light of knowledge
  Casts its rays o'er every land.

In place of the sermon came an address, "What Happens to a College Student's Religion?" showing how the study of sciences makes God improbable and unnecessary. This was followed by an "Offertory" played by the string trio, during which the collection was taken, offered not to God but to the society to defray expenses of the meeting. The final hymn was a poem, "Youth," by Robert Bridges.

There was no benediction, but instead "Closing Words" by the leader, followed by an organ postlude. Mottoes headed the pages of the calendar with the sentiments: "Enlightened Reason Our Guide in Religion," "Mental Freedom Our Method in Religion," "Human Service Our Aim in Religion." The first page declared: "We cannot fathom the Infinite. It is enough for us to love and serve humanity."

This was an hour well spent, for the address was eloquent, the thoughts read were noble, the music was delightful. But was it worship? There was no prayer, no recognition of God, no confession, offering, or dedication to God. To affirm human values is good; but the deeper needs of life, conscious and unconscious, cry out for higher resources. Worship is that deepest of hungers seeking by ultimate concern to commune with Thou. The health-giving whole-making power of worship aims in this meeting to be a creative source of new life.

## 4. *The Art of Worship*

Worship is a fine art. It is the highest of all arts in aim, for it seeks to reach divine perfection. It is the broadest of all, employing every art—architecture, painting, sculpture, stained glass, rhythm, music, literature, drama, speech—in the creative syntheses of worship. It is the deepest of all arts in significance, portraying the adventure of the human soul, the dramatic issue of man's eternal destiny. It is the most difficult of all arts, requiring insight to true values and skill in presenting their infinite mysteries. It is often a neglected art, for many do not comprehend its meaning or learn how to progress in its difficult attainments.

Worship is a journey. It is a quest for real beauty, the beauty that is objective and enduring, the beauty of God the altogether lovely. It seeks to incarnate the beauty of holiness, that human life may be possessed of divine beauty. It hopes to achieve the elevation of spirit from the sordid to the sublime. If religion is the human search for divine good, worship is the highway of this search. It is a search for the ultimate answer, the eternal good beyond our limitations and frustrations.

There is room and need for both objective and subjective aims in worship. Yet Pratt is correct in maintaining that objective worship achieves the best subjective effects. To meet ultimate Reality in the eventful experiences of adoration, prayer, and dedication renews the worshiper. If one cannot believe or find an objective Thou, the problem of worship is baffling. Humanists meet to affirm their beliefs or aspirations toward enlarging human values. By honest sharing and noble utterances they give social support to the values essential to human service and progress. To hear but the echo of one's own voice is reassuring to that extent. Yet those who feel a response from the God they worship will find the effects are very different. They taste the joy of communion with Thou, in whose presence are fulfillment and peace. "Our hearts are restless till they find rest in Thee," said Augustine. Worship is an ardent preference for the highest perfection in beauty, goodness, and reality. It is therefore a pilgrimage from this world to another, from human to divine perspective, from man to God.

Worship follows a rhythm. Seeking and finding, asking and receiving, calling and answering, indicate the responsive action and reaction of man and the mysterious energy he calls God. Worship is the response of man to the invitation of God and the response of God to the petition of man. In this way an order of worship is to be understood. Beneath these responses flows a deeper rhythm, the rising tide of worship's flood from lower to higher levels, the progressive movement of devotion to heights of spiritual communion. Hindu and Hebrew prayers reveal this outreach and upreach for the divine.

From the unreal lead me to the real.
From darkness lead me to light.
From death to Immortality. [6]

Out of the depths have I cried unto thee, O Lord.
Lord, hear my voice; let thine ears be attentive to the voice of my supplications. (Ps. 130:1-2.)

[6] *Brihadaranyaka,* I, iii, 28.

The arts of worship are devoted to meeting God. Each religious group has its characteristic way of conducting worship. The ritual arts of Protestant Christianity have a long history, rising from primitive Hebrew cults to priestly rites of temple and synagogue, through centuries of Greek and Roman Catholicism, then diverging into spontaneous evangelical expression. Rediscovering the deep emotional power and unity of Christian tradition, modern churches are reviving neglected arts of worship. Orders and contents of worship are constructed to provide better vehicles in the contemporary search for God. What are the psychological effects of such worship?

The processional and recessional provide a formal opening and closing for the service. Processionals, as noted above, are dramatic invitations to advance into the presence of God, moving from a natural point of departure directly toward the altar. Processionals represent man's journey to God, an urgent forward march that lingers not, nor wanders, but moves onward to a definite goal. A congregation that joins in the processional hymn with understanding is advancing to meet Thou.

Invocation and call to worship offer salutations to God and invitations to worship him. They declare that

> God is in his holy temple,
> Let all the earth keep silence before him.

This is the summons to attention, to waken from absent-minded apathy. Indifference has many causes—weariness from standing and singing, stupor of Sunday relaxation, lack of understanding and realization of what the summons means, negligence and unwillingness to believe, or the spectator attitude of letting the minister and choir do it. Yet these invitations are opportunities to recognize the solemn privilege of meeting God.

The hymn is a rhythmic emotional outburst to express praise, rejoicing in gratitude, faith, and consecration. But hymns fail for a variety of reasons—weak sentiment or uncongenial ideas, careless attention, singing absent-mindedly without comprehension, a reluctant spirit that begrudges the effort and prefers not to participate. Yet people can learn to enjoy singing and, as they join together in song, become unified into one body. Objective hymns address God to express religious devotion.

The Creed has long held an honored place in Christian worship, but it is often mumbled unwillingly or defiled by the dishonesty of saying what one does not actually believe. There is value in confessing the faith that binds the worshipers to a common heritage. Yet language may become archaic and theology only empty words unless reinterpreted. Creeds need to grow with the expanding faith of believers through honest thinking, constant education, and rebirth of religious experience.

Collects and responses interweave united prayers through the service in a rhythm of dialogue with God. Short prayers known to the people and repeated in unison are religious experiences of high meaning when participation is genuine. The Lord's Prayer is a model of Christian prayer, but familiarity may breed inattention. The earnest worshiper who unites with friends in such prayer renews the devotion of religious living. Choral responses and litanies are very effective. Music gives wings to prayer and creates a sense of nearness to invisible splendor. Audible affirmations, responses, and amens add the weight of personal testimony.

The scripture lesson is significant as a religious meditation guiding thought to spiritual verities. It fails when carelessly selected, poorly read, or taken as a mere device to lecture the people. A reader who is absorbed in the message to the point of forgetting himself becomes a voice for the utterance of truth. The Bible holds a central place in Christian worship as the voice of divine revelation.

The pastoral prayer is a meeting of mutual concerns. Extempore prayers may wander far or settle into ruts of well-worn phrases. Yet to read prayers is often to miss the sense of direct address to God. Here, if anywhere, worship is seeking to meet and commune with God. One who is equally aware of the divine Presence and of human dependence is in the mood of prayer. To voice the needs of men and the desire of God to meet those needs is a priestly privilege.

The offering dramatizes the generous impulse to give. The gift without the giver is bare, yet if the giver offers himself, there is encounter. It may be the climax of the whole service if one makes it a complete offering in dedication to God. The historic devotion of sacrifice is re-enacted here, when the worshiper brings forward to the altar his sacrificial gift to offer his best to God. A genuine offering has the emotional release of surrender and the votive act of dedicating oneself as a living sacrifice.

The sermon is central in many Protestant services, bringing a united search for the deeper meaning and concerns of the religious life, to declare and decide to follow this way.

The benediction offers repose easily lost in closing the service and hastening to other pursuits. In these final moments of quiet before dismissal, the value of the whole service may be summed up in perspective. Then from the poised moment of rededication the benediction sends the worshiper forth with the guiding and sustaining presence "even unto the end of the world" (Matt. 28:20).

We have been asking what are the psychological effects of worship. But we do not find the answer piecemeal in examining one form, symbol, or item of worship at a time. The actual effect of worship can be appraised only in considering the experience of worship as a whole, not to be completed in one hour but as a journey of faithful ongoing devotion that becomes a way of life. In this larger sense we may see that worship can have the effect of psychotherapy. In the previous chapter we noted that as prayer becomes a discipline of devotion, it is not unlike the encounter of individual psychotherapy. Our study of worship leads to a similar conclusion that worship can represent a group psychotherapy.

For in worship a group come together to support the individual in his search for the meaning of his life. They reinforce his self-examination, facilitate his confession of sins and mistakes, explore the frustrations and perplexities of finite existence, and search with him for a better way of resolving his conflicts. They enter into responsive relationship with him, whereby he is prepared to confront the ultimate Thou, to undergo the anguish of humility in acknowledging his own insufficiency, and to invite the healing response of forgiving love, by which to restore his broken self-respect and feel accepted as a person again. They return again with him each week at the appointed hour to continue the process of searching and finding, of open expression of feelings and the integration of life purpose into a crucial decision.

This is no doubt what psychiatrist Moreno had in mind when he spoke of Christianity as a therapeutic community:

> Christianity can be looked at as the greatest and most ingenious psychotherapeutic procedure man has ever invented compared with which medical psychotherapy has been of practically negligible effect. It can be said that the goal of Christianity was from its very beginning the treatment of the whole of mankind and not of this or that individual and not of this or that group of people. [7]

## 5. *Learning Through Worship*

If worship is an art, it must be learned, for no art is a native condition. Every art consists of skills learned to improve original nature. A naïve sense of wonder, awe, and reverence may be a natural response, but it does not become worship until one learns how to approach Thou and realize the joy of his presence.

Can the art of worship be taught? There is no reason to doubt that either children or adults can learn to worship. It is true that worship is the most subtle of the fine arts. Worship is directed to an invisible Being whose revelations are not audible to the ear. For this reason visible symbols and audible sounds are needed if vivid experiences are to be openly and mutually shared. The forms of worship described above are employed to unite all who par-

[7] *Who Shall Survive?* p. 4. Used by permission of Beacon House, Inc.

ticipate. One learns to worship by worshiping, as any art is best learned in practice.

Forms and methods of worship can be taught verbally to instruct the understanding. But the deeper emotional responses of worship are not achieved in that way. The motivating advances of purpose, devotion, dedication, and encounter are dynamic interpersonal acts. They are learned by contagious attitudes of reverence observed in others, by melodies and harmonies, by chants and responses, by familiar settings and symbols rich in funded meanings, by memories of former experiences and hopes that echo unforgettable expectations. The projection of these emotions and meanings into living relationships and the active participation in group responsiveness awaken religious attitudes and motivate religious actions.

Worship in the profound sense of meeting God is essentially dramatic and may well be one of the most moving events of human experience. With no intent to belittle the ultimate significance of worship, we can perceive that it may have the psychological effect of a reverent psychodrama. There are three important outcomes of psychodrama, which may be recognized as catharsis, therapy, and learning. The person who participates in psychodrama brings his conflicts and stresses upon the stage and acts them out with all the emotional vigor of which he is capable, with deeply beneficial catharsis. In responding to other actors on the stage who represent the significant relationships of his life, he has a direct encounter with them in open give and take that works through blocks and defenses with therapeutic effect. In such encounter he learns to understand better both himself and the other person, with practice in learning what for him is to be his role behavior.

The psychodrama of worship is also action therapy. In the dramatic encounter of I with Thou the defenses blocking insight and love may be worked through, and the person now free of crippling restraints and deceptions is able to find a full and cleaning catharsis in confession of sins and repentance of his follies. He brings forth what was hidden behind defenses and holds the secret motives up to the illuminating light of this encounter. He can no longer shelter his illusions or turn away diffidently to evade the crucial issues of his own behavior and the consequences of his folly upon himself and other persons or events. If he enters into the profound tragedy of the life drama in which he participates, he will be stirred and shaken to the depths of his being. As he responds to Thou, he must recognize that every human relationship in the constellation of his own involvements will come into this searching light and call for definite action to make right what has been wrong and what is now seen to be his responsibility.

There will be new decisions to make which are to emerge from the psychodrama of worship. With intensified humility of the encounter comes also intensified power to decide and act out through each step of his journey the purpose so decided. In his *Psychodrama of God,* Moreno sees man as cocreator with the Creator by enacting in his finite way the spontaneity which streams forth from God. This is therapy to discover through encounter the sources of conflict and creation, and to learn how to integrate the conflict in creative action.

There is, to be sure, ever more to learn through each new event of worship. It must be far more than rote learning by repetition of words. It will in psychodramatic encounter be existential learning, involving the whole of life in the struggle of conflicting emotions to fulfill one's role in society with wisdom and courage. The ongoing devotion of worship becomes the guiding spirit of the vocation that the person is to make his own by finding the meaning of his life before God and the work that is his before the needs of his fellow creatures. All learning must first come from beyond, to become a living part of him, and then to be given forth in the outpouring of his newly learned resources in response to every meeting with another person.

It is possible to worship anywhere, but it is more awakening and releasing in one context than another. The stage must be set for psychodrama and the participants need to warm up for the forthgoing encounter. So in coming to participate in the drama of worship, there are preparations to be made.

Some do not worship unless the setting is conducive to it. Thresholds of stimuli keep one constantly semiconscious of his surroundings. Church architecture with arches and symbols may be eloquent in traditional meaning, but these elements will divert and distract unless they converge upon a worship center to draw the attention of the worshipers to religious focus. A quiet hush of expectancy prepares for worship. To eliminate noise, distractions, or whispering, and withhold latecomers, will establish a mood of reverence upon coming into the sanctuary. Music is a pervasive creator of atmosphere, as artistic lighting may also be. The leader's voice needs to be modulated by an inner spirit of quiet, repose, and reverence. If these contributing factors are brought into harmony, the moment may be right for worship. For atmosphere is the mood of a community that arises from persons mutually aware of a significant reality.

Learning to worship is an artistic creation compounded of profound interest, devoted practice, and emotional understanding. Without interest there would be no practice, without practice no experience, and without experience no understanding. Worship values are increased by the wise use of these factors. Alvin Maberry[8] prepared two types of worship services,

[8] "Psychology of Religious Symbolism" (Unpublished M.A. thesis, Syracuse University, 1939).

one with symbols and one without, which were presented twenty-eight times to seven different congregations of young people. The value of symbols in worship was convincingly shown. At the beginning of a service without symbols there was noise and confusion, talking and shifting of chairs. Upon entering the symbol service, with a worship center of cross, crown, picture of Jesus, and candles, the subjects became markedly quiet—conversation ceased, chairs were not shuffled, and the attention was good even before the call to worship. Fifty-eight of seventy questioned, 74.6 per cent, said this was because the setting was so worshipful, peaceful, prayerful, beautiful, churchlike. Nonparticipation (not singing, praying, or reading) in all items of the service without symbols was 18.4 per cent, in contrast to 8.18 per cent in the service with symbols. Nonattention (gazing about, fidgeting, manipulating hands, and the like) in the service without symbols was 24.55 per cent in contrast to 7.37 per cent in the service with symbols. Attention and participation were three times better in the service with symbols, indicating how symbols aid in communicating the deeper meaning of worship.

No one can communicate what he has not. If the leader does not sense God's presence, it is quite unlikely that the congregation will. It is the sense of this Presence that makes an ordinary man a religious leader. In so far as he loses the sense of the encounter, he becomes hollow, artificial, and futile. Constant daily prayer is the best psychological preparation for public worship. Then worship becomes a crescendo of ultimate concern, arising from genuine inner experience of meeting Thou. The deeper attitudes of religious faith, hope, and love seeking the answering response of Thou are basic causes and effects of worship. When such attitudes permeate the whole personality, there is calm courage for the sharp demands of crisis or for the weary routine of drudgery.

Worship, as we have seen, is a social discipline regulated by institutional tradition. The ordering of this united journey toward God is the priestly discipline which conserves and distills the authentic notes of previous encounters and sets them into a continuing melody orchestrated in a symphony of outpouring devotion. In this way a permanent form is recorded by which the congregation may return to experience again the lyric beauty and profound emotion of the encounter with Thou. It is a priceless heritage to have these records to use for the recollection of emotion in tranquillity. With these forms of worship available the congregation may follow the score and re-enact the great drama in flowing cadences to prepare for new encounter.

Yet in every act of conservation there is a danger of enshrining the living moment in a rigid form which commemorates the past in a tomb empty of present life. By the attrition of repetition and the easement of passive inertia the congregation may slip into the attitude of listening rather than the anguish of participation. This we have already noted as the formality of the priestly discipline, whereby one may be content to go through the motions and repeat symbolic formulas without the genuine encounter. Then the prophetic function is needed to waken the spirit from lethargy. The discipline of intelligence is needed to bring searching criticism upon routine and thoughtless ways of compulsive ritualism. And the mystical discipline is needed to bring anew one's full energies to the encounter with Thou in this moment of tragic finite incompleteness.

When prayer or worship become formal, there are both gain and loss. The form is a noble creation of religious genius by which to re-create the profound and moving drama of the ultimate encounter. But if the form becomes an end rather than a means, a thing is now the object of idolatry instead of a living encounter with Thou. In this and all conserving efforts to grasp and possess a moment of genuine significance for future use, there is the fatal loss of spontaneity. And in the social discipline of worship it is too easy for the individual to let the group act for him, while he becomes a mere spectator forgetting his own urgent need for participation in outgoing and self-giving interaction. The responsibility of the individual cannot be yielded to the group, or he will suffer serious decline instead of religious growth. In every moment of worship, no matter what the form of expression, there is need for the creative event of individual spontaneity, in which to give himself completely and without reserve to the encounter with God from breath to breath.

# 9 THE PSYCHOLOGY OF BELIEF

## 1. *Psychological Conditions of Belief*

The psychological study of belief is to be clearly distinguished from the logical question of validity. Logic treats belief as true or false. It is a normative study of standards and methods for judging what constitutes valid belief. Important as the question of truth is, it is not the problem of this chapter. We are concerned rather to investigate the nature of religious belief. What do people believe? What causes belief and doubt? What are the interpersonal effects of religious belief?

There seems to be a natural tendency to believe. Everyone is a believer. Not all persons believe the same things, but everyone believes something. Why do we believe some ideas and not others? How do we come to believe at all? The conditions of belief may be classified as sociological and psychological. While they overlap and interact, it will be well to consider the tendencies to believe from these two points of view.

Sociological conditions include all belief-making influences that come from association in social groups. The behavior of other persons suggests deeds and words to imitate. Attitudes of belief associated with deeds and words become contagious. We do as others do, feel as others feel, and think as others think because we desire to share a common life and become a part of the social group. By repetition customs and traditions arise, having the authority of group sanction—when so many believe, there must be something to it. If the wisest and best believe, there is qualitative as well as quantitative sanction, and we tend to believe on the authority of prestige as well as numbers. Each generation starts with a capital fund of beliefs accepted without criticism as axioms assumed by general agreement. These customs are social habits that become incorporated into the very life of individuals who enact them. Such believing attitudes become a frame of reference not to be questioned but upheld as the stability and order by which we live. We are so largely unconscious of the basic assumptions of belief that we take them for granted without question or defense.

Psychological conditions of belief appear in these social influences of suggestion and imitation. Why do we imitate others? Imitation occurs in stimulus-response situations. When interest directs attention to other persons, the whole organism responds in exploratory motor and perceptual responses to the observed event. Note the tendency in spectators at a football game to reproduce the efforts of the players by incipient muscular tensions. Believing is a social attitude that responds in this way to the persistent stimuli of others' belief. A man standing on a street corner looking up stimulates others to look up also, for he acts as though he believes there is something up there worth looking at. It is natural to believe what others believe, and most of our beliefs are socially conditioned.

It has been customary to refer to man as a rational animal (*homo sapiens*). In this the ancient Greeks held man in higher opinion than do contemporary psychologists who reason that man is essentially unreasonable. The paradox of this view lies in the use of reason to deny reason by addressing the reasonableness of others. But the intention is to rely upon sensible experience by appealing to the facts as perceived. On this ground who will deny that much of human behavior is motivated by irrational desires and fears? The persons we know best are not altogether rational or irrational but somewhat of both. And so it is with our beliefs; they arise from a mingling of rational and irrational tendencies.

The subrational roots of belief are deeply involved in the interests and needs, desires and aversions, ends and means, of living. Psychological analyses have often tracked religious belief down to irrational deceptions of the unconscious: (*a*) Interest in God is called a manifestation of the "father complex," indicating a childish fixation that should normally be outgrown. It is viewed as a form of nostalgia, a pathetic homesickness for the parental care of infancy. (*b*) Religious hopes are taken as overcompensation for inferiority and ego frustration. Religious satisfaction is an opiate to which the weak become addicted in trying to dull the pain of a tragic existence. (*c*) Petition to God is considered a projection of the burden of dismay and dependence upon the Everlasting Arms. In God we trust for credit in lieu of of cash. (*d*) Religious belief is called "wish-thinking" or "thobbing," luxuriating in the fantasies of believing what one wants to believe. Faith is suggestibility under the hypnotic effect of soft music and stained-glass windows or under the social pressure of group conformity.

There is much to learn from these psychological descriptions. Devious as they are, the mind of man is not less so. The amazing intricacy of behavior may well demand such elaborate explorations. Human nature can be fully as irrational and deceptive as psychology finds it. And the obvious fact is that atheists have the same human nature that theists have. They also are infected by irrationality, sentimentality, and evasion. Their beliefs are subject to the same distortions of prejudice and desire. For atheism is by every test as much a belief as theism, and it is evidently quite as incapable of escaping the waves of emotion that beat upon beliefs.

First, atheism may be motivated by revolt against authority. A growing person struggling for mature independence and responsibility will need to work through periods of rivalry and revolt toward parents and other authority figures. Freud holds this rivalry and revolt typical of modern family conflicts. Now if theism may be traced to the father complex, it is quite as logical to trace atheism to the Oedipus complex, a jealous desire to overthrow and supplant the father. Rival affections and jealous conflicts displace loyalty to God. Many a son who falls into filial disagreement casts off his father's God in revolt against his father. In wider extension this attitude becomes a generalized revolt against all authority. "Down with God!" shout revolutionary leaders, for God is a symbol of the traditional authorities they are out to destroy. The Russian Orthodox Church had so identified God with the imperialism which held the people in bondage that God must be assassinated with the czar. Revolts against God occur where oppression weighs the heaviest, where God is on the side of the imperial armies and exploiting classes. Organized party atheism is everywhere associated with revolution against tyrannical authority, a contest in the struggle of power.

A second motivation in atheism may be found in the ego needs. Freud uncovers a reservoir of psychic energy, the "id," which ever strives to gratify desire by enhancing the prestige of the ego. Adler regards the basic urge of personality as the ego striving for power. We have seen how atheism is related to the struggle for power. It is further involved in the urge for ego satisfaction. Nietzsche, denied military ambitions, turned his energy to literary conquests. His bitter attacks on Christianity as "slave morality" attempt compensation for an inferioriy complex. In *Thus Spake Zarathustra* he offers the confession: "That I may reveal my heart entirely to you, my friends: if there were gods, how could I endure it to be no god? Therefore there are no gods." [1] Obviously the conclusion of this inference is not logical but psychological—a conclusion to gratify the ego, not the canons of the syllogism. Thus may atheism feed the ego by escape from inferiority to inflated superiority. Mencken strikes a pose of superiority when he heaps scorn upon the "yokels of the Bible belt." Shaw strokes his ego by satirizing *The Adventures of the Black Girl in Her Search for God*. God is sacrificed upon the altar of conceit.

A third motive is projection. Projection is a device for avoiding condemnation by placing blame upon others. Primitive tribes have been known to

[1] Pt. II, Discourse xxiv.

vent resentment upon their gods of clay or wood by hacking them to pieces in a frenzy of wrath. It is no longer good taste to chastise gods or children with corporal punishment. We now refine our instruments of torture and resort to tongue lashings. Projection is a ready way of evading moral responsibility. If God made me, then he is responsible for my misdeeds. Or it may be more convenient to dispense with God entirely—remove God and immortality, and there is nothing to fear in this world or the next. Dostoevski reflects this outcome of nineteenth-century atheism in *The Brothers Karamazov*. Ivan returns from his university studies and reports that if there is no God, anything is lawful, even cannibalism. His father's valet, Smerdyakov, pounces upon the idea and takes advantage of this lawlessness to murder his master. Again the atheistic argument follows psychological labyrinths of irrational impulses rather than logical patterns of unbiased reason.

A fourth observation is that atheists rationalize. Rationalization is the victory of desire over reason. Belief in God is often pointed to as a conspicuous example of such wishful thinking. The same ax falls at the root of atheistic beliefs, which parade arguments in support of prepotent desires. If theists emphasize meaning and value in the universe, atheists are often as anxious to accent the evil and insignificant. If the idealist rationalizes his desire for beauty and harmony, the realist rationalizes his preference for discord and ugliness. There is an oddly prevalent desire to have the worst of possible worlds. The style of "sweetness and light" was sentimental, but no wider of the mark than the mood of bitterness and darkness. The ardor with which cynics smash the idols of theistic hope approaches sadistic delight. Rationalization flourishes in the soil of credulity. The same credulity produces both the Pollyanna and the Scrooge. A Pollyanna is begging to believe the best; a Scrooge is begging to believe the worst. Schopenhauer slept with pistols under his pillow because he distrusted his fellow men; he brooded over the hopeless evils of life because he distrusted the will of the world. In both respects he suffered delusions of persecution. Atheism is a dogma that flourishes in emotional attitudes.

It would be a serious error to assume that a belief is either altogether rational or irrational. And it would be equally serious to imply that any single cause may explain a belief, which is actually the product of many intricate causal factors. The atheist is entitled to his beliefs as much as the theist and should be treated with equal respect in the honesty and sincerity of his conclusions. What I contend is that there will be a mingling of emotion with reason in all belief, and that to understand the nature of belief we must take into account a wider span of social influences as well as a deeper sounding of emotional forces than we often recognize.

G. B. Vetter and M. Green have undertaken to do this in their study of atheists.[2] They sent 600 questionnaires to a random sample of members of the American Association for the Advancement of Atheism, from which 350 replies were received. They omitted replies from women, which left 325 to be used in the study, well distributed by ages. There were only 42 per cent of the atheists' parents who were American born, as compared with 76 per cent of all persons over 21 years of age in 1900. Protestant parents contributed more than their quota of atheistic sons, while Jews and Methodists made the largest contribution. Actually, 82.5 per cent of the parents were listed as definitely affiliated with some religious creed; while 30 per cent of the parents were of different religious faith. The intensity of the parents' religious activity is shown in the following table in four categories.

INTENSITY OF RELIGIOUS ACTIVITY

| Degree of Religious Devotion | Percentages | | |
|---|---|---|---|
| | Father | Mother | Average |
| Rigid | 33 | 40 | 37 |
| Occasional | 24 | 30 | 27 |
| Lax | 19 | 19 | 19 |
| None at all | 25 | 11 | 18 |

It is significant to note that these atheists perceive their parents as more than ordinarily religious. The highest number are rated as "rigid"; and grouping together the two upper categories ("rigid" and "occasional"), the father score is 57 and the mother score is 70. This stands in contrast to the two lower categories ("lax" and "none at all"), which together have a father score of 44 and a mother score of 30. This indicates that these atheists were generally revolting against the beliefs of their parents more than they were agreeing with them. And it gives supporting evidence to our use of the oedipal theory in explaining this tendency to identify God with the parent in revolting against authority.

Another significant factor is the mortality of parents. Of all those who had broken with the church by twenty years of age, it was found that one half of them had lost one or both parents by that time. This is at least twice the average mortality rate for that age group. From this we infer that if God was identified with the parent who died, there was consequently a loss of belief in God. Or from another viewpoint that faith in a good and just God is likely to suffer a shock from the tragic event of a parent's death, upon whom the child or young person is so dependent for security in his

[2] "Personality and Group Factors in the Making of Atheists," *The Journal of Abnormal and Social Psychology*, XXVII (1932-33), 179-94.

interpersonal relations. The answering response is stilled, and the outreach to Thou has suffered a loss in communication which disturbs religious faith.

Over 30 per cent of the atheists reported an unhappy childhood or adolescence. Also Communists in a New York study and "radicals" in a study of 706 college students indicated unhappy childhood, and even more (35.7 and 50 per cent respectively) reported an unhappy adolescence. In the same study of 706 college students, among those who classified themselves as "conservatives" none of them showed an unhappy childhood and only 4 per cent an unhappy adolescence. We cannot overweight these percentages as the samples are not exhaustive, but the correlation of unhappy childhood or adolescence with atheism and radicalism would seem to support the theory of revolt against the family.

The evidence gives support also to the view that human beliefs are not merely intellectual judgments of abstract reasoning but are existential so as to involve the whole life with strong emotional and social components. A person believes religiously with his whole being, including his interpersonal relations. Beliefs are systems of value that emerge from the central propriate strivings of the person in his encounter with other persons. It is not surprising, therefore, to find in this study of Vetter and Green that religious radicals are likely to be political radicals also. Before becoming atheists, 64 per cent were Republicans or Democrats and 26 per cent were Socialists or Communists. After becoming atheists only 29 per cent were Republican or Democrat, while 54 per cent were Socialist or Communist.

Where does reason enter this believing and doubting process? It is argued that we do not think until we have to. When life flows along smoothly, there is no occasion to think until some obstacle or problem demands solution and wakens consciousness to employ ideas as tools to serve life needs. But reason does not oversleep so long as that. Daydreaming uses imaginative reason in autistic thinking. Unconscious motives work with clever rationalizing to gain their desires. Reason is not a separate faculty, standing aloof as a *deus ex machina* until called to meet a crisis. Some degree of reasoning is present in all conscious experience that relates fleeting impressions into meaning. There is no sharp line of demarcation between experience and reason, for reason is the coherent sense of experience. We believe not entirely by reason but never without an aspect of reasonableness. The subrational roots noted above already merge into complexes of coherent experience, from which reason stems and eventually blossoms into inferences, syllogisms, and theologies.

Reason serves a double function in belief, critical and constructive. When contradictions appear, critical suspicions arise and demand more careful scrutiny. The constructive function draws data together into a coherent pattern of meaning worthy of belief. Critical and constructive efforts follow no rigid sequence but intermingle in continuous efforts to make sense out of multiple impressions. The critical function is to guard against deception and falsehood. The constructive function is to develop standards of true validity and organize beliefs to form a coherent system.

## 2. *The Problem of Doubt*

Doubt is a problem. It is a painful perplexity that puzzles and worries the mind. As a negative denial of accepted belief doubt revolts against authority, betraying and deserting established tradition. Skeptical unrest may have symptoms of acute distress, insecurity, lack of confidence, mingled with feelings of guilt. Persistent attitudes of doubt may come to moods of indifference or despair which defeat constructive action and prevent creative achievement.

For these reasons doubt is often feared and opposed. A religious editor recalls a Sunday-school teacher who said to him as a boy, "You have no right to doubt." David Nyvall in a tract on *Doubt and How to Overcome It* (c. 1930) declares that doubt is always an ill and refers to critical discerning as defeating the highest purpose of life, suggesting that there is a blind faith the better for its blindness. But if doubt is an ill, it is not cured by fearful suppression.

Is doubt always an evil? The fact is that doubt performs a useful function. It arouses critical intelligence from "dogmatic slumber" as Kant demonstrated in his three great critiques.[3] It questions hollow assumption and challenges smug hypocrisy. It demands honest investigation, exposes error, and urges correction. It stimulates discussion and exchange of opinion, which foster progress in truth seeking. Studies in superstition are instructive at this point. Without doubt superstition proliferates in rank jungles of error, confusion, and ignorant fear. Systematic doubting prunes out these errors and gives truth room to grow. The scientific obligation of psychology is to employ critical processes in thoroughgoing investigation.

American psychologists have made numerous investigations of superstition, defined as unfounded belief. Typical lists of superstitions are presented to students of different age, sex, and background to discover what factors are related to such unfounded beliefs. E. E. Emme[4] reviewed such studies and found the following implications:

[3] *Critique of Pure Reason; Critique of Practical Reason; Critique of Judgment.*

[4] "Modification and Origin of Superstition Among 96 College Students," *The Journal of Psychology,* X (1940), 279-91.

1. Superstitious belief declines with age and education. High-school students are more credulous than college students; junior students are more credulous than high-school seniors.
2. Women appear to be more superstitious than men. This is evident in various studies, regardless of the age of the subjects. Rural children are more credulous than urban children.
3. Specific instruction reduces superstitious belief. General instruction in science does not seem to have this effect, but specific teaching is effective.
4. Sources of belief vary. Home, friends, observation, educational sources (books, newspapers, school, church), are important influences.
5. The more intelligent are less superstitious. They have fewer superstitions and are better able to reduce their prejudices.

He then proceeded to study ninety-six Morningside College students by tests, instruction, interviews, and correlations in reference to a list of forty-seven superstitions. Twenty-four of these students had zero superstition scores. The ten most superstitious students had scores at the outset varying from fourteen to nineteen statements. Specific instruction reduced their scores to a range of one to six. The total mean average score was reduced from 2.96 to .67. Parents were found to be the primary factor in motivating belief or disbelief. Other factors were friends, courses, and reading. Negative correlations between intelligence and superstition were –.421 before the study and –.471 after the study.

Religion has often been condemned as superstition. It is evident that superstitious beliefs have accumulated around every area of human experience, including religion. Practices of government, war, trade, agriculture, birth, death, disease, health, and so forth have in every culture operated through a maze of popular superstitions. Religion has had its share—and more, perhaps, by virtue of its devotion to supernatural and invisible powers. But in all fairness it should be recorded that religion is also a vigorous corrector of superstitions. Even as astronomy has shaken off the superstitions of astrology and chemistry the superstitions of alchemy, so the higher religions have battled steadily against error and superstition in their traditions and popular beliefs.

Sturdy faith welcomes doubt, as democracy welcomes freedom of speech, as judicial bodies welcome minority opinions, as scientists welcome revolutionary discoveries, as true religion welcomes prophetic denunciations of error and evil for the sake of truth. Doubt, well employed, is essential to growing faith and true progress. "The doubt that a man confronts purifies his faith from error. . . . For honest doubt is a new aspect of truth standing at the door and knocking, seeking a place in the system of rational experience." [5]

[5] Henry Jones, *A Faith That Enquires* (New York: The Macmillan Co., 1922), pp. 9-10.

The problem of doubt is how to doubt intelligently rather than blindly, for blind doubt is quite as superstitious as blind faith. Open-minded doubt is more eager to learn than to win arguments or defend prejudices. Honest doubt is fearless self-criticism that dissolves indifference and cynicism. Intelligent doubt concedes a belief to be affirmed as the counterpart of denial, and persists in seeking truth to affirm.

## 3. *Religious Beliefs*

The variety and extent of religious beliefs are boundless. Agreement in beliefs has social causes, as the authority of tradition and the contagion of custom shape beliefs to conformity. Similar needs and experiences suggest parallel interpretations. Yet beliefs are diverging today. Freedom to think and speak for oneself encourages individual opinion and independent judgment. The Protestant denominations in their democratic tendencies have encouraged differences. Yet the weight of authority is often set against new ideas to uphold the old beliefs. As sciences gather new facts and social change moves along, there is persistent demand to revise beliefs. Thinkers follow promising tangents and reach divergent conclusions. As each pursues his clues in search of truth, the seekers fan out widely over the fields open to exploration. The more ardently and thoroughly each hypothesis is investigated, the more likely are these co-operative enterprises to be fruitful.

What religious beliefs do contemporary Americans hold? Many surveys have been made of religious beliefs, of which we can note only a few. In 1946 Allport, Gillespie, and Young[6] studied the religious beliefs and practices of 414 undergraduate students of Harvard College and 86 undergraduates of Radcliffe College. The questionnaire instrument was completed by over 95 per cent of those who received it. Seven out of ten students answered Yes to the question "Do you feel that you require some form of religious orientation or belief in order to achieve a fully mature philosophy of life?" This gives freedom to define religion as each student perceives it, and to this question 82 per cent of the women and 68 per cent of men gave the affirmative answer. Of the men 13 per cent were doubtful and 19 per cent said No, while of the women 6 per cent were doubtful and 12 per cent negative.

When they considered the factors contributing to their being religious, the Harvard men listed parental influence (51 per cent); fear or insecurity (43 per cent); personal influence of others (36 per cent); conformity

[6] G. W. Allport, J. M. Gillespie, and J. Young, "The Religion of the Post-War College Student," *The Journal of Psychology*, XXV (1948), 3-33.

with tradition (35 per cent), aesthetic appeal (25 per cent); church teachings (24 per cent); gratitude (23 per cent); reading (20 per cent); studies (17 per cent); sorrow or bereavement (17 per cent); a mystical experience (10 per cent); and sexual turmoil (8 per cent). In contrast to the atheists these students were freer to emphasize emotional factors in their beliefs, while reading and studies played a minor role. The Radcliffe women also rated emotional factors high, with fear or insecurity leading the list (46 per cent); personal influence of others (43 per cent); gratitude (42 per cent); and aesthetic appeal (41 per cent).

Comparing their own with their parents' faith, a rather small minority considered themselves more firm than mother (Harvard men, 7 per cent; Radcliffe women, 14 per cent) or more firm than father (Harvard men 16 per cent; Radcliffe women 23 per cent). The majority are less firm in religious belief than mother (Harvard men 51 per cent; Radcliffe women, 41 per cent) and less firm than father (Harvard men, 27 per cent; Radcliffe women 27 per cent). Comparing their religious background with their present choice, the Roman Catholic students showed little change. The Protestant students showed more change (Harvard men moved from the background of 40 per cent to choice of 28 per cent; Radcliffe women from 44 per cent to 18 per cent). The Jewish students also showed considerable change (Harvard men were 18 per cent in background and 8 per cent in choice; Radcliffe women were 17 per cent in background and 6 per cent in choice).

As to the alleged conflict between the findings of science and the principle contentions of religion, 70 per cent of the students believe either that religion and science support each other or that the conflict is more apparent than real and can probably be reconciled. Of the Harvard men 58 per cent and Radcliffe women 75 per cent endorsed some belief in God as either "infinitely wise omnipotent creator" or "infinitely intelligent and friendly being" or "vast, impersonal spiritual source." There were many students in spite of their religious beliefs who considered the influence of the church harmful (Harvard men 34 per cent; Radcliffe woman 21 per cent).

Another survey of religious beliefs was conducted in 1949 by Murray G. Ross[7] based upon a questionnaire sample of 1,935 youth and intensive interviews with 100 young people who participated in the program of the Y.M.C.A. in nine states in the eastern part of the United States. He does not claim this to be a representative sample of the population as a whole, for 81.5 claim church membership, 19.1 per cent have graduated from college, 32.1 per cent are earning fifty dollars a week or more, and 18.5 per cent are married. The ages are fairly distributed from 18 to 29. In religious

[7] *Op. cit.*

affiliation 59.1 are Protestant, 34 per cent are Roman Catholic, 3.5 per cent are Jewish, and 1.2 per cent are Greek Orthodox. As to place of birth 96.9 per cent were born in the United States. The occupations most highly represented were 28.6 per cent students; 25.6 per cent clerical, sales, and kindred occupations; 13.5 per cent professional; 8.2 per cent operatives; and 6.8 per cent craftsmen, foremen, and kindred occupations.

A general comparison with the Harvard-Radcliffe students shows that the young people who participate in the Y.M.C.A. program have a stronger belief in the church, in God, and in personal immortality. This is not surprising in view of the 81.5 per cent who belonged to a church as compared with the much smaller number of the Harvard-Radcliffe students so affiliated. Of the Y.M.C.A. group 60.1 per cent agreed that "the church is the one sure and infallible foundation of civilized life," in contrast to 6 per cent of the Harvard-Radcliffe students. Of the Y.M.C.A. group 85.3 per cent endorsed belief in God, in contrast to the 58 per cent of Harvard men and 76 per cent of Radcliffe women. Of the Y.M.C.A. group 52.3 per cent believed in personal immortality or reincarnation, in contrast to 26 per cent for the Harvard men and 35 per cent for the Radcliffe women. Church attendance and prayer were more frequent in the Y.M.C.A. group.

Two other surveys were conducted of religious beliefs in 1948. Lincoln Barnett [8] obtained data in personal interviews by Gallup-poll methods with a "cross section of Americans from coast to coast." In response to the question "Do you believe in God?" 95 per cent said Yes, 2 per cent were agnostic, 2 per cent atheistic, and 1 per cent declined to reply. Of those believing in God 29 per cent thought of God as a "Supreme Power"; 26 per cent in a supervisory capacity ("He cares for us, answers our prayer"); 17 per cent thought of God primarily as "Creator"; while 7 per cent vaguely referred to him as "spirit." It is notable that 26 per cent thought of God in intimate relation to their own lives and that 95 per cent affirmed belief in God.

*Fortune Magazine* conducted a survey of the opinions of youth 18 to 25 years of age in the United States, and the survey was published in the issue of December, 1948. In response to the question "Do you think there is a God who rewards and punishes after death?" 74 per cent replied Yes, 16 per cent No, and 10 per cent had no opinion. This is higher than the Y.M.C.A. group, 52.3 per cent of whom replied in the affirmative to a similar question. As to church attendance 83.8 replied in the affirmative with 15.8 per cent saying they never attended. Of those who attended church 36.5 per cent went "weekly or more often" (as compared with 47.8

[8] "God and the American People," *Ladies Home Journal* XXXVII (September, 1948), 230-40.

per cent for the Y.M.C.A. group), 22.1 per cent two or three times a month; 10 per cent monthly, 15.2 per cent "less often than monthly."

From these studies there is indication that the general population is more ready to claim religious belief than college students and their teachers, as we shall note in the following section. Leuba in his studies of scientists seemed to find a decline of religious belief among them. We may be asking if higher education, and particularly as influenced by the sciences, reduces the tendency to hold religious beliefs. Such education, if it succeeds in its avowed intention, will foster critical thinking by which all assumptions previously held on a naïve basis may be subject to re-examination. We should be surprised, therefore, if any person could undergo higher education without changing his beliefs all along the frontiers of his investigation. This we expect in the sciences, from which have come the notable advances in human knowledge and invention. Shall we expect that religious beliefs will be untouched in their confrontation with scientific knowledge and critical analysis?

## *4. Ideas of God*

It is evident that religious beliefs are subject to change. Beliefs are modified by developing experiences of the individual and by social conditions in a world in which nothing stands still. Churches have employed the authority of apostolic succession, inerrant Scripture, and infallible judgment to resist the forces of change. But even so, variations occur, and new views alter the religious perspective. Within social patterns of belief individuals show even more flexibility in private reservations and personal opinions. Social change is speeding up in our mobile civilization, and religious beliefs are not impervious to these new viewpoints.

J. H. Leuba has sampled the religious beliefs of American scientists in two surveys, conducted in 1914 and 1933.[9] In 1914 he submitted questionnaires on God and immortality to 1,000 scientists listed in *American Men of Science* in two groups of 500 each, selected at random from 5,500 names. In 1933 he sent the same questionnaire to a sample number of 23,000 scientists.[10] listed in the 1933 edition of *American Men of Science,* supplemented by lists of the American Sociological Society (1931) and the 1933 yearbook of the American Psychological Association. Replies came from at least 75

[9] *The Belief in God and Immortality* (New York: Sherman French & Co., 1916; Chicago: Open Court, 1921) and "Religious Beliefs of American Scientists," *Harper's Magazine,* CLXIX (1934), 291-300.

[10] Leuba does not give the exact number of these scientists to whom the questionnaire was sent in 1933. The number of sociologists was 157 and psychologists 164.

per cent of selected scientists, classified in four fields: physicists, biologists, sociologists, and psychologists. These were further classified as greater scientists (starred as eminent by a poll of their fellow scientists) and lesser scientists. Each scientist was asked to check one of the following three statements on God:

1. I believe in a God to whom one can pray in the expectation of receiving an answer. By "answer" I mean more than the natural, subjective, psychological effect of prayer.
2. I do not believe in God as defined above.
3. I have no definite belief regarding this question.

A statistical comparison of the believers in God among these scientists in 1914 and 1933 is shown as follows:

THE BELIEVERS IN GOD

| | *Lesser Scientists* | | *Greater Scientists* | |
|---|---|---|---|---|
| | 1914 | 1933 | 1914 | 1933 |
| Physicists | 50% | 43% | 34% | 17% |
| Biologists | 39 | 31 | 17 | 12 |
| Sociologists | 29 | 30 | 19 | 13 |
| Psychologists | 32 | 13 | 13 | 12 |

Leuba has conducted his surveys with a commendable effort to be objective and accurate. His figures seem to indicate (*a*) that scientists tend more to disbelief than to belief in God; (*b*) that greater scientists believe less than the lesser scientists; (*c*) that belief in God is generally declining among scientists in these nineteen years. No one can deny the facts presented or fail to be impressed by the trends revealed. But there are dangers of hasty generalization in statistical surveys that need careful scrutiny before coming to final conclusions.

*First,* one must not confuse these scientists with all scientists. While Leuba employed his sampling method with care to have a random selection that would be representative, the fact is that we do not know what the other scientists would have said. The number not consulted is obviously much greater than those consulted; and approximately 25 per cent of those questioned did not reply. Some replied to protest that the three statements were inadequate to define their position. The inductive leap from some to all, or even to others not examined, is notably hazardous. This is a general difficulty affecting all scientific induction and should not be forgotten in this study.

*Second,* one must not mistake this definition of God for any or all belief in God. Ideas of God are so variously understood that no single view of him could be acceptable to all believers in God. In this case the definition of God is so obviously narrow and unscientific as to exclude scientists in particular from belief. By ruling out "natural, subjective, and psychological effect of prayer" Leuba defines God as a being who works externally and magically by setting aside natural laws. Scientists who believe in a God working in nature through uniform laws and subjective experiences have no choice but to reject Leuba's definition of God and be counted as disbelievers. Yet they may be earnest believers in a God who employs lawful means.

*Third,* the apparent decline of belief among greater and more recent scientists is probably influenced by the phrasing of the questionnaire. A statement of belief that is antiscientific will force a disjunction between such religious belief and science. The more devoted one is to science, the more surely will he defend his scientific system of beliefs when challenged by antiscientific statements. Furthermore it should be noted that surveys of public opinion are important factors in influencing opinion as shown in the use of the Gallup Poll in political contests. The published returns of Leuba's survey in 1914 evidently influenced the furtherance of trends reported in 1933. When students of science find that scientists disbelieve and that greater scientists are greater doubters, they are naturally impressed. The prestige of scientific authority may overshadow religious authority in our time. The separation of education from religion and the preponderance of time which children and youth spend in secular schools joins with the prestige of teachers and the wonders of science to give scientific belief a favored position.

*Fourth,* it should be evident that the questionnaire confuses the existence of God with the effects of prayer. One may believe in God without subscribing to the kind of prayer that sets aside natural processes. It might be argued that the decisive issue of the question is not God, but rather what one believes about prayer and miracles. At this point it is interesting to note that only 21 per cent of the theological students and 64 per cent of the ministers whom Betts surveyed believed that prayer has the power to change conditions in nature such as drought. Yet 58 per cent of the students and 83 per cent of the ministers believed that prayer for others directly affected their lives. With the variation of belief on a redefinition of prayer it is evident that subtle distinctions make a wide difference in statistical returns. Though narrow in one sense, Leuba's statement is too complex to be selective at the point of the existence of God. Other issues latent in the statement are: (*a*) How does God hear prayer? (*b*) How does God answer prayer? (*c*) What is supernatural? (*d*) Why are subjective effects discounted? (*e*) Are psychological processes impervious to God's influence?

In defense of this definition Leuba says, "That is the God worshiped in every branch of religion. In the absence of belief in a God who hears and sympathizes with man, who under certain conditions answers his prayers, traditional worship could not go on." [11]

But there is enough loose play in this statement also for it to be ambiguous. We may believe that God sympathizes without answering in ways defined, or we may hold that worship need not be traditional. The net is much too large to separate worshipers of God from nonworshipers. To assume that scientists do not believe in God because they reject a given formula, or do not pray because they expect a different kind of answer, is not exactly clarifying.

A more refined instrument for measuring belief in God was employed by Daniel Katz and F. H. Allport in studying students' attitudes at Syracuse University.[12] A scale of seven steps was devised to distinguish different concepts of God, and 1,321 liberal arts students were asked to select the statement most nearly representing their beliefs. Only the first of the seven items could possibly agree with Leuba's definition of God, and this was acceptable to just 21 per cent of the students. Yet only 4.7 per cent of the students (items 6 and 7) denied belief in God.

Factors influencing changes in students' religious belief were: teaching in certain courses, 72.4 per cent; contacts with fellow students, 46.2 per cent; general process of becoming more mature, 37.5 per cent; reading outside of courses, 29.7 per cent; personal influence of professors in courses, 21 per cent; other influences outside of college life, 19.7 per cent; religious services in churches of the city, 6.7 per cent. These changes in religious belief were accompanied by a new and satisfying philosophy of life for 62.4 per cent of the students, though of these 38.4 per cent said that certain doubts remained.

A. H. MacLean has published a study of what children think of God.[13] Interviews were held with seventy-five Protestant children eight years of

[11] "Religious Beliefs of American Scientists," p. 292.

[12] *Students' Attitudes* (Syracuse, N.Y.: The Craftsman Press, 1931), pp. 257-318.

[13] *The Idea of God in Protestant Religious Education* (New York: Teachers College, Columbia University, 1930).

age or younger living in New York City. The following responses were given by the children:

God is like a man with long white robes. He looks very kind.
God is an old man and has long white whiskers all over his face.
I just can't tell.
God is a spirit and can get into places without being seen.
God is like a spirit—like that part of you which goes to heaven when you die.
God is a very good man.
God is nature.
God is a man with power who uses his power in the right way.
God is quite different from man. He has power to create things.
God is a powerful doctor.
God has a different spirit from us. Mamma told me so.
God is a spirit. He doesn't really live, but gives you thoughts to do things to help people.
God is as big as a cloud. He wears a long dress and a blackish beard.
Mamma has a picture of God. He has hair down to his shoulders. He is old.
God has a smiling face.
God is like us.
God is like a fairy.
God is a young man.
God is a king—the greatest king of all.
God has a head.
God is the same as Jesus.
Nobody ever saw God.[14]

General trends appear from these responses. Forty per cent think of God as a man with flesh and bones and whiskers; 20 per cent think of him as a spirit, ghost, or fairy; 25 per cent refer to his kindness or goodness and 12 per cent to his power.

In response to the question "Where do you think God is?" the majority said that God is away up in the sky or in heaven. Many others said that God is everywhere and 27 per cent that he is near us all the time. "God is down inside of me," "God is in our hearts."

Four hundred and forty-three intermediate children (ages 9 to 14) in New York Protestant church schools were given a true-false test of 218 statements concerning God. Grouping these scores by deciles, MacLean gives the following summary of the children's beliefs.

Over 90 per cent of the children believe that God is omniscient; that he is changeless in nature; that in character he most resembles a loving father or mother, or the man Jesus; that He is present everywhere; that the addressing of prayers

[14] *Ibid.* Used by permission of Teachers College, Columbia University.

to Him is primarily useful in quest of moral guidance; that God's love is universally extended to mankind; that He will forgive even murder; that He protects children at night and supplies man's every physical need; that He loves all classes and races, even our enemies; that He desires us to help the underprivileged share advantages; that war should be speedily terminated; and that we should believe all the Bible says about God.

Between 80 and 90 per cent of the children believe that God is a wonderful person—He is three persons in one; He could make the sun stop and go back the other way if He wished; He lives in Heaven and will supply anything we ask; He will not grant every wish, but only what we need; He is found in the call of duty and ethical relations; He reveals Himself in blossom and sunshine; He provides a Heaven for the faithful; He has made laws we must discover and obey; He created the world and life in six days; Adam and Eve brought disaster on mankind, but God is redeeming us; He asks us to work for a world free of poverty and privation; He wants us to participate in war only when our cause is just and every peace effort has failed.

Between 70 and 80 per cent of the children believe that God has a face, hands, and feet like a man; no one really knows what God is like; God answers prayers in doing only what we cannot do ourselves; He reveals Himself through dreams, miracles, inspired men, storms, earthquakes; He uses natural forces in punishment of wrong doing; He needs human co-operation in His work of mercy and redemption; He will save a man from drowning even if he cannot swim a stroke; He desires songs of praises, church membership, and unquestioning obedience to parents; to participate in war under any circumstances is against His will; He wants us to go to war whenever our government asks us to; only those will go to heaven who believe in Jesus; it is Jesus' exemplary life that saves from sin; Jesus rose from the grave, and will come to the world again.

From 60 to 70 per cent agree that no one knows where God is; the Bibles of Chinese and Buddhists contain some knowledge about God; angels bring word from Him; He dictated the Bible to some of his followers; no one would be sick or meet with disaster if he had faith enough in the Father; God will not save the good from accidents any more than the wicked; He is responsible for only the good that is done in the world; He planned all things from the beginning; He created woman from man's rib; He will give the sinner a chance to redeem himself after death; He will send some to Hell; Jesus possesses unlimited power.

Wider disagreements appear in the group of replies from 40 to 60 per cent. God is not like a person at all; He cannot make men good unless they desire to be good; He lives especially in church buildings; He is up in the sky; to know Him one must join the Christian church; scientists can tell us something about Him; He appeared in material form to men but does not now; He created life in the world by slow degrees developing from lower to higher forms; He will not do anything for us that we cannot do for ourselves; God will slay by lightning a man who cursed Him; He will someday come to the world to destroy it; He asks us to love Him more than we do people and animals; the cross of Jesus is essential to salvation; it is hard to understand the saving mystery of the cross and the miracles of Jesus; the nativity stories are make-believe; Jesus was God's son as Lincoln and other good men are; Jesus was God himself.[15]

The contradictions in these ideas of God indicate something of the confusion that arises in this area of knowledge. The items of highest agreement (above 90 per cent) are quite consistent except for the last one, believing all the Bible says about God. For the Bible says contradictory things about God and may be considered one of the sources of the confusion. The statements in the deciles of 40 to 80 per cent show wider disagreements and more striking contradictions. There are good reasons why agreement on the questions of God is difficult.

If God is an invisible being, he is not directly observable to the senses of all. Each person has to interpret and infer what God is like from his own experience and the reports of others.

Imagination weaves the visual context of knowledge. When sense objects are not present, we imagine them as we have seen them. When we have not seen an object, we use imagination to portray it. God is portrayed in whatever imagery best seems to suggest his attributes—as the spacious sky for omnipresence or the kindly face that indicates fatherly love.

Picture thinking is vivid but misleading in giving form to the formless. The crude anthropomorphic pictures of God soon become inadequate to a thinking mind. For concepts of God expand so that no picture frame is able to contain the greater vision. The pictures of God are a delight to childhood but a limitation to maturity.

Theologians then turn to word thinking to convey the larger meaning of Deity. Words are also symbols but more flexible and less limiting than the spatial forms of pictures. The attributes of God may be defined in abstract and unlimited terms as far as thought can reach, even beyond present experience. Creeds sculpture God in language, to view his nature and describe his traits in the subtle distinctions of speculative thought. Yet this linguistic art has its dangers too, for it may substitute words for reality or cling to symbols as unreal as the pictures.

It is evident that no one can think without content of some kind. The media of words, images, and relations are essential to whatever knowledge we have. If they are not taken as final, they may sharpen concepts by debate and mutual criticism. Each thinker may wrestle with Thou and discover for himself a conviction of personal experience. And together seekers for God have learned much from social experience, from scientific experiment and systematic philosophy.

Awareness of God is a total experience, a perspective of all impressions together. Robert Browning portrays this multiple revelation of God in Pippa's song:

[15] Condensed from *ibid.*, pp. 106-9.

The year's at the spring
And day's at the morn;
Morning's at seven;
The hillside's dew-pearled;
The lark's on the wing;
The snail's on the thorn:
God's in his heaven—
All's right with the world!

No single impression but all impressions in a perspective of beauty and harmony mean God to this singer. It is the total intuition that "all's right with the world" that brings the conviction, "God's in his heaven." All things taken together yield a unity, order, and purpose that one understands to mean God.

Such experiences arise from intrasensory perception, the participation of many sense modalities in a single perceptual experience. Most perceptual experience is intrasensory, a product of co-operating sensitivities and relations in judgments of meaning. Perceptions of space and time require perspectives of here and there, of now and then. The scientific labor of constructing hypotheses and generalizing data into universal laws is similar to awareness of God. Belief in a system of orderly nature follows psychological processes equivalent to belief in God. Both employ total experience of many clues to reach a perspective of what it all means. Theist and atheist are both employing the same psychological powers to attain a universal integration of empirical evidence.

Different views of God and the universe are not a scandal of confusion but a richness of supplementation. No finite mind can comprehend the infinite range of truth and reality. Every honest view of what appears real is a contribution to our growing understanding of truth. Truth is enlarged and verified by interpersonal communication and integrating of fragmentary insights into larger patterns of whole meaning. If revelation comes from God, that is also interpersonal encounter. What appear as contradictions at the moment may in the process of expanding discovery become complementary. Paradoxes should not be scorned as false but valued as pregnant suggestions to deliver new truth.

Personal experiences have emotional depth and vivid first-person meaning. Vital knowledge of God is personal experience. Pictures and words about God may be borrowed from others, yet they are poor substitutes for experience of one's own. Forms and symbols are convenient to pick up and pass along but often prove counterfeit without the ring of reality. Yet personal experiences need to be enlarged and corrected by interpersonal discoveries, thinking together and seeing together what reality means in larger perspective. Pratt [16] tells of a man who described God as a kind of oblong blur. He had rejected the anthropomorphic pictures of childhood and put nothing in their place. He had also neglected the means of grace and growth—religious education and social participation in a stimulating religious community. Reality is too large for lonely individuals to comprehend. Truth seekers wisely form associations, schools, and churches to provide the interpersonal activity that makes education a social achievement.

## 5. *Functions of Faith*

Faith is more than belief. The terms may be synonymous in current language, but psychological analysis shows a deep distinction between belief as an intellectual nod and faith as a venture of one's whole existential being. Faith may include belief, but it is a larger experience than intellectual assent. It is not confined to one aspect of personality but is rather a dynamic intention of personality as a whole.

Belief is judgment. Faith is devotion of total personality in loyal assurance. Belief may be less than knowledge, but faith is more. "Faith is reason grown courageous." The dynamic quality of faith is indicated in a volitional activity of purpose, commitment, and steadfastness. Regardless of contrary evidence, opposition, or suffering, one who has faith in Thou will continue to give unswerving loyalty. This is the meaning of faithfulness—an act of willing and persevering devotion. The emotional quality of faith is indicated in a basic confidence and security that gives one assurance. In this sense faith is the opposite of fear, anxiety, and uncertainty. Without emotional security there is no relaxation, but tension, distress, and instability. Assurance is the firm emotional undertone that enables one to have steady nerves and calm poise in the face of danger or confusion.

A religious faith may integrate the contradictory impulses of life into the ongoing purpose of religious devotion. For this reason religious beliefs are difficult to correct and criticize. They have grown into one's life and permeated one's whole manner of living. As the very existence of the family rests upon mutual love and faith in the beloved, so the entire manner of living is involved in religious faith. It is natural to identify faithfulness with unchanging beliefs. If a person is devoted to a religion, he may come to hold his religious beliefs with all the tenacious force of his personality. In this way men become dogmatic and intolerant, defending beliefs against all evidence and critical attack as a matter of personal honor. In this mood of passionate devotion religious people may unknowingly support

[16] *Op. cit.*, p. 200.

error and give their lives to a false cause. Religion is then discredited as falsehood by the blind determination of its followers to be true to uncritical beliefs.

Static beliefs need to become dynamic, ready to change as new perspectives show the way to larger faith. They need to be tested and pruned by a loyalty too alert to accept a belief as true without inspection. Untested beliefs prevent us from seeking further; they shut us out from new discovery and full participation in true reality. On the other hand, beliefs that are constantly tested by observation and reason direct us toward reality in following the open possibility of enlarging truth.

In conclusion we may note that faith has five productive functions at work in the human venture.

*First,* faith explores the unknown. It is customary to exalt the daring of explorers, who leave the comforts of settled and familiar backgrounds to venture forth into the unknown. Deeper understanding shows that this daring stems from faith, the fundamental trait of such personalities. Columbus persisted beyond his contemporaries because he had more faith. Galileo invented the telescope and challenged the authority of astronomical tradition by faith in his hypothesis. Lincoln challenged slavery and Wilson international discord by larger faith in freedom, peace, and justice. Faith in the undiscovered impels its discovery.

*Second,* trust creates values. Faith sees the invisible and foresees the not yet attained. Truth advances in every field by this power of the mind to see the invisible. Mathematicians construct laws and scientists fling out universal systems from their confidence in reason and the orderliness of reality. Business credit structures arise from mutual confidence in the intangible values of economic exchange. Governments maintain law and order by public confidence in mutual welfare. Civilization is the sum total of human values achieved by trustful relationships.

*Third,* creeds unite believers. This is a paradox, for creeds have also divided men into rival sects and denominations. But underlying the surface tensions of division are the deeper unities of common faith. Every social unity and co-operation rises from common beliefs. If we did not believe in the same values, we would not work together for them. If we did not trust one another, we would not dwell in peace and harmony as largely as we do. Creeds are not only religious; they are also political, economic, social, and scientific. But religious creeds seek to go higher in cosmic perspective and deeper in the tide of eternal destinies.

*Fourth,* assurance releases tensions. Tensions arise in seeking and striving to reach goals. These are dynamic springs of constructive achievement. Other tensions, such as fears and anxieties, are paralyzing and thwarting. These are destructive of peace, poise, and efficiency. They may become obsessive fixations or neurotic compulsions, leading to nervous disorders and mental diseases. There is no cure for these functional disorders short of faith. Without faith every other effort fails. Faith is an antidote to fear and anxiety, the specific condition essential to relaxation and facilitation of normal functions.

*Fifth,* faithful devotion integrates personality. Devotion to a cause becomes a major purpose that gathers up all the energies of life and channels them into unified expression. Distractions of scattered interests and conflicts of contrary desires are integrated into complete devotion. Faith in a religious way of life makes it worth every effort and sacrifice. Such faith in religious values transforms all values in reference to its norms. Actions are judged by their service to the religious cause. Desires are rejected or approved as they meet the requirements of the religious life. A center has been found whereby every impulse may be oriented in the direction of unselfish love and service. Nothing so integrates personality as faithful devotion to a cause, and no cause demands more faithfulness than a religious mission led by eternal imperatives.

# 10 RELIGIOUS BEHAVIOR

## *1. Unconscious Motivation*

Behavior is overt. What persons do in public is open to observation. Actions have objective effects in the space-time world that can be noted and described. But motives are covert. Why persons do what they do is their own business, not open to public observation. They belong to the secrets of private life, well kept and closely guarded by their owners. Motives may be hidden even from the one who obeys them. And yet without knowing these motives, behavior cannot be understood.

The terms "motive" is derived from the Latin *movere,* meaning "to move." It is related to "emotion"—derived from the Latin *e* + *movere,* "to move out" or "stir up." Motivation is therefore the process of arousing energies of personality leading to action. To understand religious behavior, we need to investigate its motivation, that is, what causes people to act as they do and what goals they move toward. Psychology that explores *motives* is called a dynamic psychology. It goes beyond description of what to a bolder search for why. Various concepts have been employed: instincts, propensity, impulse, urge, drive, need, interest, desire, attitude, sentiment —each claiming to explain why we act as we do.

An older rational psychology may have viewed all human behavior as directed by conscious choices. But motives are unconscious as well as conscious. The age of reason is yielding to a more comprehensive view of the complex forces, conscious and unconscious that incite and inhibit action. And so intricate are the complexities of human nature that the chief danger in all interpretations is oversimplification. It might appear simple to distinguished "conscious" from "unconscious," so obvious are the symptoms. Yet few words are used with less clarity than these.

Of all views of the unconscious the most influential in our generation are the psychoanalytic interpretations of Freud and his associates. Freud diagnosed nervous disorders by analysis of the emotional history of the patient. Originally psychoanalysis referred to certain therapeutic methods;

later it became a systematic theory of unconscious psychic processes in dynamic interplay of urging and checking forces.

The psychic life, according to Freud, is divided into unconscious, preconscious, and conscious activities.[1] The "unconcious" he considered to be the larger part of mental life, never conscious or else repressed from consciousness. Unconscious drives consist of nonmoral and asocial cravings of primitive lusts, infantile wishes, and painful memories repressed as unacceptable to conscious standards. The "preconscious" was his name for that part of the psychic life which may at any time become conscious. It consists of verbalized material, nearer consciousness and more accessible to voluntary control. The "conscious" is that fragmentary and fleeting part of the mental life of which the individual is aware at any moment. It consists of transitory impressions and ideas that are relatively less significant, Freud believed, in determining behavior.

Later Freud offered another triple division of the mental life to classify the forces of personality: *(a)* The "id" is the source of instinctive energy in each individual. It is the unconscious reservoir of the libido (psychic sex energy), aiming to gratify the pleasure principle and avoid pain. It is unmoral and illogical, with no unity of purpose or sense of time. *(b)* The "ego" is a coherent organization of mental processes derived from the id by interaction with the external world. It is partly conscious and partly unconscious, seeking to regulate personality by repression and sublimation. It strives to be reasonable and moral, to mediate between the world and the id by submitting the pleasure principle to the reality principle. *(c)* The "superego" consists of the affirmative identifying ego-ideal and the negative punishing conscience, representing the permanent influence of parents and society in modifying the ego and id. It is largely unconscious and inaccessible to the conscious ego, yet it gives rise to religion, morality, and social ideals to guide the course of human development. It constitutes the higher nature of man, the ideals of parents and teachers as absorbed by the individual and wrought into the values of this culture.

The energy of personality accumulates in tensions and attractions (cathexes). Libidinal energy may concentrate in ego-cathexis, becoming narcissim, or affectionate regard for oneself; or it may concentrate on objects in object-cathexis, directing motor striving outward to some person or thing. It may concentrate in a fantasy-cathexis, directing the libido toward the inner world of imagination (introversion). Primitive desires are often in conflict with social standards. Confronted by the reality principle of social requirements, yet unwilling to surrender the pleasure principle of libidinal satisfaction, the ego seeks compromise solutions by such defense

[1] *The Ego and the Id*, tr. J. Riviere (London: The Hogarth Press, 1927).

mechanisms as repression, regression, reaction-formation, isolation, undoing, projection, introjection, turning against self, reversal, and sublimitation. The most notorious of these defenses is repression, the unconscious disposal of painful memories and unacceptable wishes. Yet there is confusion among psychoanalysts as to what forces do the repressing. Among the agents accused of repression are the censor, the ego, the ego ideal, the superego, the ego instincts, the death instinct, fear, anxiety, the pleasure-pain principle, guilt feeling, self-esteem, the master sentiment of self-regard, and the sex instinct.[2]

When these libidinal urges are fixated in conflictual neuroses, they disturb the normal functioning of personality and require therapeutic treatment. Diagnostic methods included hypnosis (rejected later), dream analysis, free association, analysis of resistances, mistakes and forgetting, exploring childhood incidents and emotions, translation of symbolism, interpretation of social relations (Oedipus complex) and ambivalent conflicts. Psychoanalytic therapy includes catharsis, abreaction, insight by bringing the unconscious complexes to conscious attention, and transference and sublimation to more acceptable modes of expression.

The pioneer work of Freud has been a target for criticism. In the early violence of psychoanalytic controversy one was either Freudian or anti-Freudian. Followers of Freud were apt to claim (as did mystics of their noetic experiences) that no one could understand Freud unless he had been converted and believed the whole gospel. The unconverted who rejected the teachings of Freud were unfortunately suffering from repressions that resisted and distorted the truth. Yet many of his most able associates have parted from him on major issues and taken their independent ways.

The fate of the pioneer is to be a storm center of controversy, and Freud was no exception to this destiny. His theories were at first met by the scorn and disbelief of his scientific colleagues. In his *Autobiography* he esays:

> For more than ten years after my separation from Breuer I had no followers. I was completely isolated. In Vienna I was shunned, abroad no notice was taken of me. My *Interpretation of Dreams*, published in 1900, was scarcely reviewed in the technical journals.[3]

But as he gathered data from the case studies of patients, the analysis of dreams and symbolism, wit and errors, folklore and literature, his own behavior and that of his fellow beings, the evidence accumulated. And as he continued to write his views in lucid and well-knit exposition, the un-

[2] Anna Freud, *The Ego and the Mechanism of Defence,* tr. C. Baines (London: The Hogarth Press, 1937).

[3] J. Strachey, tr. (New York: W. W. Norton & Co., [1923]; 1935), p. 95.

folding argument began to win supporters first in Vienna, then Germany and other countries. It was in 1908 that friends of psychoanalysis met at Salzburg and agreed to meet regularly and publish a journal, the *Jahrbuch für psychopathogische und psychoanalytische Forshungen.* At the second congress held at Nuremberg in 1910, an "International Psychoanalytical Association" was formed consisting of local societies but having a common president, who was Carl G. Jung. Other journals were also started: the *Zentralblatt für Psychoanalyse,* edited by Adler and Stekel; and a little later *Imago,* edited by Sachs and Rank.

Yet within two years Jung published a book, *Transformations and Symbols of the Libido,*[4] declaring a basic divergence which was unacceptable to Freud, and the breach was never reconciled. The book was an extended commentary on a case of schizophrenia with symbolic parallels drawn from religion, mythology, ethnology, art, literature, and psychiatry. In this view the libido is not primarily sexual but represents psychic energy as a whole, "a continuous life urge, a will to live," which expands into a "conception of intentionality in general" (p. 137). Jung says that the whole thing came upon him as a landslide, an "explosion of all those psychic contents which could find no room, no breathing space, in the constricting atmosphere of Freudian psychology."

In going his divergent way, Jung has steadily in the forty-five years since then carried forward his research and theory independently under the banner of analytical psychology. He refers to his difference with Freud in terms of the narrow conceptual framework of Freudian psychology, the reductive causalism, the disregard of teleological directness so characteristic of everything psychic, outmoded rationalism, and scientific materialism. Jung also employs free association, analysis of dreams and symbols, comparative study of the cultures of mankind, and the basic themes of human interest, which he calls archetypes. Yet he charts the course of psychic life from other motives, ground, and goals than Freud—giving large place to the collective unconscious that links the personal with the universal concerns of human existence.

One of his aims, he declares, has been to free medical psychology from the "subjective and personalistic bias" of Freudian psychology, which emerged from nineteenth-century individualism and left no room for objective impersonal facts. "The psyche is not of today; its ancestry goes back millions of years." Knowledge of the subjective personal consciousness means very little, as he sees it, until by comparative study one comes to understand the collective unconscious. To him personality has no fixed boundaries but merges and submerges in the endless sea of psychic ex-

[4] *Wandlungen und Symbole der Libido;* now in a new edition, *Symbols of Transformation,* tr. R. F. C. Hull, as Vol. V of the *Collected Works* (New York: Pantheon Books, 1956).

istence. Contrary to rational expectation, it is the irrational factors that play the decisive role in the processes of psychic transformation. Yet there are no purposeless psychic processes, for the psyche is essentially purposive and goal-directed.

Both Freud and Jung with their followers, have undertaken psychological studies of religion, as we have seen in Chapter Two. In his *Autobiography,* Freud gives a significant place to his work in the psychology of religion:

> I myself set a higher value upon my contributions to the psychology of religion, which began in 1907 with the establishment of a remarkable similarity between obsessive acts and religious practices or ritual. Without as yet understanding the deeper connections, I described the obsessional neurosis as a distorted private religion and religion as a kind of universal obsessional neurosis.[5]

In this study he regards the obsessional neurosis as a pathological counterpart to the formation of a religion, as both arise from unconscious guilt against which one seeks to protect himself by performing ritualistic acts with compulsive repetition. The resemblance between neurotic ceremonial and religious rites lies in the fear of pangs of conscience after their omission. But equally obvious are the differences so startling as to "make the comparison into a sacrilege." Neurotic ritual is private and without awareness of meaning, while religious rites are public and communal, full of meaning and symbolic understanding. Yet in each of these the conscientiousness is set to oppose a repressed impulse felt as a temptation; the anxiety is produced by the repression and directed to the future in fearful expectation. "The ceremonial acts arise partly as a defense against temptation and partly as a protection against the misfortune expected" (p. 32). A progressive renunciation of the instincts and their satisfaction is one of the foundations of human civilization. Religion has served this function in yielding up evil and asocial impulses to the divinity and so helping man to free himself from them.

Six years later in 1913 Freud published *Totem and Taboo,* going to the primitive religions to find psychological roots for these prohibitions and rituals of unconscious guilt. In totemistic tribes he was impressed *(a)* with the incest taboo that required exogamy or marriage outside the tribe, and *(b)* with the feast in which the totem animal was eaten as a sacred meal. He saw in the totem animal a symbol of the primal father who deprived the young men of the women until in revolt he was slain and devoured by the younger men to take his place and possess his virtue. Then in remorse for their "original sin" they sought to be reconciled with the father, to carry out

[5] P. 134. He refers to his article "Obsessive Acts and Religious Practices," *Collected Papers of Sigmund Freud,* tr. J. Riviere II (London: The Hogarth Press, 1924), 25-35.

his injunctions by tabooing the women sexually, and to honor him by ceremonial rites in the sacred meal. This Freud saw as confirmation for the Oedipus complex to substantiate the typical triangle in every family in which the son is rival to the father for the affection of the mother.

In his later studies of religion[6] Freud extends this point of view in expounding the psychological meaning of religion as a way of alleviating unconscious guilt arising from libidinous impulses against the requirements of social and moral conduct enforced by the superego. Actually this is a needed and important service wherein religion assists in the development of character and responsible self-control. Otherwise if the primitive impulses of the id should triumph, life would destroy itself. Yet to overrepress the libido by complete denial would be to extinguish the instinctual desire to live and create. The essential task of religion, as of morality and law, is to control and yet at the same time sublimate these lusty primitive impulses until the pleasure principle comes to terms with the reality principle, and blind raging may be converted into conscious adjudication of these conflicts to fulfill the needs of life in socially acceptable expression. If religion is an illusion, it has been a useful means of guiding raw impulses into identification with other persons, in the ideal of social love.[7]

In calling religion an illusion, Freud does not insist that it is error but that wish fulfillment is a prominent factor in its motivation. Yet he does foresee a declining future for religion as youth are less subject to its beliefs and as this phase of human evolution passes on to scientific knowledge. In his *Civilization and Its Discontents* he is more emphatic to say that popular religion is "patently infantile" and "incongruous with reality." Admitting that religion may save many people from individual neuroses by unconditional submission to God's inscrutable decree, yet he concludes that man could arrive by a shorter road. In 1933 he asks if the truth of religion may not be altogether discarded:

> Its doctrines carry with them the stamp of the times in which they originated, the ignorant childhood days of the human race. Its consolations deserve no trust. Experience teaches us that the world is not a nursery. The ethical commands, to which religion seeks to lend its weight, require some other foundation instead, for human society cannot do without them, and it is dangerous to link up obedience to them with religious belief.[8]

To Jung religion appears in a very different light. He also works with dreams and other data of the unconscious in psychiatric practice and observes how important religion is to persons who are deeply concerned with

[6] *The Future of an Illusion* and *Moses and Monotheism.*

[7] *Group Psychology and the Analysis of the Ego,* tr. J. Strachey (London: Hogarth Press, 1922).

[8] *New Introductory Lectures to Psychoanalysis,* p. 215.

their destiny. But to him religious experience is no illusion, no invention of the individual mind or fantasy of an obsessive neurosis. Rather it is an event that comes to one from beyond and makes its effects known in his experience. Religion is a careful and scrupulous observation of some revelation or significant energy, which Rudolf Otto termed the *numinosum*, that is, "a dynamic agency or effect, not caused by an arbitrary act of will." [9] One has the experience of being seized and controlled by an external power which has the quality of a psychic force or an invisible presence exerting its influence upon consciousness.

Such religious experience he distinguishes from dogma and ritual, which are shaped by human invention to explain or even to protect against the disturbing experience. While religious practices may be voluntary and carried out to produce desired effects, yet the belief in an external divine cause always precedes any such performance. Each experience contains something which is unknown, extending beyond the conscious realm of well-ordered knowledge. Religious intuitions seem to come to a person from the collective unconscious, as do all the basic concerns of human life.

Freud distrusted religion because it was not scientific and doubted that we could know by other means what science does not give. But Jung holds scientific theory of less value from the standpoint of psychological truth than religious dogma. A theory is highly abstract and rational while the dogma is better able to convey irrational facts, such as the psyche.

> Dogma expresses the soul more completely than a scientific theory, for the latter gives expression to and formulates the conscious mind alone. Furthermore, a theory can do nothing but formulate a living thing in abstract terms. Dogma, on the contrary, aptly expresses the living process of the unconscious in the form of the drama of repentance, sacrifice and redemption.[10]

When science puts in place of the certainty of faith the uncertainty of knowledge, the conscious mind sees itself isolated in a world of psychic variables with no roots or connecting relationships. The energy and conviction of religion, as well as its universality, indicate it to be of the nature of the archetype. It is a natural and original function that influences man as persistently as the instincts of sexuality and aggression. The symbols of religion coincide in every age and culture with these ever-recurring primordial images. The archetypes are the numinous, structural elements of the psyche that are productive of faith resting upon experience. They belong to the race from time immemorial emerging out of the collective unconscious.

Religion serves to discover what is deepest in the soul of man and relate this to what is deepest in the world around him. In thus opening a channel

[9] Jung, *Psychology and Religion: West and East*, p. 7.

[10] *Ibid.*, p. 46. Used by permission of Pantheon Books.

between the subjective and objective psychic energies, the tide has flowed both outward and inward. In the early history of religions man projected his unconscious images and deepest needs into objective symbols and external gods. The gods first lived in super-human power on mountaintops. Then they came together in one God bringing order and unity to the psychic world. At length the God became man. The projections are withdrawn, and the divine energy is known to us in the psychic functions.

For Jung it does not matter whether the gods are inside or outside of man. Most important to him is the reconciling of opposites, that the subjective and the objective may be integrated into one. Wherever the external objects stand apart, they are lifeless images or empty dogma. While if the God is only subjective, he must then be an illusion. The God-image is to be the reconciling symbol for drawing together the divisive fragments of conflicting life. Such integration of personality is the achievement of maturity and the goal of psychotherapy. To Freud psychoanalysis was to be the successor of religion, but to Jung religion is essential if psychotherapy is to fulfill the meaning of life.

What man seeks by every device and devious pathway is the experience of wholeness. To this end he may long for a religious solution of ultimate reconciliation to assuage the guilt of rebellion against the Father or the anguish of interminable strife and fragmentation. In these psychological dilemmas the controversy is whether religious experience is regression or progression, illusion or revelation, neurotic or therapeutic, repressive or releasing, motivated by guilt or growth, obsessive or purposive, evasive or invasive, reductive or productive, ego centric or outgoing through enlarging relationships.

Along the line of these dichotomies Freud and Jung stand counterpoised against each other. One is the scientist doubting the value of mystical faith; the other is the mystic doubting the finality of scientific theory to comprehend the larger mystery and meaning of the soul. Who is on the side of the angels, and who is the devil's advocate? To those who welcome Jung as the friend of religion, Erich Fromm[11] has a caustic refutation. Jung, while apparently favorable to religion, reduces it to a relativism of popular opinion that whatever is experienced is true psychologically, with no distinctions in a morass of psychological subjectivism. Freud, while apparently unfavorable to religion, attacks religion from the ethical core of religion as truth, brotherly love, reduction of suffering, independence, and responsibility. It is the neurotic and infantile forms of religion that Freud would have us outgrow.

But there is more truth in Jung than Fromm recognizes from his partisan

[11] *Psychoanalysis and Religion* (New Haven, Conn.: Yale University Press, 1950).

viewpoint. And there is more than stinging cross winds of controversy in the rival contentions of the analysts. When we view their pioneer explorations in historical perspective, we come upon significant lines of continuous development in the depth psychology. It was Freud more than anyone who opened the uncharted territory of the unconscious to psychological investigation. Yet he was bound by his preconceptions of nineteenth century materialism from which he was unable to free himself. After developing his systematic theory, Freud in his later years concluded that mind is deeper than rationality and consequently goes beyond his earlier analytic concepts.

The integrity of his work, however, enabled others who learned from him to carry on to new frontiers. Alfred Adler came to see man as a spiritual being who more than medical healing must find a meaning of life toward which he can work. To restore meaning to life, he believed the "social feeling" must be experienced in religious dimensions. To him this meant to "love thy neighbor" in a deep sense of connection to life evolving toward a universal community of mankind. This does not come as a conscious decision in rational terms; it must be a direct personal experience of the inner continuity of life in harmony with cosmic purpose and human wholeness. Only in this way can we be healed of emotional isolation and the neurotic dilemmas of sterile individualism.

Jung also perceived man as a spiritual being with religious dimensions beyond the limits of rational scientism. Beginning with Freud's conception of the unconscious, he extended the libido to psychic energy at work in collective continuities that underlie individual personality. To reconcile the conflicts of the inner life, he came to the *self* as a deeper center than ego, in whose larger relationships the integration of personality may be achieved. Speaking not as a theologian defending any creed but as an empiricist who reports what he finds in human experience, he observes that man is lost without a religious context. He then becomes a prey to political ideologies and state religions with the ruthless abandon of demonic passion and destruction. The very nature of human personality carries metaphysical overtones, something more ultimate of which man is but a partial reflection. It would be unempirical to deny man's insatiable longing to find the ultimate meaning of his life and to participate in it. Though he sought to interpret man in strictly psychological terms as archetype symbols of the collective unconscious, he found his psychological hedge flimsy and artificial. The psychologist cannot stand apart as a neutral observer; he is also a human being who is involved with the ultimate spiritual problems of his existence.

Otto Rank, who was close to Freud for over twenty years, came in his final work, which he called *Beyond Psychology,* to affirm the need for a religious dimension to fulfill the meaning of life. "Man is born beyond psychology and he dies beyond it, but he can live beyond it only through a vital experience of his own—in religious terms, through revelation, conversion, or rebirth."[12] From his historical studies he found this vital experience at a deeper level than rationality, in a sense of relationship that extends beyond the present moment in all directions of time. This he called immortality not merely as continued existence but as a sense of larger participation in everlasting life. As this new outlook comes from a psychic source beyond the rational consciousness, it gives the impression of a revelation whose transcendent significance changes the meaning of life as a conversion. As the person emerges with a new soul, this is experienced as rebirth. With such a vitalizing experience of immortality experienced in all present moments, a new life opens before us in which art and religion meet in a creative work that fulfills the meaning of life.

The unfolding of this larger meaning from psychoanalysis has been described as "the death and rebirth of psychology." Ira Progoff, the author of a book which bears this title,[13] comes from a thoughtful study of Freud, Adler, Jung, and Rank to conclude that "the foundation of the new kind of psychology is its conception of man as an organism of psychological depth and of spiritual magnitude." Its aim is to do its psychological work with the unconscious levels of personality so as to free the potentialities of the spirit to emerge, to establish the basic connectedness of life in larger wholeness, and to nourish the creative capacities of man in a cosmic community.

## 2. *Religious Conduct*

In this topic we come to the most practical problem of religious living. Religion may be respected for its noble ideals, long history, and impressive institutions. But does it work? How does religion affect conduct? Does religious instruction make children honest? Do chapel exercises in college make less cheating in examinations? Does church membership increase brotherhood, social justice, and economic equality? The most urgent question asked of religious people is, What are you going to do about this? The crucial test of religion is the test of conduct. "One hour of justice is worth more than seventy years of prayer," said Mohammed. "He that would wait upon me, let him wait upon the sick brethren," said Buddha. "Inasmuch as ye have done it unto one of the least of these my brethren, ye have done it unto me," said Jesus.

[12] (Camden, N.J.: Haddon Craftsmen, 1941), p. 16.

[13] (New York: The Julian Press, Inc., 1956).

As the experimental test is to science, so is the test of conduct in demonstrating the genuineness of religion.

Conduct is voluntary behavior. This is the field of ethics, in which one is responsible for what he is able to control by conscious choice. It is the meeting point of ethics and religion at which point one does good from religious motives, and religious motives produce good works. How shall we know what behavior is religious? Two answers are given: *(a)* By their fruits you shall know them. This is the test of action, looking toward the ends or consequences to see what the effects are. Surely these are not to be ignored, but religious acts are confusing to behold. For what deed has not been done in the name of religion? The variety of religious acts is almost infinite, and the contraditions are quite perplexing. Acts that are criminal in other circumstances—for example, murder or prostitution—may be sanctioned by religious authority. Or the same act—for example giving alms—may be done for either religious or secular motives. So we turn to motives. *(b)* By their motives you shall know them. No act is meaningful until the motive is comprehended. Deeds of service may be grudgingly given under compulsion of slavery, or shrewdly offered for economic gain, or cleverly displayed for political power. In contrast to these religious service is loving devotion to God offered freely in outgoing concern for other persons. It is the motive that makes the essential difference and governs the quality of the deed. And effects of conduct are different because motives so direct them.

Religious motivation is that which incites to religious conduct. Religion has been defined as ultimate concern. Whatever concerns you will become a motivating force to restructure and focalize the field of your experience. When you perceive this concern in reference to the whole meaning and destiny of life, it is a religious motive. The distinction noted between primary and secondary religion is one of motivation. The primary religious person is more completely involved in his religious concern. His religious dedication will make a decisive and notable difference in his conduct. But the secondary or tertiary religious person will be much less involved, and his weak religious motives will make little effective difference in his conduct.

At primitive religious levels fear of punishment and hope of reward are likely to be dominant motives. Natural evils, such as famine, flood, barren womb, illness, misfortune, or failure in enterprise, are seen as intended by angry spirits for corrective punishment. If the deity is capricious, he must be appeased; if he is moral, then man must repent of his sins and mend his ways. Beyond the vicissitudes of this life loom the mysteries of death with prospects of torture in hell and reward in heaven.

Other motives that come to have enlarging appeal are social approval, ideal imperatives, and loving devotion. Social influences operate constantly in human relations by example and imitation. The tendency to follow the crowd and do as others do is almost irresistible. It is odd to be different and lonely to stand aloof; man hungers for the unity and solidarity of association. The Soviet Union has demonstrated the strength of social approval as greater than economic motive, while in other nations patriotic devotion is a cause for which men live and die. The approval of the religious community, whether primitive or modern, is always to be reckoned with.

And yet heroic nonconformists like Jesus, Socrates, Spinoza, and Luther will accept excommunication and death for an imperative ideal. They prove that ideal motives can outreach fear of punishment, hope of reward, or social approval. This sense of duty is conscience, no fractional part of the self, but the whole mind in the act of moral judgment. Conscience has been taken as the voice of God, and again as the voice of the crowd. Yet the independent conscience is an inner authority, often revolting against the established codes and creeds of the crowd. In this way social, moral, and religious progress is pioneered by the individual person acting from inner-directed convictions. Conscience is no wiser than its owner. Yet it is capable of growth through education. A growing conscience utilizes all the resources of social tradition and moral custom, the teaching of scripture, the advice of friends, the mistakes of the past, the lessons of history, the logic of events, and the revelations of divine purpose.

Is it possible for religion to be overconscientious? That depends upon the conscience. An ignorant, superstitious, fear-ridden conscience may be the undoing of a neurotic victim of anxiety. A misguided, intolerant, persecuting conscience can do great damage, as the history of inquisitions, witch burning, and anti-Semitism shows. Conscience operates with powerful dynamics, which may be used recklessly and even destructively. The power of strong convictions when empowered by religious motives of ultimate concern has often proved explosive in human history. The primary religious person who takes his religion seriously will need to clarify the motives of his ultimate concern lest he act unwisely as an irresponsible fanatic.

Every motive comes to focus upon action. Fears and hopes point to acts of punishment and reward. Social approval is a mutual program of action agreed upon as desirable. Duties are imperatives, and love is devotion to serve a desirable cause. These and other motives intermingle in the complex network of interests, desires, and purposes. Purity of motive is often lauded as if superior to mixed motives. But all motives are mixed; the only purity is not simplicity but harmony of many co-ordinating motives in symphonic chords of ongoing purpose. Motives, as we have seen, arise from needs of which the most basic and persistent is the affiliative need for interpersonal relationship. They arise from and lead to social interaction in the dialogic relation of address and answering response.

Such interpersonal goals are the crucial factors in human motivation. If one sees nothing worth striving for, he will give up the effort. Motives strike out from desires. They are tensions goalward that release energies in direct action. But desires are not determined by innate instincts or mechanical chains of causation. At least we have no empirical knowledge of mysterious forces pushing from behind. What we know from experience is the pull of goals. Human persons are incomplete and seek to find a larger life in meeting one another. There are surely limits to the freedom of choice. No one can have everything he wants. Yet within limits we are choosing all the time. No psychology can make sense of human behavior, or follow motives, without noting preferences and choices. Determinism is determination, and destiny is destination. Conduct is directed by motives, and motives are controlled by goals at which we decide to aim. The final cause, as Aristotle saw, is purpose. However it may be in the world at large, this is psychologically true for persons and societies. We are what we are moving toward. Religious conduct is action along the line of religious purpose to meet and respond to Thou.

## 3. *Character and Religious Education*

For a century the hopes of mankind have been invested in education. In one country after another educational reforms have gained momentum until better education for all is the accepted goal. Education has been trusted as a panacea for illiteracy, ignorance, error, ill health, and most of the other ills of persons and society. Education has become a major business of local and national governments, whether democratic or totalitarian. Propaganda and advertising have so cleverly utilized educational facilities that whole populations believe what they are told. Human nature is viewed as pliable clay in the hands of educators, who can shape it as they choose for good or for diabolical ends.

When public education was established in the American way, there was general belief in the separation of church and state to avoid the control of either by the other. To avoid doctrinal controversies religion has largely been excluded from public schools, and character education has also been neglected in the emphasis on scientific methods and secular interests. To correct this oversight our generation has promoted religious education in churches and character education in recreational organizations such as the Y.M.C.A. and Y.W.C.A., Boy Scouts, Girl Scouts, Campfire Girls, clubs, camps, and such. Public schools have shown their interest by releasing one or two hours of school time a week for religious education or by fostering character interests in extracurricular activities.

How effective is this education in promoting character and religious values? Attempts have been made to appraise our current educational practices. The most notable of these investigations is the Character Education Inquiry, directed by Hugh Hartshorne and Mark A. May. With commendable thoroughness and scientific objectivity forty-one tests of deception were constructed and administered to eleven thousand school pupils, aged eight to sixteen, ranging from the fourth grade through high school. Three types of deception were tested: cheating, lying, and stealing. Concrete tasks provided twenty-two opportunities to cheat in classroom work, four in athletics, two in party games, and one in homework. Lying tests consisted of thirty-six questions in one case and ten in the other which could be answered falsely. Stealing tests offered two opportunities to steal money and one to steal articles.

Conclusions drawn from statistical treatment of the data are as follows: [14]

1. Older pupils are slightly more deceptive.
2. Sex seems to make no difference.
3. Honesty is positively related to intelligence.
4. Emotional instability is related to deception.
5. Physical condition seems to have no effect on deception.
6. Members of higher-income families show less deceit.
7. Those with better manners and cultural background show less deceit.
8. Deceit is associated with other home conditions, as parental discord, example, bad discipline, unsocial attitudes, poverty, and changing socioeconomic status.
9. Religious affiliation shows no general differences not attributable to social and intellectual level.
10. Kinship means similarity.
11. Differences in school grade are not significant, except that retarded children cheat more.
12. Those who get high marks in classes cheat slightly less.
13. Those who are good in deportment cheat less.
14. Associates are much alike in cheating.
15. Those who show greater resistance to suggestion cheat less.
16. Children who attend movies more often cheat more.
17. There is less cheating when teacher-pupil relations are cordial.
18. Students in progressive schools cheat less.

[14] *Studies in Deceit* (New York: The Macmillan Co., 1928), pp. 408-14. An exhaustive study by C. F. Chassell, *The Relation Between Morality and Intellect* (New York: Columbia University Press, 1935), incorporating the findings of three hundred other studies, concludes that correlation in restricted groups is extremely variable and as low as .10 to .39.

19. Those enrolled in Sunday school cheat less. But those who attend Sunday school regularly cheat as much as those who rarely or never attend.
20. Members of character organizations cheat as much as nonmembers.
21. Deceit is not a unified trait. Honesty is a specific function of specific situations.

The concomitants of deceit are, in order of importance: (*a*) classroom association; (*b*) general personal handicaps, as low intelligence, poor resistance to suggestion, emotional instability; *(c)* cultural and social limitations in the home background.

Implications of these studies in deceit are: (*a*) No child is dishonest by nature, but merely as a mode of adjustment. Upon this there is general agreement. *(b)* Urging honest behavior or discussing ideals of honesty has no necessary relation to honest conduct. Such methods are variable and overrated, yet discussion may prove an aid to desirable conduct. *(c)* Prevailing methods of teaching ideals do little good. This inference is taken from the low correlation between membership in character organizations and the practice of honesty. Those who attend Sunday school regularly make no better showing than those who do not. Better methods of education are urgently needed. *(d)* The specific situation holds large influence. Teaching vague generalities and abstract concepts is futile. Honesty in one situation (as telling mother the truth) may not transfer to another situation (as telling a policeman the truth or telling one's age correctly when it is disadvantageous to do so). Honesty in paying a debt to a friend may not transfer to returning over-change pennies from a stranger in a crowded store. Unless teaching comes to specific situations with effective motivation and practice, ideals are remote from actual conduct.

It would be hasty to conclude, however, that persons have no general traits or attitudes to carry over from one situation to another. Allport [15] shows the significance of traits in personality and replies cogently to Hartshorne, May, and other exponents of specificity: *(a)* Low correlations "prove only that children are not consistent *in the same way*, not that they are inconsistent with themselves." They do not all have the same trait, but each does have his own traits. *(b)* The research is based upon artificial ethical concepts—from the point of view of society rather than the actual mental organization of the individual. *(c)* Socialized traits are not to be found in younger children so much as in older persons who have assimilated prevalent ideals gradually through years of social adjustment. (*d*) While the coefficients of correlation are low, yet it is notable that they are positive and that twenty-three of the tests intercorrelate +.30 on the average. Complex statistical results are inevitably ambiguous. From the same data Maller, one of

[15] *Personality*, pp. 248-58.

the associates in the study, reports a general factor of character, "c," readiness to forego immediate gain for the sake of remote but greater gain. *(e)* Conclusions naturally depend on methods used, and others using different methods may find consistent general traits of honesty and deceit.

The net outcome of such studies is to startle us awake to the need for clearer understanding of psychological principles and more effective character and religious education. No one can blink away these facts or be complacent in the face of these studies, which conclude:

> There is little evidence that effectively organized moral education has been taking place. There is abundant evidence, however, that children have been acquiring habits which are important for character. . . . What they are learning at present of self-control, as also of service and honesty, is largely a matter of accident. . . . Anarchy in the leadership of moral education is not likely to produce order in the character of the child.[16]

Further investigation and experimentation are needed to develop a program that achieves desired results in religious and ethical conduct. Constructive suggestions may be taken from these studies in planning a more adequate education:

1. What is to be learned must be experienced.
2. What is to be experienced must be represented in the situations to which children are exposed.
3. These situations must be opportunities to pursue interests which lead to the conduct desired.
4. This conduct must be carried on in relation to the particular situations.
5. A common and potent factor in such situations is the established practice and code of the group.
6. Standards and ideals . . . must be tools rather than objects of aesthetic appreciation.
7. The achievement of specific standards, attitudes, and modes of conduct does not imply their integration. Integration is itself a specific achievement.

Civilization has been described as a race between education and catastrophe. In this crucial hour of history the race appears frantic. Catastrophe has already overtaken millions of our contemporaries in war and violent revolution. The revolutionary surge of these events provides no time for leisurely consideration of distant reforms. It demands an immediate program of social reconstruction in which education will be related to clearly defined goals of social and personal attainment. And yet in the welter of emergency measures there is danger of losing true perspective and doing

[16] Hartshorne and Maller, *Studies in Service and Self-Control* (New York: The Macmillan Co., 1929), p. 453.

the wrong things too efficiently. In other desperate hours of history notable progress has been won by seeing clearly true goals and choosing the right methods to achieve them. Grundtvig in Denmark and Pestalozzi in Switzerland led their people in educational reforms that created a democratic society in which each one could seek values and find life meaningful in the meeting of person with person.

### *4. Sin and Guilt*

What is sin? Is it a sin to break a promise or tell a lie? Is it a sin to break a traffic rule? Is it a sin to ignore the rights of others? Strictly speaking, sin is a religious problem. It is related to other offenses such as crime, immorality, and selfishness. To avoid confusion it is well to see these relations clearly. Crime is antilegal behavior, an offense against the civil law. Immorality is antimoral conduct, flouting the moral code of accepted ideals and customs. Selfishness is antisocial behavior, disregarding the good of one's fellow men. Sin is distinctly antireligious conduct, contrary to the order of religious values. Not all offenses are sins, not all sins public offenses. Any selfish, immoral, or criminal act may be a sin, but not for social, moral, or legal reasons. To those who believe they stand before God in the encounter of mutual response, a sin is any act or attitude that violates relationship to God.

Does this mean that atheists are incapable of sin? Atheists may be unconscious of sin, yet their disbelief in God does not dispense with the realities of the situation. The ultimate realities are questions for philosophy and theology. Psychology is concerned with the consciousness of guilt, whether religious or nonreligious, arising in relation to approving and disapproving persons. Yet from the psychological standpoint it is evident that guilt does not always coincide with feelings of guilt. Ignorance of the law does not excuse one from the penalty in courts of justice. Nor does ignorance of natural law save one from unforeseen consequences. An innocent child who has not heard of the law of grativation does not escape the results of falling from a window to the pavement below. The human experience which psychology studies is engaged in causal relations with realities which affect the nature of that experience.

How do anxious feelings of guilt arise in a growing person? First of all, a person sallies forth to meet other persons and events in his expanding world in personal experiments that have notable consequences. Life is a series of experiments in which every organism acts and observes reactions. Some acts bring favorable results; others bring unfavorable results. Adventures in tasting foods result in bitter or sweet flavors, satisfying nourishment or distressing poison. Social experiments in approaching, threatening, persuading, attacking, or aiding other persons produce results that are viewed as desirable or undesirable. By such trials and errors individuals come to distinguish good from evil consequences as reactions to good or evil deeds. The good so demonstrated wins social approval.

At this point in experimental learning, a second factor is the sense of personal responsibility. After numerous crucial experiments, every evil may be taken as the result of some act or failure to act. "What have I done to bring this evil upon me?" Seeking to find the causes of evils like sickness, misfortune, or defeat, one may find the cause in himself. To find one's self personally responsible for evil is to feel guilty. The fault may have been ritual neglect, or it may have been a moral failure to do what one knew to be right. In a religious sense this personal guilt may be viewed as sin in offending and impairing the approved relationship with God, which like every relation has implicit or explicit agreements and expectations. "Against thee, thee only, have I sinned." (Ps. 51:4.)

A third factor in guilt is a margin of consent or choice. Personal responsibility implies voluntary choice in which one may do either this or that. If one has no choice in the matter, how can he be responsible? The Hebrew consciousness of sin arose from this sense of ethical freedom. Under the stirring preaching of the prophets and the zealous devotion of priests to the law of God all evil became moral evil. Every man was accounted free to choose good or evil; consequently every one was responsible for his own evils. If Job suffered, he must have sinned; if Israel prospered, God must have approved.

A fourth factor in the experience of guilt is the feeling of necessity. Protests against the undeserved sufferings of Job and Prometheus, Socrates and Jesus, have the note of sincerity. They represent the unjust ills of mankind, struggling from age to age against cruel necessities. The Greeks call this inescapable destiny "fate"; the Hindus name it "karma." The doctrine of karma is perceived as a law of inheritance whereby the consequences of past deeds carry over from birth to rebirth on the wheel of existence. The Christian doctrine of orginal sin recognizes in the structure of finite existence that which makes sin inevitable. The tendency of the person to error and evil is further complicated by social evils and continuing traditions that infect and distort human perceptions.

The concept of sin reveals the level of religious development. Lack of awareness of sin indicates lack of religious concern and responsibility to Thou. Dull response to religious events suggests lack of interest and appreciation. Primitive ideas of sin mistake the trivial for the significant. Taboos may be based on ignorance and superstition. Magic and ritual often take precedence over ethical considerations of justice and mercy. To fulfill higher religious laws Jesus and the prophets set aside ceremonial requirements. Mature ideas of sin show moral awakening and better understanding of true values. A growing consciousness of sin means clearer insight and more intelligent devotion to the ethical imperatives of religious encounter.

In our time the sense of sin appears to be declining, and many moderns welcome the decline. There are psychologists who consider the feeling of sin an abnormal, unhealthy, morbid condition. There are sociologists who regard fear of sin as a social lag in which old taboos no longer apply to new conditions. The conclusion is that sin is our own bad thinking, worry, and fret over a past already gone. They advocate forgetting it and insist we will be all right if we think we are.

The sense of guilt is a serious psychological problem. It is the accusative personal and interpersonal sense of failure. Under stress of self-accusing guilt neurotic patterns may develop: anxieties and fears, rejecting oneself, evasion of responsibility in projection and repression, or defensive attitudes of aggression and obsessive compulsion. The burden of guilt is hard to bear, and suffering minds are not easily relieved of these tensions. If guilt feelings become a threat to health, a disturbing factor in personality, would it not be better, we are asked, to give up the idea of sin? Why should religious teachers and preachers encourage this uncomfortable feeling of guilt? Some answers to this question need to be considered.

*a*) Guilt feeling is a normal psychological experience. It is one of the natural tensions between psychic energy and goal, even as interest, need, desire, intention, hope, or affection.[17] All desires and efforts goalward face the risk of not reaching their goal. The sense of failure to reach a goal is equivalent to a sense of guilt. Life might be more comfortable without tensions of striving and failing, but the tensions keep us going in persistent efforts to reach goals.

*b*) Guilt feeling is inherent in ethical character. Ethical awareness is recognizing an ideal as imperative. Ethical responsibility is working and growing toward ideals. Without guilt as a feeling of personal failure or as sense of urgency to do better, there are apathy and indifference with no serious concern, and the best is like the worst. Admitting inadequacies is essential to striving more adequately.

*c*) Guilt feeling is an outgrowth of interpersonal relations in which persons care for one another enough to offer approval and disapproval. The survival as well as the usefulness of society depends upon the willingness of its members to work for one another. Social justice rests upon the responsibility of each for all and all for each. The sense of guilt is recognition of in-

[17] "Guilt feeling is actually a positive, constructive emotion. It is a perception of the difference between what a thing is and what it ought to be."—Rollo May, *The Art of Counseling* (Nashville: Abingdon Press, 1939), p. 70.

terpersonal responsibility, the feeling of shame in not doing one's part, and the sense of obligation to maintain the rights of others. The best servant of society is the conscientious person who knows and cares enough to do his best for the common good.

*d*) The person who feels no guilt is psychopathic. His character structure is so impaired that he does not respond to the interests and ideal goals of his human kind but deceives himself that they do not matter. Sinless religion is also deceptive. It deceives all who think it makes no difference what one believes or does. It brings confusion of truth and error, good and evil, not recognizing the distinction between values and disvalues. If religion is the search for divine good, it matters supremely whether one is achieving good or evil. With lack of concern about sin there is failure to define, to declare, and to realize values. A false complacency of careless neutrality is the nadir of religious deception.

*e*) Yet guilt may be an intolerable distress, crippling sensitive persons and distorting interpersonal relations. Religious parents and teachers with high and imperative ideals often bring perfectionist demands upon growing children and youth, constantly alert to every shortcoming and failure. Children who live under the pressure of such rigid codes and accusing words or glances suffer acute anxiety in the loss of security and sustaining approval. Spontaneous expression of attitudes and feelings is then guarded, and all behavior is put under heavy restraint lest it bring reprisal or rejection by parents and religious authorities. A child may either withdraw in anxious timidity from open communication or hide his mounting hostility in slow-down inertia or obstructive resistance. He may not be able to study or succeed in either creative or routine achievement if he is entangled in conflict and preoccupied with deep feelings of anger, fear, and guilt.

Psychiatrists have sought to reduce guilt and relieve anxieties, while the clergy have induced and magnified guilt. It may thus appear that they are working against each other, each with mutual suspicion that the other is mistreating the deepest needs of life. But actually there is a middle ground at which the needs of health and religious concern meet. With no anxiety we have apathy, which is a serious resistance to motivation, and at the other extreme overanxiety, which may bring disturbances in the emotional life. We cannot rest with either extreme or its neurotic complications. Between these extremes we seek healthy guilt to feel responsible and constructive anxiety to be concerned that we do our best. But we also need release from the burden of guilt and relief from overanxiety about trivial things. For those who worry most frantically are apt to disable and deprive themselves of participation in the outgoing relationships of life.

Psychoanalysts in particular have seen the dangers of a punitive superego, turning aggressive hostility inward to deny and repress the instinctual energies of the id. By such inner warfare life is caught in a binding network of contradictions and reaction formations, with no freedom to live fully or productively in mature realization of its potentialities. In seeking to correct this blockade, the aim of therapy has often been to reduce the power of the superego and release the captive libido.

O. H. Mowrer,[18] however, from his experiments with learning and the neurotic paradox comes to a different conclusion. He finds that neuroses result not from overlearning of the repressing functions but rather from underlearning of the responsible conscience. Nor is pleasure the exclusive right of the id, for he finds a "conscience pleasure" that is quite as satisfying in its fulfillment and even more dynamic in the regulation of behavior. It appears that conscience, like the ego-ideal in mature development, is a function of the ego, which takes responsibility to integrate and regulate all of the conflicting impulses and desires of personality. For the integrated life desire and guilt each play an important role, not to punish but to repent and forgive, and in this reconciliation to become a new and more effective person.

## 5. *Seeking Reconciliation*

The problem of guilt is not easily untangled. Guilt feeling is a disturbing factor in personality, yet it is inherent in normal persons and societies, and it is essential to ethical character and religious growth. It is a painful blessing—dangerous to have and fatal to be without. Like electricity, it is a dynamic current whose high-tension potentiality flows from pole to pole in widening circuits. Electricity must have an outlet; if denied an outlet, it will force its way by burning or shattering all opposition. Guilt feeling is like that—when denied an outlet into open interpersonal relations, it creates havoc in the personality that resists it. Yet its dynamic power may create values through outlets in reconciling relations to constructive action. The historic religions have procedures for alleviating guilt and reconciling broken relationships.

*Repentance* is the first step from guilt toward reconciliation. This is not the same as remorse. Remorse looks to the past with vain regret; repentance looks to the future with hope. Remorse is a sense of hopeless frustration that adds to the fixation of guilt. Repentance is a change of heart, attitude, and purpose. It works from within outward and so dissolves resistance from the very center of the guilt complex. To repent is to stop denying and evading the guilt, to give up the resistance that pre-

[18] *Learning Theory and Personality Dynamics* (New York: Ronald Press, 1950), pp. 483-530.

vents the cure, and to admit freely the evil one has done. Acceptance of personal responsibility releases the neurotic defense and brings welcome relief in honesty that ends the uncertainty and indecision of conflicting impulses. Without this basic inner release of genuine repentance, to accept the blame and desire a new start, there can be no freedom from anxious remorse.

*Confession* is another step toward reconciliation. As long as a sin is secret, it must be concealed, repressed, and guarded. The neurotic tensions play around evasion and defense. Confession is therefore cathartic, purging and releasing the pent-up guilty tensions into open expression. To give forth the secret is to expel and cast it out, to deliver it into the keeping of others, whose hearing verifies and acknowledges the declaration. To talk with a counselor about one's anxieties is to objectify them, to detach them from secret inner rootage and hold them out in public view as seprate from the self who surrenders them. Confession is vital to religious health. It cures the spreading disease of disloyalty and dishonesty. Confession to God, who forgives, is a way of deliverance from sin.

*Forgiveness* is a third step in resolving guilt and moving toward reconciliation. The tensions of guilt arise in interpersonal relations. Crime produces guilt in reference to the civil body and its legal authorities. Selfishness and immorality infect with guilt one's social obligations. Sin impairs one's relationships to God and the value system that constitutes religion. In each of these relations the wrong needs to be righted in reference to others. And the guilt is not erased until the wrong is forgiven. Forgiveness is therefore a social achievement in restoring broken relations to harmony. Unless one can forgive himself, he does not have a forgiving spirit to reconcile another person. And until another forgives, one is not at liberty himself. If he has done his best to win forgiveness, his conscience may be clear, but his social relations have not yet been restored. To the religious mind the final release from guilt is confession to God and forgiveness by God. When this is attained, men may misjudge and persecute in vain; a deeper security of divine approval is able to withstand the surface ripples of hostile injustice.

*Reparation* is a fourth step from guilt to reconciliation. No emotion is adequately expressed until it finds release in appropriate action. Reparation is the act of making amends for a wrong or injury. It is not to be confused with retaliation. To return evil for evil in revenge and reprisal is a frequent outlet for emotions of injured pride and anger. But here is no cure for guilt, only additional wrongs to be forgiven. Two wrongs do not make a right or justice either; for reprisals are bound to add an extra punch for good measure, and getting even is impossible by this method. True reparation is a voluntary desire to overcome evil with good. The act of making restitution for injury is a demonstration of sincere repentance, a public confesson of one's desire to right a wrong. It therefore carries emotions and decisions into effective action, overcoming the frustration of remorse and inertia with constructive repair of damaged relationships in overflowing love.

Guilt, as Lewis J. Sherrill [19] perceives, may be a prison of interlocking anxiety and hostility. Disapproval of hostility induces anxiety, while the pain of anxiety induces hostility, causing and caused by guilt. This vicious circle is so confining and endlessly repetitive that escape is extremely difficult. It is a neurotic condition caused by pathological human relations which tend to perpetuate themselves. The only cure is to change the pathological relations to therapeutic relations by introducing a new and ever-forgiving love. Such love is equivalent to the New Testament agape, which is that divinely faithful and self-giving love able to heal the self-seeking and fatal alienation of human striving. God is perceived as a loving and forgiving Father who loves where it is unmerited and, knowing the full evil of sin, yet accepts the sinner in spite of his offenses. Only as such love becomes incarnate in human relations are healing and release to be found from the prison of guilt. Conditional love ("if you please me") is unpredictable and fosters anxiety. Nothing less than unconditional love is sufficient to meet our human need, and this may be more than a finite person can always provide.

The greatest tragedy of human existence is to be homeless. Who suffers more acute misery than the child who is lost or the castaway of any age uprooted and torn from those he loves? When death severs the close bond of a family relationship, the survivors may be plunged into grief so profound as to endanger life and health. The violence of wars and forced migrations have hurled forth whole populations to become homeless refugees and spread their misery around the earth, doomed to be strangers wherever they go. Yet voluntary separations may exceed the involuntary, whether due to personal ambition or anger or resentment which motivate many persons to break away from intimate supportive relationships and leave them behind.

If we agree that relationship is the basic need of human life, we cannot take a light view of these separations. The finite person is fragmentary at best, and though he may go off in the excitement of anger or adventure ardently seeking freedom, he will nonetheless be impoverished by the loss of his most significant relationships. There is a rising tide of individualism in our new world culture that facilitates the breaking of family ties and provides ready access to mobility. Consequently, it is customary for young

[19] *Guilt and Redemption* (rev. ed.; Richmond, Va.: John Knox Press, 1957).

people to leave home as early as possible and for older people to retire and leave it all behind by going far away to live among strangers who will let them alone and make fewer demands upon them. What follows separation and loss of relationship, each person must answer for himself; but we cannot hide the accentuation of delinquency, divorce, and suicide, though we may conceal the empty loneliness of secret despair and loss of the meaning of life.

Whether by choice or necessity these separations will come to every finite person sooner or later. This no one can deny, and the fate of this finitude places upon every person the burden to prepare some means to cope with his separations. One way is well known to many, that is, to reduce the value of what you have so you will not miss it when it is gone. One person schooled herself to meet disappointment and losses by saying, "Nothing matters very much." This may provide a discipline to reduce the suffering, but at the expense of joy. The art of living is then to dodge encounter and turn away in detachment from the fully engaged vitality of wholehearted participation. This withdrawing tendency is schizoid and vacates the meaning of life before the crisis by a slow leaking away of esteem in deflation.

A more positive and outgoing way to cope with separation is to replace the loss with new relationships. But this is difficult, for each relationship is unique and irreplaceable; the stranger is unknown and at first inaccessible. The line of least resistance is to grieve over one's losses and relive the past in fantasy to deny the loss and avoid the pain of separation. In the toils of grief a person is torn between conflicting and ambivalent feelings. He recalls the moments of anger and resentment when he was unkind or secretly rebellious and disloyal to the person he loved. He feels a guilt the more intolerable because the loss is final and not to be healed. His anger then turns against himself as the guilty one who is punished by this separation and not entitled to enjoy peace or new relationships. He condemns himself under the lash of his punitive superego to the prison of self-accusing wrath, preoccupied with hatred and doomed to unrelieved misery.

### 6. *Forgiving Love*

The predicament of tragic separation is well demonstrated in the parable of the prodigal son. He was an impetuous youth, weary of his family relationships and resentful of the restraints and responsibilities required of him. Coming to manhood, he decided to tolerate no longer this dependence upon his family, but to claim his inheritance from his father and go forth to be independent and have his freedom. In this he succeeded, and going far away into another country, he sought other relationships by reckless spending to win the favor of new friends. But when he had spent all, the new friends vanished, and he was reduced to poverty in his empty independence. Then realizing he was better off at home, he admitted his folly and returned to his father. The home-coming was significant first by the joyous welcome from the father who loved and forgave him, and second by the bitter hatred of the brother who refused to forgive or restore the broken relationship.

In this portrait of our human situation the problem of guilt is etched in bold relief. The basic need of life is shown to be a relationship without which a person feels lonely and empty of meaning. Yet there are stresses and strains in every relationship which induce frustration and anger. When these hostile attitudes show forth, they invite a response of one kind or another which is bound to change the relationship into the complexity of ambivalent feelings. From these conflictual dilemmas offenses are given and received that further complicate the relationship, inducing anxiety and guilt. Words are spoken and actions taken that separate the persons from one another. Then follow the consequences of separation in losses that impoverish life unless they are reconciled or replaced in new wholeness.

The guilt of the son is obvious to perceive. He would be likely to repress it at first in the glow of his exciting adventure to live his own life. But then as his resources diminished and his efforts to establish himself in new relations broke down, he would have more acute distress of guilt. "What a fool I have been," he might say, "to waste my inheritance to no avail, to cut myself off from those who loved me, and to fall into this miserable state in which no ones cares whether I live or die. I can at least admit my folly and learn from this bitter lesson to value relationships of genuine love. I will arise and go to my father, confess my sin and say: 'Make me as one of your hired servants.' "

At the same time the father was mourning the loss of his son. Not expecting him to return, he gave him up with the finality of death. In his acute grief he would review their relationship through the years to see what led to the separation, how it might have been otherwise, and where he had failed. Would he not also feel guilty to realize that he too must be responsible in some degree for the conditions that provoked the separation? And how could he assuage his grief in the absence of the son with no opportunity to talk over the situation and come to a better understanding? In his searching anguish the father no doubt decided that his son was not altogether at fault, and even if he were, he would want to forgive and restore him to a relationship of love.

At last when the son did return, the father was so hoping and longing for his return that he saw him a long way off and came running to meet him. But not so with the older brother, who cherished anger and self-righteous indignation against the one who had deserted the family and failed to carry his share of the responsibilities. He had made his choice; let him take the consequences of his own folly. The elder brother was technically correct; he was in the right and his brother in the wrong. By the canons of justice he might well insist that the prodigal bear the full penalty for his folly with no claim upon the family he had renounced. Yet we can infer that the older brother would also feel the pangs of guilt, against which he needed the ego defenses of repression, projection, and rationalization. To repress his guilt feelings, he would project the blame upon the younger brother and rationalize that this fool does not deserve another chance but should bear the destitution he had brought upon himself. There is sibling rivalry here as in every family, and it may seem that the younger is the favored one who displaces the older in the affection of his parents.

Now as he returns wearily from a long day of honest toil in the fields, he finds that his upstart brother who was unwilling to work has returned and is enjoying a royal welcome of joyous feasting. The old jealousy came upon him in an overwhelming flood, and he could not bear to go in the house to make merry with the prodigal brother who had once more come into the favored place with the father.

There is more than one way to be homelesss. The prodigal had gone to a far country to separate himself from the family, but the older brother was homeless at home. He felt left out and forgotten in the feasting prepared for his brother, and in the outer rim of self-pity he felt so estranged that he excluded himself in the hopeless misery of a castaway. In the mingling of anger and self-rejection he would plunge the more deeply into guilt. Even when the father came out to invite him in, it was too late to make amends, for the prodigal was in the favored position while he had been forgotten. The words of explanation by which the father sought to comfort him only wounded him the more as they spoke of the brother and told how he was to be restored to favor again in spite of and even because of his misdeeds. In the generous act of forgiving the one son the father was offending the other son the more. The breakdown of family relations was not yet restored and could not be so long as one remained the rival of the other.

The problem of guilt is apparently not to be resolved. Whatever a person may do or not do, he will suffer guilt as he fails to reach a goal for which he strives. And if he would avoid the pain of seeking a goal, he falls into apathy or despair and empties life of its meaning. The dilemma of the finite person centers in his basic need for relationship and the guilt he suffers in relation to a person who disapproves of him. The closer is the relation to a person who cares, the more intolerable is the anxiety of fearing his disapproval. Such a feeling of guilt in relation to the person on whom one is dependent for love is probably the most refined torture that we can know. Out of this anguish steps are taken and decisions made to break the relationship at any cost. A broken relationship is not easily healed, and many prefer the impoverished state of isolation in which pride can be stoutly defended rather than to yield in humility and seek a reconciliation.

The several facets of this human predicament are illuminated in the family relations of the prodigal son. This is only a parable to be sure, but the family portrait is so accurate and revealing that almost anyone can project himself into it and find something of his own experience in seeking to relate to those for whom he cares the most. Involved in the parable is the real life of the one who told it, and the psychologist will be interested to know why it was told. Was Jesus portraying himself in the role of the young man who left home to seek new relationships? His mother and brothers sought him and invited him to return home, but turning to his disciples, he said, "Behold my mother and my brethren!" He spent himself as generously for his new friends as the prodigal, and calling them away from their former employment, he lived with them in poverty with only the barest of possessions. The father in the parable is generally conceded to represent God, who agrees that the son shall go forth alone, who does not cease to love him at any time, and who welcomes him home with overflowing and forgiving love.

Though it is said that Jesus was without sin, he was not without temptation, and as he wrestled with conflictual tendencies, there is reason to believe that he would know the full meaning and anguish of guilt as a disturbing human concern. In fact, we may agree that his ultimate concern was the I-Thou relationship and how to work through alienation and guilt to forgiving love. While the prodigal might go forth to please himself, the going forth of Jesus was a vicarious dedication to minister to the needs of others. He went forth in the great tradition of the Hebrew prophets, responding to the call to speak for God and do his work among the people as the servant of all. And he seemed to believe that he would not be alone, that God would always be with him. In prayer he often turned to God and in every encounter sought to know and to do his will. He was ever seeking to bring other persons into relation with God and to one another "that they all may be one" (John 17:21). He showed to them that God is a loving and forgiving Father, to whom they may bring their sin and guilt, trusting that he will reconcile and heal and restore the broken relationship.

Recognizing that finite persons have a basic need for a relationship of forgiving love, Jesus offered this reconciling relation as a religious way of life. His ultimate concern was to know God and the mercy of his forgiving love so abundantly that the overflow might come into every relationship of life. The overflow of this unmerited love to the undeserving is the agape love which in the New Testament is God's love for every creature no matter how sinful he may be. It is through this forgiving love that man is to be reconciled to man in the spirit of the I-Thou relationship.

The therapeutic value of forgiving love is now well recognized by psychologists and other professions working for mental health. Growing children are entitled to such love, and parents are generally instructed in the wisdom of tempering stern discipline with tender mercy. The lack of such love is understood to be the principal cause of neurotic anxiety, juvenile delinquency, resistance to learning, the blocking of potential achievement, mental illness, and psychosomatic disorders. If forgiving love is this important, the need for it is confirmation of our interpersonal theory of religion.

In this chapter we recapitulate the interpersonal theory to understand religious behavior. Believing that the basic need of the human person is for relationship, it is our theory that religious behavior is seeking the answering response with ultimate concern. From deep unconscious dynamics as well as from his conscious strivings, the person is restlessly and relentlessly seeking Thou. He concerns himself most with persons who care for him enough to uphold him in approving relationships. Yet in his ambivalent emotions and conflictual strivings every such relationship will invite disapproval, and the person will suffer the pangs of guilt. He will feel estranged from the persons he loves the most, and his anxious guilt will alienate him through attitudes of hostility whether open or veiled in passive resistance. To be homeless is so intolerable, however, that he will eventually seek some way of reconciliation or else he will suffer the impoverishment of his values in isolation. Forgiving love is the ultimate concern of religious behavior.

# 11 RELIGION AND HEALTH

## *1. Health and Wholeness*

Health and wholeness are linguistic brothers who share a common ancestry in many languages. The word "whole" appears in Old English as *hál*, in Middle Dutch and Danish as *heel*, in German as *heil*, in Swedish as *hel*, in Gothic as *hails*. The word "heal" appears in Old English as *hal*, in Old Saxon as *heli*, in Middle Dutch as *heile*, in old High German as *heili*, and in Gothic as *haileri*. Both words are closely related to "hale" and "hail." The northern dialect of the Old English hál was *hale* or *heal*, while the southern and middle form was *hol*, *hole*, or *whole*.

The words are affiliated not only in form and derivation but also in content of meaning. "Whole" means to be sound or in good condition; in good health, free from disease or defect; well, restored to health, recovered from disease. In reference to mental powers it means sane. "Heal" means to make whole or sound, to recover from sickness or a wound; to restore a person from some evil or unwholesome condition to wholeness. "Hale" means free from injury, disease, or infirmity; in good health, robust, vigorous, whole, entire, complete, no part wanting. "Health" means soundness of body, that condition in which its functions are duly and efficiently discharged; also spiritual, moral, or mental soundness; and well-being, welfare, salvation, wholesomeness. "Holy" is another more distinctly religious word from the same root meaning to be spiritually whole.

From this semantic study, it is clear that health means wholeness. It is to have abundant life and overbrimming energy, the fulfillment of human capacities and the efficient functioning of all parts in unified co-ordination. Illness, by sharp and painful contrast, is the crippling disability and restraint of disease. Disease is an abnormal state of the body, recognized by objective examinations. But illness is subjective and consists of health disturbances experienced and recognized by the individual affected. Positive health, therefore, includes the normal functioning of body and mind in harmonious unity experienced in well-being or happiness. Health is the exercise and enjoyment of the powers and functions of life as a whole. Dynamic wholeness is the norm of health. It is the fulfillment of growth and efficiency.

This is not the newest discovery of medicine; Hippocrates (460?-377? B.C.), the Greek founder of medical science, saw that "in order to cure the human body it is necessary to have a knowledge of the whole of things." [1] And yet it is one of the most significant rediscoveries of modern medicine. For specialism, valuable as it is for scientific research, has proved inadequate for medical practice. Physicians are now declaring that the whole is more than its organic parts and are re-emphasizing "treatment of the patient as a whole." Psychosomatic medicine is demanding a holistic approach to the whole man. No man can be wholly understood without taking into consideration his social relationships and the environment in which he lives.

Health problems are not confined to organic processes. They include emotional and social factors as well, for health is a state of the whole personality, and whatever affects the person in all his relationships concerns his well-being. H. F. Dunbar has reviewed two thousand publications, submitting evidence to show that the functions of virtually all the organs of the body are disturbed by excessive or repressed emotions.[2] Whatever affects adversely any aspect of life threatens health.

Stanley Cobb [3] finds the interaction of living processes so intricate that the popular distinction between organic and functional diseases is misleading. Organic diseases are affected by psychological factors, even as psychological disorders are affected by organic conditions. He classifies diseases by etiology into four groups:

1. *Geneogenic* disorders arising from heredity
2. *Histogenic* disorders due to nonhereditary lesions
3. *Chemogenic* disorders from effects of chemical agents or their lack
4. *Psychogenic* disorders arising from disturbed interpersonal relations

Interpersonal relations are the source of emotional anxieties, fears, grief, guilt, and inferiority feelings, which are very influential in a variety of illnesses.

Robinson's study of 174 unselected patients admitted to Johns Hopkins Hospital from an urban community [4] showed that (*a*) adverse social conditions were present in 80 per cent of them, (*b*) these adverse social conditions caused harmful emotional reactions in 58 per cent of the patients,

[1] Quoted by C. A. Wise, *Religion in Illness and Health* (New York: Harper & Bros., 1942), p. 9.

[2] *Emotion and Bodily Changes* (4th ed.; New York: Columbia University Press, 1954).

[3] *Foundations of Neuropsychiatry* (Baltimore: Williams & Wilkins Co., 1941), pp. 205-25.

[4] G. C. Robinson, *The Patient as a Person* (New York: The Commonwealth Fund, 1939).

(*c*) emotional factors were the chief cause of illness in 26 per cent of these cases, and of 10 per cent more whose relation to social conditions was not established.

Thornton and Knauth studied one hundred cases in the Presbyterian Hospital of New York City.[5] They found adverse social factors in 80 per cent of the patients and conditions definitely related to the illness of 65 per cent of the patients. A comparison of these two studies is shown below:

ADVERSE SOCIAL FACTORS RELATED TO ILLNESS

| *Social Factors* | *Presbyterian Hospital* | *Johns Hopkins Hospital* |
|---|---|---|
| 1. Inadequate physical protection (undesirable habitat, shelter, clothing, food, personal service) | 44% | 24% |
| 2. Inadequate economic protection (undue effort and inadequate means to secure subsistence) | 36 | 52 |
| 3. Faulty personal habits influencing health (unfavorable to health or following medical directions) | 31 | 14 |
| 4. Dissatisfaction connected with family or other group relationships (broken home, incompatibility, lack of satisfying status) | 30 | 44 |
| 5. Dissatisfaction connected with restricted outlets (lack of satisfying work, recreation, or social life) | 34 | 12 |

Measures taken by the Presbyterian Hospital to remedy adverse social factors in the lives of these patients indicate how far-reaching are the conditions of health.

A. Measures designed to control environment:
   1. Supplying deficiencies
   2. Helping patient utilize available resources
   3. Removing obstacles to care
   4. Removing to more favorable environment

[5] Janet Thornton and M. S. Knauth, *The Social Component in Medical Care* (New York: Columbia University Press, 1937).

B. Measures designed to influence conduct:
   1. Imparting information on problems
   2. Explaining
   3. Elucidating by reiteration
   4. Demonstrating by example
   5. Influencing choice by incentives
   6. Fostering habits
   7. Standing by and following up

The boundaries of personality are never final as a confining wall. They are open frontiers with freedom to explore and expand into enlarging relationships. Our focal awareness sets a tentative boundary at the border of conscious experience. Beyond this conscious area are the unconscious relations, and beyond them the biological relations of the body, and beyond that the social relations of the human world, and beyond that the physical and metaphysical relations of the universe, including the reality that religion calls God. The relations of personality are infinite. Where can one draw a line of demarcation to declare that here a person reaches his final limit? For the limits of today are exceeded by the adventures the person may undertake tomorrow. Boundaries are useful for definition and logical distinction, but they are artificial abstractions that living persons persist in leaping over.

One of the widely accepted definitions of personality is offered by Allport after a systematic review of etymology, history, and contemporary use: "Personality is the dynamic organization within the individual of those psychophysical systems that determine his unique adjustments to his environment." [6] This seems to draw the boundary at the circumference of the body and to treat all that is outside the skin as not mine. But what of one's clothes, glasses, false teeth, artificial limb, fountain pen, radio, and other instruments of his unique adjustment to his environment? What of one's family, school, clubs, church, country, vocation, in all of which his personal values are invested? These may be classified as environment, but if so, why not the body and the unconscious processes also? All are beyond experience and inferred as object, not known as subject. If one is to be strictly empirical, then only the conscious unity is personal. But if one is to expand the range of personality to include the biological relations of the body, is it not quite as consistent to include the social relations? Are they not essential to the actual sphere of personal living and integral in the organizing unity of insights and purposes?

Personality is more or less than a psychophysical system. If empirically subjective it is less. If behavioristically interactive, it is more. From the

[6] *Personality*, p. 48.

holistic point of view personality is bio-psycho-socio-physical. A person is a complex unity of dynamic relationships among these interacting spheres of the body-mind-society-physical world. To mechanistic and fragmentary psychologies which reduce life to segments we offer the more dynamic integrative concept of *wholeness*. Every experience either is itself a whole or belongs to a whole. Wholeness does not exclude internal multiplicity, nor external relationships. As an open totality of outreaching intentions the person has incessant intercourse with the world. Of utmost significance in this world are the persons whom we meet in interpersonal relations.

To possess health, a person needs to have all functions of his multiple relationships in harmonious accord. L. J. Henderson[7] has shown that 214 environmental conditions have to be present in accurate proportion for life to exist at all on this planet. No less intricate and delicate are the internal adjustments of the psychophysical organism. Far more subtle and variable are the social adjustments of interpersonal relations, and their effects upon the individual are beyond measure. In all these interactions nothing less than a total adjustment of the inner and outer relations constitutes normal personality. When Spencer[8] defined life as "the continuous adjustment of internal relations to external relations," did he comprehend the full implications of that happy phrase? Or in fact, do we?

## 2. *Emotional Factors in Health*

Faith healing has the mystery and appeal of an unexplored continent, in which fact and fancy mingle. Extravagant claims and denials clash in controversy. Cures often appear miraculous yet remain incredible to many doubters. After centuries of superstition and legend it is no wonder that scientific medicine in the nineteenth century turned from faith to fact. Medical scientists have accumulated a vast array of accurate information on health and disease by specialized research in bacteriology, biochemistry, histology, physiology, and neurology. Now in our time the psychic factors, once ruled out as unscientific, are demanding attention as decisive causes in illness and health. The functional disorders as well as numerous organic diseases are clearly related to anxieties and emotional problems. Faith is evidently a fact to be investigated along with other emotional attitudes in understanding the conditions of health. The question of faith in healing has new significance as emotional factors in

[7] *The Fitness of Environment* (New York: The Macmillan Co., 1931).

[8] *Op. cit.*, I, 80.

illness are recognized. What are the facts about faith and other emotions in reference to health?

W. B. Cannon[9] conducted pioneer studies in the effect of emotions on bodily processes. He found that a cat frightened by a barking dog has the following bodily changes: (*a*) increased pulse rate and blood pressure; (*b*) increased adrenalin in the blood; (*c*) increased sugar in the blood; (*d*) decreased coagulation time; (*e*) increased muscular tension; (*f*) increased motor activity, restlessness; (*g*) deep and rapid respiration; (*h*) dry mouth pilomotor and vasomotor activity; (*i*) dilation of the pupils; (*j*) defecation and urination; (*k*) immobility of the stomach.

In a study of voodoo death Cannon[10] examined reports of death among primitive peoples following a magical spell or curse. Careful observers have seen men die within a few hours after a curse has been put upon them. The physiological reactions are similar to shock conditions arising in war, accident or surgery. Shocking emotional stress (obvious or repressed terror) affects the sympathetic nervous system, which controls the internal organs and blood vessels. Severe emotions of fear and rage stimulate increase of adrenalin and sympathin, causing a persistent constriction of the small arterioles, inadequate supply of oxygen, and escape of plasma through the capillary walls into the perivascular spaces. This leaves the red corpuscles more concentrated, dehydrates the circulation, and reduces the blood pressure. Deterioration then occurs in the heart and the nerve centers, which become less able to keep the blood circulating effectively. In the cursed man, who believes death is inevitable, this vicious circle is fatal unless the curse is withdrawn and he is persuaded to believe he is able to live. Belief controls life and death.

H. F. Dunbar[11] has also conducted studies on emotions and bodily changes, showing that emotional factors are present in virtually all diseases. There are four ways in which emotional tensions predispose to organic illness: (*a*) by inducing accidents; (*b*) by upsetting physiological functioning by inhibiting, overstimulating, or contracting; (*c*) by indirect emotional causation with organic complications; and (*d*) by perpetuation of physiological changes by chronic emotional stress. Diseases of the heart and circulation; asthma and hay fever; laryngitis and the common cold; diseases of the stomach, pancreas, and liver; intestinal ailments (peptic ulcer and colitis); infectious diseases such as tuberculosis and typhoid; convales-

[9] *Bodily Changes in Pain, Hunger, Fear and Rage* (New York: D. Appleton-Century Co., 1915; 1936).

[10] "Voodoo Death," *American Anthropologist*, XLIV (1942), 169-81.

[11] "Problems of Convalescence and Chronic Illness," *American Journal of Psychiatry*, Vol. XCII (1936).

cence and chronic illness, together with all personality disorders, have emotional components.

If emotional responses are so important in disease and death, they are equally so in life and health. If malignant anxiety is fatally distressing, then adequate faith is specifically curative. These medical investigations give scientific answers to the question of faith healing. Faith healing is not impossible, for emotional factors play a decisive part in illness and health. Not all healing miracles are authentic. In fact, many are fraudulent, deceptive, or temporary in results. The agent employed for the healing may be as ineffectual as patent medicines or bread pills, and yet results may be surprisingly good if only the patient believes firmly enough to provide the needed emotional support. For without faith no one can be well, and with this basic confidence there is ground for better health.

The urgent need for emotional health has given rise to various healing cults. The most influential of these is the Christian Science Church, whose expansion since the first incorporation of twenty-six members in Boston in 1879 has been phenomenal. Coming at a time when mental factors in healing were overlooked by physicians and ministers alike, this church demonstrated the value of Christian faith in promoting health. Devotion to this truth may lead to neglect of other truths, denial of organic diseases or the refusal of the services of physicians. To reject medical services is to endanger the health of individuals and delay public health improvement. Progress in health, public and private, has come by collaboration more than by rivalry. There are signs today of heartier co-operation between medical and religious health workers. Human welfare demands larger understanding of intricate health needs and constant teamwork among social, psychological, religious, and medical services.

### 3. *Spiritual Healing*

The miracle of healing has never been so impressive as in this age of science.[12] Every step forward in the history of the medical sciences deepens the mystery of healing. Along the vast frontier of scientific research we know more each year about the causes of illness. New drugs are powerful allies in the battle for health. The actual healing is what we wait for when we have done all we can by scientific means, and the wonder of it is the more profound in the light of medical knowledge. It is evident that health arises from a complex network of many intertwining causes so intricate as to involve the whole man in all

[12] Material in this section appeared in *Religion In Life*, XXV (Spring, 1956), 195-204. Used by permission.

his relationships. To disturb the delicate balance of any one of these vital factors may invite illness.

The National Council of Churches of Christ in America has for many years shown a continuing interest in this question of health. Since 1938 a Commission of Religion and Health has brought together representatives of the healing professions (especially physicians, psychiatrists, and nurses) to consider with religious leaders the interrelation of health with spiritual resources. So many inquiries were received about such healing that in 1948 a Committee on Spiritual Healing was established to study it.

Professor Charles S. Braden[13] of Northwestern University was asked by this committee to conduct a survey of healing experiences known to pastors of Protestant churches. After a pilot study in the Chicago area he selected a key pastor in each of twenty-seven cities and asked him to distribute questionnaires to pastors in the major denominations in his community. Altogether 982 questionnaires were sent out and 460 replies received, or 46.7 per cent of the total.

For the purpose of this study spiritual healing was defined as "healing effected through other than the recognized methods of scientific medicine and those of the trained psychiatrist, that is, healing wrought directly through religious faith in some sense." Many who replied insisted that religion should not be set over against scientific healing as though no relationship existed between them. It was often noted that all healing, by whatever means, is of God and that religion is not to work apart from but along with the use of every available scientific procedure. Others insisted that healing is not always spectacular but proceeds in quiet and often gradual changes for the better.

In reply to the question "Have you ever as a minister attempted to perform a spiritual healing?" 142 or 34.5 per cent of those replying gave an unqualified "yes" and 248 or 54 per cent gave an unqualified "no." Forty-eight or 10.4 per cent gave a qualified "no," such as "if you mean this, no," but would then go on to allege that healing came from prayer or counseling which was equivalent to a spiritual healing ministry. Summing up the total number of qualified and unqualified "yes" replies with the qualified "no" replies gives 206 or approximately 43 per cent of the pastors reporting some use of spiritual healing in one way or another. Of the 982 questionaires sent out 21 per cent actually report spiritual healing.

It is impossible to know how those who did not return the questionnaires would have replied, but Braden infers that these would raise and not lower the percentage of affirmative replies, because more time and effort are required to fill out the questionnaire affirmatively with the detailed infor-

[13] "Study of Spiritual Healing in the Churches," *Pastoral Psychology*, V (May, 1954), 9-15.

mation requested. He had particularly urged those having negative replies to fill in the one or two easy questions with "no," and return the blank in the stamped addressed envelope provided. A spot check further indicated that some not replying said they would say "yes," but did not find the time to fill in the detailed responses required.

In what kind of churches does spiritual healing occur most frequently? According to this study it occurs in churches of all sizes and economic classes except the upper class. We find 20 per cent of the healing in churches of more than one thousand membership, 38 per cent in churches with five hundred to one thousand members, and 37 per cent in churches of less than five hundred members. As to economic level only 11 per cent were in the low income group, 54 per cent in the lower middle group, and 39 per cent in the upper middle group.

On tabulating the variety of diseases reported healed, it appears that sixty-four are different enough to be listed separately. But on closer scrutiny these fall into broad classifications. The largest number of healings, twenty or 12½ per cent of the total, are from mental illness such as extreme anxiety, hallucinations, neuroses, depression, abnormal fears, schizophrenia, and nervous fatigue. All but one of the mental cases had been medically diagnosed and treated. About half had been pronounced hopeless. In all but three cases the cure was reported as permanent.

Of the organic diseases the largest number, eighteen, were of cancer, as of the lungs, the spine, the mouth, the duodenum, the bone, and so on. In almost every case we are informed the diagnosis had been made by a competent physician with medical attendance. A Methodist minister in the Midwest reported a case diagnosed as lung cancer by a group of physicians in consultation, who gave the patient, a woman of thirty-seven years of age, one week to live. The minister prayed with her, she confessed, and forgave a person she hated. The next day the lungs were found to be clear of cancer, and after two years the woman was still well.

Heart trouble was next in order with fifteen healings reported. A man of fifty who suffered a coronary thrombosis had been so diagnosed and treated but was considered incurable. Following prayer he was healed and lived six years. Most of the cases were reported as permanently healed, and only two experienced a recurrence.

Five cases of paralysis were reported healed. A two-year-old child, who was diagnosed by a physician as having infantile paralysis, was permanently cured following prayer by a Presbyterian minister. In another case a woman of fifty-five, diagnosed and treated by a physician as incurable, gained permanent recovery following group prayer. Four cases of tuberculosis were reported healed.

Other cases were reported of pneumonia, spinal meningitis, arthritis, stomach ailment, ulcers, alcoholism, brain hemorrhage, severe burns, crushed or broken bones, yellow jaundice, kidney trouble, varicose veins, concussion, ruptured appendix, intestinal blockage, diabetes, influenza, chronic asthma, mastoiditis, excessive bleeding after childbirth and so on.

The method of healing employed may be seen from the following table.

### METHODS OF HEALING REPORTED BY PROTESTANT MINISTERS IN TWENTY-FIVE CITIES (160 CASES)

| | *Total Organic* | *Per cent Using Each* | *Total Mental* | *Per cent Using Each* | *Total Cases* |
|---|---|---|---|---|---|
| Prayer | 98 | 70 | 19 | 95 | 117 |
| Forgiveness | 44 | 31.4 | 13 | 65 | 57 |
| Affirmation | 35 | 25 | 14 | 70 | 49 |
| Laying on Hands | 33 | 23.6 | 4 | 20 | 37 |
| Anointing | 24 | 17.1 | 2 | 10 | 26 |
| Rituals | 14 | 10 | 4 | 20 | 18 |
| Others | 18 | 12.8 | 6 | 31.6 | 24 |

*Prayer* is most frequently used of all the methods employed, with assurance of forgiveness, affirmation of faith, laying on of hands, anointing with oil, and rituals, in descending order. Other methods were in most cases not specified, though scripture reading, listening, and counseling were indicated. The laying on of hands, rituals, and anointing were used less with mental patients. Affirmation and forgiveness show larger percentages in reference to mental than to organic illness, though ranking next to prayer in both.

Distribution by age is widespread, ranging from ages one to seventy-nine. The majority, eighty-nine, were above the age of thirty, while only twenty-five were under thirty. The number of men and women was about equal. Of the 123 pastors who reported both healings and denominational affiliations, forty-six were Methodist, nineteen were Episcopalian, eighteen Presbyterian, fourteen Lutheran, seven Baptist, five Disciples, three United Brethren, two each Congregational, Evangelical and Reformed, and Nazarene. Five other denominations reported one each.

It is significant that 80 per cent of the healings were declared permanent. Only nine cases were listed without indicating medical diagnosis, and only ten failed to specify adequate medical treatment. More than half of the patients healed became "more religious," and only six reported no change religiously. More than half of the pastors who reported healings had participated in more than one. When asked, "Do you preach healing as an integral part of religion?" 80 per cent answered in the affirmative, and 55 per cent thought it should be a part of the regular work of the pastor.

The facts uncovered by this survey are in many ways remarkable. It is surprising (*a*) to find that 43 per cent of the pastors responding and 21 per cent of all those questioned have participated in spiritual healings. We may have assumed that such healing was confined to the minority religious groups, and it is notable to discover it is widely practiced in the major Protestant denominations. It is also significant (*b*) to find medical diagnosis and treatment reported in all but nine or ten cases. This indicates more than scientific appraisal of the disease and the healing. It also implies the collaboration of the physician and the pastor in team work for health, or at least that medical and religious resources have both been called upon, not neglecting one for the other. (*c*) The miracle of healing is baffling to both science and religion. It may occur in a variety of ways, now sudden and dramatic, or again a quiet and gradual growth.

The results are particularly remarkable in view of the limiting way in which the concept of spiritual healing was defined, to set it in contrast to "the recognized methods of scientific medicine and those of the trained psychiatrist." The contagious faith which the physician brings to the patient by his own integrity and confidence is a recognized method of scientific medicine, which may also characterize the pastor in his healing ministry. In all healing the spiritual factors, therefore, interact with the physical and social factors. If this is so, then the definition used by the committee would seem to rule out many valid situations of spiritual healing and lead to negative rather than affirmative replies from the pastors surveyed.

Another form of spiritual healing likely to escape the net of this questionnaire is pastoral counseling. For it is excluded by the phrase which rules out the methods of the psychiatrist, who proceeds by a therapeutic relationship of listening to feelings expressed, accepting the person with distressing conflicts, and helping him to work through them by insight and personal growth. This is also the method of the pastoral counselor who enters a healing relationship in religious perspective. It would not be a rash observation to note that among Protestant churches today, pastoral counseling is the most prevalent form of spiritual healing.

To look more closely at the healing work of pastoral counseling, a case study will be introduced with the permission of a person whom we will designate by the pseudonym Joel Mark. He came to the Pastoral Counseling Service at Boston University on November 4, 1952, on referral from a psychiatrist. During the three years in which he saw a counselor once a week his progress in health was notable, after which he met with the staff to consider the situation together. At regular intervals he consulted with and was examined by his physician, who reports the medical examination of December 9, 1955, as follows:

Joel Mark came in to see me on December 9 for a complete physical examination and proctoscopic evaluation of his old ulcerative colitis. I must say that I was very delighted to find Mr. Mark in excellent physical condition without any significant abnormalities. Examination of his lower bowel with the sigmoidoscope revealed what was essentially a normal bowel for a distance of 20 cm. There is no evidence of bleeding or irritability of the lower intestinal tract and I believe that we can consider his ulcerative colitis healed at this point.

This is the third consecutive year in which this physician has reported an essentially normal colon, after twelve years of ulcerative colitis. The story to follow was told by Mr. Mark to the staff of the Pastoral Counseling Service.

Joel Mark was born in Nebraska (names of places will be changed to respect the confidential nature of the information given) in 1914, one year after the marriage of his parents. His mother was nineteen years old at the time of the birth, and his father, then twenty-four, was a Methodist minister. The father had wanted to be a surgeon, but from the day he was born he was destined by his mother to be a minister, for in her words "the ministry is the only honorable profession." When Joel's father, whom we may call Isaac Mark, completed his theological course he started for the Ph.D., but health problems interfered and he became pastor of a church in Nebraska. A year after the birth of Joel he returned to continue work on his Ph.D., but again his health failed and he had to give up the attempt to become a "Doctor." When the war came, he volunteered for the Medical Corps, and after two epidemics of influenza in which he and the medical doctor were the only two men in the unit on their feet, Isaac developed genitourinary tuberculosis, which afflicated him the remainder of his life.

The family then moved to Colorado, where Isaac Mark became head of the Department of History at the State Teachers' College. Joel was the only child, and due to the illness of the father, his mother was occupied in caring for him and seemed to have no margin of affection left for the son. Isaac was in politics as chairman of the school board and in trying to clean up corruption aroused opposition that reflected adversely on the son. To keep the family record above reproach, the son was never permitted to attend private parties or have social dates with young people of his age in the home town. On the other hand, he could take the car and drive to another town where his activities were not directly supervised, and Joel came to feel that his father cared more for his own reputation than his son's happiness. When Joel brought home good grades, his father would take the credit by saying, "Look whose son he is," but when the grades were not so good, no sympathy was shown, and the father would scornfully say, "We can't all be Phi Beta Kappa!" (which he was).

Joel secretly longed to be a surgeon but thought his father wanted him to be a minister, which he would not be. Yet he did try desperately to win his father's approval. He completed high school in three years, matriculated at the state university when he was fifteen, and had his Master of Arts degree before he was twenty-one. Early in the fall of this same year his father died, after having made groping attempts but never reaching a reconciliation with his only son. The mother, who was unprepared for her husband's death, went to pieces and for over ten years lived in complete emotional darkness before psychiatric aid helped her recover perspective.

Joel was married nine months after his father's death, but with the father's apparent approval of the prospective bride. Six months after the marriage Joel was out of work due to the recession of 1937, and he decided to return to school.

At the age of twenty-four he entered a technological institute to become a chemical engineer. His background in engineering and mathematics was insufficient, and it was a struggle to make the grade. The dean called him into his office and said, "The most serious mistake we have made in ten years was to admit you to this engineering program. If you ever amount to anything, I will be surprised." He failed part of the course but recovered and came through with some A grades and a Bachelor of Science degree in chemical engineering. In 1940 at the age of twenty-six, just after Joel finished this academic work, their first child was born and trouble started with his wife. It was in February, 1940, that he began to suffer with ulcerative colitis.

For three and a half years he was in the research department of a paper mill in Wisconsin. The director of research was a driver and could not tolerate a worker who was sick from time to time. Joel consulted physicians at the Mayo Clinic but was not helped by the strictly medical treatment. He felt insecure in his job and so transferred to the research department of a large chemical company, which in two and one-half years made him a group leader in charge of the paper laboratory. As a result of his work twelve patents were granted, upon which the company since earned in excess of five million dollars per annum.

In spite of this he was discharged in 1952 with no satisfactory explanation, but as he said, "personalities entered into it." By this time he and his wife had three growing children and were buying a home, with a good deal of tension and distress in their relationship. He was seriously ill with a disease that could easily become fatal.

About a year before this last crushing experience, Joel had been referred to a psychiatrist in a Boston hospital by his family physician. The psychiatrist was unable to continue treating him and referred him successively to three other psychiatrists, but none of them was able to continue or satisfy him. Finally the first psychiatrist said, "Joel, I don't know what you're going to do. You're going to have to learn to live with yourself."

"Doctor," said Joel, "don't you even know a minister I can go to?"

Then it was the psychiatrist referred him to the Pastoral Counseling Service. That day Joel telephoned to ask for an appointment, and two days later he came for the first interview with a pastor who had specialized at the Ph.D. level in psychology and counseling. The first session with the counselor was described by Joel as a very warm meeting, yet without any sentimental sympathy. "It was just plain, downright understanding. We were at the bottom, and we actually started up then."

The fourth interview, from the minute he walked into the counseling room, was particularly significant.

I felt a third presence. Now this, remember, I am relating as I felt it, and it is a reasonably objective proposition, I believe, because of my training. We have been taught unless you can measure it, forget it! Well, this is a case of something we could not measure in physical terms. Yet it was just as *real* as if you could measure it with a yardstick.

With the counselor he worked through his emotional difficulties. He explored his feelings toward his family and his vocation, and came to see their relatedness. The psychiatrist had helped him to discover his focal problem as hatred toward his father. This hostility was evidently transferred to his professors in school and later to his superiors in chemical research. He was engaged also in a running combat with God. He was not easy to live with at home, his relation to his wife was very aggravating, and his children suffered from his inability at that time to give them the affection they needed.

He was re-enacting the frustrations and conflicts of his own childhood. The turning point came as he found himself accepted, when everyone else had seemed to reject him, by a pastoral counselor who stood for his father and his God. He sensed that the counselor cared what happened to him, and he began to feel that God also cared. Toward the close of an interview it became natural to pray, first Joel and then the counselor praying, acknowledging that the task was too big for them alone and seeking to draw on the resources of God with which to grow.

*Joel:* I have said that we could sum up the experience here in one word of four letters, spelled L-O-V-E, and for the first time in my life I have felt its impact. I have never felt here that I was a burden, unwanted, impossible, a dumb dodo, nothing like that. In fact, sometimes I felt insecure because somebody didn't lay the whip on me. . . .

*Staff II:* So you felt that you counted as a person.

*Joel:* I counted as a person, yes; I wasn't a case, but a *person.* I've always been an individual here and the personal approach helped plus the fact that I have felt continuously that I was understood on the basis of being a Methodist minister's son who had, shall we say, strayed from the path. . . . Basically I wanted to be accepted by my own father. I think that I wanted to be loved by my own father. I felt that I was not loved, and here I have found a very reasonably healthy substitute.

*Counselor I:* It seems to me we arrived at some conclusion that your inability to establish or continue a relationship with your father, who died, had prompted your physical difficulty; and from then on you began to improve physically.

*Joel:* No question about it.

*Counselor I:* That to my mind was the turning point. . . .

*Staff II:* That he couldn't recover the losses in his relationship to his father?

*Joel:* No, that I couldn't battle my father any more, that's right.

*Counselor I:* Father was not there.

*Joel:* I didn't have anything to beat on. I didn't have any—anything any more. I mean my father was all I had. I had no brothers, no sisters. My mother was helpless in that picture.

*Staff II:* He was the emotional focus of your life.

*Joel:* He certainly was.

*Staff III:* At what point in the counseling did this take place?

*Counselor I:* This was fairly early—I'd say it was in the first two months.

*Joel:* That is correct. By December there was a marked decrease in the hemorrhaging, and by the following November when my family doctor examined me, he said it was wonderful; he had never seen anything like it. . . .

*Staff I:* At one time did you feel God was against you?

*Joel:* I felt that until I came here. I mean I never wanted to believe that God really cared. If he did not care then he would not want me to be a minister—and I would not have to be a hypocrite such as I saw in my father.

*Staff I:* Has your feeling toward God changed in these experiences?

*Joel:* Definitely, yes. And the turning point, as I say, was that fourth interview. It was—it was almost as if you could see the light over the hill. I still can't see over the top of the hill quite—but it's getting there. The walls no longer exist. We're beyond the walls, but we're not quite over the top of the hill.

Further, it was at about this same time that my counselor began to get to me with the idea that God is a forgiving Father, always ready to accept us, but that for him to make himself felt, we must forgive ourselves even as he forgives us. This was a difficult concept to accept, at the time, in the face of my deep-seated feelings of guilt.

In conclusion, what have we learned about a healing like this?

*a*) Illness afflicts the whole personality and not one organ. It affects the inner spiritual life and cannot be cured unless there is healing of the spirit.

*b*) The sense of well-being we desire affects our relationships with other persons too. If the relationships are loaded with feelings of anxiety, guilt or hostility, then we may expect health to falter.

*c*) To regain health, a new wholeness is needed in the person and his relationships to other persons. Counseling, to be effective, must be a healing relationship of accepting and understanding love.

*d*) While a turning point may come early in the counseling, there is often need of a continuing relationship to work through the emotional conflicts and grow into larger wholeness.

*e*) The pastor who gives healing love may help to fulfill the unmet need for an accepting parent and open the way to a forgiving heavenly Father.

We have no desire to force conclusions upon anyone. The skeptical pastor or scientist is entitled to his doubts and he should be heard. He may appeal to the lack of conclusive evidence or the principle of logical coherence in the face of contradictory evidence. Whatever laws are known to characterize the natural order should be consulted and respected in the work of healing. But who knows enough to say with finality, "This cannot happen"? It may be contrary to known laws and yet follow other laws not yet known. It may appear contradictory in our limited view and yet come to higher consistency in a larger perspective than we now have. The mystery of healing is greater than our best knowledge today. It is this challenge which invites ever-new discoveries in the search for health and wholeness.

## 4. *Therapeutic Services of Religion*

Health is a vital issue, basic to human values. Organic vitality is the tide of life supporting personality in every experience and expressive behavior. Healthy interests, attitudes, and emotional responses are essential to every constructive achievement. Disease is for this reason a crisis, striking terror and impotency into life. Illness is a threat to the values for which men live, a danger to combat with all resources at hand. Religion is devoted to fulfillment of the whole person and committed to human life in its growing needs and ultimate concerns. It is therefore the task of religion to promote health and wholeness.

Through the long centuries of religious history the need and art of healing have not been forgotten. In primitive communities the medicine men were priests, guardians of the mysteries in which magic, medicine, and religion mingled. Scientists who reject religion because of its association with magic might examine the history of science. For science is the child of magic, which was the primitive system of controlling the forces of nature by experimenting with assumed causes and effects. Lingering superstitions have retarded both science and religion, yet in the long advance both have won, they stand together as allies against the errors of magic.

The art of healing has always been empirical and pragmatic. With so many unknown factors in illness and health, it is impossible to exclude all but one causal agent and control this isolated variable. Methods of healing have developed from experience of what worked in previous cases. True and false remedies have grown up together until the winnowing of time and more accurate understanding. Neither science nor religion is specifically to blame for these errors, so long as every effort is made in theory and practice to sift the true from the false.

The Ebers papyrus, dated before 1552 B.C. describes the Egyptian treatment of healing by the laying on of hands with ceremonial formulas. The Hebrews, deriving their medical knowledge from Egypt, practiced similar treatment with prayer. The Greeks practiced healing by reference to the god Asclepius before 500 B.C. Excavations at Epidaurus produced inscriptions giving the rites used. Patients brought sacrifices, cleansed themselves with holy water, submitted to ceremonial acts performed by priests, and fell into a deep sleep (hypnotism?). Visits to shrines have been popular in various religions: Moslems go to Mecca to touch the black Kaaba stone; Hindus go to bathe in the sacred Ganges; Buddhists go to touch sacred relics supposed to have healing power. Faith in persons, whether religious leaders or physicians and psychiatrists, is undoubtedly one of the most effective resources for healing at the point where emotional attitudes affect health.

Christianity has been a healing religion throughout its entire history. Jesus responded to the needs of the sick as one of the foremost concerns of his mission. His disciples believed it was their responsibility to heal in his name, no less than to preach and teach. They did not claim to heal by their own wisdom or skill but by spiritual power from God. This charismatic healing was continued by the church fathers, who employed prayers, the laying on of hands, anointing with oil, and the Eucharist to this purpose. Disease was held to be not a punishment of God but a deficiency which God would be ready to supply through spiritual means, quite apart from the medical services of physicians.

By the fourth century, however, the leaders of the Eastern Church were praising medicine and giving honor to physicians as ministers of God. Gregory of Nyssa recognized natural causes for illness of mind and body, yet physicians labor in vain without the Lord, as Jerome said. The first Christian physicians practiced in the vicinity of Syria. Early in the fourth century Christian hospitals were founded in many cities, with deaconesses, widows, or virgins as nurses. The hospital was caled *Xenodochia* or "house of lodging for strangers," indicating a compassion to serve anyone in need. A famous hospital was established by St. Basil at Caesarea in Cappodocia which had many houses staffed with physicians and nurses to provide care for the sick, lodging for the travelers, homes for the poor and the lepers. St. Chrysostom founded hospitals in Antioch and Constantinople.[14]

The mentally ill were given special attention. Exorcism of evil spirits may be considered a primitive approach, and yet it does recognize the psychogenic factor in such illness. The aim was not only to free the afflicted person from his obsessions or delusions but also to lead him into the positive growth and grace of the Christian life, thus preparing him to deal with future problems and distresses when they might arise. The mentally ill were respected and loved; they were accepted as worthy of regard and visited regularly. Not being segregated as a different species to be shunned or put away, they were given the kind of treatment which is now recognized as conducive to mental health.

What therapeutic values beyond promoting medical programs does Christianity offer our generation? Other religions have their values too, but in order to be specific, we shall consider the ways in which Christianity contributes to health. The following items are not exhaustive. Nor do they influence all Christians equally, but they are representative of emotional forces and dynamic relationships which have a vital part in health of body and mind.

*a*) *The worth of every person* is a cardinal belief of Christianity. To realize one's personal worth is essential to mental health, a needed corrective to the inferiority feelings so common in our competitive society. To realize the equal worth of other persons is quite as useful in correcting the superiority feelings of ego-inflation. To view every personality as sacred corrects indifference and makes health a religious obligation.

*b*) *Membership in a loving fellowship* is a responsive relationship. The Christian Church as a therapeutic organism cultivates wholeness of personality through loyal devotion of person to person and open communication with inclusive rather than exclusive membership. Every person needs to belong to an intimate fellowship in which he is well known and loved and expected to do his best for all.

*c*) *Faithful companionship is health-giving.* Loneliness and isolation are a recurrent problem which group membership does not entirely solve. For no one can be with others at all times; moreover there come inner separations that create loneliness in the midst of a crowd. Belief in God as a faithful companion, who is present at all times in all places, meets this need. The sense of this constant relation to Thou brings an inner stability, the moral support of feeling "I am not alone."

*d*) Christian faith means *trust in the ultimate victory over evil.* Life

[14] Victor G. Dawe in "The Attitude of the Ancient Church Toward Sickness and Healing" (Unpublished Th.D., dissertation, Boston University, 1955) finds a wealth of material on healing in the documents of the ancient church.

values are constantly threatened and at times overwhelmed by evils. Who is not plagued by anxiety and fears, insecurity and despair? Persistent anxieties make life miserable and unhealthy. The fear of evil may, in fact, become the greatest evil of all. To these toxic emotions Christian faith offers the antidote of trust in God and the hope that evil can be overcome by spiritual resources. Without faith there are insecurity and nervous despair; with faith there are hope and confidence to sustain peace of mind and health of body.

*e*) *Worship* is a therapeutic experience. For worship seeks the highest attainable reality. The individual worshiper who is earnestly sincere lays aside the hypocrisies and deceptions of daily living and tries to be honest with his Creator and himself. He aspires to become more worthy. He shares with fellow worshipers a unity of purpose and rededicates himself to a new life. He meditates upon dynamic symbols and resolves to translate ideals into realities. Life may be reoriented and re-created in meeting the reality he calls God.

*f*) The religious purpose is an *urge and guide to growth*. The aspiration of worship and the challenge of prophetic preaching is a rousing experience, shaking one out of complacency, rejecting the *status quo* as inadequate, and demanding further growth. Religious education guides this growth through scripture, ethical analysis, problem-solving, study of life situations, and projects for putting principles into action. We have seen that health is normal growth toward wholeness. Christian activities urge and guide such growth.

*g*) Another therapy is *unselfish devotion to human needs*. The unselfish purpose of Christianity is fulfilled not in words but in deeds. It is not healthy to have a purpose unless one is doing something about it. The gap between theory and practice is well known. This failure to practice ideals is a human failure which Christianity seeks to overcome by a program of specific action and a commitment to that program. Occupational therapy finds work a means of healing human ills. The serving of human needs gives meaning and dignity to life.

*h*) *Confession* is needed because the repression of anxiety and guilt increases the tensions that disturb personality. It is difficult because isolation, timidity, shame, dignity, and fear of being misunderstood block the way to expresssion. "There appears to be a conscience in mankind which severely punishes the man who does not somehow and sometime at whatever cost to himself, cease to defend and assert himself, and instead confess himself fallible and human." [15] The Roman Catholic Church has made confession a required institution. Protestant churches may accomplish much by the

[15] Jung, *Modern Man in Search of a Soul*, p. 39.

intimate association of members and by the sympathetic interest of pastors in personal problems. The training of pastors in counseling will facilitate confession, insight, and reconciliation at time of stress. Serious psychopathic problems should be promptly referred to psychiatrists, but a majority of the people who have psychoneurotic problems will go unaided except as pastors, teachers, parents, and friends hear confessions in permissive counseling relationships.

*i*) *Forgiveness* is one of the most essential therapies to relieve the anguish of guilt and restore healthy relationships. It is the healing response to confession. Confession is the honest admission of one's mistakes, a first step in the repudiation of an unworthy past in order to start a more worthy future. Forgiveness is the willingness to show mercy and to be reconciled in a new beginning. As long as men do wrong, forgiveness will be urgently needed. Peace cannot resolve public war or private quarrels until enemies are forgiven. The family will fall apart unless husband, wife, and children are able to forgive. No one can endure to live with himself unless he can forgive his own mistakes.

*j*) Christianity is a *way of life*. A promise of new life is empty without a specific program of action. Physicians prescribe exercise and posture, sleep and relaxation, diet and regular habits, as more important in the long run than medication. Mental health requires wholesome attitudes, emotions, and a philosophy of life. There are those who make a cult of health, "whose god is their belly," who seek to perfect the body and have peace of mind at any cost. They flee every ache and pain as a curse; they run from counter to counter hoping to find salvation in a pill or a bottle of patent medicine. But this is not the good news of the New Testament. Health is not sought as an end in itself; it is subservient to and may be sacrificed for a more ultimate goal. "This is life eternal, that they might know thee the only true God." (John 17:3.)

There is a greater wholeness than physical or mental health to which the follower of this way dedicates himself and for which he is willing to suffer all things. The willingness to suffer in compassion for others rather than to choose one's own comforts, and to give all even life itself for this way, is what distinguishes the true disciple from the pretender. Jesus for the joy that was set before him endured the Cross. Paul was not relieved of his "thorn in the flesh" but found grace sufficient to fulfill his mission at the cost eventually of his life. In this self-forgetting devotion the ills and losses suffered are incidental and not to be compared with the joy of giving one's life into the vocation of God's calling. No one can demand health or take it as a measure of God's favor; the Christian aim is to be thankful in whatever condition to stand before Thou and serve him as one who may know that he does not labor in vain.

Jung considers religious orientation crucial for mature wholeness of personality.

> Among all my patients in the second half of life (over 36 years) there has not been one whose problem in the last resort was not that of finding a religious outlook on life . . . and none of them has been really healed who did not regain his religious outlook.[16]

One may have partial integrations, but they are apt to be unstable unless devoted to a cause larger than self-interest. A religious cause is the ultimate concern that seeks with God the largest integration of the outgoing, forth-giving relationships of life.

[16] *Ibid.*, p. 264.

# 12 A RELIGIOUS VOCATION

## *1. The Sense of Vocation*

No psychological study of the religious life would be complete without considering the sense of vocation. More attention has been given to the beginnings of religion in childhood and adolescence or to conversion and religious awakening. These are worthy of study, but they are not the whole of the ongoing religious life whose culminating devotion comes to maturity in a sense of religious vocation. It is here that the religious search, when serious and continuous, will eventually come to focus and follow a faithful discipline with ultimate concern.

The religious life, as we see it from the interpersonal point of view, is an irresistible search for encounter. The basic need of the person is for responsive relationship. The lonely infant cries out of his need for an answering response, in which we find the prototype of address in prayer and language. Out of this dialogic relationship will come the growing interests and activities to enrich personal life, as well as the social resources and associations, the arts and sciences, the ethics and religion of human civilization.

The lonely person calls and listens for the answering response. At first he is so helpless and dependent that his very life and survival require some person to answer his call. Then as he learns to walk and talk, someone will call him and listen for his response. When this occurs, the address is reciprocal, and each one in the dialogic relation becomes responsible to answer the call of the other. The growing person learns that someone wants him and needs him, and he finds it good to be wanted and needed, knowing that he is valued by and significant to the other person.

In the human family in which these lessons are learned, there is work to do, so he is given tasks to help other persons and participate in the social enterprise of family life. The mother may call him to put away his playthings, wash his hands, and come to the table to eat dinner with the family. The father may call him to help in the garden or return some tool to a neighbor. He will be asked by siblings and playmates to do things with them, and later by teachers or employers to perform the tasks assigned.

Thus he will learn the meaning of respons-ibility, which is to be able to respond to the call of another.

One time he will respond gladly and another time sadly according to his mood or readiness. If he is wondering what to do next and wishing for an invitation to participate, he may welcome the call. But if he is occupied with some other interesting activity or enjoying leisure, he may find the call unwelcome. Ambivalent feelings will consequently develop around the tasks he is called to do, and caught in emotional conflicts, he will approach his work with a divided mind. Most labor is perceived as "hard work," which is fatiguing because of strenuous effort or repetitive routine monotony. His freedom is restricted by the attention which his task demands. Though he accepts the task and knows it must be done, he is likely to have unconscious resistance that reduces the motive and obstructs efficient performance. We see this in a student who has been so urged to achieve excellence that strong unconscious resistance prevents his conscious effort to succeed. He cannot drive himself to do what he unconsciously rejects, and after many delays he may come to defeat in "educational suicide."

When the person leaves school, he will probably engage in one of the forty thousand occupations listed by the United States Bureau of Census. He may be glad to be through school and take a man's place in the world, but the same compulsions will be apt to follow him into the occupation he chooses. He will work for the rewards of labor, such as wages and social participation with status and recognition, and the satisfaction of being a productive person. But he will also have unconscious resistances, which will enhance fatigue and slow down his efficiency. No one is free from these emotional conflicts, for the dynamic forces of personality are ever at work in the conflictual nature of man. Many workers resent the work they have to do and count the hours until the end of the day when they can have their freedom to enjoy leisure activities. The urgency of this dilemma is so widely recognized that many schools and business organizations are staffed with personnel and vocational counselors to guide and improve the conditions of work.

The sense of vocation arises when the person's basic relationships give a new depth of meaning to his occupation. An occupation is any activity to keep one busy or occupied in space and time, as the root meaning of the word indicates. A vocation, however, is literally a calling which signifies address and response. To have a vocation is to feel called to do a work and to accept that call. This re-enacts the family scene in which a child is called by his father or mother to do a work that needs to be done, but now in larger context. As the person grows into maturity, he goes beyond his parents to other authorities to whom he responds in his community. The vocation becomes fully religious when the person sees his vocation in its most ultimate context and feels called of God to do his work. Even as I seek Thou for his answer, he is seeking me for my answer. The religious meaning of vocation is to live always before God to do his will and be faithful in his work.

A vocation calls for a mature person to undertake a work that is endless. It is not a task like piecework to finish and set aside or an occupation that closes when the clock strikes or the whistle blows. A vocation is never done but goes on as long as life continues. It is in fact a profession that surrounds many tasks with one ongoing purpose which we profess at all times wherever we are and whatever we do. If I have a calling to fulfill, this becomes my destiny and ultimate concern. To fulfill a calling, I must respond by giving my life without reservation to this cause for which I dedicate myself.

## 2. *The Religious Layman*

It would be false to assume that a religious vocation is only for the priest who is ordained to be the leader of a congregation. The layman has his vocation, and it would be unhistorical to imply that his calling is less religious than that of the holy man set apart from the world. Prophet, priest, mystic, and intellectual have been noted as distinct religious types. But they do not exhaust the list of religious vocations. Far more numerous and equally important to the community are those who serve as religious laymen. They too may be faithful in their work and fully devoted to the call of God.

The idea of a call is a biblical concept, as we have seen in the religious experience of the prophet and the basic relationship to God known as the covenant, in which God would care for his people in return for their faithful obedience. This was dramatically portrayed in the Garden of Eden as God called to Adam "Where art thou?" (Gen. 3:9), to examine his faithfulness and appoint him to his task in the sweat of labor. All the children of Israel were to participate in the covenant to keep the law and be responsible to God in their daily lives. In the early Christian community there were different offices to which persons were called according to their gifts (Rom. 12:6), yet each one was to be faithful to God in his calling (I Cor. 12). In his letters to young Christians, Paul emphasized the hope of this calling (Eph. 1:18), to which they should be worthy and in which they should abide (I Cor. 7:24).

With the Protestant reformers the idea of a religious calling became central. In this democratic awakening every layman was a member of the universal priesthood with direct access to God in the relation of I and

Thou. And every layman must be responsible in his daily work to answer the calling of God and prove his faith in faithful deeds. Max Weber[1] has shown the far-reaching effects of this Protestant ethic upon the economic and social life of the modern Western world, motivated by a new concept of the religious life as a vocation in the world. The German word *Beruf*, which is equivalent to the English word "calling," is not found in lexicons in its present secular use before Luther's translation of the Bible. A similar word was used only to indicate a candidate for holy orders and referred to leaving the world to enter a monastery or church. Luther introduced the term in reference to a secular vocation in the world as the task to which one is assigned by God. He saw the monastic life as a selfish tendency to withdraw from temporal obligations, while to labor for God in the world appeared to him as the expression of brotherly love.

To Calvin, God had predestined each individual to work out his own salvation, not knowing whether he would be saved but proving his faith in the world by social usefulness for the glory of God. In Holland and England the Pietists and Puritans further developed the theory of Protestant asceticism, requiring the faithful man to labor in the world and to control his impulses and temptations by the discipline of faithful work in the calling. The Methodists valued such conduct as a sign of rebirth and took their name from methodical devotion to the disciplines of a holy life in the daily task as their religious vocation. John Wesley set a strenuous example for his laymen. He was up at four o'clock in the morning, saying, "Leisure and I have parted company," to pray and work the long day through, calling on the destitute in prisons, teaching his lay preachers, organizing class meetings, preaching to the workers in mine or village, reading books on horseback and writing tracts to awaken England. To the Puritan Richard Baxter waste of time was the first and deadliest of sins. Baptists and Quakers were also insisting that every layman is called of God to labor urgently in the world to fulfill his religious vocation.

Weber traces the rise of the modern capitalistic society from this religious motivation. The mark of capitalism, he contends, is not the profit motive, for this has been present in all economies. The basic pattern of this industrious, scientific, and inventive economy is the labor of free men who discipline themselves to a rational organization of resources and efficient work. The ethic of Protestant asceticism he finds in the belief that God calls every man to be productive and bear the burden of daily toil as his religious duty to God and the neighbor. By such industry we have become a working society in which money is earned, not to spend on

[1] *The Protestant Ethic and the Spirit of Capitalism*, tr. T. Parsons (New York: Charles Scribner's Sons, 1930).

luxuries or to buy leisure, but to hold in stewardship to God through self-denial. Where this ethic is followed, capital accumulates to expand business, while those who deny themselves pleasure and leisure continue to work with undiminished zeal to fulfill their calling.

In the secular world the fruits of this ethic are abundant. It is likely that the religious motive is receding today. The Protestant ethic may be giving way as other theories of luxury and leisure are amplified through the mass media of press, screen, and radio. But still the compulsive worker drives himself to his task and feels guilty whenever he ceases to work, for he has found in his vocation the meaning of existence. Work is central to him, for life is empty without it. Many are caught in the conflicting motives of puritanism and paganism, one driving restlessly to ascetic labor and self-denial, while the other drives restlessly to leisure and self-indulgence. Such conflicts in motivation result in a frustration of self-defeat in which unconscious resistance blocks efficient work and full devotion to goals which are chosen and at the same time rejected.

From such defeat a sense of religious vocation may save the person who dedicates himself anew each day to the work he feels God calling him to do. If he finds with Luther that labor in a calling is worship of God, this becomes his religious encounter. He will undertake a rational planning of the whole of life according to God's will. Each task is to be for God, so he will seek what God would have him do and work in this larger perspective with the earnest devotion of ultimate concern. Before God he will know his weaknesses and temptations, which betray him into repetitive error and require self-criticism. Yet in humility he is ready to admit his mistakes, to learn what they will teach him, and to offer himself with new devotion to do better next time. He may be lonely, especially in a competitive society, yet he is not alone, for he works as a colaborer with God. He may be pressed upon by difficult circumstances that obstruct and baffle him, yet he is not to give up in despair or wait for the flattering words of men, for he is responsible to One who calls him to the vocation he desires to fulfill.

This sense of vocation has brought dignity to every honest work. In this view there is no one task that is sacred and preferred of God above all others. The priest or pastor may be called to serve at the altar or bedside of the dying as a man of God. But every layman is called of God to work faithfully, and there are many tasks to do in the service of human need to fulfill the divine purpose. The Society of Friends has declined to ordain priests or pastors on the theory that all men and women are equal before God, and every member of the body of Christ is equally responsible to uphold and instruct and serve the whole community. The democratizing effect of the Protestant ethic is to give the layman a place of responsible leadership in the loving community in which each is the servant of all and in which all are the servants of each. Then every meeting is a religious encounter, and all vocations are given in love, in which I am responsible to Thou in utmost devotion.

The professions of our contemporary society emerge from this sense of vocation. The mood of the religious vocation in the world has descended upon their shoulders, clothing them with the authority of those who are devoted to the unselfish service of mankind. They do not work by the piece or the clock, for their tasks are never done and their devotion is endless. They prepare by arduous training to meet high standards to give more effective service, and this service is withheld from none but given to all who have need whether they can pay or not. There are fees, to be sure, and the cost of professional services is high, yet for those who cannot pay there is service freely given. We think with gratitude of physicians, nurses, and other medical workers who care for the sick, of lawyers and social workers who care for those who are caught in social conflict, teachers and counselors who care for growing persons, psychologists and psychiatrists who work to understand and guide the human mind into health and maturity.

These are secular professions, yet their representatives work as if they were motivated by religious dedication. Their sustained, willing, and uncalculating service given to those in need has the quality of religious devotion. And the human community seems to recognize it as such by setting them apart in contrast to the "laymen" they serve. When a physician comes to church to worship, he is a layman in reference to the minister, and when the minister is a patient in the hospital, he is a layman in reference to the physician. There is this juxtaposition among the professions implying that they are all engaged in a common service to mankind. Each profession has its supporting community to define standards and validate role behavior within its guild without always clarifying the relations to other professions, though in the clinic there is teamwork among related specialists.

In these days when young people are largely free to choose their own vocations, it is not surprising to find how often a secular profession is chosen from religious motives. Young people with religious orientation talk about choosing a vocation in the world as their call to give altruistic service and make the world a better place to live in. We have noted that many psychologists and psychiatrists are sons of ministers. Studies of persons known for their public service as listed in *Who's Who* are shown to originate from the families of ministers twice as often as from the homes of other professions. Visher conducted a large-scale investigation of this in 1925 with such results and confirmed them with another study in 1947 of scientists starred in *American Men of Science*.[2]

Clark in his study of factors leading to achievement and creativity gathered questionnaire data from 116 biographees of *Who's Who in America* and 186 alumni of Williams and Middlebury colleges. He also found that twice as many of the more eminent group come from ministers' families. In considering the constructive factors leading to creativity, these respondents ranked (*a*) interest and satisfaction in the work for its own sake; (*b*) the desire to know and to understand; (*c*) the desire to aid society; (*d*) the desire for new experience; (*e*) the desire for economic security; (*f*) the desire to please someone; (*g*) the desire to see others do things properly; (*h*) the desire to find and create beauty; (*i*) the desire to fulfill one's religious destiny; (*j*) the desire to overcome handicaps; and (*k*) the desire for social recognition.

This seems to place religious motivation as a separate item rather far down the list. Yet in a broader view of the situation religious motives may be diffused throughout the entire list, if we see religion as ultimate concern for intrinsic values with a sense of responsibility to fulfill a vocation in service of others. Clark notes that individuals in his study tend to rate the religious item either very high or very low to a greater extent than other factors, and he infers that many of them may have rejected religion as a particular creed rather than a broader way of life.

While generalizations on such data are valid only to a point, he does find that 107 indicate that religious beliefs had a greater influence on secular achievements in comparison with 32 who said their secular achievements were more influential on their religious beliefs. His hypothesis is that creativity often results from a tension between faith and skepticism. Religious belief he finds to be a durable and intense form of motivation with attitudes of social responsibility, ethical obligation, and a sense of the reality of nonmaterial value which are conducive to creativity. Yet under the pressure of orthodoxy the energy is often turned into a defensive emotional effort to protect the verbalized belief in bigoted and repressive ways. The function of skepticism is to extend horizons and direct energy away from defensive restrictions to broader areas of creativity in art, literature, social service, or political and business enterprise.

In seeking to understand why people are religious, C. S. Braden [3] col-

[2] For a review of such studies see W. H. Clark, "A Study of Some of the Factors Leading to Achievement and Creativity, with Special Reference to Religious Skepticism and Belief," *The Journal of Social Psychology*, XLI (1955), 57-69.

[3] "Why People Are Religious—A Study in Religious Motivation," *The Journal of Bible and Religion*, XV (1947), 38-45.

lected answers which he eventually reduced to a check list of 65 items and compiled data from over 2,500 respondents. The leading motive, checked 5,293 times, was that religion gives meaning to life. Other motives, in descending order, were that religion motivates human kindness, provides help in time of stress, enriches life, furnishes a moral ideal, arises from belief in a supreme being and early training, furnishes an aim and purpose for being, gives guidance, and makes life worth living. While college students predominate in this group, the age ranges from under twenty to over fifty, with a wide geographical, economic, occupational, and denominational distribution among Protestants in the United States. There is a congruence among these high-ranking motives indicating that many people find in their religion a central purpose for living an altruistic goal-seeking way of life with a continuing sense of meaning even in times of stress and difficulty. This may sum up the experience of religious laymen who feel responsible to a supreme Being for their conduct in daily life.

### 3. *Role Perception Is Interpersonal*

Human behavior is guided by role perception. We respond from moment to moment to each situation as we perceive it. And in each situation we ask what is expected of us. We may be instructed by another person if he tells us explicitly what he expects us to do. If not we look sharply for cues and draw upon previous experience to perceive his expectations. Or by empathy I may project myself into your situation and ask what I would do if I were you. In meeting a stranger, you may search his face and posture to recognize his intention, whether to avoid encounter or to meet you openly. If he smiles and nods to you, then you are encouraged to take the role of a friend and respond to him in a friendly manner.

Role behavior, as analyzed by social psychologists, is seen to be a product of personal intentions and the expectations of other persons. As we enter a new situation, we wonder what role to take and look to see what other persons expect of us, then decide what under the circumstances we intend to do. Every role is thus mutually given in the constant interaction of persons with one another. David Riesman classified persons as other-directed and inner-directed. But in the process of perceiving our role, we are both inner-and other-directed. This is the nature of every true encounter as I offer myself to Thou alert to perceive and respond in behavior appropriate to the relationship.

A religious vocation has this inner and outer aspect. There is the secret call or inner experience whereby a person believes that he is summoned by God. This may impel him to offer and prepare himself for the vocation which he feels called of God to perform. Yet in his preparation he must meet the standards set by his society, and in offering himself he must measure up to the qualifications for acceptance into his vocation. This is the public call to answer the inner call by social approval of his intentions. His private revelation may be a delusion to mislead him unless he is accepted by the community as one whose role behavior meets their expectations.

When a young person enters one of the vocations of the secular world, his qualifications will be appraised by the secular standards. If he asks to be a licensed electrician or certified public accountant, he must take examinations and meet the requirements of his city or state for that work. If she desires to be a registered nurse or a public-school teacher, her qualifications are tested and validated by a state board. The public call is a social approval that must be earned by meeting high standards carefully defined by society. Applicants are not to be discriminated against by reason of their religious affiliation, lest bigotry and prejudice defeat equal opportunity and fair treatment for all.

But the inner motives and decisions which lead to the vocation may be deeply religious. A young person who feels called of God to enter this vocation in the world is likely to be guided and empowered by a steady and unswerving motive. Not only will he sacrifice competing interests to devote himself faithfully to his work. He will also, if his motive is genuinely religious, hold each task in the larger perspective of his ongoing purpose, constantly submitting his efforts in humility to God and seeking ever to do better. His interest in other persons will be unselfish and compassionate to serve those in need, to love and care for them. Whatever he does in the religious mood will be sincere from ultimate concern to fulfill the I-Thou relationship.

Nothing has been more distinctive and authentic in the religious life than this sense of vocation. Religious history has been made time and again by persons who believed they were called by divine initiative, often against their own desire and inclination, to do God's work. This was a characteristic experience of the Hebrew prophets, who like Moses, Elijah, and Jeremiah at great cost to themselves responded to the call to speak for God. Jesus and his disciples heard the call to forsake all else to follow the way of God's love. The prophet Mohammed and his followers responded as they believed to the call of God as the central meaning of life.

To explore the motives in choosing the vocation of the Protestant ministry, seventy-six first-year theological students at Boston University were asked to write an autobiographical sketch on "Motives for Entering the Ministry." Of these students sixty-two were male and fourteen female whose mean age was 24.9 years and who had reached their decision an average of 4.6 years before. The majority of them were Methodist. A content analysis[4] of the autobiographies revealed twelve frequently occurring motives, which may be expressed in the following statements:

1. A minister is respected, has personal prestige, and is a leader. (Prestige)
2. I was called by God. (Call)
3. I wanted to serve the needs of other people and to help them in their troubles. (Altruism)
4. My parents urged me to become a minister. (Parental influence)
5. I was interested in the things that ministers do. (Interest)
6. I wished to express my natural aptitude for the ministry. (Aptitude)
7. I wanted to learn about and understand religious matters. (Curiosity)
8. The ministry is a reasonably secure profession. (Security)
9. A successful minister usually has a steady financial income. (Monetary gain)
10. I wanted to make the world a better place in which to live. (Reform)
11. A minister's job is glamourous. (Glamour)
12. I was anxious and fearful and believed the ministry would help to solve my emotional problems. (Emotional inadequacy)

Six weeks after this analysis of the autobiographies, these statements minus the categories were distributed to the same first-year theological students. They were asked to rank the twelve statements in a forced choice so that each one would be sorted into an order descending from the most to the least important. If an item did not appear in their own vocational decision, they were to rank it as such a motive would have been sorted if it had been present. Other relevant motives they were invited to write in at the bottom of the page, but only one student needed to do this. To record changes in motivation, they were asked first to rank the statements as they considered them important at the time of deciding to enter the ministry and then rank them again according to present motives for continuing in the ministry.

The results of these rankings are given in the table below. It should be noted that the actual motives in their relative strength and intermingling are no doubt far more complicated than would appear in this list. Furthermore, the actual motives in their entirety are unknown. What we have here is a ranking of motives as perceived by the students some time after the actual decision was made.

[4] See Orlo Strunk, Jr., "Theological Students: A Study in Perceived Motives," *Personnel and Guidance Journal*, XXXVI (January, 1958), 320-22.

RANKINGS OF 12 STATEMENTS BY 76 THEOLOGICAL STUDENTS

| Statement Category | Ranking of Entering Motives | Ranking of Present Motives |
|---|---|---|
| Altruism | 1 | 1 |
| Call | 2 | 2 |
| Reform | 3 | 3 |
| Interest | 4 | 5 |
| Curiosity | 5 | 4 |
| Aptitude | 6 | 6 |
| Prestige | 7 | 7 |
| Security | 8 | 8 |
| Emotional Inadequacy | 9 | 11 |
| Parental Influence | 10 | 10 |
| Monetary Gain | 11 | 9 |
| Glamour | 12 | 12 |

Of these 76 students 81.58 per cent placed "altruism" as first, second, or third choice; and 65.79 per cent placed "call" as first, second, or third choice. The most idealistic and religious motives are firmly entrenched at the top of the ranking scale. They do not change over the period of 4.6 years. The lesser motives change more readily as occurs with interest, curiosity, emotional inadequacy, and monetary gain. As the students mature, interest becomes stronger and curiosity and monetary gain are more openly recognized as significant even for a religious worker. The hope that the ministry will help to solve emotional problems recedes as the students become more mature, with two possible interpretations. Either the maturing student feels less anxious or he does not consider the intention of a religious vocation to be for the purpose of helping himself emotionally in view of the altruistic motive, and perhaps a more realistic view of the emotional demands of the ministry. It is evident in comparison with avowed motives of persons in other vocations that the idealistic motives play a leading role in the choice of a religious vocation. The most distinctly religious motive is the call of God to love and serve the neighbor in a community of mutual concern.

## 4. *Dilemmas of a Vocation*

Vocations are defined by a community. Every profession has a supporting community to guide and authenticate the vocation. Professional associations elect qualified members, accredit and regulate them by official standards. So leadership in any vocation is supported by the group of people who uphold and appreciate it. The religious community ordains the priest and the pastor; it approves the teacher and elects the religious officer. The prophet may form his own community, yet he is constantly oriented to the needs of the group to whom he prophesies. He may decline to conform to the expectations of the community and even be rejected by others, but he does not reject them for he is responsible to God for them whatever they may do.

Yet vocation is also response to the call of God. This dual focus frequently results in conflict between a religious person and his group, and causes what is known as role stress. If the individual knows what the members of the group expect of him, but his own intention is otherwise, he will be impaled on a painful dilemma. If he feels responsible to a higher authority in God or his own conscience, he may decide not to conform at the expense of his leadership or even his life. If on the other hand he does conform and win the approval of his group, he may feel discredited in relationship to God and his own sense of vocation.

It is because of this stress that laymen may lose their sense of vocation and find it more convenient to conform to the behavior and motives of the secular world. Many persons drift away from religious affiliation altogether and give up the severe requirements of discipleship for other comforts and successes. Or they may hold membership in a church to which they give minimal and nominal participation. Instead of going the whole way, they make a "halfway covenant." Instead of giving all to the religious calling, they give a fraction of time and interest. This becomes a retreat from the full meaning of religious vocation to the specialized form of behavior which is a token of neglect rather than a devotion of the whole life. It is secondary or tertiary rather than primary religious behavior. This is self-defeating, for it separates religion from life and will ultimately mean that such religion loses all power to shape life.

This problem of role stress, which affects us all in the conflict of inner intentions and outer expectations, is particularly acute for the person whose sense of vocation leads him into the service of the church. If he is to lead a congregation or teach others, he will be apt to suffer from a sense of unworthiness. He may also feel trapped by the expectations of those he comes to serve. They may have very narrow and rigid ideas as to how a minister should conduct himself. Or they may expect him to set an example of perfection in all the virtues which they find lacking in themselves. He may either resent their expectations or come into open conflict with them over his perception of the role he seeks to fulfill. Then he may have secret feelings of guilt for disappointing them or himself or God in the conduct of his vocation.

To explore this dilemma, Richard W. Boyd[5] constructed a role perception interview which he gave to nine Protestant ministers before and after group therapy as part of clinical training in a mental hospital, and to another group of ministers two years after similar therapy. He desired to learn (*a*) what these young men perceived to be their role as ministers, (*b*) what they thought their parishioners would expect in such role behavior, and (*c*) what the ministers felt they ought to do in their role behavior. Each item consisted of two or three questions to be answered in five degrees of emphasis, and these were classified under general headings. Economic factors referred to expected income in ten years, salary increase, and living conditions. Social life factors referred to church control over social life, the choice of friends, and freedom to express negative feelings. Goal factors referred to the goals of the minister in his church work. Professional factors included the preaching of controversial sermons, the range of topics, and community activities for the minister and the parishioner. The final section was on interpersonal relations with preferred groups and the minister's affect for workers and nonworkers, heavy givers and nongivers.

So much conflict was found between the role intentions of these ministers and their perception of what parishioners expect of them that great stress was evident in the pretest. After therapy, however, the role stress was reduced especially in economic factors, goals, and interpersonal relations. Yet the conflicts remained in control of social life and the professional activities in which the ministers considered it was their right to act contrary to expectations of parishioners. The sample of ministers was too small for wide generalization, and there would be value in a study of larger proportions, including also the perceptions of laymen, as for example, Murray H. Leiffer[6] has conducted in his survey of how laymen look at the minister. Other studies, however, confirm the role stress under which the minister seeks to fulfill his vocation.

One of these is the study by Samuel H. Blizzard[7] of 690 Protestant clergymen widely distributed geographically, denominationally, and in population of community. He distinguishes six practitioner roles within the work of the parish minister: administrator, organizer, pastor, preacher, priest, and teacher. The ministers were asked to evaluate these six roles from three perspectives: importance, effectiveness, and enjoyment. They were ranked from the most to the least important as follows: preacher, pastor, priest, teacher, organizer, administrator. Considering their own sense of effective-

[5] "The Use of Group Psychotherapy in the Professional Training of Ministers" (Unpublished Ph.D. dissertation, Boston University, 1952).

[6] *The Layman Looks at the Minister* (Nashville: Abingdon Press, 1947).

[7] "The Minister's Dilemma," *The Christian Century*, LXXIII (April 25, 1956), 508-10.

ness in these roles, they ranked them from most to least effective: preacher, pastor, teacher, priest, administrator, organizer. The intention here was to assess the minister's level of personal involvement in relation to each professional role as a clue to his motivation and goal tension. Another index of motivation was taken to be their enjoyment of each role. The role of pastor was most enjoyed, followed by the roles of preacher, teacher, priest, organizer, and administrator. It will be noted that preacher and pastor hold ascendancy in all three of these ratings, with administrator and organizer given least value.

A time study was then made of daily activities reported by 480 rural and urban ministers, distinguishing the professional from the nonprofessional. Professional activities were classified according to the roles noted above except that preaching and priestly roles were combined as one unit. The professional work day averaged approximately ten hours, of which two fifths were spent as administrator. Slightly more than one fourth was devoted to the role of pastor. Preaching and priestly functions together took up one fifth of the average work day. Organizing required more than one tenth of the day and teaching about one twentieth. This order of priority was the same for the rural and the urban parish ministers.

The dilemma of the minister herein studied is the conflict between his perception of the most important roles and the amount of time he is able to give to them. The conflict and resultant stress are most acute between the roles of pastor-preacher versus the roles of administrator-organizer. The administrator and organizer roles are viewed by the minister as least important, effective, and enjoyable. Yet he spends considerably more time in administration than any other role. For example, the average time devoted to daily sermon preparation is thirty-four minutes for the rural ministers and thirty-eight minutes for the urban ministers. But time required for stenographic tasks is one hour and four minutes. Not only is this obstructive to efficiency in the roles perceived as most important, but the motivation for his work is seriously frustrated by his having to give the least time to what he enjoys the most and the most time to what he enjoys the least.

Such acute stress in the exercise of roles is not conducive to either mental health or integral effectiveness in a vocation. Were it not for strong religious devotion, more ministers would evidently be in distress or turning to other vocations. For the minister must do his work in roles that seem to be basically equivocal. These ambiguities are complicated by three different norms: (*a*) the traditions of the church, (*b*) the expectations of the parishioners, and (*c*) the intentions and norms by which the minister himself perceives his roles. There is need for open communication and reappraisal of the work of the minister by all concerned, which may lead to clarification of goals and the means to advance toward them.

We need to be aware of projective tendencies whenever we seek to appraise our interpersonal relations. It is true that other persons make demands upon us by their expectations. In the dilemmas of a vocation as we suffer the conflictual pressures of role stress, we are quite likely to project the blame upon other persons. We may feel that we are victims of unwelcome demands imposed upon us by the authorities for whom we work in our vocation. A minister who is responsible to a congregation may feel he has too many masters who come at him from all sides with contradictory expectations which make unreasonable demands upon him. A sociological study, like the Blizzard report, will naturally point to social structures and procedures that appear determinative of the minister's behavior. This may give support to the martyr complex of one who projects the cause of his predicament outward upon others.

This tendency to suspect the boss or the organization of overworking one is quite typical of workers in all vocations. And this may mislead our perceptions rather than to provide true understanding of our dilemmas. A psychological dimension is needed here to reveal the part which inner motives play under cover in ways so stealthy as to deceive us. The minister who enjoys and values most the role of preacher-pastor yet involves himself more largely in the role of organizer-administrator may need to look at the hidden motives here. Even while he is idealizing one role as more worthy of his calling, he is choosing many times a day to occupy his time with office details as a clerical worker. Even while he protests that he is a victim of necessities imposed upon him, he is actually doing first what he wants to do first. The minister is an executive in the sense of planning his own work and deciding from hour to hour how to spend his working time. It would appear that he is more comfortable with routine tasks that demand less emotional stress than the anxious encounters in face-to-face relationships in which he meets persons as pastor and preacher.

If he insists he is not choosing the lesser and cannot do otherwise, he reveals a glimpse of how deeply the conflict is working at unconscious levels. There is re-enacted here the conflictual dilemma of every man's finite predicament. He is caught in the contradiction of two alternatives both of which are unwelcome at many levels of his behavior. The general predicament of man, as we have noted before, is to have infinite desires with finite limitations to constrict their realization. In his sober moments he knows that he cannot have everything he desires and certainly not at one time. Yet this is so unwelcome to him that he continually strives as if he thought he could. The other alternative is to give up these unruly desires, as Buddha would recommend. But this is also unwelcome, for without desires life appears to be empty and becalmed, useless and meaningless. So we try to compromise on a wider front than we can manage by failing to give up either side of the contradictory desires and acting as if we could do the impossible. The consequence of this predicament is to defeat the unity of intentional living and undermine effective action by unresolved conflicts that block and cancel one another.

## 5. *Deterrents and Disciplines*

In conclusion we need to recognize some of the psychological deterrents and disciplines of a religious vocation.

Among the psychological deterrents we may first note the distraction of many interests. It is natural for a person to have many interests, as he is sensitive to a wide range of stimuli and goes forth eagerly to meet whatever confronts him. The whole bent of education in our culture is to increase the range and intensity of human interests. The aim is to be more alive and have more to live for, to waken us from the stupor of unconsciousness, to call forth response to every invitation to learn, and to develop every potentiality to fulfillment. But the very richness of these multiple interests we seek to cultivate draws us in all directions and leads to distraction in a welter of profusion. And this becomes a deterrent to the single-minded purpose of a vocation which requires concentration upon essentials to the exclusion of the extraneous. In a religious vocation there is need for a constant discipline to remember one's calling, to keep the true purpose ascendant and devote one's energies by a faithful following in every detail of the ultimate concern. This is contrary to our nature, and the many desires clamoring for freedom deter the singleness of the vocation.

To complicate the struggle further, we find that our many desires are charged with conflictual ambivalence. They are dynamic in pressing us impulsively to and fro before we make up our mind, not waiting like flowers to be plucked but like roots that grow ever deeper in the intertwining and grasping tenacity of unyielding life. If I say I will now choose this or that, the outcome is not so decisive as I might expect. For these contradictory impulses hold me in counterpoise, not quite able to give up the one for the other. Publicly and openly I may vow to follow one, but secretly and covertly I hold on to the other for the time when I may indulge it in a moment of unguarded leisure. We may dignify our oppositions by calling them the abundant life and be the more reluctant to deny ourselves any good thing. But this ambivalence deters a religious vocation with the impedimenta of excess baggage and otiose overweight. Our secret indulgence may be a pleasant retreat from weary toil, but it slows and retards the swift runner who is handicapped by unwillingness to give up one good for a greater one. It is this ambivalent hesitation to give up the secondary desires that prevents the whole-hearted devotion to what we intend to make the primary goal.

A third complication is the cross-pulling tangle of our interpersonal relations. In the lonely recesses of my self-conscious being I take my stand determined to hold my separate identity as an independent person. Even before a little child has words to say, "I want what I want when I want it," he is eloquent in acting out this unyielding self-affirmation. And yet he is so incomplete in himself that he cannot endure his "splendid" isolation and will cry in hopeless or angry despair for someone to answer his dependent need. When we come to maturity, the ground is firmer under our feet, and yet we find ourselves inextricably entangled in contradictory relationships with other persons. Their expectations at once define and distort my sense of vocation and precipitate the role stress we have noted above. Our vocation is devoted to these persons whose conflictual demands are so often confusing. How to live with those we cannot live without is a constant tension, however much we desire to uphold the relationship.

Another deterrent is the attrition of devotion by fatigue and routinization in the daily tasks of a vocation. Repetition inevitably tends to make a routine of any regular operation. And the performance of daily tasks is bound to generate fatigue either from exertion or from monotonous boredom. Chronic fatigue is an emotional and often unconscious protest against situations that irritate or bore us. Boredom reduces sharp attention to careless inattention as the active mind seeks escape in wandering fantasy. These symptoms are so typical and characteristic of the daily worker that we are likely to take them for granted. But this detensioning is fatal to the intention of a religious vocation to be always alert to the call and faithful to the calling. The line of least resistance is to let down rather than to rise up and press forever on to the unfinished tasks. A religious vocation asks more than we have and invites us to become more than we are. This calls for heroic and persistent self-giving against the drift of easy inclination.

Recognizing these deterrents to a vocation, what may the religious person do to counteract them? Are there psychological controls to correct the drift and facilitate the vocation he seeks to fulfill? Some discipline is needed if the recalcitrant impulses of life are to converge and give unfailing energy to serve a vocation. We may dislike discipline by associating it with the repressions and punishments of our childhood. But actually a discipline is a positive way of affirming our intention to make the most of the life that is ours. It is a systematic procedure to enact a purpose and move forward to a goal. A student seeking to prepare for a vocation enters upon the discipline of learning that will guide him to the goal. A disciple offers himself to follow a chosen master in a way of life that transcends all other interests. There can be no vocation unless the worker, the artist, or the scientist is willing each new day to submit to the discipline essential to its fulfillment.

To cope with distraction, we can employ the discipline of selectivity. Psychologists find this one of the distinctive abilities of a living organism from the amoeba to man, to select the stimuli to which one will respond. The educated man is responsive to an amazing range of stimuli, and this invites the distraction we have noted above. For his span of attention is strictly limited, and he can focus sharply upon just one configuration at a time. It is therefore important to the efficient worker that he discipline himself to concentrate his attention steadily upon the task before him. Yet the vocation is more than one task; it is a forward-moving purpose that gathers up a maze of details into clear perspective. For this a high degree of skill is required in holding a span of attention so as to relate many discrete items into a Gestalt or whole pattern of central meaning. Yet it will call for more than routine practice; it will be a constant redefining of goal and renewing of purpose. It will mean a constant willingness to give up the irrelevant interests for the most relevant concerns. There must be a constant reorganizing of strategy and mobilizing of resources to achieve the vocation through effectual selectivity.

To do this will take more than mechanical or technical skills. For we work with and against the ambivalent and conflictual motives within ourselves. These we may repress, but they continue to struggle in the counterplot of underground resistance. By what discipline can we undertake to resolve these inner conflicts?

Buddha taught the cutting off of desire, and holy men practice renunciation of material goods or worldly ambitions. Can we and do we want to uproot these unruly desires of our human striving? If so will life be empty and the vigor of our Western civilization to invent and produce be lost? Freud believed the primitive impulses can be neither uprooted nor stifled. He offered the way of sublimation, to elevate and transform them into useful energies moving out through acceptable channels to creative expression. This we learn also from the great religious and ethical teachers, that the passional nature of man is to be refined in the crucible of suffering and the grace of forgiving love to become a new creature. The disrupting conflicts must be worked through to integrating wholeness. Religion and psychiatry have their disciplines and agree that without the discipline there is no salvation. There will be renunciation of present for future satisfactions and of lesser for greater good. There must be honest self-examination to understand motives and willingness to seek the whole above segments of life.

This working through of conflicts we cannot do alone, for they involve our relationships with other persons. The inner conflicts must come out in the open, and the hidden grievances must be made known between us. This is the discipline of open communication. But this we are reluctant to do, for the load of anxiety and anguish is heavy, and we fear the relationship cannot bear the strain. So we hold up our defenses and let communication break down to our deeper sorrow and insufferable loss. The counsel of religion and psychiatry is united here in showing the need of this open discipline. "Confess your faults one to another and pray one for another that ye may be healed" (Jas. 5:16), we learn from religion. In the language of psychiatry the words may be different, but the meaning is the same. Otherwise health and human relations both suffer; the hurt is deeper and wounds do not heal. We deceive ourselves as much as another when we fail to bear the brunt and take the risk of communication. There is no other way to understand or clarify our tangled relations. Only by this discipline do we educate, negotiate, and converge upon common agreement. To ventilate our concerns in open communication is to release the stiffling defenses and reach out hopefully, even faithfully, to the persons we distrust.

This we know is difficult and often contrary to the drift of our inclination to self-protection. Consequently we shall need a discipline to counteract the defensive closing in upon ourselves and what we note above as the attrition of our best intentions. This discipline will call us to frequent and regular encounters with other persons, from those nearest to us in our human relations to the Ultra-Person we address as Thou. It will be easier to turn aside from encounter and hold our feelings apart in covert isolation. A discipline of courage will be needed to break through the barriers into open communication. Humility will be needed to confess failures and negative feelings that threaten self-esteem, as well as to accept the strictures of finitude. Grace is a constant need to forgive oneself and graciousness to forgive the other his offenses of omission and commission.

It is only in such encounters that re-creation is possible in the largest sense. No man is sufficient to be his own physician or to heal himself, for true healing is a gift from the Creator mediated to us through relationship. We may seek to accomplish it on a "do-it-yourself" procedure, but we are so adept in deceiving ourselves that we are unable to achieve true honesty apart from the relation of dialogue. It is the encounter that confronts me with reality when I must answer to another for my behavior and view of life. In this sense no vocation, least of all a religious vocation, can be a one-man job. For a calling is from one to one, and in this living relation it is to be fulfilled. The encounter with the One who calls me is my summons to vocation. Out of this meeting will come again and again the occasion to seek renewal of the central and integrating purpose by which to rededicate a whole life to an endless vocation.

# 13 THE RELIGIOUS COMMUNITY

## *1. A Social Theory*

In these chapters we have been studying religious behavior from the viewpoint of interpersonal psychology. This is not to deny the truth in other contemporary theories of religion. We have acknowledged the conflictual nature of man in the contradictions of infinite desires beating against finite limitations. With the collective theory we can see that no person is complete within himself but is profoundly related to the whole human race, whose archetypes or psychic meanings speak to him in ageless symbols. With the personalistic theory we affirm the unique integration that each individual person must achieve in the goal-seeking intention of his own becoming. There is much to learn from each of these psychologists as we seek to comprehend the complexities and perplexities of the religious seeker.

Yet as we follow the trails they blaze through the thick undergrowth of psychological fact and theory, we find them converging upon another pathway to which they lead. This is the interpersonal theory which draws together the individuality of unique persons who emerge from social groups, wrestle with dynamic conflicts, and reach out beyond themselves to other persons. There is partial truth in each theory, which may come to fulfillment in interpersonalism. The individual, unique as he may be, does not and cannot stand alone but seeks encounter with other persons. The collective unconscious may indicate the vastness of psychic energies and resources beyond the individual, yet it will remain a bottomless abyss of fleeting impressions until its energy comes to focus in persons who reach out one to another. The dynamic conflicts that beset the goal-striving personality are not to be understood or healed except through the relations of person with person.

To proceed in this way is to invite the charge of eclecticism. In so far as truth is found in rival theories, the eclectic mood of tolerance is not altogether banished to the outer darkness. Strictly speaking, an eclectic method does select from various sources and systems of thought, but this need not imply a careless attitude of piecing together a collection of unrelated items with no critical analysis. If theorists are unable to learn fron one another, there would seem to be less concern for the whole truth thai for rival positions. For as the evidence accumulates, there must of necessit be facts and principles acknowledged as common ground among divers points of view.

The interpersonalist is open to learn from other theories, and this is one ( the assets which accrue to such a theory. But more than a collection c observations, it is a systematic theory in its own right that moves fron data to orderly hypotheses. We have seen Moreno and Buber as two pioneers who have opened trails worth following. There is reason to note contributions also from those associated with George Herbert Mead in social psychology; with Harry Stack Sullivan, Eric Fromm, and the cultural ar alysts in psychiatry; with Kurt Lewin and researchers in group dynami and human relations. Among psychologists of religion Fritz Kunkel h emphasized the we-psychology, and I have emphasized interpersonal ps chology.

The major hypothesis of the interpersonal theory is that because the fini person is incomplete in himself, he will inevitably reach out of his huma need to relate to other persons. Persons have many needs, to be sure, but the affiliative need is the most basic and persistent of all. Out of thi insatiable hunger for reconciling love (in the social sense primarily, thoug sexual and other components are never absent from biological life), th lonely person will seek ever and again to orient himself to other persons. H will be troubled by their demands and by his own anxiety in desiring thei approval. He will fumble and fail in his relationships, and so react against and away from other persons in the anguish of his distress. Yet he will be so fractional that even though he may endure isolation and rationalize his preferences, he will yet long for the answering response.

Religion cannot well be understood, it would seem to me, apart from the hypothesis of the basic need for relationship. You may well question the novelty of this idea. Does interpersonalism offer, as James said of pragmatism, only a new name for some old ways of thinking? The social nature of religion has surely been recognized before. If the eighteenth century is known for the awakening of the individual, the twentieth century will be known as the era of social awakening. With the rise of the social sciences there has been increasing recognition and exploration of man in society. Sociologists and anthropologists have long been interested in religion as a social phenomenon.

Comte (1830) in his hierarchy of the sciences placed sociology as one of the "psychics" at the apex, predicting that it would replace theology with the "religion of humanity." To him society was the "Great Being" to be worshiped. Durkheim (1912) held that religion is a "collective representation" to which the individual is exposed. Religious beliefs and practices unite believers into one single moral community. It is society that sanctions the sacred and becomes the real object of worship. Lévy-Bruhl (1910) traced the origin of religion to the prelogical "participation" of primitive societies in which it was born of ignorance before science.

These are actually collective theories, however, which view society as a crowd or mass of anonymous and faceless numbers. It was once easy to talk of the herd instinct or the gregarious instinct impelling the individual to merge himself in the crowd. Laws of sympathy, imitation, and suggestion were invoked to explain the social behavior of individuals and show why they were religious. Psychologists of religion in the early period of this century were also explaining religion in these terms. Hall (1904) protrayed conversion as a socializing process at puberty similar to the tribal initiations from boyhood to manhood in primitive societies. Ames (1910) expounded religion as the consciousness of the highest social values, which is the end of all its forms and strivings. To him there was no distinction between morality and religion as both were devoted to the social consciousness.

Interpersonal theory stands over against collectivism as much as it does against individualism. Granting that the lonely individual cannot find his ultimate fulfillment in isolation, neither will he find it in "the lonely crowd." To flee from oneself to the crowd is not to escape either one's self or one's loneliness. What the individual person most needs is an answering response from another person in a relationship of mutual recognition and regard in which the dialogue is a true encounter of I and Thou. The crowd reduces the unique person to the impersonal mass. But religious encounter is a meeting of person with person that enhances the value of each in his unique individuality and enlarges the meaning of life in the disclosure of relationship.

Social psychologists were at first engaged with either a unitary principle such as imitation or a plural set of instincts by which to explain social behavior as pushed from behind. Cultural determinists have been engaged with social influences upon the individual to show how he is pushed by lateral pressures from all sides. But these mechanistic pressures give an artificial, external, and dehumanizing view of man. What we are most concerned to know is what the person himself is trying to do in his social behavior. What goal does he want to reach? Does he not want to meet another person who will respond to him in mutual respect and self-giving?

The need for community is not to lose oneself in the anonymous crowd but to find oneself in relation to other persons in the dialogue of address. I want to talk with someone who will care enough to listen and talk to me. We desire to know persons who know us and to whom we count in a unique and qualitative sense of personal value. This is more than a desire to be together with our kind or to have the primitive We-feeling that Kunkel would cherish in the infant or Lévy-Bruhl in the tribal experience of mystical participation. The goal of interpersonal theory is encounter of the person with other persons, who stand in opposition to one another and yet who meet as I and Thou in reverent appreciation for the otherness that draws them together in responsive relationship.

G. H. Mead approaches this view in his self-other system as a duality of subject and object to know and be known at the same time. We know ourselves only in the presence of another, or as we imagine another person would perceive us. "We are in possession of selves just in so far as we can and do take the attitudes of others towards ourselves and respond to those attitudes." [1] Yet we do not find the full encounter in Mead, for this activity seems to be going on within a person as subjective awareness rather than among persons who address one another with social response in the living moment. Increasingly social psychologists have been concerned with the interaction among persons in view of what they perceive one another to mean.[2]

There were two psychologists of religion in this period who also approached the interpersonal point of view. When Coe was writing on religion as group conduct, he considered the religious crowd as motivated by suggestion and the sacerdotal group by authority. But the deliberative group he described as welcoming free variation of thought and stimulating the individual to self-discovery. He agreed with Mead that society arises through the individuating process and "the increasing notice that one takes of another as an experiencing self." [3]

Another approach toward interpersonalism is found in the writing of Pratt, who defines religion in terms that imply encounter. "Religion is the serious and social attitude of individuals or communities toward the power or powers which they conceive as having ultimate control over their interests and destinies." [4] While he is not explicit in portraying the religious encounter as interpersonal, he does show that religion is immediately subjective and that it will also involve the acceptance of the objective. He does not insist that religion must have a personal object, yet it must not be mechanical or coldly intellectual. "Attitude" refers to the "responsive side

[1] *The Philosophy of the Present*, ed. A. E. Murphy (Chicago: Open Court Publishing Co., 1932), p. 189.

[2] Robert MacDougall employs the term "interpersonal relations" as early as 1912 in his article "The Social Basis of Individuality," *American Journal of Sociology*, XVIII (July, 1912), 1-20.

[3] *Psychology of Religion*, p. 143.

[4] *Op. cit.*, p. 2.

of consciousness," and the social quality consists of feeling ourselves in relation to something that can make response to us. He goes further to show the fragmentary impoverishment of subjective worship and points to the larger and more fully religious meaning of objective worship as aiming to communicate with the Deity as a direct address of the soul with God. It is this relation of encounter that distinguishes interpersonal theory.

## 2. *The Need for Community*

If persons need above all the response of other persons, how is this to be provided? The need will evidently have to be met in the dynamic and responsive relations of group life. The numerically simplest structure of social interaction is between two individuals. And we have agreed that no individual could become a person without becoming aware of a self-other relation. Whenever we think of a singular individual, we have extracted him from the context of relationships to which he belongs. The concept of isolation does not refer merely to the absence of other persons, but actually to an intentional turning away from them. Simmel[5] describes isolation as interaction between two persons, one of which leaves after exerting certain influences.

It is this dyad which is the basic structure of group life. Here we have the encounter of person to person which we have seen as the I-Thou relation. Each of the two feels himself to be confronted by the other, and the social structure rests upon this one to one relation. There is no superpersonal collectivity, but each is directly responsible to the other, and if one gives up, the structure breaks down.

A triad has a very different social structure. For in such a group each one acts as an intermediary between the other two, and his effect is to both separate and unite. There is a further division of responsibility, and if one drops out, there are still two to continue the group. The intensity and intimacy of the two are somewhat diminished by the third person, who may be regarded as an intruder who distracts and disturbs the relation of two. But when the two are in conflict, a third person may become the mediator, and work to effect a reconciliation.

Preferences may be shown for the dyad, as in the proverb "Two is company, three is a crowd." It is evident that Buber prefers the two in what he considers the primary relation of I and Thou. Freud also preferred the dyad, as he indicated by devoting his life to individual psychotherapy in one to one relationship. Moreno evidently prefers the multiple relationships to which he devotes himself in sociometry and group therapy. In

[5] Kurt H. Wolff, *The Sociology of Georg Simmel* (Glencoe, Ill.: Free Press, 1950).

his sociometric testing to show the emotional preferences of persons for one another, he finds various designs in a social atom of psychosocial networks such as dyads, triads, quadrangles, pentagons, and chains. Josiah Royce believed that three persons are the minimum required for a community. Where there are two, he perceived them as a dangerous pair set in opposition conducive to conflict and needing a third person to serve as interpreter of each to the other.

The idea of community is rich in meanings and so variously perceived that we may well pause here to consider how to define it. A good working concept is offered by Baker Brownell [6] in saying that a "community is a group of people who know one another well." In so defining the human community, he notes five characteristics: (*a*) a group of neighbors who know one another face to face; (*b*) a diversified group in age, sex, and function; (*c*) a co-operative group in which main activities of life are carried on together; (*d*) a group having a sense of belonging or solidarity; and (*e*) a rather small group in which members know one another as whole persons, not as functional fragments.

These characteristics may not be definitive of all groups who enjoy community, but they are descriptive in a general sense of communities we know and can designate as the concrete situation to which we refer. The term is derived from the Latin meaning "common," the past participle of which yields the word "communicate." A group of persons who know one another well enough to communicate and impart one to another concerns they have in common is what we mean by a community. It becomes an extension and multiplication of the dialogic relation of address by which each person may give to and receive from other persons the answering response.

There may be a difference of opinion as to whether the dyadic relation of two can be a community, though we may expect general agreement upon a triad of three. How large a community may be will depend upon the facilities for meeting, knowing, and communicating within it. For there is in large centers of population the constant pressure to mass into impersonal crowds of faceless individuals who are unknown to one another.

It is not the sheer mass of numbers in a crowd thronging a subway that makes a community. Nor is it anonymous co-operation that binds together; for training in mass groups as military, industrial, or political regimentation may either breed indifference or set people against one another and defeat community. Training in special interest and pressure groups may lead to propaganda and struggle for power in divisive ways. The fragmented roles of urban society cause people to serve others in one function only, such as a salesclerk at a ribbon counter or a policeman directing traffic with

[6] *The Human Community* (New York: Harper & Bros., 1950), p. 198.

no opportunity to know whole persons. In these ways we are losing community in the crowding bigness of cities as much as in the rural isolation of man from man.

The need for community grows more urgent in the urbanization and mechanization of modern society. Automation of industry reduces the creative joy of the craftsman working as a whole person with other persons to the silent and shadowy machine tender performing a fractionated operation in the monotonous repetition of the assembly line. If he lives in a congested urban apartment, he may not know persons who dwell in the same building or who ride the same bus or trolly car. He will then turn away from them in his leisure to the mass media of the newspaper, radio, and television in which he becomes a passive spectator or listener, hermetically sealed off from other persons with whom he might converse. To counteract the trend of this depersonalizing massiveness, new centers of employment and business are locating in smaller satellite towns in which people can live and associate together as neighbors in community.

What the person needs to fulfill his potentialities and heal his fragmentation is a primary group characterized by "intimate face-to-face association and co-operation." C. H. Cooley,[7] who in 1909 defined the primary group, referred particularly to the family, the play group, and the neighborhood. Such relationships are practically universal, belonging to all times and stages of human development. These groups, as he pointed out, are the springs of life, not only for the individual but for social institutions. They give the individual his first and completest experience of social unity in which he knows life in psychic wholes rather than artificial separation. Institutions of religion, school, and government may develop elaborate and austere forms that seem alien to us, but they emerge from the family and small groups of the common life and "with them we can always make ourselves at home."

The intimacy of family and neighborhood has been desiccated into intricate patterns of diversified individuality and mass uniformities which leave us strangers to one another. The general confusion of rapid social mobility and frequent migrations in our time has uprooted many persons from their sustaining social context, sorely wounding the primary relationships of life. To recover from separation and loss, there are many who become frantic joiners of secondary associations that give status or connections but little more. Others grow weary of massive functional associations and seek to recover wholeness in the family or friendship circles.

This need for primary relationship motivates the religious search. As the anguish of finite loneliness mounts to intensity, I seek with ultimate concern

[7] *Social Organization* (New York: Charles Scribner's Sons, 1909).

to encounter Thou. As the sense of alienation becomes acute, religious seekers come together in face-to-face relations to confess their human need and reach out for the answering response. The return to religion is one of the significant social trends in the United States, where church members have increased 59 per cent in twenty-five years. What we observe in this social trend is persons coming together in religious groups. They may return to a neglected church membership or try another church in which the relationships seem more congenial and vital. Where they feel unwelcome or not at home in established churches, they form new sects of their own to have a religious community.

There are many theories as to why persons join a church and participate in religious activities. And there can be no single answer, for the reasons are many and the motivations intricate. It is suggested that we live in an age of anxiety and instability in which the distresses of chronic insecurity lead many persons to the religious "cult of reassurance." Another view would see church membership as a badge of respectability with social prestige and perhaps economic gain in associating with "the right people." Where there are political committees to expose and drive out the radical, it might be safer to follow the conservative tradition of a well-established church. Where there is confusion, the affirmations of religious faith may give a note of certainty by the truth of infallible authority. Where there are feelings of guilt, one may turn to defensive operation in compulsive rituals and well-repeated dogmas. One study[8] shows church members to be more authoritarian than nonmembers.

There is no reason to deny that such motives may operate consciously or unconsciously in some of those who turn to religion. For human motives are subtle and intricate, tinged with neurotic anxieties and compulsive defenses. And such motives are surely at work in every human enterprise in the secular quite as much as the religious pursuits. What we would refute is the implication that this is the whole story with nothing more to explain. For we find a deeper and truer motivation in the finite sense of estrangement and the incessant need to offer oneself with ultimate concern to Thou, to seek the answer to lonely yet creative potentialities in mutual response. This need will seek a primary community in which such relationships may enhance the meaning of life in moments of self-giving communion.

Churches may also suffer loss of community and decline to conventional formalities that are little more than hollow echoes of a receding past. No church or religious society will survive unless it has the vitality of a primary group, with lively interest and cherished sentiments, common activities carried on by mutual participation, and norms to guide the behavior of

[8] T. W. Adorno, *et al.*, *The Authoritarian Personality* (New York: Harper & Bros., 1950).

members. Without a community a church is but the shell or façade of what may once have been a corporate life.

In his study of "Hilltown," a declining New England village, George C. Homans[9] traced the fatal loss of what had once been community life. The spires of two white churches rise as landmarks from Main Street, but the churches are scarcely used. Before splitting into rival churches, the village life centered in the church from its founding in 1767. Due to many dispersive tendencies the present citizens have lost interest in one another and do not share a life together. Many of the families have no children, or the children have left home. The residents do not visit in one another's homes and are not concerned about the moral behavior of their neighbors. They decline to support the churches or to maintain a full-time minister in town. The disintegration of primary relations has undermined the community, and the village though still on the map no longer holds the people together in mutual concern and response.

When a church is a living community, it will revive and renew primary relationships through regular practice of religious encounter. If so it will aim to be a *corporate society* of Christian life, a body of Christ, as Paul declared, in which all members participate in organic interdependence to share resources and bear one another's burdens. This organism will seek to be a worshiping society devoted to God, the creative source of life for each one and the incarnate unifying spirit of all. It will intend to be a *loving society,* the members respecting and upholding one another in reverent appreciation for the joy of being present together and the privilege of caring each for the other in unfaltering devotion. As a beloved community it will unite to be a *faithful society,* the members responsible one to another, motivated by faith in God, and keeping faith with one another in a continuing life for the sake of all in the ongoing purpose of this love.

In a study H. Richard Niebuhr and others [10] note a prevalent confusion arising from unclarity in defining the nature of the church as religious community. The church has various activities and objectives, but central among them all is the one goal which is the *increase among men of the love of God and neighbor*. Amid the pressures of many social compulsions, this religious community is a voluntary association of colleagues who believe in one faith and uphold one another as loving members of one family of God. The church is an intentional community, whose representatives declared at Amsterdam in 1948 in forming the World Council of Churches: "We intend to stay together." There have been closed communions going apart to defend their particular way of life. But the intention of a world community

[9] *The Human Group* (New York: Harcourt, Brace & Co., 1950).

[10] *The Purpose of the Church and Its Ministry* (New York: Harper & Bros., 1956).

like this is to be open to all who are willing to enter into the responsibilities of its membership—"a voice for those who have no voice, and a home where every man will be at home."

### *3. Leadership in a Religious Community*

In religious communities there are two kinds of leadership evident, which arise from external and internal relationships. External leadership holds the leader superior to the group, upon which he exerts influence from another plane. This may be observed historically in Hinduism, in which a priestly caste of Brahmans was set apart, and their descendants perpetuated religious laws of avoidance, declining to dine or intermarry with members of other castes lest they suffer ceremonial uncleanness. Social distance became so rigid and separatist that Buddha in the sixth century B.C. founded a protestant movement, identifying himself with the common people as an internal leader to abolish the caste system. Though he was influential in his religion of mercy to relieve the sufferings of life, Buddhism in India was eventually absorbed into Hinduism by "fraternal embrace," and the caste system was upheld. The protest against external religious leadership continues, however, in the holy man who takes the vow of poverty and the begging bowl to identify himself with the poor.

We may observe these contrasting forms of religious leadership as well in Judaism and Christianity. In Judaism the priests of Yahweh become a hereditary caste, occupied with religious laws designed to maintain ceremonial cleanness in diet and personal behavior as the acme of faithful devotion. This legalism was intensified by a series of national disasters and exiles, interpreted as the punishment of God and requiring more zeal in obeying the religious laws to recover divine favor. In their external leadership representing the authority of the Holy One, they became the taskmasters of the people to enforce the religious laws. Then came the prophets to speak for God with another voice of authority, claiming ethical righteousness as the true way rather than ceremonial rightness. In one sense the prophets were internal leaders who identified themselves with the common people and ethical common sense against the priests who held themselves aloof and the institution above the man. Yet in another sense the prophet brought external leadership in speaking for God as a higher authority often against the comfortable wishes of the people.

In Christianity, Jesus came in the role of a prophet to speak for God contrary to the priests of the temple. By this time religious teachers who exercised the intellectual role were living among the people as rabbis. Jesus who was also known as a teacher, left his home to go among the common people to talk with them of God and the way of religious love, to heal the sick and train disciples to carry forward the kingdom of God. By some he was identified as the long-expected Messiah and the son of God, which the priests violently opposed in demanding his crucifixion. In one sense he offered internal leadership, as he came from the common people to the common people and so identified himself with them. Yet in another sense he spoke for God as a higher authority to whom he gave unswerving allegiance in spite of all opposition, in his effort to reconcile man and God.

In portraying himself as a shepherd, Jesus defined the role of pastor which has developed in the Christian Church as a significant expression of religious leadership. A pastor is one who cares for his people in loving concern, who goes to them in their sorrow and distress, who guides them in their perplexities and ministers to them according to their individual needs. He also represents the loving community and not only comes for them to serve the one in need but also encourages and instructs the people in ministering one to another. In this mission of forgiving and sustaining love, he becomes the reconciler of each to the other and of all to God, weaving their separate individualities like many colored threads into a whole fabric, in which all are united and each supports the other as members of one body. The vocation of the pastor is to foster the primary relationships of individual persons and their families so as to join them into one living and loving community. It is evident that the pastor who so identifies himself with his people is practicing internal leadership.

Protestant churches have emphasized internal leadership in the religious community. The reformers stood for the common people against the hierarchy of priests, seeking to be justified by faith rather than by ceremonial or ritualistic correctness. The priesthood of all believers as taught by Luther, his translation of the Bible into the common tongue, and his turning from the monastery to marriage and the religious family had the democratizing effect of dignifying the common man. The concern for the layman to have a religious vocation in the world furthered this reconciliation between religious castes. The Calvinist and Puritan churches, as well as the pietist movements eventuating in the Methodist, Baptist, and Quaker churches elevated the laymen to leadership from within the community.

Yet as in all religious communities there are tensions between higher and lower authorities. This is inevitable wherever man as a finite creature addresses himself to God as ultimate Being. The tension may accent the otherness and transcendent distance of God as omniscient, omnipotent, and eternal. Or it may accent the nearness and immanence of God as omnipresent spirit in whom we have our being and who is not far from any one of us. In the ardent search to meet God the mystic may depart from the community in lonely external vigil or he may seek God through the common fellowship of the congregation at worship. The priest may turn his back on the congregation to face God or he may turn to the people to bless them as a mediator who leads them to God. The prophet may like Moses go apart to commune with God and speak his word, or he may enter into their captivity as one who seeks with them the way to a land of freedom. The intellectual may go into his study to labor for truth which he hands down to the people, or he may start where they are in a discussion group and go with them toward goals chosen by the group. The pastor may be "the minister" who is ordained to another order of apostolic succession, or he may be the leader who emerges from the people to draw them into a ministering community.

The religious leader is evidently caught in a serious dilemma: shall he hold his position above the people as external and authoritarian or identify himself with them in a relationship that is internal and democratic. This dilemma confronts the leader of every group whether secular or religious, and it may be well to consider the psychological effects of these alternative ways of leading a group. One series of experiences[11] with authoritarian and democratic leadership in clubs of ten-year-old children has sought to clarify this question.

In the authoritarian groups all policies were determined by the leader. Techniques and activity were dictated by the authority one step at a time. Work tasks and work companions were assigned by the leader. Praise and criticism were "personal" as given by the leader, who remained aloof except when demonstrating what to do.

In the democratic groups all policies were made by group discussion and decision, encouraged by the leader. Activity perspective was gained during discussion period, steps were considered, and when technical advice was needed, the leader offered alternatives from which a group choice could be made. The members were free to work with whomever they chose, and the work decisions were made by the members of the group. The leader was "objective and fact-minded" in his praise and criticism, and tried to be a regular group member without taking the responsibility away from the other members.

In a careful recording and analysis of what happened, Lippitt and White found striking contrasts. The quantity of work done in the autocratic groups was somewhat greater, but the motivation and originality were greater in democratic groups. There was much more hostility (ratio 30 to 1) in autocratic groups, more demands for attention, and more destructive and scapegoat behavior. There was also more discontent in autocratic groups,

[11] Ronald Lippitt, "An Experimental Study of the Effect of Democratic and Authoritarian Group Atmospheres," *University of Iowa Studies in Child Welfare,* XVI (1940), 43-195; R. Lippitt and E. R. White, "The Social Climate of Children's Groups," in *Child Behavior and Development,* ed. Roger C. Barker *et al* (New York: McGraw-Hill Book Co., 1943), pp. 485-508.

with four boys dropping out and nineteen out of twenty boys preferring the democratic leader. There were more dependence and less individuality in autocratic groups, and conversation was less varied and less spontaneous.

In the democratic groups there were more group-mindedness and friendliness. The pronoun "I" was used less and "we" more often. Spontaneous subgroups were larger, and group-minded remarks were more frequent. Friendly remarks were also more frequent, with mutual praise and more friendly playfulness. The democratic groups showed more readiness to share property and participate as if they had a sense of belongingness.

In religious groups there is usually a mingling of authoritarian and democratic procedures. We have noted the tensions that inevitably arise between higher and lower authorities. Where each member is entitled to search for himself and have direct encounter with God, anyone is free to report what is revealed to him as the word of God. It is in this way that new leaders arise from the ranks and new sects may gather around them. Authorities are needed in democracy as much as autocracy, but the sources and shifts of authority tend in a democratic society to move upward from the common people rather than downward from the hereditary ruling caste. Continuity is provided in the oral tradition or the written documents such as a scripture or a constitution.

We may observe with sociologists a strong upward mobility in contemporary societies. When oppressive and rigid social structure denies this, the outcome may be a revolution. When the social structure is fluid and open to change, the upward movement may be evolutionary. Protestant sects most often emerge from the common people as lay groups who agree on some principles of special concern to them. At first they are homeless and gather on street corners, in camp meetings or tabernacles in temporary shelters. Their leaders are often passionately emotional and may without formal training exercise charismatic gifts that draw a following. Then as they prosper and take a course of upward mobility, by another generation or so they have become established churches with cathedral-style buildings of brick and stone, with members who are comfortably at home in the rising middle class, and leaders who are educated for their calling as a profession. As the membership enjoys upward mobility, the leaders do also with mutual responsibility for the life and direction of the religious community. But when the gap widens between laymen and clergy, the leadership becomes authoritarian and is likely to be more external.

Do we have evidence that internal leadership is likely to be more effective in a religious community than external leadership? Historically there is evidence that the most rapidly growing religious movements have manifested internal leadership. Among the religions of the world the most expansive in moving across frontiers have been Buddhism, Christianity, and

Mohammedanism. The founders in each case have shown strong internal leadership in identifying themselves with the common people and representing them in their forward thrust. Judaism is not a missionary religion, but the Jews have crossed many frontiers in their dispersion and have increasingly relied upon the internal leadership of the rabbi, who dwells among the people and invites lay participation.

Among the Protestant groups the most expansive have also manifested strong internal leadership, as in the Methodist and Baptist movements. On the American scene today the Pentecostal sects who show the most rapid expansion are essentially lay groups who produce their leaders from the ranks. They may be zealous and authoritarian in their Bible-centered gospel, but the leadership is close to the common people and works from within clusters of lay workers.

From the Protestant Episcopal Church comes another piece of evidence. W. G. T. Douglas[12] in his study of ministerial effectiveness interviewed lay officers of Episcopal churches, in New England mostly, asking them to rate seventy of their ministers. The composite portrait which they give of the effective minister consists of five characteristics: (*a*) a genuine love for people as people regardless of their color, class, economic status, or educational level; (*b*) definite convictions with respect for the convictions of others; (*c*) ability to sacrifice immediate impulse satisfaction to long-range goals and personal desires to the slow working out of group purposes; (*d*) flexibility of temperament, including the ability to plan realistically in terms of one's own abilities, to try new ways, and to sacrifice accuracy to speed when the occasion demands it; and (*e*) concern for the organizational life of the local church, involving the ability to get others to work with him and to relate all group activities to the central function of the church as a redeeming fellowship.

There is need to clarify the role of the minister in the context of his religious community. He has many tasks to perform such as the priest who mediates, the preacher who brings the good news, the counselor and teacher who guides, the administrator who organizes and promotes a working program. Yet in all of these he has one vocation: to increase the love of God and neighbor. The study of theological education by Niebuhr, to which I have referred, gives further evidence in support of internal leadership. He reports a trend among churches and theological schools toward a pastoral leadership that is integrated with lay workers as an organism of close-knit relationships. This emerging concept is called the "pastoral director" to in-

[12] "Predicting Ministerial Effectiveness" (Unpublished Ph.D. dissertation, Harvard University, 1957).

dicate that the minister is to co-ordinate and draw the fellowship together as a ministering community.

We have seen a pastor go about church work assuming that "I am the one who has to do the job, and everything depends on me." But this egocentric view induces anxiety and makes him a compulsive driver who works under tension with a burden of lonely despair. He is the external leader, the man up front who stands above and against the group to put over his program in a way that invites their opposition. In his anxious perfectionism he may overextend the range of his office and underestimate the potential and co-operative responsibility of the laymen. If he will identify himself with rather than against his people, he will move from external to internal relationships. Instead of one superior leader who stoops down to minister to lost souls, we may see the whole church ministering as a religious community in which each shares in mutual responsibility for all.

### 4. *Communication*

The life of the community is mediated through relationships. It is the awakening responsiveness of person to person that gives living vitality to the relationships of community. And the weakening of interpersonal relatedness is the fatal decay that foretells the death of a community. If community is to flourish, there must be communication, the dialogue of address and response.

The loss of community in our time is due to the breakdown of primary speaking relationships. We have mass communications extending far and wide through commercial and political enterprise. Newspaper, radio, and television are keying attention to professional entertainers, informers, and persuaders who have something to sell. Will the religious community survive mass communication in a secular society? Religious leaders may utilize mass media to propagate their message, but without face-to-face relations the cement of community will crumble and dissolve. Here again external leadership will not be an effective substitute for internal relationships.

Experimental studies bear out the hypothesis that leadership is a function of accurate perception of the attitudes of associates. Four groups were studied by K. Chowdhry and T. M. Newcomb:[13] a religious group, a political group, a medical fraternity, and a medical sorority, to gather the opinions of individuals and to test their perceptions of group opinions. Then sociometric testing was employed to discover leadership within each group. Leaders in each group proved superior to nonleaders and isolates in their

[13] "The Relative Abilities of Leaders and Non-Leaders to Estimate Opinions of Their Own Groups," *The Journal of Abnormal and Social Psychology,* XLVII (1952), 51-57.

ability to evaluate group opinion accurately. This ability to judge group opinion was successful particularly in familiar issues that were relevant to the specific group. These results concur with studies of other groups by Newcomb and by Jennings. They recognize that leadership depends upon effective internal relationships within the specific group. Those persons who are chosen by the group as leaders have greater sensitivity to and understanding of other members of the group. The leaders show aptitude for fuller communication with their group. They are group-oriented in contrast to nonleaders and isolates, who are "self-bound" and unable to bridge the gap between themselves and other persons.

How is the pastor communicating with the people around him? To whom does he talk about what? Who communicates with him and why do they communicate? David B. Chamberlain[14] has studied the communications of 50 Protestant ministers of 21 denominations in Lynn, Massachusetts, a city with its satellites constituting 130,000 people. Each minister was given a notebook with printed categories to use in recording each item of incoming and outgoing communication for one weekday and, with the assistance of a trained observer, one Sunday. These days were distributed over the week for a period of four months to provide a broader sample of conversations. Group meetings were omitted to concentrate upon individual items of communication, of which 2,640 items were recorded and submitted to content analysis. The average membership of the churches was 524. The average age of the ministers was 44. Their education came to an average of 8 years beyond high school, and their length of service in the ministry was an average of 17 years. Additional data were gathered in a three-hour structured interview with each minister.

For the content analysis eight categories were used to classify the items of communication. Considering all topics of conversation, pastoral events (personal, religious, general) account for 48 per cent of the total, administrative for 31 per cent, organizational for 11 per cent, and matters pertaining to worship, sermons, and teaching were less. What is most surprising to these ministers was that specifically religious talk occurs only 2 per cent of the time in these conversations. Personal topics initiated by the minister outweigh business topics 55 per cent to 44 per cent. When parishioners initiate communication, however, administrative concerns outnumber personal concerns 53 per cent to 47 per cent.

Sunday conversation does not differ in content from weekdays, but there is 92 per cent increase in volume. Insiders and outsiders talk in general about the same topics except that insiders talk of administrative matters

[14] "Communication Problems in the Parish Ministry" (Unpublished Ph.D. dissertation, Boston University, 1958).

twice as often as personal matters. Analysis of the minister's function in communication shows 46 per cent of semiprofessional and nonprofessional activity and only 13 per cent of spiritual guidance. Mass media are used largely; 80 per cent use the public newspapers, 82 per cent use a weekly bulletin, and 58 per cent a church paper.

The use of various means of conversation follows a pattern of telephone calls in the morning, home and hospital visitations in the afternoon, and group activities in the evening. As much as 55 per cent of the communications are less than four minutes in duration. Communication with those inside the parish occupies 60 per cent and outsiders 40 per cent. The largest group of insiders consists of housewives (33 per cent) and of outsiders the professional group (also 33 per cent). The majority (80 per cent of all communications) are with the white-collar group. Men outnumber women in communications and talk slightly longer.

While ministers communicate with all ages, they talk more with persons in their thirties and forties. At least 90 per cent of communication is with persons well liked by the ministers. Of the weekday communications 70 per cent are rated as pressing, quite pressing, or very pressing. Ministers communicate more to give something (61 per cent of the time) rather than to get something (39 per cent). Parishioners communicate more often to get something (60 per cent) than to give (40 per cent).

It appears that only 62 per cent of the ministers are happy in the present-time distribution among their roles. They want more pastoral work and less administrative detail. There is serious lack of equipment and office facilities, and even more serious lack of personal assistance. Seventy-eight per cent report concern about neglected areas of work, 70 per cent do their own typewriting; and 25 per cent do the stenographic and secretarial tasks in getting out the weekly bulletin. Fifty-eight per cent of the ministers work alone, only 10 per cent have secretarial help, and only 8 per cent have any professional help of any kind, full or part-time.

This will indicate something of the dilemma of the Protestant minister in trying to meet the rising demand today for his services. The rate of communication is very high, but the pressure of time limits the opportunity to consider the deeper concerns of life. There is a strong tendency toward superficiality when 55 per cent of the conversations last less than four minutes. Much of the communication is fleeting and unplanned "passing conversation," with a minimum discussion of ultimate concern and the meaning of the religious life. The large proportion of time which the minister gives to nonprofessional detail robs him of fully exercising the profession to which he is called and dedicated.

Of course any communication has overtones of personal interest which say, "You are a person who counts for something, and relationship with you is significant." What might seem a trivial and passing conversation may actually symbolize very significant meanings in the language of relationship. There are also nonverbal cues and signs, given and received, which may carry both emotive and cognitive meaning of great significance. Every communication is actually an address of person to person and will therefore have something of the value of encounter.

In the secularizing of modern society and diversification of multiplying interests and activities, there is obviously less talk about religion in the doctrinal sense. Theological controversies may rage among the scholars and specialists, yet among the laymen, except the fanatical, the religious sense appears to be diffused over a wide range of activities often classified as secular. The Protestant emphasis on religious vocation in the world has facilitated this dispersion and diffusion of religious concern in a fine spray over the entire landscape.

And though there is a publicizing of many concerns today, with religious themes also appearing on billboards, yet the content is of the most general kind as a vague sentiment put in terms to offend no one. There is no little privatism in modern religious feeling or opinion in which many persons, to avoid argument and prejudice, insist that "It is my own affair" and not to be exposed to prying eyes. This shyness may be due in part to the fact that religion shares with other concerns of deep significance the difficulty of being put readily into words. But we cannot well measure the amount or value of the unspoken and inarticulate religious feelings, except to infer that for many people they are not easy to talk about.

The tendency to hide behind defenses appears in religious matters as much and perhaps more than in other matters which do not so seriously call for a decision in reference to the whole meaning and destiny of life. It is often easier and safer not to expose one's true feelings, for they may invite criticism, ridicule, or demands for explicit responsibilities we are not prepared at the moment to meet. This may be due in part to unclarity of thinking on religious issues and in part to the existential character of religious faith that calls for personal decision and a forthright living out of this decision in the open in relation to other persons even when it may be inconvenient.

If the members of a religious community, whether a family or a church, were more supportive one of another and able to manifest true personal regard for one another in faithful and forgiving love, it would perhaps be easier for the lonely person to expose his private feelings. We say "perhaps," for closeness of relation especially with emotional responses is often threatening to our ego defenses. It may be easier to give and receive hostility than love, and this predicament indicates why the requirement of the religious life in full communion of I and Thou is so terrifying even while the encounter is so ardently desired. Jung notes that Protestants are, by virtue of their intention to meet God directly, more seriously exposed and charged with anxiety, guilt, and dread in such encounter.

Marx looked upon religion as an opiate to tranquilize the person deprived of material goods. The finite person must always wrestle with his deprivations and somehow come to terms with his limitations. But religion also has the effect, better known to those who experience the religious encounter, of a stimulant to waken a person from lethargic inertia or enervating despair. It may be difficult to put into words what this meeting of I and Thou means to a religious person, but he needs to communicate the meaning both to give and to receive the fuller relationship of community. Many churches fall short of true community through the unwillingness of their members to become more deeply involved in their relationships. Due to preoccupation with other interests or defensive anxieties, the easier way may be to hold themselves aloof in nominal rather than existential relatedness. Then to find the answering response, new religious groups will be formed outside of established churches, in which more vital encounter is sought in the emotional depth and interpenetration of a ministering community, each to be responsible to the other.

### 5. *Frontiers*

In conclusion, what may we say as to the psychological frontiers of religion? Psychology of religion has been at work for two generations of some sixty years, engaging interested persons in considerable activity which is recorded in countless publications. And yet in the long perspectives of history we have taken but a few faltering steps along the shore of a vast mystery. We may have some theories about why man engages in religious behavior and a few facts as to what it means to be religious. New scientific methods are needed to cope with the broader horizons opening before us. Methods are also needed to explore religious experience in dimensions of greater depth. There is work for younger minds who may free themselves from the prejudices and limited perceptions of the past. There are new inventions awaiting the creative minds who will integrate the insights of the present and project into sharper focus the devices of research and discovery.

One frontier that will surely concern the next generation will be the problems and resources of communication. The science of communication is in reality a synthesis of many sciences concerned to understand and develop the means and content of our vast communicative network for the welfare of all people. Mass communications hold a crucial role as so many people are affected by them every hour of every day. As people around the world are aware of one another and how much they have in common, the number and effective services of world organizations are steadily increasing. Many dimensions of religious communication need to be explored, in the small group as well as the large, to engage in authentic dialogue instead of double talk or talking past one another.

A second frontier of crucial importance will be the life of the primary group, which now concerns psychology as much as religion. It is in the face-to-face relationships of the family that persons first reach out to one another and come to know the meaning of human life in its complex interrelatedness. Amid the pulverizing forces of mass migration and mass congestion many are threatened with loss of community in this "century of the homeless man." To find the answering response which is the basic need of every person, there can be no substitute for the primary group in which persons may know one another well as whole persons. Otherwise man is estranged in the grief of his separations and alienated from the joy of belonging and counting as a uniquely contributing member of a group. There is new research to follow in group dynamics, sociometry, and interaction analysis. The church is a natural home for small groups meeting to share mutual concerns in affectionate devotion, and if churches become too austere or massive, new religious groups will form apart from them. The primary group is not to be overlooked, for it is the essential source of vitality for the community as well as the individual person.

A third frontier that urgently calls for workers is some therapy to resolve social conflicts. These conflicts may be as old as the human race but in our time, due to invention and the unleashing of atomic energies, they have been magnified to lethal destructiveness. In the frantic struggle for power the passionate violence of these conflicts is inflamed and mounts to ever-greater intensity. "Since wars begin in the minds of men, it is in the minds of men that the defenses of peace must be constructed." This declaration from the preamble to the constitution of UNESCO points to psychology and religion as two responsible parties in the resolving of these conflicts which emerge at every level and group in human society. Moreno has brought forward the need for "sociatry," the healing of social relations, which is as urgent as individual psychiatry. To understand these conflicts is not enough, intricate and disturbing as that challenge may be. There is also occasion to practice everywhere in all human relations the healing so urgently needed. And this is a labor of love in which religion and psychology are destined to meet.

A fourth frontier of perennial concern is to understand the dynamic nature of the individual person. If wars do begin in the minds of men, there is basic work to do in the realm of personal motivation. We can neither deny nor hide the conflictual nature of man, so we shall have in one way or another to come to terms with it. What drives or lures the impulsive forces of personality into such entangling and excruciating conflict? And how can we release the creative energies so entangled into freer and fuller realization of our creative potentialities? Here again psychology and religion are destined to meet in the depths of the human soul, whose secrets so profoundly elude us.

A fifth frontier which persistently baffles and insistently calls us is the encounter. The meeting of person with person is the great drama of human life, comical in its surprising revelations yet tragic in its unrealized potentialities. To explore what each person brings to his encounter with other persons is an inexhaustible task, as great as the mystery of what he will be able to make of such a meeting. Religion brings to this mystery of the horizontal dimension a greater one in the vertical dimension that may seek and confess a meeting with God. Here religion becomes a theology that goes beyond the limits of psychology. And yet psychology of religion is concerned with the human side of this encounter and will seek to capture and if possible domesticate in scientific framework the meaning that such an event has for a finite person. Of all the frontiers this one is probably the most difficult and therefore the most challenging to comprehend, and the workers on this line of march will require, even as those on the other frontiers deserve, a steady reinforcement of hardy and tireless pioneers.

In now completing this journey we have traveled together, there is time for little more than a person-to-person farewell. We have been together a long while, and the number of wordy miles is quite appalling; but if we have earnestly searched together, we have sought to enter into genuine dialogue. As I perceive you at the moment, the reception is a little dim while I wait for your answering response. But if you will respond, there will be communication, which is the life of community.

# BIBLIOGRAPHY


Adler, Alfred. *The Individual Psychology of Alfred Adler*. Ed. H. and R. Ansbacher. New York: Basic Books, Inc., 1956.

Adorno, T. W., Frenkel-Brunswik, E., Levinson, D. J., and Sanford, R. N. *The Authoritarian Personality*, New York: Harper & Bros., 1950.

Akhilananda, Swami. *Hindu Psychology*. New York: Harper & Bros., 1946.

Allport, G. W. *Becoming: Basic Considerations for a Psychology of Personality*. New Haven, Conn.: Yale University Press, 1955.

———. *Personality: A Psychological Interpretation*. New York: Henry Holt & Co., 1937.

———. *The Individual and His Religion: A Psychological Interpretation*. New York: The Macmillan Co., 1950.

———, Gillespie, J. M., and Young, J. "The Religion of the Post-War College Student," *The Journal of Psychology*, xxv (1948), 3-33.

Ames, E. S. *The Psychology of Religious Experience*. Boston: Houghton Mifflin Co., 1910.

Ancilla. *The Following Feet*. Greenwich, Conn.: The Seabury Press, 1957.

Athearn, W. S., *et al. Indiana Survey of Religious Education*. 3 vols. New York: George H. Doran Co., 1924.

Augustine, Aurelius. *Confessions*. Tr. E. B. Pusey. New York: E. P. Dutton & Co., 1932.

———. *The Soliloquies of St. Augustine*. Tr. R. E. Cleveland. Boston: Little, Brown & Co., 1910.

Axling, William. *Kagawa*. New York: Harper & Bros., 1932.

Barnett, L. K. *The Universe and Dr. Einstein*. New York: William Sloane, Associates, 1948.

Bergler, Edmund. *The Battle of the Conscience*. Washington, D.C.: Washington Institute of Medicine, 1948.

Bertocci, P. A. "A Critique of G. W. Allport's Theory of Motivation," *Psychological Review*, xlvii (1940), 535-45.

Betts, G. H. *The Beliefs of 700 Ministers*. New York: The Abingdon Press, 1929.

Blake, R. R., and Ramsey, G. V., eds. *Perception: An Approach to Personality*. New York: The Roland Press, 1951.

Blizzard, S. W. "The Minister's Dilemma," *The Christian Century*, lxxiii (April 25, 1956), 508-10.

Blos, Peter. *The Adolescent Personality*. New York: D. Appleton-Century Co., 1941.

Boisen, A. T. *The Exploration of the Inner World*. Chicago: Willett, Clark & Co., 1937.

———. *Religion in Crisis and Custom*. New York: Harper & Bros., 1955.

Boring, E. G. *A History of Experimental Psychology*. New York: Appleton-Century-Crofts, Inc., 1950.

Boyd, R. W. "The Use of Group Psychotherapy in the Professional Training of Ministers." Unpublished Ph.D. dissertation, Boston University, 1952.

Braden, C. S. "Study of Spiritual Healing in the Churches," *Pastoral Psychology*, v. (May, 1954), 9-15.

———. "Why People Are Religious—A Study in Religious Motivation," *The Journal of Bible and Religion*, xv (1947), 38-45.

Breuer, J., and Freud, S. *Studies on Hysteria*. London: Hogarth Press, 1955.
Brooks, F. D. *The Psychology of Adolescence*. Boston: Houghton Mifflin Co., 1929.
Brownell, Baker. *The Human Community*. New York: Harper & Bros., 1950.
Buber Martin. *Between Man and Man*. Tr. R. G. Smith. New York: The Macmillan Co., 1948.
———. *I and Thou*. Tr. R. G. Smith. New York: Charles Scribner's Sons, 1937.
———. "The William Alanson White Memorial Lectures," *Psychiatry*, xx (May, 1957), 97-129.
Cannon, W. B. *Bodily Changes in Pain, Hunger, Fear and Rage*. New York: D. Appleton-Century Co., 1929.
———. "Voodoo Death," *American Anthropologist*, xliv (1942), 169-81.
Chamberlain, D. B. "Communication Problems in the Parish Ministry." Unpublished Ph.D. dissertation, Boston University, 1958.
Chowdhry, K., and Newcomb, T. M. "The Relative Abilities of Leaders and Non-Leaders to Estimate Opinions of Their Own Groups," *The Journal of Abnormal and Social Psychology*, xlvii (1952), 51-57.
Clark, E. T. *The Psychology of Religious Awakening*. New York: The Macmillan Co., 1929.
Clark, W. H. *The Psychology of Religion*. New York: The Macmillan Co., 1958.
———. "A Study of Some Factors Leading to Achievement and Creativity, with Special Reference to Religious Skepticism and Belief," *The Journal of Social Psychology*, xli (1955), 57-69.
Cobb, Stanley. *Foundations of Neuropsychiatry*. Baltimore: William Wood & Co., 1941.
Coe, G. A. *The Psychology of Religion*. Chicago: University of Chicago Press, 1916.
———. *The Spiritual Life*. New York: Abingdon Press, 1922.
Cole, W. C. *Sex in Christianity and Psychoanalysis*. New York: Oxford University Press, 1955.
Conklin, E. S. *The Psychology of Religious Adjustment*. New York: The Macmillan Co., 1929.
Cooley, C. H. *Social Organization*. New York: Charles Scribner's Sons, 1909.
De Sanctis, Sante. *Religious Conversion*. Tr. H. Augur. New York: Harcourt, Brace & Co., 1927.
Dewey, John. *A Common Faith*. New Haven, Conn.: Yale University Press, 1934.
Douglas, W. G. T. "Predicting Ministerial Effectiveness" Unpublished Ph.D. dissertation, Harvard University, 1957.
Dunbar, H. F. *Emotions and Bodily Changes*. New York: Columbia University Press, 1938.
———. "Problems of Convalescence and Chronic Illness," *American Journal of Psychiatry*, xcii (1936).
Durkheim, Émile. *The Elementary Forms of the Religious Life*. Tr. J. W. Swain. London. George Allen & Unwin, Ltd., 1915.
Emme, E. E. "Modification and Origin of Superstition Among 96 College Students," *The Journal of Psychology*, x (1940), 279-91.
Ferm, Vergilius, ed. *Religion in Transition*. New York: The Macmillan Co., 1937.
Flower, J. C. *An Approach to the Psychology of Religion*. New York: Harcourt, Brace & Co., 1927.
Flugel, J. C. *Man, Morals and Society: A Psychoanalytical Study*. London: Gerald Duckworth & Co., 1945.
Freud, Anna. *The Ego and the Mechanisms of Defence*. Tr. C. Baines. London: Hogarth Press, 1937.
Freud, Sigmund. *Autobiography*. Tr. J. Strachey. New York: W. W. Norton & Co., 1935.
———. *Civilization and Its Discontents*. Tr. J. Riviere. New York: Cape & Smith, 1930.
———. *The Collected Papers*. 5 vols. Tr. J. Riviere and A. and J. Strachey. London: Hogarth Press, 1924-50.
———. *The Ego and the Id*. Tr. J. Riviere. London: Hogarth Press, 1927.
———. *The Future of an Illusion*. Tr. W. D. Robson-Scott. London: Hogarth Press, 1928.

———. *Group Psychology and the Analysis of the Ego.* Tr. J. Strachey. London: Hogarth Press, 1922.
———. *Moses and Monotheism.* Tr. K. Jones. New York: Alfred A. Knopf, Inc., 1939.
———. *New Introductory Lectures on Psycho-analysis.* Tr. W. J. H. Sprott. London: Hogarth Press, 1933.
———. *Psychopathology of Everyday Life.* Tr. A. A. Brill. New York: The Macmillan Co., 1917.
———. *Totem and Taboo.* Tr. A. A. Brill. London: G. Routledge & Sons, 1919.
Fromm, Erich. *Psychoanalysis and Religion.* New Haven, Conn.; Yale University Press, 1950.
Hadfield, J. A. *Psychology and Morals.* New York: Robert M. McBride & Co., 1925.
Hall, C. S., and Lindzey, Gardner. *Theories of Personality.* New York: John Wiley & Sons, 1957.
Hall, G. S. *Adolescence.* 2 vols. New York: D. Appleton & Co., 1904.
Hartshorne, H., and Froyd, M. C. *Theological Education in the Northern Baptist Convention.* Philadelphia: Judson Press, 1945.
———, and Maller, J. B. *Studies in Service and Self-Control.* New York: The Macmillan Co., 1929.
———, and May, M. A. *Studies in Deceit.* New York: The Macmillan Co., 1928.
———, and Shuttleworth, F. J. *Studies in the Organization of Character.* New York: The Macmillan Co., 1930.
Heiler, Friedrich. *Prayer.* Tr. S. McComb and J. E. Park. New York: Oxford University Press, 1932.
Henderson, L. J. *The Fitness of the Environment.* New York: The Macmillan Co., 1913.
Hocking, W. E. *The Meaning of God in Human Experience.* New Haven, Conn.: Yale University Press, 1912.
Homans, G. C. *The Human Group.* New York: Harcourt, Brace & Co., 1950.
Hooke, S. H., ed. *Myth and Ritual.* New York: Oxford University Press, 1933.
Horney, Karen. *The Neurotic Personality of Our Time.* New York: W. W. Norton & Co., 1937.
———. *New Ways in Psychoanalysis.* New York: W. W. Norton & Co., 1939.
Horton, W. M. *A Psychological Approach to Theology.* New York: Harper & Bros., 1931.
James, William. *The Varieties of Religious Experience.* New York: Longmans, Green & Co., 1902.
Johnson, P. E. "The Contribution of Psychology to the Teacher of Religion," *The Journal of Bible and Religion,* xxiv (July, 1956), 167-72.
———. *Personality and Religion.* Nashville: Abingdon Press, 1957.
———. "Spiritual Healing," *Religion in Life,* xxv (1956), 195-204.
Jones, Ernest. *The Life and Work of Sigmund Freud.* 3 vols. New York: Basic Books, Inc., 1953-57.
Jones, Henry. *A Faith That Inquires.* New York: The Macmillan Co., 1922.
Jung, C. G. *Modern Man in Search of a Soul.* New York: Harcourt, Brace & Co., 1933.
———. *Psychology and Religion: West and East.* Tr. R. F. C. Hull. New York: Pantheon Books, Inc., 1958.
———. *Symbols of Transformation.* Tr. R. F. C. Hull. New York: Pantheon Books, Inc., 1956.
Katz, D., Allport, F. H., and Jenness, M. B. *Students' Attitudes.* Syracuse, N. Y.: The Craftsmen Press, 1931.
Kierkegaard, Soren. *The Concept of Dread.* Tr. W. Lowrie. Princeton, N. J.: Princeton University Press, 1944.
———. *Fear and Trembling.* Tr. W. Lowrie. Princeton, N. J.: Princeton University Press, 1941.
———. *The Journals.* Tr. A. Dru. London: Oxford University Press, 1938.
———. *The Point of View for My Work as an Author.* Tr. W. Lowrie. London: Oxford University Press, 1939.

———. *The Sickness unto Death.* Tr. W. Lowrie. Princeton, N. J.: Princeton University Press, 1941.
King, Irving. *The Development of Religion.* New York: The Macmillan Co., 1910.
Knudson, A. C. *The Validity of Religious Experience.* New York: The Abingdon Press, 1937.
Künkel, Fritz. *In Search of Maturity.* New York: Charles Scribner's Sons, 1943.
Kupky, Oskar. *The Religious Development of Adolescents* Tr. W. C. Trow. New York: The Macmillan Co., 1928.
Lee, R. S. *Freud and Christianity,* New York: A. A. Wyn, Inc., 1949.
Leiffer, M. H. *The Layman Looks at the Minister.* Nashville: Abingdon Press, 1947.
Leuba, J. H. *The Belief in God and Immortality.* Chicago: Open Court Publishing Co., 1921.
———. *A Psychological Study of Religion.* New York: The Macmillan Co., 1912.
———. *The Psychology of Religious Mysticism.* New York: Harcourt, Brace & Co., 1925.
Ligon, E. M. *The Psychology of Christian Personality.* New York: The Macmillan Co., 1935.
Lippitt, Ronald. "An Experimental Study of the Effect of Democratic and Authoritarian Group Atmopheres," *University of Iowa Studies in Child Welfare,* xvi (1940), 43-195.
———, and White, E. R. "The Social Climates of Children's Groups," in *Child Behavior and Development.* Ed. R. G. Barker, J. S. Kounin, and H. F. Wright. New York: McGraw-Hill Book Co., 1943.
Maberry, A. T. "Psychology of Religious Symbolism." Unpublished M.A. thesis, Syracuse University, 1939.
McCann, R. V. *Delinquency: Sickness or Sin?* New York: Harper & Bros., 1957.
MacDougall, Robert. "The Social Basis of Individuality," *American Journal of Sociology,* xviii (July, 1912), 1-20.
McDougall, William. *An Introduction to Social Psychology.* Boston: J. W. Luce & Co., 1908.
MacLean, A. H. *The Idea of God in Protestant Religious Education.* New York: Teachers College, Columbia University, 1930.
Maslow, A. H. *Motivation and Personality.* New York: Harper & Bros., 1954.
May, Rollo. *The Art of Counseling.* Nashville: Abingdon Press, 1939.
———. *The Meaning of Anxiety.* New York: The Ronald Press Co., 1950.
Mead, G. H. *Mind, Self and Society.* Ed. C. W. Morris. Chicago: University of Chicago Press, 1934.
———. *The Philosophy of the Pressent.* Ed. A. E. Murphy. Chicago: The Open Court Publishing Co., 1932.
Money-Kyrle, R. *The Meaning of Sacrifice.* London: Hogarth Press, 1930.
Moreno, J. L. *The Psychodrama of God.* New York: Beacon House, 1947.
———. *The Theater of Spontaneity.* New York: Beacon House, 1947.
———. *Who Shall Survive?* Boston: Beacon Press, 1953.
Mowrer, O. H. *Learning Theory and Personality Dynamics.* New York: The Ronald Press Co., 1950.
Murray, H. A. *Explorations in Personality.* New York: Oxford University Press, 1938.
Niebuhr, H. R. *The Purpose of the Church and Its Ministry.* New York: Harper & Bros., 1956.
———, Williams, D. D., and Gustafson, J. *The Advancement of Theological Education.* New York: Harper & Bros., 1957.
Niebuhr, Reinhold. *The Nature and Destiny of Man.* New York: Charles Scribner's Sons, 1941.
Nietzsche, Friedrich. *Thus Spake Zarathustra.*
Otto, Rudolf. *The Idea of the Holy.* Tr. J. W. Harvey. London: Oxford University Press, 1923.
———. *Mysticism, East and West.* Tr. B. L. Bracey and R. C. Payne. New York: The Macmillan Co., 1932.

Parker, J. I., ed. *Interpretative Statistical Survey of the World Mission of the Christian Church*. New York: International Missionary Council, 1938.
Perry, R. B. *A General Theory of Value*. New York: Longmans, Green & Co., 1926.
———. *The Thought and Character of William James*. 2 vols. Boston: Little, Brown & Co., 1935.
Plotinus. *The Essence of Plotinus*. Ed. G. H. Turnbull. New York: Oxford University Press, 1934.
Pratt, J. B. "The Psychology of Religion." *Harvard Theological Review*, I (1908), 435-54.
———. *The Psychology of Religious Belief*. New York: The Macmillan Co., 1907.
———. *The Religious Consciousness*. New York: The Macmillan Co., 1920.
Progoff, Ira. *The Death and Rebirth of Psychology*. New York: The Julian Press, 1956.
Rank, Otto. *Beyond Psychology*. Camden, N. J.: Haddon Craftsmen, 1941.
Reik, Theodor. *Dogma and Compulsion: Psychoanalytic Studies of Religion and Myths*. New York: International Universities Press, 1951.
———. *Ritual: Psycho-analytic Studies*. London: Hogarth Press, 1931.
Robinson, G. C. *The Patient as a Person*. New York: The Commonwealth Fund, 1939.
Ross, M. G. *Religious Beliefs of Youth*. New York: Association Press, 1950.
Sanders, B. J. *Christianity After Freud*. London: Geoffrey Bles, 1949.
Schaub, E. L. "The Psychology of Religion in America During the Past Quarter Century." *Journal of Religion*, VI (1926).
Sherrill, L. J. *Guilt and Redemption*. Richmond, Va.: John Knox Press, 1945; rev. 1957.
Spencer, Herbert. *Principles of Biology*. 2 vols. New York: D. Appleton-Century Co., 1897.
Sperry, W. L. *Reality in Worship*. New York: The Macmillan Co., 1925.
Starbuck, E. D. *The Psychology of Religion*. New York: Charles Scribner's Sons, 1899.
Stern, William. *General Psychology*. Tr. H. D. Spoerl. New York: The Macmillan Co., 1938.
Stratton, G. M. *The Psychology of the Religious Life*. London: Macmillan & Co., 1911.
Strickland, F. L. *Psychology of Religious Experience*. New York: The Abingdon Press, 1924.
Strunk, Orlo. "The Present Status of the Psychology of Religion," *The Journal of Bible and Religion*, xxv (October, 1957), 287-92.
———. "Theological Students: A Study in Perceived Motives," *Personnel and Guidance Journal*, xxxvi (January, 1958), 320-22.
Thorndike, E. L. *Human Nature and the Social Order*. New York: The Macmillan Co., 1940.
Thornton, J., and Knauth, M. S. *The Social Component in Medical Care*. New York: Columbia University Press, 1937.
Tillich, Paul. *The Dynamics of Faith*. New York: Harper & Bros., 1957.
Trout, D. M. *Religious Behavior*. New York: The Macmillan Co., 1931.
———. *Twelve Steps and Twelve Traditions*. New York: Harper & Bros., 1952.
Underhill, Evelyn, *Mysticism*. New York: E. P. Dutton & Co., 1911.
Underwood, A. C. *Conversion: Christian and Non-Christian*. New York: The Macmillan Co., 1925.
Vetter, G. B., and Green, M. "Personality and Group Factors in the Making of Atheists," *The Journal of Abnormal and Social Psychology*, xxvii (1932-33), 179-94.
Wach, Joachim. *Sociology of Religion*. Chicago: University of Chicago Press, 1944.
Weber, Max. *The Protestant Ethic and the Spirit of Capitalism*. Tr. T. Parsons. New York: Charles Scribner's Sons, 1930.
Wieman, H. N. *Religious Experience and Scientific Method*. New York: The Macmillan Co., 1926.
———, and Wieman, R. W. *Normative Psychology of Religion*. New York: Thomas Y. Crowell Co., 1935.
Wise, C. A. *Religion in Illness and Health*, New York: Harper & Bros., 1942.
Wolfe, K. H., tr. and ed. *The Sociology of George Simmel*. Chicago: Free Press, 1950.
Wundt, Wilhelm. *Elements of Folk Psychology*. Tr. E. L. Schaub. New York: The Macmillan Co., 1916.

# INDEX